Principles of Rorschach
Interpretation

The LEA Series in Personality and Clinical Psychology

Irving B. Weiner, Editor

Principles of Rorschach Interpretation

Irving B. Weiner
University of South Florida

 LAWRENCE ERLBAUM ASSOCIATES, PUBLISHERS
1998   Mahwah, New Jersey   London

Lawrence Erlbaum Associates, Inc., Publishers
10 Industrial Avenue
Mahwah, New Jersey 07430

Cover design by Kathryn Houghtaling Lacey

Library of Congress Cataloging-in-Publication Data

Weiner, Irving B.
    Principles of Rorschach interpretation / Irving B. Weiner.
        p.   cm.
    Includes bibliographical references and index.
    ISBN 0-8058-3108-8 (alk. paper).
    1. Rorschach Test—Interpretation. I. Title.
    RC473.R6W45 1998
    155.2′842—dc21   98-7193
                                                              CIP

Books published by Lawrence Erlbaum Associates are printed on acid-free paper,
and their bindings are chosen for strength and durability.

Printed in the United States of America
10 9 8 7 6 5 4 3 2

Contents

Preface

This is a comprehensive textbook of Rorschach interpretation addressed to clinicians who use the Rorschach Inkblot Method in assessing personality functioning. Intended as a manual of principles for effective application of Rorschach findings in professional practice, the text integrates structural, thematic, behavioral, and sequential Rorschach data into systematic guidelines for describing personality characteristics and their clinical significance.

The book is divided into three parts. Part I addresses basic considerations in Rorschach testing and comprises chapters dealing with conceptual and empirical foundations of the inkblot method and with critical issues in formulating and justifying Rorschach inferences. Chapter 1 discusses the nature of the Rorschach as an instrument that contains both objective and subjective features, measures both perceptual and associational processes, and assesses both structural and dynamic aspects of personality. This chapter also discusses the advantages of considering the Rorschach as a multifaceted method of collecting data, rather then merely as a test, and it concludes with an overview of research findings that have demonstrated the sound psychometric foundations on which Rorschach assessment rests.

Chapter 2 discusses key considerations in approaching the interpretation of Rorschach data. These include (a) distinguishing between respectable ways of justifying interpretations, which are defined as empirical and conceptual approaches, and inadequate ways of justifying interpretations, which are designated as "Ouija board" and "authoritative" approaches; (b) formulating interpretations on the basis of strategies involving attention to structural, thematic, behavioral, and sequential features of the data; and (c) modifying the significance attached to interpretations in light of considerations related to subjects' age, gender, and cultural background.

The six chapters in Part II are concerned with the elements of interpretation that contribute to thorough utilization of the data in a Rorschach protocol. Chapter 3 describes the Comprehensive System search strategy and indicates the conceptual and practical benefits of grouping Rorschach variables into clusters related to discrete personality functions and of determining a particular order in which to examine clusters of variables. These benefits include (a) ensuring a thorough, efficient, and person-centered rather than test-centered manner of approaching the data; (b) promoting a flexible and clinically relevant approach to Rorschach interpretation; and (c) facilitating differentiation between adaptive and maladaptive functioning and between symptomatic and characterological patterns of psychopathology.

Chapter 4 elaborates the complementary roles of projection and card pull in determining the characteristics of Rorschach responses. The text illustrates ways in which projection (which refers to properties that subjects attribute to the blots) and card pull (which refers to stimulus properties inherent in the blots) jointly shape the response process, and the chapter concludes with a review of the objects, themes, and affects most commonly suggested by each of the 10 cards.

Chapter 5 delineates the significance of Rorschach structural variables in relation to their implications for six dimensions of psychological adaptation: attending to experience, using ideation, modulating affect, managing stress, viewing oneself, and relating to others. Specific guidelines are presented for utilizing various Rorschach scores, indices, and percentages as a basis for identifying personality strengths and weaknesses in each of these dimensions of adaptation.

Chapter 6 provides systematic guidelines for conducting content analysis of the thematic imagery in Rorschach protocols. Procedures are outlined and illustrated for identifying which responses in a record are likely to contain particularly rich content themes, for generating associations to these themes and using them to formulate interpretive hypotheses, and for judging the plausibility of the thematic interpretations thus formulated. The chapter concludes with consideration of particular symbolic meanings likely to be associated with certain types of content themes.

Chapter 7 turns to the interpretive significance of test behaviors that yield valuable information about subjects' personality style and their attitudes toward being examined. The text categorizes and illustrates several such aspects of how subjects handle and turn the cards, what they reveal through personal comments and asides, and how they generally express and conduct themselves in the examination situation.

Chapter 8 calls attention to how the structural, thematic, and behavioral characteristics of responses can be analyzed conjointly or in sequence to amplify the implications of Rorschach data for personality dynamics. The text presents a model for sequence analysis in which monitoring changes in response quality can be used to identify subjects' sources of concern, the impact of these concerns on them, and the nature and adequacy of the ways in which they seek to ward off or defend themselves against distressing experience.

The guidelines presented in chapters 3 through 8 for translating Rorschach findings into descriptions of structural and dynamic aspects of personality functioning are grounded as much as possible in available research data. Because of their immediate relevance in clinical decision making, normative criteria are identified in detail in Part II and are cited regularly in case illustrations in Part III. Occasionally, reference is also made to specific research studies bearing on the validity of a particular point being made. For the most part, however, this is not so much a book about the Rorschach (i.e., what the research shows) as it is a book about how to use the Rorschach (i.e., what to do with the data in attempting to answer a referral question).

Accordingly, Parts II and III do not regularly cite or describe relevant research. Research support for most of what is said can be found in the basic volumes of the Rorschach Comprehensive System (J. E. Exner, 1991, 1993; J. E. Exner & Weiner, 1995) and in the contemporary journal literature. However, empirical data are not the only road to truth. Clearly formulated concepts and logical reasoning concerning their implications can also yield conclusions that serve useful purposes and stand the test of time. With this in mind, and without ever stating as fact something known to be false, I have not hesitated to base interpretive guidelines on concepts as well as data, while being careful to distinguish speculation from certainty and tentative possibility from probable likelihood.

Part III is devoted to case illustrations of how the interpretive principles delineated in Part II can be used to identify adaptive strengths and weaknesses in personality functioning and apply this information in clinical practice. Chapter 9 provides an introduction to these case illustrations, following which chapters 10 through 14 present and discuss 10 Rorschach protocols. As elaborated in chapter 9, these 10 protocols were given by persons from diverse demographic backgrounds and demonstrate a broad range of personality styles and clinical issues. Discussion of these cases touches on numerous critical concerns in arriving at differential diagnoses, formulating treatment plans, and elucidating structural and dynamic determinants of behavior.

ACKNOWLEDGMENTS

The information presented here builds on the previous contributions of Rorschach clinicians and scholars who have labored fruitfully over the years to generate creative ideas and sound research concerning the utility of the

Rorschach Inkblot Method in assessing personality functioning. This book could not have been written without their work, and their creativity, clinical wisdom, and scientific sophistication are gratefully acknowledged. I would also like to acknowledge the professional value and personal pleasure of my long relationship with my good friend and colleague, John Exner, who graciously gave me permission to use some of his material in the preparation of this book. I am also indebted to Leonard Handler and James Murray for their comments on a draft of the manuscript.

—Irving B. Weiner

BASIC CONSIDERATIONS
IN RORSCHACH TESTING

1

The Nature of the Rorschach

The centennial of Hermann Rorschach's birth was observed in 1984, and more than 80 years have passed since he began in earnest to show inkblots to patients being treated in the Krombach Mental Hospital in Herisau, Switzerland. His "psychological experiment," as he called it, led to the 1921 publication of his monograph, *Psychodiagnostics: A Diagnostic Test Based on Perception* (1921/1942), and eventually to the standardization of a personality assessment instrument that has been administered to hundreds of thousands of people, generated thousands of research studies, and become widely familiar to professional persons and the general public around the world. Despite its high visibility and broad recognition as an assessment technique, however, the Rorschach has not always been adequately conceptualized with respect to the kind of instrument it is and how its data can best be interpreted. Accordingly, this presentation of principles of Rorschach interpretation begins with two introductory chapters on basic considerations in Rorschach testing, one concerning the nature of the Rorschach as a measuring instrument and the other addressing approaches to Rorschach interpretation.

The nature of the Rorschach revolves around the following five questions, each of which has received considerable attention in the literature:

1. Is the Rorschach an objective or a subjective assessment technique?
2. Does the Rorschach function as a measure of perception or as a measure of association?
3. Does the Rorschach assess primarily personality structure or primarily personality dynamics?

4. Is the Rorschach a test or a method?

5. Is the Rorschach a psychometrically sound measuring instrument?

This chapter discusses each of these questions and answers them in ways that provide a conceptual overview of the nature of the Rorschach as a measuring instrument.

OBJECTIVE AND SUBJECTIVE FEATURES OF THE RORSCHACH

Hermann Rorschach (1921/1942, p. 13) undertook his so-called psychological experiment as an objective way of sampling, codifying, and drawing inferences from individual differences in styles of cognitive structuring. To this end, he developed a single set of inkblots to be used with every subject;[1] he formulated a standard procedure for asking subjects what the inkblots might be; he delineated specific criteria for categorizing subjects' responses in terms of such features as location, determinants, and content; and, on the basis of differences he observed among patient and nonpatient groups of various kinds, he proposed interpretive guidelines for inferring personality characteristics from such summary scores as *W%*, *Erlebnistypis (EB)*, and *A%*.

Rorschach's codification of responses was addressed to how subjects solve the problem of having to say what the inkblots might be while recognizing that they are in fact merely inkblots. To accomplish this task, subjects must choose what portions of the blots to consider, which involves focusing their attention in certain ways; they must decide what these portions of the blot look like, which involves forming perceptual impressions of blot characteristics such as shape and color and comparing these impressions with object impressions stored in memory; and they must ponder what interrelationships, if any, exist among the impressions they form. In contemporary language, these elements of producing Rorschach responses identify the instrument as a cognitive structuring task involving processes of attention, perception, memory, decision making, and logical analysis.

As a cognitive structuring task that comprises uniform stimuli, standard administration, formal coding, and specific interpretive guidelines, the Rorschach is in many ways an objective assessment technique. To be sure, most Rorschach responses cannot be coded with as much certainty as a

---

[1]As described by J. E. Exner (1993, pp. 5–6), Rorschach experimented with a large number of inkblots, out of which 15 were used most frequently. Of these 15 inkblots, 10 were included in the *Psychodiagnostics* and, after some modifications during the process of printing the monograph, became the standard set of plates that have been used worldwide since 1921.

true-or-false answer on a self-report inventory. Yet, there is ample evidence that Rorschach coding can proceed in a reliable and largely objective manner. Empirical studies indicate that examiners trained in the Rorschach Comprehensive System can be expected to achieve better than 90% agreement on codes for Location Choice, Pair, Popular (*P*), and Organizational Activity (*Z*); more than 80% agreement on determinants, form quality, content category, and Special Scores; and an overall mean percentage interrater agreement of just under 90% (J. E. Exner, 1991, pp. 459–460; J. E. Exner, 1993, p. 138; McDowell & Acklin, 1996; Meyer, 1997).

Reliable coding by conscientious examiners who hew strictly to well-established coding criteria for basic structural variables should not be unexpected. Whether or not Rorschach responses include the entire blot, articulate color, or identify human figures are objective facts. Likewise, the corollaries of *W* emphasis, low *SumC*, and infrequent *H* can be investigated as objectively as the corollaries of variables drawn from any other test, including those commonly described as objective instruments. Thus, for example, coding *W* for a whole response, tallying the total number or percentage of *W* in a record, and comparing the result with some behavioral index of preference for a global approach to experience is an entirely objective process. Without doubt, then, there is considerable objectivity in identifying personality and behavioral correlates of formally scored dimensions of the cognitive structuring style that subjects bring to bear in saying what the Rorschach inkblots might be.

On the other hand, in the years after Rorschach's death in 1922, scholars came gradually to recognize that the inkblot method could assess many more aspects of personality functioning than were tapped by his focus on objective measurement of cognitive structuring. Of particular importance in this regard were the contributions of psychoanalytically oriented Rorschach clinicians who elaborated numerous ways in which the thematic content of Rorschach responses can provide clues to a person's underlying feelings and concerns. Especially influential among these contributions were B. Klopfer, Ainsworth, W. G. Klopfer, and Holt (1954), who endorsed psychoanalysis as the best theory for understanding the Rorschach, especially the content of responses; Schafer (1954), who developed a broad conceptual framework for psychoanalytic interpretation of thematic imagery; and Lindner (1950), who wrote that "*what* the patient under Rorschach scrutiny produces is quite as important as *how* he produces it" (p. 76).

From this psychoanalytic perspective, the production of Rorschach responses involves processes of association, attribution, and symbolization. These processes lead subjects to attribute characteristics to their percepts that go beyond the actual stimulus features of the blots, as in saying that two human figures "are arguing about which way to go," or that an animal "has been shot and wounded," or that some object "is a weapon that could be used to hurt you." Similarly, descriptions of the inkblots may involve associations to what is seen, as in a male subject describing the bottom center detail (D6) of Card VII (for which "vagina" is an ordinary form) as "something you could fall into and get trapped," or they may include such symbolic references as saying about Card III that "the red heart-shaped object in the center indicates that these two people are in love."

In contrast to Hermann Rorschach's structural focus, the emergence of attention to these types of thematic imagery introduced a new and less objective Rorschach tradition in which the inkblots are regarded not only as a cognitive structuring task but also, or even primarily, as a stimulus to fantasy. In this subjective tradition, fantasy productions provide important and personally relevant information independently of any objective features of the stimuli, the mode of administration, or the subject's cognitive structuring style. The distinction between objective and subjective features of Rorschach responses encompasses two key considerations in specifying the nature of the instrument. The first of these is the role of projection in the formulation of responses, and the second is the extent to which a Rorschach examination involves ambiguity.

Role of Projection

Projection is customarily considered to occur when people attribute their own internal characteristics to external objects or events without justification and without being consciously aware that they are doing so. Rorschach did not refer to projection in his monograph, even though he was familiar with the psychoanalytic literature of his day and presumably with Freud's (1911/1958) discussion of the mechanism of projection in his analysis of the Schreber case. Projection was not mentioned in connection with the Rorschach until 1939, when L. K. Frank suggested that personality tests in which there is relatively little structure induce a subject to "project upon that plastic field . . . his private world of personal meanings and feelings" (pp. 395, 402). Frank's linking of the concept of projection to the response process in such measures as the Rorschach led to the designation of assessment methods involving some ambiguity as "projective tests" and to Rapaport (1942) proposing to "call this principle underlying projective techniques 'the projective hypothesis' " (p. 213).

The role of projection in Rorschach responses was subsequently elaborated by others, most notably Schachtel. Schachtel (1966, chaps. 2, 7, 9) described in detail how projection influences Rorschach responses through subjects' attributions to their percepts of their own qualities, feelings, experiences, and strivings, especially in movement responses and in personally meaningful form responses partially determined by the subject's drives, needs, and emotional states.

These formulations of projection in the Rorschach led to the now well-entrenched distinction between objective and projective tests and the customary classification of the Rorschach as a projective test. In retrospect, this classification has proved regrettable, in two respects. First, classifying the Rorschach as something other than an objective instrument implies that it is an entirely subjective measure. Being thus tarred with the brush of subjectivity has at times provided the basis for unwarranted criticism of Rorschach assessment as a method in which interpretations say as much about the examiner as about the subject. Although ill-prepared examiners may in fact err in this way, such personalized interpretations represent poor Rorschach practice rather than anything inherent in the instrument.

Second, classification as a projective instrument implies that projection is inevitable in Rorschach responses and essential to their providing any useful information. Like allegations of its being an entirely subjective method, however, conception of the Rorschach as an entirely projective measure is faulty and misleading. Projection is neither inevitable nor essential in the Rorschach because adequate, interpretively meaningful responses can be given without recourse to association, attribution, or symbolization. The basic instructions recommended by Rorschach and used in the Comprehensive System ask "What might this be?", "Where do you see it?", and "What made it look like that?" Subjects can comply with these instructions and produce a valid protocol without using projection in formulating their responses.

For example, suppose a subject says to Card I, "The whole thing looks like a black bat." Card I does in fact look like a bat or butterfly to most people, and it is gray-black in color. Hence, this "black bat" response does not attribute any characteristics to the stimulus that are not already there, and it accordingly does not involve projection. Although records composed entirely of such unelaborated responses as "a black bat" do not have much interpretive richness, they can nevertheless provide valuable information about a subject's personality style. This is especially the case when otherwise impoverished records comprise numerous responses that, like the black bat, are popular, use the entire blot, or articulate achromatic color.

Allowing that responses can thus be formulated and protocols interpreted in the absence of projection, it remains the case that projection does occur frequently and sometimes dramatically in the production of a Rorschach record. Suppose a subject looking at Card I—instead of a black bat—responds with "A vulture swooping down to get its prey." Now the response involves an uncommon and inaccurate percept ("A vulture"), the attribution of movement to a static inkblot ("swooping down"), and the fantasy of imminent victimization ("to get its prey"). Responses that are perceived inaccurately or embellished in these ways usually involve projection, because what is being reported is not present in the stimulus and therefore must have emerged from attitudes and concerns internal to the subject.

The fact that projection can and does occur in the formulation of Rorschach responses but is neither inevitable nor essential in the response process is consistent with the recognition that the instrument elicits responses containing both objective descriptions and subjective impressions. As for the extent to which Rorschach protocols are likely, in general, to be influenced by projective mechanisms, there is no single answer to this question. Depending on the richness of subjects' fantasy lives and their inclination to be forthcoming in revealing these fantasies, protocols will vary in the amount of projection they involve. At the same time, however, note should be taken of an observation by Schachtel (1966) that projection does not occur in the majority of Rorschach responses and is not the only significant aspect of responses in which it does occur: "In other words," he wrote, "only a small fraction of the many processes underlying Rorschach responses are of a projective nature" (p. 10).

Heeding Schachtel's caution, those who use and study the Rorschach should keep in mind that an interpretable record can be produced without much involvement of projective mechanisms and the subjectivity they entail. In discussing this aspect of the response process, J. E. Exner (1989) argued that the Rorschach should no longer be classified and referred to as a projective test. Given what has been said here about the nature of the instrument and the disadvantage of its being erroneously considered an entirely subjective method, Exner's point seems well-taken. Long-established customs die hard, however, and logical argument is not likely in the foreseeable future to alter common categorical distinctions between objective and projective tests.

Moreover, there may be sound definitional basis for retaining the identity of the Rorschach as one among a group of personality assessment instruments known as "projective." Some years ago, following in the tradition of Frank, I offered the following definition of projective tests: "Projective tests are psychodiagnostic instruments in which some degree of ambiguity prompts subjects to 'project' their underlying needs and attitudes into the responses they give" (Weiner, 1977b, p. 112). I noted then that this ambiguity could reside either in the test stimuli or in the instructions given to subjects, and I concluded that "the definition of a 'projective test' rests largely with the extent to which it emphasizes stimulus or response ambiguity as a means of obtaining information about personality processes" (p. 113). By this criterion, the Rorschach would appear to resemble a projective test by virtue of the relatively unstructured nature of the subject's task, which introduces ambiguity into the examination situation independently of how much projection is involved in the subjects' responses.

Role of Ambiguity

To elaborate the preceding observation concerning the extent of ambiguity in the Rorschach situation, the role of projection and the corresponding relative importance of objective and subjective elements in response production is closely tied to the amount of structure that is inherent in the inkblot stimuli and the nature of the subject's task. The basic theory of projective mechanisms holds that the possibility and probability of people attributing their internal characteristics to external objects and events is directly proportional to the lack of structure in these objects and events. That is, the less clarity there is in a stimulus field, the less it truly resembles anything, and the fewer well-defined properties it has, the more likely it is that observers will see and define it in their own terms.

Conversely, the more structure and clarity there is in a stimulus field, the less opportunity there is for observers to perceive it in an idiosyncratic fashion and the less likely it is to foster impressions based on projection—even though people on occasion may misinterpret even seemingly clear situations on the basis of projective mechanisms. The psychological principles involved in this relationship between ambiguity and projection parallel those that relate the frequency and intensity of transference reactions among psychotherapy patients to the extent to which their therapists present themselves as ambiguous figures rather than real objects (see Weiner, 1998a, chap. 10). Accordingly, the most truly ambiguous stimulus among widely used assessment techniques and the one most likely to elicit responses based on projection alone is Card 16 of the Thematic Apperception Test (TAT), which is a totally blank card with no stimulus characteristic other than being white.

Although it has become commonplace to speak of the Rorschach as an unstructured test, the 10 inkblots have nowhere near the ambiguity of Card 16 of the TAT. To the contrary, the inkblots contain many reasonably definite shapes, and each has some readily identifiable characteristics of color and shading. There is very little ambiguity with respect to Card I being black, Card V resembling a butterfly, Card VI being heavily shaded, and Card VIII being multicolored. On the other hand, subjects are told when being administered the Rorschach that the stimuli are just blots of ink, and there is no blot characteristic that is uniformly articulated by all subjects. Hence, it would be as mistaken to regard the inkblots as lacking ambiguity as it would be to regard them as completely unstructured.

The subtle relationship between ambiguity and structure was thoughtfully addressed some years ago by Klein and Arnheim (1953), in the following way: "A visual stimulus should be called unstructured or amorphous only when it is impossible to find an organized perceptual pattern in it.... But an outstanding perceptual factor of the ten standardized cards is that—

mainly, because of their symmetry—they offer to the first glance a striking total picture, which is far from being unstructured" (p. 91).

As for the nature of the task, the degree to which an assessment instrument is ambiguous or unstructured depends on what the subject is asked to do as well as the nature of the stimuli. Even the presentation of Card 16 of the TAT would be a structured and clearly defined situation if the instructions were, "I'm going to show you a blank card and I want you to tell me what color it is." To carry this example further, suppose Card 1 of the TAT were presented with the question, "What is this a picture of?", and suppose the subject responded, "It's a picture of a boy and a violin." Then the TAT would be functioning as an objective measure, and no projection would be involved in the response process.

What about the Rorschach task in this regard? There is considerable ambiguity in the free association portion of the administration, because subjects are asked "What might this be?" without being given any further guidance concerning how they should go about responding. When subjects ask such questions as how many responses they should give or whether they can turn the cards, they are told, "It's up to you." On the other hand, during the inquiry phase, subjects are asked to indicate where their percepts were seen and what made them look as they did, and these are unambiguous questions that call for specific kinds of answers. Hence, in the Rorschach task as well as in the inkblot stimuli, there are elements both of ambiguity and of structure, neither of which should be overlooked in contemplating the nature of this instrument.

Conclusions

How then should the first of the five questions at the start of this chapter be answered: Is the Rorschach an objective or a subjective measuring instrument? Clearly it is both. It is an instrument that constitutes in part a problem-solving task and provides objective assessment of cognitive-structuring style; that constitutes in part a stimulus to fantasy that provides subjective assessment of thematic imagery; that may and often does involve projection but can also function independently of it; and that embraces both ambiguous and clearly defined stimulus and task elements and, whether or not called projective, is best regarded among personality assessment techniques as a relatively unstructured instrument.

RORSCHACH MEASUREMENT OF PERCEPTION AND ASSOCIATION

When Hermann Rorschach subtitled his monograph "A Diagnostic Test Based on Perception," he established not only the objective tradition in Rorschach assessment that has just been discussed, but also a subsequently widely held belief that the Rorschach functions primarily as a measure of perception. From this perspective, Rorschach responses identify personality characteristics because the manner in which subjects impose perceptual structure on the inkblots mirrors the ways in which they are likely to see and respond to other relatively unstructured situations (i.e., stimulus fields) in their lives.

Rorschach himself paid scant attention to fantasy in his basic monograph. In part II of the monograph, which was concerned with "The Factors of the Experiment," he discussed form, movement, color, and location choice but devoted just two pages to content, most of which concern the implications of a high Animal percentage for stereotypy. In part V, on "The Use of the Form Interpretation Test in Diagnosis," he went a step further and wrote the following frequently quoted conclusion concerning the minimal significance of associational processes in Rorschach interpretation:

> The test cannot be used as a means of delving into the unconscious. At best, it is far inferior to the other more profound psychological methods such as dream interpretation and association experiments. This is not difficult to understand. The test does not induce a "free flow from the subconscious" but requires adaptation to external stimuli, participation of the "fonction du réel." (Rorschach, 1921/1942, p. 123)

Interestingly, however, on the very same page as he came to the previous conclusion, Rorschach also wrote that "certain tendencies in the subconscious are occasionally revealed by comparison of the content of the interpretation with the rest of the findings" (p. 123). He then gave as an example a subject who sees Christ-like figures, halos, and martyrs and can therefore be identified as someone "who considers himself quite holy." Clearly, the content elaborations to which Rorschach referred derive not from perceptual functioning alone but instead involve associations by the subject to what was being seen in the inkblots.

Of further interest in fully grasping Rorschach's own views of the instrument is his posthumously published manuscript, "The Application of the Form Interpretation Test," which he completed a few weeks before his death in 1922 and is usually included as an addendum in bound volumes of the basic monograph. Here he wrote the following:

> Thus we see that the kinaesthetic [movement] interpretations furnish a deep insight into the unconscious. They reveal the unconscious tendencies of the subject, the basic attitude, whether it be active or passive. The color interpretations are symbols corresponding to the symbols in dreams. In the unconscious they represent something else, namely, the latent content, revealing the tremendous affective relationships of the latent content. (p. 214)

Traditional Views

A close reading of the work of Rorschach's most traditional followers reveals that they were as adamant as he about the irrelevance or minor import of thematic content but shared with him, whether or not consciously, a sensitivity to subjects' associations as well as their percepts. Thus, S. J. Beck (1968; S. J. Beck, A. G. Beck, Levitt, & Molish, 1961) regarded the inkblots as visual stimuli and Rorschach interpretations as a process of quantifying features of perception; as far as he was concerned, qualitative impressions of what subjects say or do while responding "are not the Rorschach test" (S. J. Beck et al., 1961, p. viii). Yet, one of S. J. Beck's (1968) most carefully delineated and enduring interpretive strategies involved attending to what he called "personal F-" responses, which he defined as "erratic misperceptions that can be shown as mirroring interests or needs of serious personal importance to the subject" (p. 132).

Like Beck, Piotrowski (1957, 1977) pursued the understanding of personality with the Rorschach mainly through perception; in his opinion, "the primary visual response is much more valid than the secondary verbal comments" (1977, p. 195). At the same time, however, Piotrowski made some of his most enduring contributions to Rorschach knowledge by addressing how elaborations of M responses can identify subjects' customary roles in interpersonal relationships and the attitudes they hold toward other people.

Bohm (1951/1958) advocated a very structured approach and ignored the content of responses as much as Rorschach. However, he also wrote about the special significance of "M responses with double meaning"; he gave as an example of such responses, "Two men want to shake hands, or are drawing back," which he interpreted as indicating "tendencies toward flight or splitting" (p. 115).

These observations in the structural core of the Rorschach literature implicitly endorse interpretations based on thematic imagery, that is, on characteristics attributed to or projected onto the inkblots through associational processes. There seems little doubt, for example, that Beck's interpretive use of "personal F-" closely parallels what Schachtel proposed doing with personally meaningful form perception.

Historically, however, with the previously noted emergence of expanded attention to subjective features of the Rorschach, some Rorschachers came to believe that the instrument functions primarily not as a measure of perception but as a measure of association. From this perspective, Rorschach responses identify personality characteristics because the associations subjects form to the inkblots reveal how they are inclined to think and feel about life experiences. The scholars who contributed most to establishing the importance of associational data in Rorschach responses, mainly by bringing psychoanalytic insights to bear on the thematic imagery of

Rorschach content, influenced many practitioners to disregard the perceptual aspects of the Rorschach task and abandon traditional coding of structural variables. As reviewed by Rosenzweig (1951), this regrettable trend
had become quite apparent by the end of the 1940s, and vestiges of it are
still to be found.

However, neither disregard of perceptual processes nor abandonment of
coding was intended by the pioneering advocates of attention to Rorschach
imagery whose contributions were noted earlier. Lindner (1950), for example, while recommending content interpretation as a way of enriching the
clinical value of the Rorschach, opposed relying on content alone: "It cannot
too often be stressed that the approach through content is only an *additional*
approach, adding another dimension to the Rorschach responses, and that
it must take its proper place among other approaches" (p. 78).

Klopfer (B. Klopfer et al., 1954), while endorsing psychoanalytic formulations of the Rorschach, developed a formal psychogram for assessing formally scored structural features of Rorschach responses. Like Lindner, Klopfer advised clinicians to avoid excessive reliance on content, and he also
advised them to avoid interpreting symbols as if they have fixed or universal
meaning. According to Klopfer (B. Klopfer et al., 1954), "Rorschach records
will differ greatly in the extent to which we can profitably approach them
from the standpoint of content analysis. . . . The school of content interpretation that proceeds from the assumption that reactions to a specific card
can be taken to give the pattern of the subject's relations to his mother or
father is in fact without adequate justification" (p. 545).

In this same vein, while writing about the importance of utilizing symbolic
imagery contained in Rorschach responses, Miale (1977) argued for an integrated approach to interpreting structure and content: "The point of view
which I have found most useful in understanding Rorschach responses is
that the formal characteristics and contents are not different in kind. Rather,
the same symbolic characteristics which determine the meaning of the
content of a response also determine the meaning of the scorable aspects
of the Rorschach stimuli" (p. 448).

The integrationist perspective favored by Miale had its origins in the
seminal contributions of Rapaport, who maintained that reactions to the
Rorschach inkblots involve both a perceptual organizing process that has
a continuity with perception in everyday life, and associative processes that
reveal underlying personality dynamics (Rapaport, Gill, & Schafer, 1946/1968,
chap. 9). Rapaport expressed his views in the following way:

> According to Rapaport, both perceptual organization and associative proc-
> esses "are always implied in every Rorschach response. . . . One can learn
> more about the subject sometimes by looking at a responses from the point
> of view of its perceptual organization, and at other times by looking at it from

the point of view of the associative process that brought it forth. However, one must never neglect the integration of the two processes.... Clearly, then, it would not be correct to reason that the Rorschach response is to be considered mainly either a perceptual product or one of free association." (pp. 274, 276)

Contemporary Views

Historically, then, although there were purists of both perceptual and associational persuasions who disdained each other's approach and urged colleagues and students to do likewise, major figures in the development of the Rorschach either inadvertently or by design consistently answered the second question posed on page 3 by describing the instrument as a measure of both perception and association. And what of present-day thinking in this regard? Contemporary developments in perceptually based Rorschach interpretation have for the most part been embodied in the Comprehensive System introduced by J. E. Exner (1974). With its strong emphasis on carefully coded structural variables, the Comprehensive System has sometimes been regarded as inimical to content interpretation and has evoked concern that, because it links test signs to clinical characteristics on an actuarial and impersonal basis, "reports based on such an approach give too little sense to what is unique and idiosyncratic about the individual's personality structure" (Sugarman, 1991, p. 131).

In fact, however, neither disdain for content interpretation nor disregard for individual uniqueness influenced the formulation of the Comprehensive System. The development of the system was motivated primarily by the need for a consistently administered, adequately normed, reliably scorable, and psychometrically sound method of Rorschach assessment, and a relatively small number of structural variables provided the most promising place to begin. There was neither animus toward content interpretation nor any intent to exclude it from consideration; content variables were less well understood than structural variables and more complex to study, and they would merely have to wait their turn to be adequately examined and incorporated within the system. The Comprehensive System sought to exclude from the Rorschach only that which was unreliable and invalid and hence of illusory value only.

From 1974 to the present, the Rorschach Comprehensive System has expanded considerably in scope and diversity. New ideas and additional data have resulted in refinement of many of the original structural variables in the system and the introduction of new variables as well. At the same time, research demonstrating the significance of various content categories and elaborations has led to new indices based largely or entirely on content, such as the Isolation Index and the Intellectualization Index, and to thematic imagery analysis as part of the Comprehensive System interpretive process.

Presently, then, as elaborated by Weiner (1998c) and in current editions of Exner's basic texts (J. E. Exner, 1991, 1993; J. E. Exner & Weiner, 1995), Comprehensive System interpretation calls in every case for reading the content of responses involving people, movement, form distortion, or unusual elaborations, in order to derive information about subjects' attitudes toward themselves and other people—which is exactly what Schachtel recommended. Chapter 3 amplifies the role that these features of the interpretive process play in the Comprehensive System search strategy. Thus with respect to the nature of the Rorschach, the Comprehensive System, while exemplifying a basically structural approach to the Rorschach, treats the instrument both as a measure of perception and a measure of association.

As for contemporary psychoanalytic perspectives on Rorschach testing, scholars both in the United States and abroad continue in the tradition of Klopfer, Rapaport, and Schachtel to endorse the intermingling of perceptual and associational features in Rorschach responses (Baba, 1995; Blatt, 1990; Lunazzi de Jubany, 1992; Rausch de Traubenberg, 1993). Even the contributions of Rorschachers interested primarily in the development of and promulgation of psychoanalytically derived interpretations of thematic imagery typically attend to the coding of basic perceptual variables. Leading examples in this regard include P. M. Lerner's (1991) work on content analysis, which is accompanied by scoring along the lines of the Rapaport/Schafer system, and the approach of Aronow, Reznikoff, and Moreland (1994) to content interpretation, which involves scoring basically according to the Klopfer system with some supplementary reliance on Beck, Hertz, and Exner for coding Populars and form level. B. L. Smith (1994) suggested further that a psychoanalytic approach to the Rorschach should be defined not by an interpretive emphasis on thematic imagery, but rather by a psychoanalytic theoretical perspective that is applied equally to all of the data, both qualitative and quantitative.

Leichtman (1996a, 1996b) interjected a third alternative conception of the Rorschach by arguing that it measures neither perception nor association but rather is a measure of representation. The Rorschach is not a perceptual task, according to Leichtman, because the inkblots are in reality only inkblots. Borrowing concepts introduced by J. E. Exner (1980), Leichtman observed that perception is involved and necessary in the Rorschach response process, but that the task calls for subjects not to perceive but to *misperceive* what is there—as by saying that Card I is a butterfly when in fact it is an inkblot. At the same time, however, Leichtman argued that associations alone cannot constitute the basis for Rorschach responses, because associations do not occur without their having been some prior perception.

Leichtman concluded from his observations, then, that the Rorschach can best be conceived as a measure of representation in which perceptions and associations combine to create in subjects' minds certain impressions of the inkblots, which they report as their responses. Summarized in this way, Leichtman's representational perspective on the Rorschach, although logically reasoned, constitutes basically an integration of perceptual and associational perspectives and a preference to regard Rorschach responses as impressions. Although responses may indeed be best regarded as impressions, the lumping of perceptual and associational processes risks blurring useful distinctions between them in their own right. As is elaborated in chapter 4, the differential contribution of projection (which is primarily an associational process) and card pull (which is primarily a perceptual process) to the response process has important implications for how interpretations should be derived and formulated.

As for vestiges from the past, one does hear from time to time about practitioners who say they use the Rorschach but never bother to score it. One can wonder whether this lack of bother is based on some firmly held conviction concerning advisable assessment technique, or whether it reflects instead inability or unwillingness to score properly. Questions can also be raised concerning whether, in light of present knowledge, such incomplete use of the instrument borders on incompetent practice (see Weiner, 1989). Whatever one chooses to think in this regard, there is almost no one currently writing with authority who recommends a solely thematic approach to the Rorschach. Examiners may prefer to view the Rorschach as mainly a measure of perception or mainly a measure of association, even while recognizing that to some extent it is both. These preferences in turn have implications for whether Rorschach responses are interpreted primarily in terms of the perceptual structuring they involve or the thematic imagery they contain, which is discussed in chapter 2. In both concept and practice, however, attention to the complementarity of perceptual and associational processes in Rorschach responding, rather than an exclusionary focus on one or the other, presently prevails.

Nomothetic and Idiographic Perspectives

Finally, with respect to the perception/association distinction, these complementary processes in Rorschach responding bear on whether the instrument should be considered a nomothetic or idiographic technique. Aronow, Reznikoff, and Moreland (1995), in concert with their preference for interpretations based on thematic imagery rather than perceptual structuring, argued for an idiographic perspective. In their opinion, the associational features of Rorschach responses are unique to subjects' state of mind and therefore provide the basis for idiographic interpretations that help to define their individuality as people. Perceptual features of responses, by contrast, are shared by all subjects to a greater or lesser degree (e.g., all subjects have some percentage of good form responses and some number of Populars) and hence, they say, allow only for nomothetic interpretations that compare people with normative standards or expectations.

According to Aronow et al., idiographic interpretations are preferable to nomothetic interpretations (and thematic imagery thus more important than perceptual structuring) because they provide more information about what people are really like. However, there is some flawed logic in equating association with idiography and perception with nomothetics. This equation can be challenged in three respects that help to clarify the nature of the Rorschach further.

First, why must associations be exclusively idiographic? To be sure, it may be unusual (although not impossible) for two people to express the very same association in precisely the same words. In fact, however, Rorschach examiners do not interpret associations by repeating them just as they were given, but by attempting to categorize them in some way. Some associations may be categorized as suggesting fear of domination by powerful male figures, for example; some associations may point to a view of oneself as being fragile or damaged; still other associations may contain a common thread of concerns about becoming merged with or engulfed by others. Having categorized psychodynamically significant associations, as has been done with numerous content scales that have been developed over the years (see, e.g., Aronow & Reznikoff, 1976; Stricker & Healey, 1990), examiners can then count how frequently these categories occur in a subject's record and compare this frequency with that observed in certain other people. In this process, associations become nomothetic data.

Second, why must perceptions be exclusively nomothetic? A subject may be determined on the basis of comparisons with normative data to have very poor form level and an elevated Hypervigilance Index. Nevertheless, the impaired judgment and paranoid tendencies inferred from these findings become idiographic characteristics of the individuals that are part of their own individuality.

Third, why must idiographic information be considered preferable to nomothetic information, or vice versa for that matter, in describing what people are like? The idiographic and nomothetic perspectives in personality theory derive from the work of two prominent scholars: Allport (1937), for whom the essence of personality resided in the uniqueness and individuality of each person independently of comparisons to other people; and Cattell (1946), for whom the essence of personality resided in traits or dimensions of functioning that all people share to some degree and on which they can be compared with each other.

There was a time when the idiographic and nomothetic traditions spurred theoretical debate concerning whether people could be described better in terms of how they differ from other people or how they resemble them. Such debates are long out of fashion, replaced by more sophisticated awareness that people can best be described by attending to both how they differ from and how they resemble each other. Likewise, with respect to contemporary personality assessment, the fullest possible understanding of people requires both idiographic and nomothetic information. Neither kind of information is preferable to the other; they complement each other, and both emerge from Rorschach data.

Conclusions

There can be little doubt concerning the answer to the question of whether the Rorschach functions as a measure of perception or as a measure of association: Clearly, it functions as both. As noted in discussing the objective and subjective features of this instrument, most Rorschach protocols will include some responses influenced by projection and others in which projection plays little or no part. On the other hand, most responses are likely to be the joint product of perceptual and associational processes, each of which contribute to their final form. Paying adequate attention to both aspects of their subjects' responses will help Rorschach examiners maximize the richness and utility of the interpretations they formulate.

RORSCHACH ASSESSMENT OF PERSONALITY STRUCTURE AND PERSONALITY DYNAMICS

The previous two sections have considered what the Rorschach is and how it functions. It is a relatively unstructured personality assessment instrument having both objective and subjective features and constituting both a perceptual-cognitive task and a stimulus to fantasy, and it functions both as a measure of perception and as a measure of association. The next question to address concerns whether the Rorschach serves primarily as a way of assessing personality structure or a way of assessing personality dynamics.

For purposes of definition, *personality structure* can be said to refer to the nature of people as defined by their current thoughts and feelings, which constitute personality *states*, and their abiding dispositions to conduct themselves in certain ways, which constitute personality *traits*. Personality states comprise a broad range of relatively transitory affects and attitudes that are elicited by situational circumstances, such as being happy or deeply in thought at the moment. Personality traits comprise a broad range of fairly stable characteristics and orientations of the individual, such as being a persistently dependent or suspicious kind of person.

Personality dynamics can be said to refer to the nature of people as defined by the underlying needs, attitudes, conflicts, and concerns that influence them to think, feel, and act in certain ways at particular times and in particular circumstances. Personality dynamics also refers to the manner in which states and traits of the individual may interact to influence each other, as, for example, in the case of a high level of trait anxiety causing one person to become situationally anxious in circumstances that do not produce state anxiety in another person who is less disposed to becoming anxious.

As might be expected, historical traditions associated with Rorschach assessment of personality structure and personality dynamics parallel the distinction between perceptual and associational processes discussed in the previous section. Rorschach pioneers who regarded the instrument primarily as a measure of perception tended to regard it mainly as a way of identifying states and traits, that is, structural elements of personality. Rorschach scholars who pioneered attention to associations in Rorschach interpretation tended to regard the instrument mainly as a means of revealing a subject's underlying needs, attitudes, conflicts, and concerns, that is, dynamic aspects of personality.

Contemporary rapprochement between these divergent traditions regarding Rorschach assessment of personality structure and personality dynamics has proceeded somewhat differently from the evolution of widespread agreement that the Rorschach is a measure of both perception and association. In the first place, holding a primarily perceptual or associational view of the Rorschach has been and continues to be a matter of preference not susceptible to proof or disproof by empirical data, and the generally recognized complementarity of perceptual and associational processes in Rorschach responding represents a sensible advance in conceptualization but not in established fact. By contrast, whether the Rorschach assesses personality structure or personality dynamics can be directly put to empirical test by examining the validity of Rorschach-based inferences concerning these aspects of personality functioning.

As is elaborated later in the final section of this chapter with respect to psychometric properties of the Rorschach, both structural and dynamic interpretations of Rorschach data have been found to demonstrate substantial validity. Hence, the capacity of the Rorschach to assess both personality structure and personality dynamics is not merely a sensible way to look at the instrument, but a matter of established fact.

As a second contrast with the sharp distinction that can be drawn between perceptual and associational features of Rorschach responding, the types of Rorschach data that can generate structural and dynamic inferences are not mutually exclusive. In times past, it was commonly suggested that Rorschach assessment of personality structure proceeds through structural variables and assessment of personality dynamics through content variables (e.g., J. E. Exner & Weiner, 1982, chap. 1). Current developments in Rorschach interpretation indicate that this distinction has probably been overdrawn. As illustrated in the case discussions later in chapters 10 through 14, detailed analysis of structural data can reveal many aspects of personality dynamics as well as personality structure, and careful consideration of thematic imagery can generate useful information concerning personality states and traits as well as underlying needs and concerns.

Accordingly, the Rorschach should not be considered either as a measure primarily for assessing personality structure or as a measure primarily for assessing personality dynamics. It is a measure for assessing both the structure and dynamics of personality functioning. To use the Rorschach adequately, examiners need to be schooled in both structural and dynamic personology and versed in how both structural and dynamic personality characteristics can be inferred from Rorschach responses. In the hands of examiners thus schooled and versed, Rorschach protocols will on some occasions provide information mainly about subjects' personality structure and on other occasions be particularly revealing of their personality dynamics. Which turn occurs will be determined by the openness of subjects' coping style and how they approach the testing situation, not by the nature of the instrument itself. The Rorschach is equally capable of assessing personality structure and dynamics when administered to responsive subjects and interpreted by knowledgeable examiners.

THE RORSCHACH AS TEST OR METHOD

What's in a name? Often more than is immediately apparent, especially when labels carry far-reaching implications. Tradition would suggest that the Rorschach is best identified as being a test. As mentioned previously, Rorschach (1921/1942) called it "a diagnostic test" in the subtitle of his monograph; Beck (1930a, 1930b), who introduced the Rorschach into the English language, used the title *Rorschach's Test*; and contemporary terminology commonly places the Rorschach within the category of "psychological tests" and refers to administration of the Rorschach as an aspect of "psychological testing."

Early on, however, question was raised about the advisability of regarding the Rorschach as a test. Krugman (1938) and Ainsworth (1954) concluded that it would be advantageous to regard the Rorschach as a *method* rather than as a test, and Klopfer (B. Klopfer et al., 1954) used "Rorschach Technique" in titling his books on it. Both Krugman and Ainsworth were troubled by the difficulty of demonstrating the reliability and validity of Rorschach findings; conceived as a method of observation rather than as a test, they argued, the Rorschach could be judged according to whether it was useful and productive without being held accountable to statistical analysis of its psychometric properties.

As matters have turned out, standardization of administration and scoring in the Comprehensive System have made it possible for the Rorschach to demonstrate substantial psychometric sturdiness, the data concerning which are presented in the concluding section of this chapter. Nevertheless, with respect to the purposes that tests are designed to serve, Krugman and Ainsworth seem to have been on the right track in suggesting that the Rorschach is more than a test.

Tests are intended to measure the extent to which some phenomenon is present. Thus tests of intelligence yield scores that are taken to indicate how intelligent a person is; tests of memory measure how good a person's memory is; tests of depression show how depressed a person is, and so on. By this standard, the Rorschach includes numerous scales and indices that function as tests and measure various personality characteristics, such as receptivity to emotional stimulation (Affective Ratio), extent of disordered thinking (*WSum6*), and degree of interpersonal isolation (Isolation Index). At the same time, the previous discussion concerning subjective features of the Rorschach and the role of associations in the response process indicate that there is more to the Rorschach than its quantitative measurements as a test. Idiographic response characteristics not presently codified and aspects of the subject's behavior during a Rorschach examination contribute important qualitative information about personality functioning. Hence, in common with other complex and multifaceted personality assessment instruments, the Rorschach serves not just as a test but as a method of generating data that identifies many different aspects of personality functioning.

In previous commentaries on what the Rorschach should be called (Weiner, 1994, 1995b), I encouraged replacing the traditional designation of the Rorschach as a test with referring to it as the *Rorschach Inkblot Method* (RIM). As I indicated then, identifying the Rorschach as a method of generating data rather than merely as a test has important implications for how the instrument is conceptualized. In particular, identifying the Rorschach as a method rather than as a test signifies that there can be no single, overarching theory of the Rorschach. The data generated by the Rorschach method can be interpreted from many different theoretical perspectives, and the utility of these data does not require any theory to account for them. What is required is only to know why the RIM generates useful information, and two well-documented reasons why it does so have already been explicated in this chapter.

First, the Rorschach generates useful information about personality functioning because it confronts subjects with a problem-solving situation to which they respond as they usually respond in problem-solving situations in their lives, thereby revealing many facets of their personality style. Second, the Rorschach generates useful information about personality functioning because it presents subjects with an associational situation in which they often attribute personalized characteristics to what they see, thereby revealing many of their underlying needs, attitudes, conflicts, and concerns.

This account of why the RIM works is not theoretical; it merely provides a description of what takes place when subjects tell examiners what the inkblots look like to them. This account is also not new to the literature, but instead constitutes a distillation of two traditional perspectives on the nature of the Rorschach discussed previously: The RIM is (a) a measure of cognitive structuring involving processes of attention, perception, memory, decision-making, and logical analysis, and (b) a measure of thematic imagery involving processes of association, attribution, and symbolization.

Clinicians and researchers who regard the RIM as a test have at times attempted to formulate theoretical positions stressing either the cognitive or the thematic aspects of the instrument. Narrow formulations of this type do a disservice to the richness and complexity of the method and mistakenly imply that there is just one adequate theory of the Rorschach already available or waiting to be formulated. Moreover, conceptualizing the Rorschach solely as a measure of perception or as a measure of association tends to foster an interpretive process that makes only partial use of the data and paints an incomplete picture of the subject—for example, extensive coverage of personality structure without much delineation of dynamics, or considerable attention to personality dynamics without much articulation of structure. Appreciating how the RIM functions as a method helps to discourage fruitless pursuit of a single test theory and promotes adequate utilization of both the cognitive and thematic features of the instrument.

Finally, viewing the RIM as a method that transcends theoretical points of view, rather than as a test held captive by some particular theory, allows Rorschach data to be interpreted within whatever theoretical framework an examiner prefers. Any valid theory of personality functioning can provide concepts that help to describe and explain the meaning of Rorschach findings, and the capacity of the RIM to generate useful information about personality functioning exists independently of any particular theory. The answer to the fourth question being pursued in this chapter, then, is that the Rorschach is better conceived as a method than merely as a test.

Although concurring with the preceding arguments for considering the Rorschach to be more than a test, J. E. Exner (1997b) expressed some reservations about referring to the instrument as being anything but a test. Exner's concern in this regard is that calling the Rorschach something other than a test may give undeserved comfort to critics of the instrument who use "not a test" in a pejorative fashion to indicate psychometric inadequacy. Exner correctly pointed out that the Rorschach fully satisfies standard criteria for being considered a test, including the following description of "test" in the *Standards for Educational and Psychological Tests* promulgated by the American Psychological Association (1974): "a set of tasks or questions intended to elicit particular types of behavior when presented under standardized conditions and to yield scores that will have desirable psychometric properties such as high reliability and high validity" (p. 2). Accordingly, Rorschach clinicians and researchers who appreciate why the Rorschach is more than a test, and who may consequently refer to it as a method, should neither lose sight of nor demur from emphasizing the merits of the Rorschach Comprehensive System as a test.

PSYCHOMETRIC FOUNDATIONS OF THE RORSCHACH

For more than 50 years after its publication in 1921, the Rorschach Inkblot Method (RIM) was frequently and sometimes harshly criticized as a psychometrically unsound instrument. To some extent, this criticism was warranted by repeated failures to demonstrate the reliability and validity of Rorschach assessment. As already noted, these "failures" led some early leaders in the development of the Rorschach to recommend calling it a method rather than a test in order avoid accountability to psychometric standards. The fact is, however, that methods as well as tests can be judged according to whether they generate reliable and valid information, and questions about the psychometric soundness of the Rorschach must be answered regardless of what it is called. Historical perspectives and current data provide a clear answer to these questions.

Historical Perspectives

In retrospect, a watershed regarding the psychometric soundness of the RIM was reached during an approximately 10-year period beginning in 1965. Thoughtful and scholarly criticisms of the psychometric foundations of the instrument peaked with Zubin, Eron, and Schumer's (1965) *An Experimental Approach to Projective Techniques*. They concluded from an extensive review of the literature that traditional Rorschach variables had not shown acceptable psychometric properties and were not likely to do so. They accordingly recommended a "global" rather than an "atomistic" approach in which the Rorschach serves not as a measuring instrument but "essentially [as] an interview" (Zubin et al., 1965, p. 239).

In the decade or so following the appearance of Zubin et al., Rorschach enthusiasts began to respond to such criticism not with the apologies and defensiveness that had previously been common, but instead with scholarly assertiveness and scientific initiatives. The inconclusive research studies that had presumably "failed" to support the soundness and utility of the Rorschach were themselves called into question by Blatt (1975), Holt (1967), Weiner (1977a), and others, who pointed out that a majority of these early studies were inadequately conceived, inappropriately designed, and poorly conducted. On those relatively few occasions when early Rorschach researchers had employed respectable methodology, their results tended to affirm rather than challenge the psychometric soundness of the RIM.

Since the mid-1970s, growing sophistication in research design has expanded the available data concerning the scientific status of the inkblot method. Contemporary advances in Rorschach research methods have included greater emphasis on theory-based and construct-oriented hypotheses, increased attention to objective and observable correlates of Rorschach variables, utilization of meta-analytic statistical methods, and appreciation for the impact of Type II error. These and other methodological issues in Rorschach research methods are elaborated by J. E. Exner (1995), Meyer (1996), and Weiner (1995a). Significantly, methodological advances over the years have confirmed a relationship first noted by Holt (1967): The better the quality of Rorschach research, as measured by the adequacy of the methods employed, the more likely it is to produce results that bear positive witness to the validity of the instrument.

With respect to scientific initiatives, the 10 years following Zubin et al. was a time when something was done about the fact that Rorschach clinicians and scholars, in their creativity, had long been their own worst enemy. S. J. Beck (1968) described this self-defeating state of affairs as follows: "The Rorschach scene is at present a chaos of sights and a cacophony of sounds. With few exceptions, so far as I can judge from published reports of Rorschach test material, everyone using the test does what is right in his own eyes" (p. 131).

Subsequent to Beck's observation, J. E. Exner (1969; J. E. Exner & D. E. Exner, 1972) confirmed with survey data that the RIM in the 1970s had evolved in the United States not only into the five major systems of Beck, Klopfer, Hertz, Piotrowski, and Rapaport/Schafer, but also into an almost infinite number of idiographic variations and combinations of administration and scoring methods employed by individual clinicians. With such enormous variability in how Rorschach data were being obtained and codified, it was a small wonder that validating research findings had failed to accumulate despite a large volume of publications.

To overcome this serious obstacle to demonstrating the psychometric adequacy of the Rorschach, Exner (1974) developed the Rorschach Comprehensive System. As noted earlier, the guiding principle in developing the Comprehensive System was to produce a rational, reliable, and standardized approach to administering the instrument and coding subjects' responses. Exner believed that standardization of the types of data utilized in Rorschach research—so that, for example, one examiner's *M:SumC* and *X* + *%* would mean exactly the same thing as another examiner's *M:SumC* and *X* + *%*—would lead to cumulative positive findings demonstrating the soundness of the inkblot method. Current data, as summarized next, have justified his belief.

Current Data

The psychometric soundness of a measuring instrument is judged by whether (a) trained examiners can reach reasonable agreement concerning their scoring of its variables; (b) estimates of its reliability indicate that it provides reasonably accurate information, that is, scores obtained from it have minimal error variance and closely approximate actual or true scores; (c) its demonstrated corollaries identify purposes for which it is reasonably valid; and (d) there are adequate normative data concerning its descriptive statistics among various populations (Anastasi & Urbina, 1997, chaps. 3–6; Weiner, 1996). The RIM, when administered and coded according to the Comprehensive System, satisfies each of these four psychometric requirements.

To review briefly the evidence in this regard, research findings reported earlier indicate first that all of the variables coded in the Comprehensive System can be coded with substantial interrater agreement. Second, the reliability of Rorschach summary scores has been documented in a series of retest studies with both children and adults over retest intervals ranging from 7 days to 3 years. Among 100 nonpatient adults who were reexamined after 3 years, 13 core variables showed stability coefficients of .80 or more (*Z frequency, Lambda, M, Active movement, FC, SumC, Affective Ratio, Sum T, Sum V, X + %, Egocentricity Index, Sum Critical Special Scores*, and *Experience Actual*); an additional six core variables had stability coefficients greater than .70 (*Response Total, Passive movement, CF + C, Popular, FM*, and *Experienced Stimulation* (Exner & Weiner, 1995, pp. 21–27).

In a further report on the 1-year retest data of 50 nonpatient adults, Exner (1997a) provided reliability information on numerous additional variables as well. Summary scores showing stability coefficients above .80 in this report included *Pairs, Reflections*, and *Dimensionality*; the *Isolation Index* and the *Intellectualization Index*; *Cooperative* and *Aggressive* movements; and *Xu%, X − %*, and *WSum6*. *Morbid* and *Blend* responses had retest correlations above .70.

Concerning the validity of Rorschach assessment, the scientific merit of the instrument was confirmed in meta-analytic reviews by Atkinson (1986) and by Parker, Hanson, and Hunsley (1988) that led to two conclusions: (a) conceptual, theory-based studies demonstrate substantially higher validity coefficients for Rorschach variables than research undertaken without a theoretical empirical rationale; and (b) conceptual validation studies of the Rorschach indicate adequate validity values approximately equivalent to those found for the Minnesota Multiphasic Personality Inventory (MMPI).

Specifically, in Parker et al. the results of 411 published studies yielded population estimates of convergent validity coefficients of .41 for the Rorschach and .46 for the MMPI, with there being no statistically significant difference between these values. In a subsequent commentary on trends in Rorschach research, Shontz and Green (1992) indicated that "definitive statements can now be made about the psychometric properties of the Rorschach," because the meta-analytic reviews have "all concluded that the Rorschach is reliable and valid when it is properly used" (p. 149).

In a subsequently published meta-analytic study, Meyer and Handler (1997) examined the predictive validity of the Rorschach Prognostic Rating Scale (RPRS), a measure developed by B. Klopfer, Kirkner, Wisham, and Baker (1951) and previously known to demonstrate good construct validity as an index of ego strength and adaptive potential (Goldfried, Stricker, & Weiner, 1971, chap. 12). The Meyer and Handler findings confirmed that the RPRS is a valid predictor of psychotherapy outcome and foretells behavior change extremely well in both child and adult patients being treated in both hospital and outpatient settings.

In commenting on the implications of their findings, Meyer and Handler concur with the argument made earlier in this chapter concerning the advantages of conceiving the Rorschach as a method rather than merely as a test. As an assessment method, they noted that "the Rorschach is on a par with other methods [that are] amenable to the development of an infinite number of specific, operationally defined scales" (pp. 29, 31). Accordingly, they concluded, recognizing this diversity rather than erroneously viewing the Rorschach as a single test can help to preserve a distinction between its general utility as a device for obtaining information and the specific validity of individual scales derived from it.

Considerable specific information concerning the validation of individual Rorschach variables is included within the volumes of the Comprehensive System (J. E. Exner, 1991, 1993; Exner & Weiner, 1995) and has been summarized by Weiner (1997a) with respect to the following four clinically relevant assessment tasks:

1. With respect to personality description, the RIM provides a well-validated basis for describing many aspects of personality structure and a rich source of hypotheses for describing numerous aspects of personality dynamics.

2. With respect to differential diagnosis, the RIM has been demonstrated to aid in diagnosing various conditions that involve specific patterns of personality functioning, and it has potential to facilitate diagnosis of any condition that is determined by or contributes to distinctive personality characteristics.

3. With respect to treatment planning and evaluation, the RIM makes well-validated contributions to identifying treatment targets and possible obstacles to progress in psychotherapy, selecting appropriate treatment modalities, and monitoring change and improvement over time.

4. With respect to behavioral prediction, the RIM is not by nature a predictive instrument, and its use in predicting the future should be limited to cautious, personality-based estimates of behavioral potentials. On the other hand, Rorschach trait variables are likely to provide reasonably accurate longitudinal predictions of personality style, especially in adults, and, the more that a particular behavior is determined largely by personality characteristics or involves foreseeable environmental influence, the more likely it is that Rorschach variables will achieve better than chance prediction of whether it will occur.

The positive reliability and validity data that have accumulated with improved research methodology and the advent of the Comprehensive System have for the most part muted the psychometric challenges to Rorschach adequacy that peaked with Zubin et al. (1965). Although harsh criticisms of the RIM continue to appear now and then, sometimes accompanied by appeals to clinicians to desist from using or teaching it, none of these critiques has approached the level of scholarship or influence of Zubin et al. For example, Dawes (1984), in a book titled *House of Cards*, referred to the Rorschach as a "shoddy" instrument that "is not a valid test of anything" (pp. 123, 146). However, as I have elaborated in a commentary on Rorschach validity, Dawes' conclusions take no account of the standardizing impact of the Comprehensive System and are not based on a balanced review of the empirical data. The fact of the matter is that well-designed research continues with regularity to affirm the utility of the RIM in providing valid assessment of personality characteristics and facilitating not only differential diagnosis, but treatment planning and evaluation as well (see, e.g., Ganellen, 1996; Hilsenroth, Fowler, & Padawer, in press; Hilsenroth, Fowler, Padawer, & Handler, 1997; Weiner, in press).

Finally, with regard to the importance of adequate normative data, the Rorschach Comprehensive System provides detailed descriptive statistics for each of its coded variables on a sample of 700 nonpatient adults stratified to represent the U.S. census; on 1,390 children and adolescents separately for each age from 5 to 16; and on patient reference groups of 320 hospitalized schizophrenic patients, 315 hospitalized depressive patients, 440 diagnostically diverse outpatients, and 180 outpatients with character disorders (J. E. Exner, 1993, chap. 12). The size and diversity of these normative and reference samples provide more standardized information than is available for most psychological assessment measures and establishes the RIM as adequately normed for a U.S. population.

To conclude this introductory chapter, then, the fifth and final question can now be answered: The Rorschach Inkblot Method is a psychometrically sound measuring instrument. With this assurance, and drawing on the answers given to the four previous questions, the discussion in this book of principles of Rorschach interpretation can proceed with the understanding that the RIM has both objective and subjective measurement features, serves both as a measure of perception and as a measure of association, assesses both personality structure and personality dynamics, and functions not just as a test but as a multifaceted method of collecting data about personality processes.

2

Approaches to
Rorschach Interpretation

Having considered in chapter 1 the nature of the Rorschach Inkblot Method (RIM) as a measuring instrument, we can now turn our attention to basic considerations in translating Rorschach responses into conclusions about the subject who gives them. These conclusions consist of descriptive statements that address structural and dynamic features of subjects' personality functioning and contribute to diagnostic inferences, treatment recommendations, and hypotheses concerning their previous life experiences and likely future behavior in certain kinds of circumstances. The descriptive statements that examiners derive from the Rorschach are by tradition referred to as "interpretations" and their derivation is called the "interpretive process."

The manner in which Rorschach examiners approach the interpretive process depends on three factors: (a) the basis on which they elect to justify their descriptions, inferences, hypotheses, and recommendations; (b) the interpretive strategies on which they rely in determining which features of the data to examine and emphasize; and (c) the extent to which they modify their interpretations in relation to a subject's age, gender, and sociocultural background.

JUSTIFYING INTERPRETATIONS:
THE OUIJA BOARD, AUTHORITATIVE, EMPIRICAL,
AND CONCEPTUAL APPROACHES

Psychologists at different times and in various places have typically chosen one of four approaches to justifying their Rorschach interpretations. Two of these approaches rarely reflect clinical wisdom or scientific sophistication and have previously been labeled the *Ouija board approach* and the *authoritative approach* (J. E. Exner & Weiner, 1995, chap. 1). The other two approaches consist of *empirical* and *conceptual* perspectives on the interpretive process that, when integrated in an informed fashion, serve effectively to indicate how and why Rorschach responses warrant the inferences being drawn from them.

The Ouija Board Approach

When examiners employ the Ouija board approach to Rorschach interpretation, they justify their conclusions by alluding to their empathic or intuitive gifts. "It's just a feeling I have from this person's record," they may say; when asked what there is about the record that gives them this feeling, they say, "I can't tell you exactly what it was in the record, but I'm pretty sure I'm right." Quite possibly there are interpersonally sensitive clinicians who can use the Oiuja board approach to good effect, deriving accurate and clinically useful hypotheses about a subject's personality functioning on the basis of a Rorschach examination without being able to specify their sources of information in the test data. However, even when it appears to work, the Ouija board approach has the disadvantages of being insufficiently generalizable, inadequately focused, and professionally embarrassing.

With respect to generalizability, the insights of highly intuitive clinicians reside in their unique capacities to grasp the psychological essence of people they are examining. However, unless these clinicians can identify generally observable phenomena that help them understand their patients, there is little they can teach or transmit to anyone else. As a consequence, their skills benefit only their individual patients and make no general contribution to knowledge. Such is the case with the Ouija board approach to Rorschach interpretation, which has little to offer the field of assessment unless intuitive assessors provide hypotheses about the interpretive significance of specific aspects of the test data—at which point they are no longer relying solely on their intuition.

With respect to focus, the problem with intuitions is that they come and go as the inspiration strikes, and they rarely provide dependable means of painting a comprehensive picture of personality functioning or answering specific referral questions. For example, a Ouija board interpreter of the Rorschach may formulate some keen insights into a subject's interpersonal orientation when the referral question concerns depth of depression and suicide potential. If asked how depressed the subject is and whether suicide precautions appear indicated, this clinician may have to say, "I don't have any feelings about that."

As for embarrassment, Rorschach assessors who base their interpretations on intuition risk jeopardizing the esteem of their professional colleagues and the respect they command in public situations, such as giving testimony in a forensic case. The professionals with whom psychologists interact are too informed and the general public is too sophisticated for examiners to prosper by cloaking themselves in mysticism. Intuitive clinicians who suggest that only Rorschach examiners with their special gifts can interpret subjects' responses isolate themselves from the professional assessment community, and those who maintain that the utility of the inkblot method falls beyond the pale of scientific scrutiny gain themselves a public identity shared with astrologists and palm readers.

The Authoritative Approach

When examiners employ the authoritative approach to Rorschach interpretation, they justify their conclusions by referring to the opinions and conclusions of presumed authorities on the inkblot method. If the authorities referred to have contributed scientifically sound and clinically meaningful formulations to the Rorschach literature, examiners who invoke their name will usually be on solid ground. In fact, the justification of interpretations by informed appeal to authority can serve both examiners and their clients well. Clinicians who keep current with the literature gain respect for their diligence and competence, and the knowledge they acquire enhances their capacities to form accurate impressions and make helpful recommendations.

On the other hand, Rorschach examiners who rely too heavily on appeals to authority may undermine their own independent capacity to account for the conclusions they draw. Examiners who customarily cite authority in support of their interpretations may not be adequately prepared to indicate why a particular authority is credible. For example, to say that a Rorschach with very poor form quality suggests the possibility of schizophrenia is justifiable, but saying that this is so because "that's what Weiner (1996) says" constitutes an inadequate justification because it lacks any explanation of why Weiner endorsed this diagnostic guideline.

Examiners who depend exclusively on authority may fare reasonably well in clinical practice, especially if they choose their authorities carefully and are seldom required to provide direct feedback to patients, referral sources, and cross-examining attorneys. When feedback must be given, however, clinicians will give a better account of themselves and command more respect if they can go beyond appeals to authority and explain in their own words why certain characteristics of Rorschach protocols suggest certain personality patterns.

The Empirical Approach

When Rorschach examiners employ an empirical approach to their data, they justify their interpretations on the basis of research evidence. Attention is focused on the extent to which a subject's responses resemble responses typically given by persons with some known condition or characteristic, such as being depressed, antisocial, or interpersonally aversive. The more closely the responses of a particular subject correspond to empirical findings concerning how people with a certain condition or characteristic typically respond, the more justifiable it is to conclude that the subject has this condition or characteristic. Examiners who are prepared to provide empirical justification for their interpretations can now say, for example, that very poor form quality suggests the presence of a schizophrenic disorder not merely because Weiner says so, but because schizophrenic patients have been found on the average to show much poorer form quality than nonschizophrenic persons.

Compared to the Ouija board and authoritative approaches, an empirical approach to justifying Rorschach interpretations is both scientifically and professionally more respectable. Being able to draw on quantitative data concerning the discriminant validity and normative distribution of Rorschach variables allows examiners to distinguish normal and abnormal conditions with confidence and to describe personality characteristics with conviction. Adequate empirical foundations thus greatly facilitate effective utilization of the RIM in personality assessment and, the more fully Rorschach clinicians can draw on hard data to document the psychometric soundness of their conclusions, the better able they will be to translate these conclusions into effective and impressive applications of the instrument.

As useful as it may be, however, a strictly empirical approach to Rorschach interpretation has two shortcomings. First, empiricism demonstrates but does not explain relationships between measured phenomena. Although empirical statements of what Rorschach research findings indicate are sounder and more convincing than appeals to intuition or authority, they do not identify the personality processes that link certain patterns of response with certain descriptive or diagnostic inferences. Thus, saying that schizophrenic patients are known to show very poor form quality does not indicate why this phenomenon occurs. The empirical correlates of Rorschach variables do not reveal why particular subjects respond to the inkblots in certain ways, or why certain ways of responding to the inkblots help to identify a broad range of personality characteristics and normal and abnormal conditions.

A second shortcoming of a strictly empirical interpretive approach involves insufficient attention to idiographic aspects of subjects' responses, particularly in their thematic imagery. Numerous features of thematic imagery can be codified along with the structural data and subjected to empirical analyses that document their normative distribution and behavioral correlates. Consider, for example, the following response to Card III: "It's two happy people, and they've got this big pot of food between them; they're making this nice lunch, and they're going to have a real good time eating it." Available content scoring schemes provide empirically based codes for the activity, cooperative interaction, mature object representation, and oral dependent imagery apparent in this response.[1] However, the codes assigned by these scoring schemes would be the same if the response were merely, "Two people cooking some food together in a pot."

Hence coding for the first version of this sample response would not take into account the people being "happy," making a "nice lunch," and being about to enjoy "a real good time," all of which are idiographic elaborations that may have important implications for the subject's state of mind, such as a highly positive outlook on life or perhaps pressing needs to deny unpleasantness. Unless examiners are prepared to go beyond strictly empirical justification of their interpretations, to include attention to idiographic elaborations for which codification and quantification may not be available, they are likely to overlook potential valuable sources of information in a Rorschach protocol.

The Conceptual Approach

When Rorschach examiners adopt a conceptual approach to justifying their interpretations, they identify aspects of personality functioning that link their test data with the conclusions they draw from them. Thus, from a conceptual perspective, very poor form quality suggests schizophrenic disorder not simply because someone has said so (authoritative approach) or because research findings have demonstrated that such a relationship exists (empirical approach). Instead, this clinically important relation exists because (a) poor form quality indicates inaccurate perception, especially when there is a substantial percentage of distorted form responses; (b) inaccurate perception constitutes the basis of impaired reality testing; and (c) impaired reality testing is a defining characteristic of schizophrenia. As this illustration indicates, interpretations in the conceptual approach revolve around personality constructs (such as impaired reality testing) that account both for the obtained Rorschach data (such as very poor form quality) and the inferences drawn from these data (such as possible schizophrenia).

A conceptual approach to Rorschach interpretation contributes to overcoming the shortcomings of a strictly empirical approach to the data and provides useful guidelines for clinical practice and research design. In assessment practice, formulating both measuring instruments and referral questions in terms of personality functions contributes to efficient use of the test data and effective preparation of reports. Identifying in advance

---

[1]These include scoring categories utilized or developed by Blatt, Brenneis, Schimek, and Glick (1976); J. E. Exner (1993); Masling, Rabie, and Blondheim (1967); and Urist (1977). The coding of thematic imagery is discussed further in chapter 6.

those dimensions of personality functioning that bear critically on whatever questions are being asked helps examiners attend selectively to features of the data most likely to measure these dimensions; such selective focusing, in turn, helps examiners organize their reports around adequately explained conclusions that are responsive to the referral. When asked about possible schizophrenia, for example, conceptually oriented Rorschach examiners anticipate paying special attention to a subject's form level and writing an organizing statement on the order of, "Mr. Smith's poor reality testing, as reflected in an unusual frequency of inaccurate perceptions of the Rorschach stimuli, is consistent with the presence of a schizophrenic disorder."

In a broader sense, formulating interpretations in conceptual terms can help Rorschach clinicians communicate their impressions to an audience beyond other psychodiagnosticians and mental health professionals. The examiner who says only, "I think this woman is schizophrenic because her form level is poor" will make little sense to listeners who are not themselves Rorschachers. The examiner who instead says, "I think this woman is schizophrenic because she tends to misperceive the meaning of events in her life" will probably be understood by reasonably intelligent people, whatever their level of psychological sophistication.

It is by facilitating such communication that a conceptual approach to Rorschach interpretation can enrich research efforts as well as clinical practice. When Rorschach findings are conceptualized in terms of personality processes, they can readily be linked to general lines of research concerning the nature, origin, and implications of personality functions, such as the causes of perceptual inaccuracy and the consequences of becoming schizophrenic. As I have elaborated elsewhere (Weiner, 1986), these linkages between Rorschach formulations and scientific study of personality and psychopathology allow Rorschach clinicians to draw on a vast array of information to help sharpen their understanding and application of the instrument. In turn, these linkages make it possible for clinicians and researchers who have minimal familiarity with applications of the RIM to utilize Rorschach research findings to expand their knowledge of normal and abnormal personality processes.

FORMULATING INTERPRETATIONS: STRUCTURAL, THEMATIC, BEHAVIORAL, AND SEQUENCE ANALYSIS STRATEGIES

As noted in the introduction to this chapter, the Rorschach interpretive process requires examiners to formulate some strategy for choosing which features of subjects' responses to examine and emphasize. The nature of the RIM as both a measure of perception and a measure of association (see chap. 1) identifies two such interpretive strategies: an analysis of the *structural characteristics* of a Rorschach protocol and an analysis of its *thematic characteristics*. In addition, because valuable information can be gleaned from the manner in which people approach taking the Rorschach, especially in their relationship with the examiner, analysis of subjects' *behavioral characteristics* constitutes a third worthwhile strategy. Finally, the amount of information derived from a Rorschach examination can be maximized by an interpretive strategy that integrates structural, thematic, and behavior characteristics into a *sequence analysis*.

Structural Characteristics

Interpretation of the structural characteristics of a Rorschach protocol derives from the conceptualization of the instrument as a measure of perception and is based on the assumption that the way in which subjects formulate their responses constitutes a representative sample of their behavior. Because the Rorschach stimuli are in fact only inkblots, being asked to say what else they might be and why presents subjects with a problem-solving task. How subjects exercise perceptual and cognitive processes to accomplish this task, and thereby deliver responses, indicates how they are likely to cope with perceptual-cognitive tasks in general and how they tend to think, feel, and act in problem-solving and decision-making situations.

Because the ways in which subjects structure the inkblots is likely to reflect how they are inclined to structure other kinds of perceptual-cognitive experiences, identifiable correlates of structuring the Rorschach in certain ways provide the basis for numerous inferences concerning a subject's characteristic dispositions and current emotional and attitudinal states. For example, individuals who respond mainly to blot details and rarely use the whole card in formulating their responses can be expected to lack capacity or willingness to integrate aspects of their experience; such people in their daily lives are the kinds of individuals who "don't see the big picture" or "lose sight of the forest for the trees."

Similarly, people who report many perceptually inaccurate or distorted forms can be expected in their daily lives to misperceive what is happening around them and misjudge the consequences of their actions; those whose determinants include frequent articulation of the black and gray features of the blots are probably people who, at least at the moment, are looking on the dark side of things and experiencing sad and gloomy affect; and various other interpretive implications are likewise conceptually and empirically attached to structural aspects of how subjects respond to the Rorschach task. Specific guidelines for the interpretation of structural characteristics of Rorschach data are elaborated in chapter 5.

Thematic Characteristics

Interpretation of the thematic characteristics of a Rorschach protocol derives from the conceptualization of the instrument as a measure of association and is based on the assumption that responses are symbolic of behavior. In thematic interpretation, the RIM is approached as a stimulus to fantasy, rather than as a perceptual task, and attention is directed primarily toward those responses that appear to involve projected attributes.

Thus, the thematic characteristics of Rorschach responses consist of ways in which percepts are elaborated beyond merely indicating what the inkblots might be. For example, a response of "Two people" on Card III has several important structural characteristics, including a probable *D* location, human content, a Pair, a Popular, and good form; however, the response has few thematic characteristics (although an unusually high frequency of "Two people" responses may without being elaborated reveal some preoccupation with people or people-related events). By contrast, saying that Card III is "Two people just standing there" involves a definite thematic elaboration that begins to suggest a passive orientation to life or an impression of people as not readily becoming engaged with each other. Should this response be further elaborated into "Two people just standing there, each waiting for the other to take the first step," then there is even further suggestion of the subject's passivity and interpersonal reticence, especially if this same theme appears in several other responses as well. In this way, thematic imagery provides the basis for interpretive hypotheses concerning many aspects of a person's underlying needs, attitudes, conflicts, and concerns, particularly in relation to self-perceptions, interpersonal orientations, and self- and object-representations. Detailed guidelines for deriving interpretations from the thematic characteristics of Rorschach responses are elaborated in chapter 6.

Behavioral Characteristics

Interpretation of the behavioral characteristics of a Rorschach protocol derives from the assumption that how people deal with this test-taking task and how they relate to the examiner provide information about their current frame of mind and how they generally tend to approach problem-solving and interpersonal situations. For example, comments about being tested ("This seems like a waste of time"; "I'm worried what this test will show") point respectively to an angry or anxious emotional state. Task-related comments can similarly reveal subjects' inclinations to be passive/deferential ("How many responses would you like me to give?") or hostile/assertive ("That's all you can get me to say about that one") in relation to authority.

The nature of the Rorschach as a measure of behavior has received far less attention than its operation as measures of perception and association, which explains in part why this concept was not included in the discussion in chapter 1. Of course, test-taking attitudes and examiner interaction behaviors are not unique to the Rorschach situation. They occur in all clinical evaluation situations, including interviewing as well as testing, and they can be interpreted meaningfully by empathic clinicians whether or not they have any specific knowledge of the RIM. This may account for the fact that test behavior did not figure prominently in the early basic texts on the Rorschach and has rarely been the subject of published research with the instrument.

On the other hand, for most people taking the Rorschach is a less familiar and more ambiguous situation than being interviewed or being administered a relatively structured test. Accordingly, a Rorschach examination may be particularly likely to evoke personally revealing patterns of dealing with the task and relating to the examiner. Moreover, there are informative features of test behavior in the Rorschach situation that are unique to this instrument, such as how subjects handle the cards and whether they turn them, and a Rorschach-based understanding of what such test behaviors signify has a definite place in the interpretive process.

Detailed and systematic consideration of the import of behavioral characteristics was introduced into the Rorschach literature by Phillips and J. G. Smith (1953), in a chapter titled "Attitudes, Role Playing, and Life Themes"; by Schafer (1954), in a chapter titled "Interpersonal Dynamics in the Test Situation"; and by Schachtel (1966), in a chapter titled "The Interpersonal Meaning of the Test Situation." These contributions from the distant past, along with an article by Masling (1960) titled "The Influence of Situational and Interpersonal Variables in Projective Testing," remain the most thoughtful and informative discussions available concerning utilization of test-taking and examiner interaction variables in the interpretive process (see also Masling, 1997, 1998). Specific guidelines for interpreting characteristics of Rorschach test behavior are discussed in chapter 7.

Sequence Analysis

Given that attention to structural, thematic, and behavioral characteristics of Rorschach protocols can each lead to useful interpretations, clinicians and scholars have often pondered which strategy to pursue. As would be anticipated from the discussion in chapter 1 concerning the nature of the Rorschach, those who have viewed the instrument primarily as a measure of perception have tended to favor structural data as a source of information, whereas those who have regarded the RIM primarily as a measure of association have been inclined to emphasize thematic and behavioral data in their interpretive strategies. At the same time, however, Rorschachers of both persuasions have long recognized that the inkblot method measures both perceptual and associational processes (see pp. 10–18) and have or-chestrated their interpretive strategies accordingly.

I have referred elsewhere to the interpretive overlap between perceptual and associational theorists as "Thematics among the structurists" and "Cognition among the imagists" (Weiner, 1995b). Taking first thematics among the structurists, S. J. Beck (1968; as noted in chap. 1) was a staunch advocate of a strictly structural approach to Rorschach data but included attention to need-determined perceptual distortions among his interpretive strategies. Among his most important interpretive strategies was attention to "personal *F-*," which he defined as "a misshaping of reality as dictated by personal needs" (p. 21). Piotrowski (1977) pursued a perceptual under-standing of personality in his work with the Rorschach but wrote at length about using response elaborations to identify subjects' attitudes toward people and their customary roles in interpersonal relationships. Bohm (1951/1958) hewed strictly to Rorschach's original emphasis on perceptual processes in Rorschach interpretation but commented on the dynamic im-plications of responses depicting human interactions.

As for cognition among the imagists, Lindner (1950) recommended con-tent interpretation as a way of enriching the clinical value of the Rorschach but cautioned against abandoning traditional perceptual approaches to the instrument. B. Klopfer et al. (1954) and Schafer (1954) placed considerable emphasis on psychoanalytic formulations of thematic imagery but did so in the context of a well-elaborated system for coding structural features of Rorschach responses. Schachtel (1966) elaborated how projection can influ-ence the content of subjects' responses and their test behavior in ways that reveal their subjective experience but also maintained that "content, by itself, is of relatively little value and unreliable as a diagnostic indicator" (p. 258).

Hence suggested interpretive strategies in the classical structural Ror-schach literature embrace attention to thematic imagery, and strategies recommended in the classical thematic literature include attention to the interpretive significance of structural variables. As noted in chapter 1, both of these enlightened perspectives are well-echoed in contemporary litera-ture. The interpretive strategies recommended in current editions of the Comprehensive System volumes (J. E. Exner, 1991, 1993; J. E. Exner & Weiner, 1995) call specifically for thematic analysis of idiographic and embellished content, and P. M. Lerner (1991) and Aronow, Reznikoff, and Moreland (1994), continuing the tradition of focusing heavily on thematic content in Rorschach interpretation, also addressed structural aspects of the interac-tion between perceptual and fantasy components of responses.

Turning now to the question of which interpretive strategy is preferable to pursue, two considerations preclude any single selection. First of all, there is no way to determine prior to considering a response carefully whether its structural, thematic, or behavioral characteristics will prove most informative; likewise, until all of the responses in a record have been considered carefully, there is no way to determine in advance which characteristic of the protocol as a whole will reveal most about a subject's personality functioning. Second, learning about people from how they respond to the Rorschach is maximized not by an emphasis on either structural, thematic, or behavioral features of a record, but rather by an integrative strategy in which inferences are derived from a carefully orchestrated integration of all three aspects of subject's responses. This integrative strategy is the essence of sequence analysis.

In support of these two assertions, consider first the relationship that exists between the nature of a response and the most informative strategy for interpreting it. Suppose a subject begins on Card I with "A black bat, the whole thing, with wings here (side details) and the body here (center detail)." This response contains virtually no thematic imagery, certainly none that is idiographic, and there are no extraneous comments or indications of an unusual approach to the task. Structurally, however, the response contributes to summary scores for W, Fo, A, P, and Z, and it also contains a C', suggestive of a negative or painful emotional experience. By virtue of being normatively infrequent in the initial response to Card I, this C' lends a noteworthy idiographic quality to the structure of the response. In this example, then, the structural characteristics of the response are particularly revealing and important to pursue, whereas its thematic and behavioral characteristics add little information. Records comprised largely of responses of this type would be notable mainly for their structural characteristics.

But now suppose that the initial response on Card I is "Something flying around, I don't know what it is, but it's lost and can't find its way home." This response contributes some structural elements to the data, in the form of what appears to be basically a $W\ FM\ A$ response, but these are common response elements on Card I and provide only a modest amount of information. Thematically, however, the association to being lost and unable to find one's way home contains compelling implications for feelings of confusion, uncertainty, and helplessness, and the thematic imagery in this response is more revealing and important to pursue than its structural elements. Records consisting mainly of this type of response would be notable primarily for their thematic characteristics.

As a third alternative, consider a subject whose first words on being handed Card I are "Doctor, is it permitted to turn the card?" Especially if this comment is followed only by a single, unelaborated $W\ F\ A$ percept, the Card I data would be notable more for their behavioral characteristics than either their structural or thematic features, and it would be the test behavior alone that begins to suggest what could well be an authoritarian personality orientation. Most examiners have had the experience of taking guarded, unelaborated, and narrowly focused Rorschach records in which the structural and thematic data provide little information beyond identifying the subject's defensiveness and in which the most revealing features of the examination involve how the subject approached the task and related to the examiner.

As an interpretive strategy that integrates structural, thematic, and behavioral characteristics of subjects' responses, sequence analysis draws conjointly on all three features of a Rorschach protocol. Sequence analysis, which was introduced to Rorschach assessment by Klopfer (B. Klopfer et al., 1954, chap. 11), involves attending thoroughly to subjects' perceptual-cognitive structuring, thematic imagery, and test behavior and then interweaving conclusions drawn from all three Rorschach facets into a description of personality functioning. As a conjoint interpretive strategy, moreover, sequence analysis goes beyond merely additive or complementary utilization of structural, thematic, and behavioral elements to consider (a) the *interplay* of all three elements in each individual response and (b) the *succession* of these elements from one response to another.

To illustrate analysis of the interplay of elements in a single response, consider the following version of an initial response to Card I: "I really don't want to do this, but I guess it could be a black albatross flying around, like it's lost its way." As is emphasized frequently in the chapters that follow, no individual response or response characteristic should be taken to mean anything for certain without being considered in the context of the entire record. However, as a basis for illustrating at this point the generation of hypotheses, this sample response is rich with interacting structural, thematic, and behavioral elements.

The structure includes a *C'*, an unusual form, and an *INCOM* (an albatross is not black); the imagery includes the possible symbolism of the albatross itself (in light of what is usually meant by having an albatross around one's neck) and of losing one's way; and the behavior contains clues to aversion to being examined ("I really don't want to do this") and a hesitant, tentative, and noncommittal manner of self-presentation ("I guess it could be"). Taken together, these multiple features of the response suggest an uncertain, indecisive person who feels unlucky and overburdened, who lacks a clear sense of direction in life, whose uncertainty and discouragement are depressing, and whose distress tends to interfere with being able to see things the way most people do and to reason logically about relationships between events.

The sequence analysis of successive responses consists of examining how the structural, thematic, and behavioral characteristics change from one response to another. Suppose, for example, that this previous subject follows the response of the black albatross that is lost by inverting the card and saying, "I like it better this way, it's a bat." Then the subject's positive comment, conventional structure ($WFAP$), and lack of thematic elaboration would appear to indicate a capacity to recover from an episode of distress, become more comfortable, and respond more realistically and adaptively, albeit at the expense of a narrowed focus of attention and a somewhat immature defensive maneuver (inverting the card) in which something bad is made to go away by ceasing to look at it.

As an alternative example, suppose the response following the lost black albatross is "I don't even want to say what I see next, but it looks like the face of an ugly person, somebody you really wouldn't want to look at, and he's got mean-looking eyes and a misshapen nose." In this complex and revealing response, there is little indication of defense and recovery from the distress associated with the black albatross. Instead, the subject's comments show continuing discomfort with the Rorschach task and what is being seen; the structure of the response shows a deterioration in perceptual accuracy, from an unusual to a minus form; and the imagery contains strong suggestions of a devalued self-image ("ugly" and "misshapen") and of concern about being under unfriendly scrutiny from others ("face" with "mean-looking eyes"). Thus, the distress associated with a depressing sense of uncertainty in the first response would appear to have led in the subsequent response to even greater distress associated with poor reality testing, negative self-attitudes, and interpersonal discomfort.

In this way, then, the interplay of structural, thematic, and behavioral elements of Rorschach responses and their succession from one response to another identify sequences of distress, defense, deterioration, and recovery that in turn reveal the key psychological concerns in subjects' lives, the nature of the coping strategies they employ to deal with these concerns, and how successful they are in sustaining an adaptive and rewarding lifestyle. This is the essence of a sequence analysis, the data from which make it possible for Rorschach clinicians to provide comprehensive personality descriptions and speak intelligently to a broad range of differential diagnostic and treatment issues. Specific guidelines for conducting sequence analysis in the interpretation of Rorschach protocols are elaborated in chapter 8.

AGE, GENDER, AND CROSS-CULTURAL CONSIDERATIONS IN INTERPRETATION

Personality assessors must always consider whether the measures they are using are applicable to the people with whom they are using them. The questions most commonly raised in this regard concern the reliability and validity of particular assessment instruments in examining subjects who differ in age, gender, and cultural background. Test developers typically address these questions by accumulating a large normative database that is representative of males and females who range widely in age and come from diverse backgrounds. Having such a representative normative sample increases the likelihood that a test will be broadly applicable to various kinds of people.

However, a single set of representative norms does not ensure that a test can be interpreted similarly regardless of a subject's age, gender, and cultural background. Including diverse groups in a normative database contributes to the generalizability of the normative standards that are derived, but such lumping of diverse groups can also obscure differences among them. Hence there may be circumstances in which test performance should be evaluated in relation to normative responses among a specific subgroup of people with whom a subject shares important demographic characteristics.

To provide demographically sensitive interpretation of personality assessment instruments, examiners need to utilize appropriate normative data for two purposes: (a) to determine whether and how the implications of certain test findings for particular personality characteristics differ from one group to another, and (b) to determine whether and how personality characteristics identified by test findings differ from one group to another in what they imply about a subject's level of adjustment. The Rorschach literature includes both normative data and conceptual guidelines that can facilitate age-, gender-, and culture-sensitive interpretation.

Considerations Related to Age

As elaborated by J. E. Exner and Weiner (1995, chap. 1), Rorschach examiners working with subjects of different ages need to learn only one set of interpretive hypotheses because Rorschach responses have similar implications for personality characteristics whatever the subject's age. On the other hand, personality characteristics inferred from Rorschach responses may differ in what they imply for adjustment among subjects who differ in age, and conclusions concerning how people who give certain kinds of responses are adapting in everyday life must be framed accordingly.

Two examples can be used to illustrate both the universality of Rorschach interpretive principles and the necessity of age-related considerations in drawing conclusions from Rorschach interpretations. Consider first the relationship between FC and $CF + C$ responses. There is good reason to believe that use of FC in determining a response reflects well-modulated, fairly stable, and somewhat reserved ways of experiencing and expressing affect. Use of $CF + C$, by contrast, correlates with relatively spontaneous, intense, and labile emotionality. A predominance of FC over $CF + C$ responses suggests tendencies to restrain feelings for the most part, to express relatively mild degrees of affect even in emotionally provocative situations, and to maintain an emotionally even keel. A predominance of $CF +$

C responses usually indicates tendencies to let emotions flow freely rather than hold them in check, to express strong feelings even with little provocation, and to show frequent fluctuations in emotional tone (see J. E. Exner, 1993, chap. 19).

This interpretive significance of color use applies equally to children, adolescents, and adults of all ages. However, after an examiner has arrived at whatever interpretation is generally indicated by a particular *FC:CF + C* ratio, conclusions about what this interpretation signifies for individual subjects must be formulated with regard to their age. For example, a predominance of *FC* over *CF + C* responses, which generally indicates restraint in emotional displays and relatively little spontaneous affective expression, is likely to signify adaptive maturity in an adult. However, the same Form–Color Ratio in the record of an 8-year-old suggests maladaptive emotional inhibition, because 8-year-olds normally do not deal with their emotions in a reserved and well-modulated fashion. Conversely, a predominance of *CF + C* over *FC*, which identifies relatively intense and unrestrained affectivity, is consistent with expectations for an 8-year-old but likely to indicate emotional immaturity in an adult.

As this example shows, effective utilization of the Rorschach with subjects differing in age does not require separate sets of age-related interpretive hypotheses, but it does call for attention to relevant normative data. In the particular case of color use, the Comprehensive System normative data relevant to the conclusions drawn in the example are as follows: Nonpatient 8-year-olds have a mean *FC* of 1.80, a mean *CF* of 2.73, and a mean *C* of .43; just 40% of persons this age have a *CF + C* exceeding *FC* by more than one, but only 8% have an *FC* exceeding *CF + C* by more than one. By contrast, nonpatient adults have a mean *FC* of 4.09, a mean *CF* of 2.36, and a mean *C* of .08; only 4% have a *CF + C* exceeding *FC* by more than one, whereas 49% have an *FC* exceeding *CF + C* by more than one (Exner, 1993, chap. 12).

As a second example, consider the interpretation and age-related implications of the *Egocentricity Index*, which is best construed as a measure of self-focusing. As such, the Egocentricity Index indicates the extent to which people tend to pay attention to or be concerned with themselves, as opposed to attending to and being concerned about others. A low level of attention to or concern about oneself, as manifest in a low Egocentricity Index, frequently serves as an index of low self-esteem. This interpretation of what the Egocentricity Index signifies for self-focusing is applicable at every age.

However, the implications of a particular level of self-focusing as identified by the Egocentricity Index vary with the age of the subject. Children are normally quite self-centered early on and become gradually less so as they mature. The normative Rorschach data for young people from age 5 to 16 closely reflect this well-documented developmental trend. The mean

Egocentricity Index is .69 among nonpatient 5-year-olds and decreases gradually in each successive year to a mean of .43 among nonpatient 16-year-olds, and the adult mean for the Egocentricity Ratio is .39. Clearly, then, a degree of self-focusing that meets normal expectation in a child would be unusually high in an adult; conversely, an Egocentricity Index that is average and thus unremarkable for an adult may be unusually low in a child and thus indicative of problems with self-esteem.

In practice, then, with respect to all of the interpretable variables in a Rorschach protocol, examiners can use the instrument effectively with people of any age provided that they (a) comprehend the interpretive significance that attaches to these variables, and (b) take into account any age-specific differences in normative expectation that are likely to influence the implications of particular interpretations for the adequacy of a subject's adjustment.

Considerations Related to Gender

In parallel to the universality of Rorschach interpretations across age groups, Rorschach variables identify the same personality characteristics in the same way for males and females alike. Although the interpretive process accordingly does not vary with a subject's gender, gender-related issues and concerns can affect the implications of certain personality characteristics identified by Rorschach data. For example, heightened concern about the normal aging process among subjects at midlife often includes worries about declining potency in men and about loss of childbearing capacity in women. Rorschach imagery involving figures seen as being pregnant or "having big stomachs" often identifies some preoccupation with the reproductive process, whether in the record of a male or female subject, but such imagery implies a much more poignant concern when given by women than men. Similarly, imagery involving cylindrical objects that are hanging down, or "gone limp," is likely to point to preoccupation with weakness or ineffectiveness in both male and female subjects, but such imagery is likely to have more focused and troublesome implications for men than for women.

Such life cycle and contextual issues that affect males and females differently should be considered in judging the implications of personality characteristics inferred from Rorschach findings. On the other hand, unlike Rorschach protocols of persons differing in age, the records of nonpatient males and females show virtually no normative structural differences that alter the implications of interpretations according to gender. Exner at one time published separate descriptive statistics for the 350 females and 350 males in the Comprehensive System nonpatient reference sample (J. E. Exner, 1991, chap. 2). However, the differences between these female and male norms were so minuscule and inconsequential that he subsequently re-combined them into a single 700-person normative table (Exner, 1993, chap. 12).

One further example may be helpful in illustrating the utility of distinguishing between the interpretive significance of Rorschach variables and the implications of interpretations for adjustment. It is sometimes suggested that men in today's society are generally more assertive than women and women are more passive than men; consequently, according to this notion, assertiveness in women and passivity in men tend to prove maladaptive. With respect to the interpretive significance of Rorschach variables, it does not matter whether these propositions are correct. Aggressive content (AG) is a measure of assertiveness, and the more such content subjects give, regardless of gender, the more likely they are to behave in a verbally or physically assertive manner. Similarly, a preponderance of passive over active movement responses ($p > a + 1$) identifies behavioral passivity in interpersonal relationships among male and female subjects alike.

As for the implications of giving Rorschach indications of assertiveness or passivity, however, it could be that the personality characteristic identified by numerous AG responses is adaptive for males and maladaptive for females, and contrariwise for a preponderance of passive movements. The Rorschach can help to determine whether such is generally the case by answering the following question: With respect to the postulated gender specificity of assertiveness and passivity, do nonpatient and therefore presumably adequately adjusted men and women differ in Rorschach indices of these characteristics?

The relevant Comprehensive System reference data on adult nonpatients are the following: (a) AG responses are given by 68.7% of males ($M = 1.70$) and 64.3% of females ($M = 1.19$); (b) a clinically significant finding of $AG > 2$ occurs in 11% of males and 16% of females; (c) active movement responses show means of 6.66 in males and 6.30 in females; (d) for passive movement responses the means are 2.76 for males and 2.62 for females; and (e) a clinically significant finding of $p > a + 1$ has a 0% frequency in nonpatient males and a 1% frequency in nonpatient females. These essentially equivalent normative levels indicate that nonpatient men and women closely resemble each other on Rorschach measures of assertiveness and passivity and that, at least in group terms, adequately adjusted women can be as assertive as men and adequately adjusted men as passive as women.

Considerations Related to Cultural Background

As in considering the significance of age and gender differences in applications of the Rorschach, the import of cultural differences must be assessed with respect to four considerations: (a) the interpretive significance of Rorschach variables for identifying personality characteristics, (b) the influence of cultural differences on the coding of responses, (c) the impact of language on the delivery and comprehension of responses, and (d) the implications of inferred personality characteristics for adaptation within the subject's cultural context.

Interpretive Significance of Rorschach Variables. In parallel with the previous discussion of differences in age and gender, Rorschach variables mean what they mean regardless of a subject's socioeconomic status, ethnicity, and national origin. Thus, wherever people live and whatever their cultural background, those subjects with an introversive Experience Balance (*EB*) are likely to be ideational people who prefer thought to action and are more likely to deal with their experience in a contemplative than expressive manner. Wherever they come from, subjects who give numerous distorted forms (high $X - \%$) tend to perceive their world unrealistically, those who underincorporate ($Zd < -3.0$) are inclined to deal with situations hastily and carelessly, and those who give several Morbid contents are concerned about the adequacy, integrity, and well-being of their bodies and bodily functions. Across the entire range of structural and thematic features of Rorschach data, those features that have been validated in relation to particular cognitive, affective, or behavioral correlates will validly identify these same correlates in people of all kinds, anywhere in the world.

In support of this conclusion, basic interpretive hypotheses derived from Rorschach data have in fact been used successfully for over 75 years in clinical assessments and research studies all over the world, with people of many different kinds and with cultures at many different levels of development. American psychologists have at times thought of the Rorschach as having languished following Hermann Rorschach's death in 1922 until Beck published the first English-language article in 1930. In truth, however, the inkblot method and Rorschach's plates were circulating in many other countries before they came to the United States, and Beck's first article was preceded by Rorschach publications during the 1920s in such far-flung places as Japan, Peru, Russia, and Spain (Burlatchuk & Korzhova, 1994; Ogawa, 1993; Quintana & Campo, 1993; Raez de Ramirez, 1994). The global utilization of the Rorschach is currently reflected in the vigor of the International Rorschach Society, which typically draws participants from more than 30 different countries to its triennial congresses and sponsors *Rorschachiana*, an annual yearbook consisting of theoretical, research, and clinical contributions translated into English from many different languages.

The utility of the Rorschach extends not only to developed cultures in which professionals have been trained to use it, but to primitive societies as well. More than 60 years ago, Vernon (1935) observed that the Rorschach is an ideal instrument for exploring cross-cultural differences because, unlike verbal or more structured tests, it involves culture-free stimuli. As reviewed by Hallowell (1956), cultural anthropologists have long capitalized on Vernon's observation by employing the Rorschach in field studies of primitive and even preliterate tribes in many different locales. Hallowell concluded from his analysis of these field studies that the Rorschach is a universally applicable and cross-culturally relevant instrument:

> Rorschach protocols wherever collected with care exhibit constant as well as variable features which, considered as group phenomenon, appear to be of the same order as the protocols of individuals within any particular group. . . . So far as practical use is concerned there is no reason whatever to believe that the Rorschach test is "culture-bound." . . . Common principles of Rorschach interpretation can be applied to the protocols of subjects with any cultural background. (Hallowell, 1956, pp. 511, 512)

In more recent times, the anthropological tradition of cross-cultural research with the Rorschach has been carried on by such investigators as Boyer (1988), De Vos (De Vos & Boyer, 1989), and Vaz (1995), who have examined such interesting matters as personality differences between members of primitive tribes who have remained in their ancestral territory and those who have emigrated to urban areas and begun a process of acculturation. With respect to developed countries, Mattlar and Fried (1993) described a large-scale normative study in Finland in which the several hundred records obtained constitute a larger percentage of that country's total population than has been sampled in any other national study. They concluded from the Finnish data that "at least as concerns Europe and the U.S., it would seem that the principal elements of the structural summary could be described as 'sturdy,' little affected by nationality" (p. 110).

In a review of cross-cultural personality assessment, Butcher, Nezami, and Exner (1998) mirrored Hallowell's statement with the following conclusions:

> Findings, especially concerning personality description and/or psychopathology, have been strikingly similar. . . . When data relating to these several features [of personality] are compared cross-nationally, differences are modest because the distribution of Rorschach scores are surprisingly uniform regardless of what culture or country a sample of subjects may be drawn from. . . . Dozens of studies from various countries and cultures suggest that common features do exist in the Rorschach that accurately differentiate schizophrenia and the major affective disorders. . . . In summary, as noted above, the distribution of scores related to various personality features, when derived either from non-patient or patient samples, seems to be very similar across cultures. . . . The validity of the substance of interpretations does appear to be reasonably uniform regardless of the culture from which the protocol is collected. (p. 238)

Cultural Influences on Response Coding.   Possible exceptions to the generally universal interpretive significance of Rorschach variables can arise in instances in which the expected frequency of certain kinds of responses influences how these responses are coded. In the case of Popular responses, for example, 13 specific responses are coded *P* in the Comprehensive System on the basis of their having occurred in at least one third of 7,500 records given by a diverse sample of adult nonpatients and nonschizophrenic, nonpsychotic outpatients in the United States. The Comprehensive System data suggest that 4 to 7 Populars constitutes the normal range for this variable, with $P < 4$ indicating inability or unwillingness to recognize and endorse conventional modes of response and $P > 7$ indicating a more than usual emphasis on conventionality.

With respect to group differences, however, there is evidence that cultural context can influence how many and what kinds of responses are likely to appear in more than one third of records. Normative studies have established that in Finland and other Scandinavian countries, where pictures of what are called "Christmas elves" appear widely in printed matter the year around, "Christmas elves" are given frequently enough on Card II to be coded as a Popular (Mattlar & Fried, 1993). Should there be cultures in which such culture-specific responses as "Christmas elves" occur frequently, and in which some of the 13 Populars in the Comprehensive System occur infrequently, *P* will provide an accurate measure of conventionality only if it is coded in light of normative standards developed for those particular cultures. According to Sendin (1995), this already appears to be the case in Spain, where just 10 of the 13 Comprehensive System Populars appear in as many as one third of adult records.

Similar considerations apply to the coding of ordinary (*FQo*) and unusual (*FQu*) form level. Both *FQo* and *FQu* are coded for accurate percepts, as defined by a reasonably good correspondence between the shape of a blot location and the object it is said to resemble. The Comprehensive System codes as ordinary those responses that were given by at least 2% of the previously mentioned U.S. sample of 7,500 adults and as unusual those that appeared in fewer than 2% of these records but nevertheless clearly resembled the blot locations to which they were given. The number of times *FQo* and *FQu* are coded for a record in turn affects its form-level summary scores for $F + \%$, $X + \%$, and $Xu\%$. Hence cultural differences in the frequency with which certain kinds of accurately perceived responses are given can yield misleading interpretation not only of *P*, but also of $F + \%$, $X + \%$, and $Xu\%$, if Comprehensive System coding criteria are used. Where such cross-cultural differences are found to exist, form level as well as Populars require recoding based on culture-specific expectations before they can be interpreted according to usual standards as measures of accuracy and conventionality in perception.

Fortunately, with respect to universal applicability of Rorschach interpretation, cultural influences do not have any bearing on the coding of minus form level (*FQ-*) or the resulting level of $X - \%$ in a record. Minus form level is determined not by response frequency, but by whether responses constitute a substantial distortion or misperception of what the inkblots resemble. The boundaries between realistic and unrealistic perception are universal and not culture bound. Thus in Rorschach terms, for example, seeing Card I as a frog or Card VIII as a pelvis is perceptually inaccurate and calls for an *FQ-* coding, wherever and by whomever either of these responses is given.

Aside from Populars and ordinary form level, the only other code in the Comprehensive System based on response frequency is the Location Choice designation of ordinary details (*D*) as distinguished from unusual (*Dd*) details. In the development of the system, inkblot details that were used in 5% or more of the 7,500 records examined were designated as *D* locations, and those responded to in fewer than 5% were designated *Dd*. Hence, *D* and *Dd* location choices, like Popular contents and ordinary and unusual form quality, are aspects of coding that depend on frequency of occurrence and can accordingly be influenced by cultural differences.

These three content, form quality, and location choice codes that potentially can be influenced by cultural differences constitute only a small portion of the Comprehensive System coding scheme. All of the remaining codes in the system are assigned on the basis of criteria that are independent of the frequency with which certain kinds of responses appear, and they are thus culture free. It is accordingly unwarranted to assume that every aspect of coding and interpreting the RIM must be based on culture-specific normative data, just as it is inappropriate to assume that U.S. Comprehensive System criteria can be applied anywhere in their entirety. Further development of culture-specific norms for those few variables for which coding may be culture bound, building on the previously noted work on Popular responses in Finland and Spain, should prove helpful in minimizing culturally insensitive Rorschach interpretation.

Impact of Language. Culturally sensitive coding and interpretation of Rorschach protocols requires careful attention to the impact of language usage on how responses are formulated and delivered. Forms of expression particular to the native tongue subjects speak, symbolic referents distinctive to their cultural heritage, and dialectical differences in what certain words mean to them inevitably give linguistic shape to the verbal content in which they frame their responses on the Rorschach.

As an illustration of differing forms of expression, Spanish-speaking persons use an abundance of articles (e.g., "a," "an," "the") in expressing themselves and Japanese-speaking persons use none at all, both of which are natural in their respective languages but in literal translation sound stilted to the English-speaking ear. Regarding symbolic referents, the concept of a "spider woman" suggests at least to some people in many cultures concern about the threat of powerful and dangerous female or maternal figures of the kind that devour their own mates or young. However, in the legends of the Hopi Indians, spider woman is the Earth Goddess who is the "Mother of all" and who "receives light and nourishes life" (see Mullett, 1979). As for differences in dialect, the Spanish word "conferencia" translates into "conference" in English but is used by Spanish-speaking people to refer to what English-speaking people would call a "lecture." Even within English as spoken in the United States, words can take on different meanings in relation to the demography or geography of the person using them. For example, the carbonated soft drinks referred to as "pop" in the Midwest are known as "soda" in the East.

With respect to the coding of responses, subtleties in language usage have a particular bearing on the Special Scores in the Comprehensive System, all of which are based on features of verbalization. The basic criteria for coding these Special Scores are universally applicable, as are the interpretive hypotheses that attach to them. However, in order for examiners to identify whether subjects are expressing themselves in a peculiar or redundant way, whether their references to symbolic representations are bizarre or inappropriate, and whether their choice of descriptive terms warrants coding for *AG*, *COP*, or *MOR*, both subject and examiner must be fluent in the language being used.

The substantial impact of culture-specific language usage on Rorschach responses leaves little room for compromise with respect to fluency. In order for a Rorschach protocol to be properly coded and correctly interpreted, subjects need to be responding in their native tongue or a very well-known second language, and examiners need to be thoroughly familiar with that language and its cultural context. Subjects describing the inkblots in a second or unfamiliar language may not be able to provide a representative picture of their personality functioning, particularly with respect to the codes assigned to their responses. Taking records in the subject's native tongue and then translating them into another language prior to their being coded and interpreted can also lead to misrepresentation of the subject's personality, unless the translator is an experienced Rorschach clinician well-versed in both the original and the translation language.

As for examiners attempting to administer or code the Rorschach in a language with which they are not extremely familiar, this is an ill-advised practice that is likely to yield an inadequate if not invalid set of data. To compound this conceptual inadequacy of a Rorschach assessment in which either subject or examiner lacks fluency in the language being used, there are no normative data pertaining to this kind of assessment. Hence, even when English-speaking examiners feel confident that they have obtained a "good" record from a subject for whom English is a second and far from perfect language, they are not justified in relying on the Comprehensive System normative data in evaluating the significance of their results. Rorschach clinicians faced with the need to evaluate a subject who is not fluent in English are well-advised either to find an examiner fluent in the person's first language or to omit the Rorschach from their test battery. An equally strong stance in this regard is elaborated by Dana (1993, chap. 6).

Implications of Personality Characteristics for Adaptation. An extensive literature addresses issues concerning whether psychological normality is an absolute or relative phenomenon (see, e.g., Offer & Sabshin, 1991). Does successful adaptation depend on having certain personality characteristics, regardless of one's surroundings, or does it depend on having certain personality characteristics that are common in and valued by the society in which one lives? Contrariwise, does adjustment difficulty derive from having particular functioning limitations that are universally maladaptive or from having particular limitations that are unusual or frowned on in one's society?

Although detailed pursuit of these important questions is beyond this discussion, cross-cultural applications of the Rorschach must certainly take them into account. As a general guideline in this regard, it can readily be observed that both absolute and relative perspectives on abnormality contribute to reasonable conclusions. With regard to mental and physical status, for example, having at least average intelligence is likely to prove more adaptive than being mentally retarded wherever people find themselves, and, as Jonathan Swift (1726/1960) showed clearly, Gulliver was too big for the Lilliputians and too small for the Brobdingnagians. Similarly for personality characteristics, at least some will prove disadvantageous and maladaptive in almost any surroundings, whereas the impact of others will depend on cultural expectations and preferences. Thus, for example, being involuntarily out of touch with reality is probably a universal handicap, whereas being highly assertive is likely to prove more adaptive in an individualistic or warriortype society than in a communal or pacifist society.

Accordingly, Rorschach examiners need always to consider the implications of the personality characteristics indicated by their test data for how subjects are likely to adapt in their cultural surround. Whereas the interpretive significance of Rorschach data involves universally applicable descriptions of personality processes, the adaptive significance of the findings rests with normative considerations. In some instances, particularly with respect to evidence of particularly good coping capacities (e.g., a high EA) or major functioning impairments (e.g., an elevated $X-\%$), the implications of the data are likely to transcend cultural differences. In other instances, particularly those involving variations in trait characteristics within a broad normal range, the translation from personality description to nature and adequacy of real-life adjustment requires taking careful account of the subject's social, educational, occupational, family, interpersonal, and cultural context.

ELEMENTS OF RORSCHACH
INTERPRETATION

3

The Comprehensive System Search Strategy

The Rorschach Comprehensive System developed by Exner (J. E. Exner, 1991, 1993; J. E. Exner & Weiner, 1995) rests on the three pillars of standardized administration, objective and reliable coding, and a representative normative database. The systematic objectivity introduced into Rorschach testing by J. E. Exner (1974), following over 50 years of highly variegated and often chaotic utilization of the instrument, made it possible (as noted in chap. 1) for cumulative research to demonstrate the psychometric respectability of the Rorschach Inkblot Method (RIM). In addition to expanding productive utilization of the RIM in empirical studies, the advent of the Comprehensive System allowed Rorschach assessors to formulate clinical conclusions with more confidence than was previously possible and to communicate these conclusions with greater effect (Weiner, 1997a, 1998c).

The Comprehensive System derives considerable value as a basis for undertaking interpretation not only from its systematic objectivity in administration and scoring, but also from the fact that a full set of Comprehensive System data, appropriately arrayed in a Sequence of Scores and a Structural Summary, facilitates efficient and wide-ranging analysis of the information available in Rorschach protocol. Of further significance, the Comprehensive System approach places a premium on empirically documented inferences that also make conceptual sense and serve some useful purpose (see J. E. Exner, 1993, chap. 13; Weiner, 1986, 1996). Hence Rorschach data obtained, coded, and presented following Comprehensive System guidelines provide examiners with a reliable and easy-to-scan set of scores and indices that have empirically demonstrated and conceptually meaningful correlates in aspects of personality functioning.

55

However, Rorschach examiners confronting a structural summary form or computer printout showing two dense pages of Structural Summary and Sequence of Scores information can easily feel overwhelmed by the abundance of data in front of them. Even putting aside for the moment the interpretive significance of the thematic and behavioral characteristics of a record, how does one begin to make sense of the well over 100 bits of information represented by the Comprehensive System summary scores, percentages, and indices? Where should one begin, and what direction should one take in examining these data?

Over the years Rorschach authorities have offered various partial answers to such questions. Perhaps most influential among these was Klopfer (B. Klopfer et al., 1954, chaps. 10–11), who recommended starting the interpretation with an analysis of the quantitative data, then turning to the sequence of scores, and finally examining response content. Klopfer's three-stage approach to interpretation became widely adopted and in fact characterized the Comprehensive System prior to 1991. However, Klopfer's approach does not specify which particular scores should be examined first, which next, and so on, nor did he suggest any strategy for examining response content other than beginning with the first response and reading on through the record.

In an early effort to add some further guidelines to the three-stage approach, J. E. Exner (1978, chap. 4) advised examiners to begin every Rorschach interpretation by analyzing the "Four Square," which was his term for the four variables *EB* (Experience Balance), *EA* (Experience Actual), *eb* (Experience Base), and *es* (Experienced Stimulation). He chose these four summary scores because of their significance for identifying basic aspects of an individual's adaptive resources and coping style, and he suggested that their comparative values would identify fruitful directions in which to proceed with the interpretation. For example, an extratensive *EB* would suggest examining color use scores prior to movement scores, whereas an introversive *EB* would suggest just the opposite.

Although better than having no rudder at all, the quantitative–sequence–content three-stage approach, even with Exner's (1978) additional suggestions, leaves examiners pretty much adrift among the data once they get underway. Unsteered and lacking a good end-to-end guidance system, the interpretive process even in the best of hands is at risk for meandering inefficiently among available bits of information. Few examiners using the three-stage approach are able to avoid instances in which they overlook at least initially some key feature of the data or lose track of the significance of some finding they have noted previously. Moreover, Exner found over time that beginning with the Four Square, although helpful in many instances, proved misleading or inefficient in records in which other characteristics, such as evidence of schizophrenia or an elevated *Lambda*, had greater bearing on the subject's functioning than the *EB*.

J. E. Exner (1991) addressed this gap in Rorschach methodology by introducing a significant advance in interpretive strategy. Although the interpretive technique he proposed was not given any formal name, the title of the present chapter, "The Comprehensive System Search Strategy," has become a common way of referring to it. As delineated in detail by J. E. Exner (1991, chaps. 5–10), this search strategy has two basic components: (a) the grouping of Rorschach variables into clusters, and (b) the formulation of a sequential search strategy that indicates the order in which these clusters of variables should be examined.

GROUPING VARIABLES INTO CLUSTERS

The grouping of Rorschach variables into clusters emerged from clinical lore and some supportive research concerning similarities among certain structural variables in the personality functions they assess. For example, Rorschach clinicians evaluating a subject's sense of reality have traditionally examined form quality and Populars in tandem, in the justifiable belief that both minus form-level responses (as an index of inaccurate perception) and infrequent Popular responses (as an indication of unconventional perception) identify impaired ability to see things as others do (e.g., Korchin & Larson, 1977; Weiner, 1966/1997b, chap. 7). Similarly, Rorschach examiners interested in a subject's emotional functioning have traditionally looked conjointly at variables involving response to color, such as *FC:CF + C* and the Affective Ratio (*Afr*), in the expectation that reactivity to chromatic features of the inkblots provides information about how people process affect (e.g., Schachtel, 1966, chap. 8; Shapiro, 1977).

As the first step in developing a new interpretive search strategy, Exner studied the validity and possible utility of such previously suggested relationships among structural variables by submitting Rorschach data to a formal cluster analysis. This formal analysis identified seven groups of intercorrelated variables, which he designated as Rorschach "clusters" or "sections." Each of these seven clusters of intercorrelated variables appeared related to a distinct aspect of personality functioning, including two clusters documenting the perceptual and emotional groupings mentioned in the previous paragraph. As named by Exner, the seven clusters of variables identified by his data analysis were the following:

1. An *information-processing* section, which concerns how people pay attention to their world.

2. A *cognitive mediation* section, which involves how people perceive the objects of their attention.

3. An *ideation* section, which consists of how people think about what they perceive.

4. A *control and stress tolerance* section, which has to do with the adaptive resources people have available for coping with demands and managing stress.

5. An *affective features* section, which comprises how people deal with emotional situations and how they experience and express feelings.

6. A *self-perception* section, which pertains to how people view themselves.

7. An *interpersonal perception* section, which addresses how people perceive and relate to others.

Along with identifying clusters of structural variables that provide information about these seven components of personality functioning, Exner recognized that certain types of thematic imagery often shed light on them as well. In previous work, J. E. Exner (1989) concluded that Rorschach responses are particularly likely to reveal underlying aspects of personality dynamics when they involve (a) movement, especially human movement and interactions between people or humanlike figures; (b) perceptual distortions, as coded in minus form-quality responses; or (c) embellishments of various kinds, especially those coded as Morbid (*MOR*), or receive other special scores. He accordingly added the thematic content of movement, minus, *MOR*, and other embellished responses to various clusters, most conspicuously in those concerned with self-perception and interpersonal perception.

The grouping of Rorschach variables into clusters has some important practical implications, particularly with respect to analyzing the data in a thorough and efficient manner. Additionally, this approach to organizing and utilizing the information provided by a Rorschach protocol, although empirically derived, has turned out to have some noteworthy conceptual implications for person-centered as opposed to test-centered interpretation and for an integrated rather than compartmentalized examination of structural and thematic data.

Practical Implications of the Cluster Approach

The practical implications of the cluster approach for thorough and efficient Rorschach interpretation derive from the composition of these groups of variables and the recommended ways of using them in the interpretive process. Table 3.1 shows the seven Comprehensive System clusters, and the variables associated with each of them, listed in order as steps to be followed

TABLE 3.1
Steps in Interpretation for Seven Clusters and One Array of Variables

Information Processing			
Step 1	*Lambda*	Step 5	*SumC':WSumC*
Step 2	*OBS* & *HVI*	Step 6	Affective Ratio
Step 3	*ZF, W:D:Dd, W:M*	Step 7	Color Projection
Step 4	Location Sequencing	Step 8	*FC:CF + C*
Step 5	*DQ*	Step 9	Pure *C*
Step 6	*Zd*	Step 10	Space responses
Step 7	*PSV*	Step 11	Blends
		Step 12	*m* & *Y* blends
		Step 13	Blend complexity
Cognitive Mediation		Step 14	Color shading blends
Step 1	*Lambda*	Step 15	Shading blends
Step 2	*OBS*		
Step 3	Populars	**Self-perception**	
Step 4	*FQx+*	Step 1	Reflections
Step 5	*X + %*	Step 2	Egocentricity Index
Step 6	*FQnone*	Step 3	*HVI* & *OBS*
Step 7	*Xu%*	Step 4	*FD* & *Vista* (review history)
Step 8	*X − %, S − %*	Step 5	*H:Hd + (H) + (Hd)*
Step 9	Sequence of minus	Step 6	*An + Xy*
Step 10	Homogeneity of minus	Step 7	Sum *MOR*
Step 11	Minus distortion levels	Step 8	*MOR* contents
		Step 9	Contents of minus responses
Ideation		Step 10	Contents of *M* responses
Step 1	*EB*	Step 11	Contents of *FM* & *m* responses
Step 2	*EBPer*	Step 12	Contents of embellished responses
Step 3	Left side *eb*		
Step 4	*HVI* & *OBS*	**Interpersonal Perception**	
Step 5	*a:p*	Step 1	*CDI*
Step 6	*Ma:Mp*	Step 2	*HVI*
Step 7	Intellectualization Index	Step 3	*a:p* ratio
Step 8	*MOR* frequency	Step 4	Food responses
Step 9	*Sum6 Spec Scores*	Step 5	Sum *T*
Step 10	*WSum6*	Step 6	Sum Human contents
Step 11	Quality *6 Spec Scores*	Step 7	Sum pure *H*
Step 12	*M* form quality	Step 8	*PER*
Step 13	*M* minus distortion levels	Step 9	*COP* & *AG*
Step 14	Quality of *M* responses	Step 10	Isolation Index
		Step 11	*M* responses with pairs
Control and Stress Tolerance		Step 12	*FM* responses with pairs
Step 1	*AjD* & *CDI*	Step 13	Human contents
Step 2	*EA*		
Step 3	*EB* & *Lambda*	**Situation-related Stress**	
Step 4	*es* & *Adjes*	Step 1	*D* in relation to *es* & *Adjes*
Step 5	*eb*	Step 2	*D* in relation to *AdjD*
		Step 3	*T* (also review history), *m*, & *Y*
Affective Features		Step 4	*V* in relation to Egocentricity Index
Step 1	*DEPI*		and history
Step 2	*EB*	Step 5	Blends
Step 3	*EBPer*	Step 6	Color shading blends
Step 4	Right side *eb*		

in the interpretive process. Although these clusters are fairly discrete, by virtue of the manner in which they were derived, they are not entirely so in four instances.

MOR responses, because they suggest both pessimistic ways of thinking and negative attitudes toward one's body or bodily functioning, intercorrelate substantially in both the ideation and self-perception clusters. The Hypervigilance Index (*HVI*), because it includes components relating to how people focus their attention, form concepts, and regard themselves and others, appears in the information-processing, self-perception, and interpersonal perception clusters. The *a:p* (active/passive movement) ratio, because it relates both to cognitive flexibility and behavioral passivity, has a place in both the ideational and interpersonal clusters. And *Lambda*, because of its implications both for situational and characterological narrowing of attention, is interpreted in both the information-processing and control clusters. Each of these interpretive meanings is elaborated in chapter 5.

As can also be seen from Table 3.1, the seven clusters are joined by an eighth group of variables labeled *situation-related stress*. The variables in this group do not all correlate with each other and hence do not constitute a distinct cluster. Technically speaking, the situation stress group is an *array* rather than a cluster. It comprises several variables that contribute to the interpretive process by measuring various components of situational stress, some of which are ideational in nature, some affective, and some related to capacity for control. By thus cutting across the individual clusters, the situation stress array serves the purpose of calling attention to several specific variables of different kinds that should be considered in interpreting records containing prominent indications of problems with stress management.

Taken together, then, the seven Comprehensive System clusters provide groups of variables that encompass all of the structural and thematic data in a protocol related to each of seven central aspects of personality functioning. To employ these clusters most effectively during the interpretive process, examiners working with variables in a particular cluster should remain in that cluster and search it completely before turning their attention to variables in a different cluster. Proceeding in this way minimizes the risk of overlooking key bits of information and ensures instead that everything a Rorschach protocol has to say about a subject's affect, ideation, self-perception, and so forth is taken into account.

In addition to promoting thoroughness, a discrete cluster-by-cluster search of the data helps examiners maintain their focus on one topic at a time. Regardless of their capacities to pursue multiple lines of inquiry simultaneously, Rorschach examiners lose efficiency if, for example, they interpret some of the affective variables in a record, then look at some form-level indices, then become distracted by the self-image implications of some dramatic content, and then return to further consideration of how the subject processes affect. Although complete inspection of all of the data in a Rorschach protocol will guarantee arriving eventually at a thorough set of interpretive conclusions, a systematically focused cluster-by-cluster search of the data facilitates arriving at that point more quickly and efficiently than would otherwise be possible.

With further respect to thoroughness, the seven named clusters and the situation stress array shown in Table 3.1 include almost all of the structural variables coded in the Comprehensive System. There are three important exceptions to this inclusiveness. The first concerns R (Response Total) and its implications for protocol validity and the interpretation of brief records; the other two involve the Suicide Constellation (S-CON) and certain content categories.

R, Protocol Validity, and Interpreting Brief Records. R is not listed in Table 3.1, even though over the years it has frequently appeared in diagnostic sign lists for neuroticism, organicity, and various other conditions (see Goldfried et al., 1971, chaps. 9 & 11). The absence of R from Table 3.1 signifies that it does not in fact load on any of the seven clusters, nor does it relate to whether subjects are experiencing situational stress. Regardless of how many responses subjects give, in other words, they may or may not display adaptive capacities or adjustment difficulties in how they attend, perceive, and think about their experience, how they manage stress and process affect, and how they regard themselves and others—and they may or may not be situationally distressed.

Despite not appearing in the clusters of variables to be searched in the Comprehensive System approach, R is nevertheless critical to the interpretive process because of its implications for protocol validity. Protocols containing fewer then 14 responses are considered "brief" records and, generally speaking, are invalid and should not be interpreted. The shortcoming of brief records was identified by J. E. Exner (1988) through an analysis of the Rorschach reliability data. As noted in chapter 1, the basic reliability of the RIM is demonstrated by retest studies that have yielded sizable stability coefficients for its trait variables. However, Exner's close examination of these retest data revealed that subjects who had given fewer than 14 responses on either their first or second testing did not show much temporal consistency in their scores. Because the reliability of tests is known to be proportional to their length, a brief test may contain too few items to provide reliable information. Hence a Rorschach protocol with fewer than 14 responses typically does not have enough "items" to achieve adequate retest reliability.

A measuring instrument is likely to demonstrate valid corollaries only if it is reliable. Variables that lack internal or temporal consistency have little chance of correlating consistently with each other or with other variables that bear on their validity for some purpose. Accordingly, measures that yield unreliable indices are always of questionable validity, and a brief Rorschach protocol ($R < 14$) is largely invalid because of its limited reliability. A protocol thus largely invalid by virtue of its brevity should not be interpreted by blithely drawing inferences from all of its summary scores and indices as if they were reliable. Doing so runs considerable risk of unwarranted interpretations and erroneous conclusions. Hence it is always advisable to regard a brief record as invalid, except when there is good reason to think otherwise.

Such exceptions do occur, however, and being largely invalid does not necessarily mean that a brief record is without value. Brief records may include certain specific findings that are highly reliable and therefore interpretable, sometimes in very telling ways. There are both psychometric and clinical reasons why a generally invalid record may, on occasion, yield some highly reliable findings. Psychometrically, the variability of any measurable phenomenon over time is known to be greatest in its middle range, whereas scores at its extremes are relatively likely to be stable, even for phenomena that in general show little stability. Thus in Rorschach testing, markedly deviant scores, such as a highly elevated $X-\%$ or a pervasively introversive or extratensive *EB*, are likely to be stable findings even when they emerge in brief records.

Clinically, the potential utility of certain findings in brief records may be indicated by their deviation from expectation in such records. Brief records typically result from guardedness on the part of subjects and include such typical characteristics of guardedness as a high *Lambda*, numerous Populars, an acceptable or even high $X+\%$, predominance of *D* locations, few Blends, a narrow range of content categories, and a minimum of verbiage. A brief record that is elaborated in ways contrary to these indications of guardedness is very likely to provide some reliable information about selected aspects of subjects' personality functioning and may even do so more clearly and dramatically than a longer record with similar characteristics.

For example, a 12-response record containing six *X-* responses and a *WSum6* of 24 provides fairly strong evidence of impaired reality testing and disordered thinking. A subject giving such a record and receiving a *SCZI* of 6 despite giving only 12 responses is very likely to have a schizophrenic disorder, even though the limited nature of the data in other respects precludes any general personality description. Likewise, a brief record in which half of the responses are Morbid constitutes substantial evidence of pessimistic thinking or negative body imagery; the presence of several Sex responses in a brief record is quite likely to indicate sexual preoccupation; and so on. Generally speaking, then, any unusual or dramatic indications of personality problems or preoccupations that break through the typical guardedness of a brief and otherwise generally invalid record are probably stable and, as such, provide useful information concerning the personality characteristics of the subject.

Because research with the Comprehensive System has identified records with fewer than 14 responses as being generally invalid, examiners may be inclined to discard such records without appreciating their potential utility. However, the Comprehensive System does not in fact call for giving short shrift to brief records, and the guidelines offered here for working with unusual structural and thematic features of brief records have previously been elaborated by J. E. Exner and Weiner (1995, pp. 33–34). Additionally, the test behavior of subjects who give brief records may also provide reliable clues to their present concerns and personality characteristics. Transparently oppositional ("I refuse to tell you any more"), self-disparaging ("I never do well on tests"), anxiety-laden ("I'm worried that the more I say, the worse it will be for me"), and support-seeking ("If you would tell me a little more about how I'm supposed to do this, I could do better") comments are often particularly revealing when they emerge in the context of a brief record. Brickman and Lerner (1992) elaborated ways in which an interpretive focus on behavioral characteristics of brief Rorschach protocols can be especially useful in examining guarded children and adolescents who give brief records.

Even while keeping in mind the possible utility of brief records in certain respects, examiners should not lose sight of the overriding fact that records with fewer than 14 responses are, in general, too short to provide reliable information and do not therefore support valid interpretations. Hence, prior to identifying the first positive key variable, the Comprehensive System search strategy should always begin with an examination of R to determine whether a record meets the minimum validity requirement of at least 14 responses.

S-CON and Content Categories. Like Situation Stress, the *S-CON* is an array of variables that relates to several different personality functions and is not itself included within any single cluster. In addition, the *S-CON* is notable as an index to which R, when less than 17, has been empirically confirmed as a contributing element. Because of the overriding importance in clinical assessment of recognizing suicidal potential, the *S-CON* merits special attention beyond what is accorded any other single group of variables. After first checking R, then, examiners beginning a Rorschach interpretation should next look at the *S-CON* as their second step.

As the third exception to the inclusiveness of the clusters of variables appearing in Table 3.1, several content categories are not considered within any of them. These include Blood, Explosion, Fire, Household, Human Experience, Science, and Sex. Their exclusion does not preclude the possibility that thematic imagery involving these contents will be revealing. Often responses containing these contents are targeted in a cluster search by virtue of their involving movement, form distortion, or some embellishment. Moreover, exclusion from the clusters does not signify that nothing can be learned from the frequency with which these contents occur. Nevertheless, whereas the other content categories coded in the Comprehensive System appear in Exner's clusters, either in their own right or as elements of such composite variables as the Isolation Index ($Bt + 2Cl + Ge + Ls + 2Na/R$) and the Intellectualization Index ($2AB + Art + Ay$), the frequency of these seven content categories was not found empirically to load on any of the clusters.

Conceptual Implications of the Cluster Approach

As previously noted, Exner's grouping of structural and thematic variables into seven clusters has two noteworthy conceptual implications for Rorschach interpretation. The cluster approach to interpretation fosters a focus on describing people and personality functions rather than test findings, and cluster-based interpretation mandates an integrated rather than compartmentalized analysis of the structural and thematic data in a Rorschach protocol.

Person-Centered Interpretation. For many years, Rorschach interpretation was a test-centered process in which examiners sought answers to various questions about the nature of the data. To be sure, competent psychodiagnosticians always recognized that their test data are but a means to an end and their findings of value only when translated into accurate personality descriptions, dependable differential diagnoses, and helpful treatment recommendations. This having been said, however, the fact remains that, even in competent hands, attention to the person being evaluated traditionally emerged following rather than prior to an analysis of the test data. Examiners would begin their interpretation by addressing to a Rorschach protocol such test-centered questions as how the subject dealt with color, what the form-quality scores were, and whether there was any striking thematic imagery in the record. After answering to their satisfaction as many such questions as they considered important, examiners would then turn to contemplating what these answers implied about the subject's personality functioning.

The cluster-based approach to interpretation reverses this traditional test-centered order in which questions about the data precede questions about personality functions. Instead of asking first how a subject dealt with color and then drawing conclusions about how this person is likely to process affect, for example, cluster-based interpretation begins with such questions as "How does this person experience and express feelings?" and then examines test data that bear on this question. Likewise, rather than seeking first to know what the form-quality scores and prominent content themes are, a cluster-based approach to the RIM organizes the interpretive process around learning how subjects tend to manage stress, handle interpersonal relationships, and so on.

The distinction between a test-centered approach to Rorschach data and the person-centered approach fostered by cluster-based interpretation may seem inconsequential, inasmuch as they lead to the same results. Both approaches, when adequately implemented, will sooner or later yield both an analysis of the data in its own right and a set of inferences about the subject's personality functioning. However, like pursuing one cluster of variables at a time rather than skipping about among them, person-centered rather than test-centered interpretation offers some distinct advantages in focus and efficiency.

In the first place, person-centered interpretation helps psychodiagnosticians avoid becoming overly invested in their techniques at the expense of adequate attention to the person for whose benefit the techniques are being used. Focusing initially on personality functions rather than test characteristics makes a clear statement concerning which are more important. Even the most conscientious and sensitive clinicians may at times become more fascinated with the nature of their test data than with using these data to address personality strengths and weaknesses that are critical to understanding subjects' personality processes. With particular respect to the RIM, mastery of Comprehensive System administration and coding and thorough familiarity with the interpretive hypotheses associated with each of its variables come to naught unless they are constructively applied to describing each individual subject's personality structure and dynamics. Because our primary purpose in using the RIM is to understand the person being examined, not the Rorschach data, the cluster-based approach gives proper focus to our priorities.

Second, the person-centeredness of the cluster-based approach provides a useful guide for organizing and communicating test results. Reports of psychodiagnostic evaluations of personality functioning should present a comprehensive personality description in clear and comprehensible language. Interpretation based on the grouping of variables shown in Table 3.1 typically enhances an examiner's efficiency in these respects. With respect to being comprehensive, the variable clusters encompass cognitive, affective, adaptational, self-referential, and interpersonal aspects of personality functioning. Although the components of personality are delineated differently by various personality theorists and authors of personality tests, it is difficult to conceive of any basic dimension of personality that would not fit somewhere under the scope of the Comprehensive System clusters.

Accordingly, unlike examiners pursuing a test-centered approach to interpretation, those using a cluster-based approach can be assured of arriving at a comprehensive personality description without having to make any special effort to be comprehensive or having to worry about overlooking important facets of the data. At the same time, cluster-based interpretation facilitates an orderly presentation of how people focus their attention, perceive events, think about their experiences, cope with stress, experience and express feelings, view themselves, and approach interpersonal situations. By taking each of these clusters one at a time and elaborating a subject's assets and liabilities with respect to the personality functions they measure, examiners can be assured of presenting a cohesive and comprehensible report, and they will also be spared having to struggle in each case with the numbing task of determining how best to organize a long list of test-centered interpretations.

Aside from helping examiners paint thorough and well-organized pictures of personality functioning, the cluster-based approach provides ordinary language terminology that simplifies the communication of results. Although such cluster names as "ideation," "mediation," and "information processing" are technical terms, reference to them as indications of how people pay attention to their experience, how they perceive what they pay attention to, and how they think about what they perceive is readily understood by most people to whom psychological examiners are likely to report their findings. For each of the individual variables in the Comprehensive System clusters, J. E. Exner (1991, chaps. 6–9) provided descriptive statements in clear and simple English that examiners can utilize or adapt to their own language style as a way of promoting effective and well-received communication of their impressions.

Integrated Interpretation. As noted earlier, Rorschach interpretation as recommended by Klopfer and employed in the Comprehensive System prior to 1991 consisted of a three-stage process. First, the structural summary data were examined for whatever inferences they appear to suggest, then the sequence of scores was used to amplify these inferences, and finally the responses were read to identify additional implications of the thematic imagery. This segmented approach to interpreting a protocol was common to most of the traditional Rorschach systems and became very widely used. In the classic literature, only Schafer (1954) in his book, *Psychoanalytic Interpretation in Rorschach Testing*, deviated from this compartmentalization of the data by attempting to look jointly at structural and thematic aspects of individual responses.

The composition of the Comprehensive System clusters as delineated by Exner (1991) mandates an integrated rather than compartmentalized analysis of the structural and thematic data in a Rorschach protocol. Consistent with the focus of the clusters on personality functions rather than test characteristics, the clusters call for consideration of all of the Rorschach information relevant to the function they measure. Thus, for example, in determining what can be inferred about a subject's interpersonal orientation, all of the structural data and all of the thematic imagery bearing on attitudes toward others and perspectives on social relatedness are examined jointly.

This shift from a segmented to an integrated interpretation changed the way Rorschach protocols are examined in clinical practice and presented in case studies and teaching exercises. Contemporary Comprehensive System interpretation begins, as previously stated, with examining R to determine the general validity of the record and the S-CON to assess suicide potential. The integrative approach then continues with analysis of all of the variables in the first cluster and ends with analysis of the seventh cluster of variables, by which time all of the test data will have been considered. With the advent of this approach, the presentation of cases by commenting separately and successively on the Structural Summary, the Sequence of Scores, and the content of responses has passed into the history of the Comprehensive System, replaced by an integrated and conjoint seven-cluster analysis of all three facets of the data in relation to assessing particular personality functions.

EMPLOYING A SEQUENTIAL SEARCH STRATEGY

With the structural and thematic data of the Rorschach grouped into clusters concerned with personality functions, interpretation could consist of searching these clusters in any sequence. Eventually, regardless of the order in which the clusters of variables are examined, all of the information a protocol contains about a subject's personality functioning will come to light. Table 3.1 lists the clusters in an order that is convenient for explaining their significance and selecting the illustrative case material presented in part III, but the very same conclusions would emerge whether a protocol was interpreted from information processing down through interpersonal perception or vice versa, from interpersonal perception up through information processing.

However, searching the clusters in some routine order or skipping among them in random fashion typically proves inefficient. In the case of a person being evaluated for depressive disorder, for example, beginning the interpretation with information processing might identify some features of depression, such as whether the person has limited mental energy as reflected in an unexpectedly low frequency of synthesis responses $(DQ+)$. Continuing on with the mediation cluster might indicate whether the subject, if depressed, is out of touch with reality and thus psychotically depressed, as indicated by an elevated frequency of inaccurate perceptions (high $X-\%$). Moving next to the ideation cluster would provide some information concerning whether the subject is having difficulty concentrating or thinking coherently and logically, as shown respectively by indications of intrusive ideation (elevated left side of the *eb*) and an unusual frequency of Critical Special Scores (elevated *WSum6*).

Each of these first three clusters listed in Table 3.1 relates to aspects of cognitive functioning, and most psychopathologists concur that impaired cognitive functions of the type just noted play a role in depressive disorder, whether as causative or derivative phenomena. However, none of these clusters addresses what is generally acknowledged to constitute the core of depressive disorder, a disturbance in mood. Although the affective cluster of variables comes fourth in the convenience listing in Table 3.1, examiners concerned about possible depressive disorder will with few exceptions find affective variables the most relevant cluster with which to begin their interpretive search.

To take another example, suppose a subject has been referred for assessment of possible schizophrenic disorder. Although affective difficulties often play a role in schizophrenia, beginning with the affective cluster in such cases would initially bypass the most critical and defining characteristic of schizophrenia spectrum disorders, namely, problems in thinking logically and coherently. Accordingly, in cases in which schizophrenia is at issue, the key to an efficiently focused search of the Rorschach data is initial examination of the ideational cluster of variables. Moreover, traditional conceptualization of schizophrenia as primarily a cognitive rather than affective disorder would argue for proceeding from the ideational cluster to the other cognitive clusters of variables to learn how the person perceives reality and attends to experience (mediation and information processing).

Using assessment questions in this way to select an initial cluster or group of clusters with which to begin an interpretation facilitates an orderly and sensible approach to effective utilization of the Rorschach data in answering these questions. Numerous additional examples can readily be generated to illustrate translation from the personality parameters associated with various psychological conditions or characteristics to a cluster or clusters of variables that should receive primary attention in the interpretive process, and the case material in part III exemplifies several different initial approaches to a test protocol.

However, using referral questions or examiner concerns to guide an interpretive search strategy may on occasion fail to utilize the clusters most effectively. The questions examiners are asked and the concerns they formulate sometimes overlook or deflect attention from the most significant features of a subject's personality functioning. A referring colleague may ask for help in assessing depth of depression in a withdrawn and emotionally blunted patient, when in fact the patient's withdrawal and flat affect are manifestations of an emerging schizophrenic disorder. Similarly, a referral question may focus on differentiating among types of personality disorder when the patient is struggling with acute and debilitating distress, or an examiner may become preoccupied with ferreting out the nuances of a subtle thought disorder in a patient whose most pressing problems involve disturbed interpersonal relationships.

If neither referral questions nor examiner inclinations provide dependable guidance in deciding which facet of a subject's personality functioning to consider first, how can one identify the most useful sequence in which to search the clusters of variables? The Comprehensive System interpretive approach answers this question by proposing that a Rorschach protocol should be allowed to speak for itself concerning the identity of its most salient features. That is, instead of allowing prejudgments to determine a starting point, examiners should review certain features of the record itself for clues to which cluster of variables is likely to yield the most important information about a subject's personality functioning, which cluster will be next most informative, and so on.

Employing this type of clinical reasoning and the notion that the RIM should be allowed to speak for itself, J. E. Exner (1991, chaps. 5–9) formulated a sequential search strategy based on a series of *key variables*. Each of these key variables, if in evidence, dictates a particular sequence in which to search the seven clusters of variables. These key variables were identified empirically by identifying especially prominent variables in groups of records that generated numerous interpretive statements related to one or another of the various clusters. For example, one group of records was noteworthy for how many interpretive statements it generated in the ideation cluster of variables, almost all of which showed a value outside the range of normative expectation. Examination of these records revealed that they were prominently characterized by an elevated Schizophrenia Index (*SCZI* > 3). Hence, *SCZI* > 3 was established as the key variable for the ideation cluster, which means that interpretation of a record in which the *SCZI* is four or more should begin with a review of the variables in the ideation cluster.

In the same way, in a different group of records noteworthy for the number of interpretive statements they suggested in relation to variables in the affective cluster, Exner found that a Depression Index (*DEPI*) greater than 5 was prominent among them. *DEPI* > 5 was accordingly established as a key variable indicating that interpretation of a Rorschach protocol should begin with attention to the affective cluster. This procedure was followed to identify key variables for the remaining clusters of variables and to determine additional key variables for groups of records that did not show the most prominent characteristic among the records with which they were initially grouped. For example, some of the records that generated numerous interpretive statements relating to ideation did not show *SCZI* >

3, but were instead most notable for an introversive *EB* (*M* exceeding *SumC* by two or more points, or by more than two points if *EA* exceeds 10). Hence, an introversive *EB* was established as a key variable that, like *SCZI* > 3, calls for interpretation to begin with the ideational cluster. This procedure yielded 11 key variables, each associated with a cluster of variables that typically serve well as the initial focus in interpreting a Rorschach protocol, following appropriate attention to *R* and the *S-CON*.

After these records had been used to identify key variables on the basis of which was their most interpretively prolific cluster, they were examined further to determine which cluster generated the second most frequent number of interpretive statements and should be reviewed next in the interpretive process. In the case of the *SCZI* > 3 records, which were most notable for the interpretive significance of the ideational variables, the second most numerous group of interpretations was generated by variables in the mediation cluster. In the case of the *DEPI* > 5 records most notable for affective variables, the second most frequent number of interpretive statements emerged from the control cluster of variables. Repeated examination of the groups of records associated with each of the key variables yielded a remaining sequence based on which cluster generated the third most frequent number of interpretive statements, which the fourth, and so on.

From this extensive analysis of Rorschach protocols, a sequence of clusters emerged in association with each key variable, in which the first cluster can generally be expected to provide the greatest amount of interpretive information concerning the subject, and the remaining six yield a gradually diminishing amount of information as the search proceeds. In actual practice, occasional findings of considerable import may emerge in the last one or two clusters searched. By and large, however, examiners can anticipate that the first cluster to which this key variable approach directs their attention will identify the most salient features of a subject's personality functioning, and the first three or four clusters they examine will provide the bulk of what can be learned from the protocol. In this way, then, the Rorschach is allowed to speak for itself: The sequential search strategy approach alerts examiners to which aspect of the data is likely to have the most interpretive significance, which the second most, and so on.

The final step in formulating the sequential search strategy for Rorschach interpretation involved assigning priorities to the key variables. For instances in which more than one of the key variables is positive, a decision must be made concerning which should receive attention first. Exner addressed this matter by considering the clinical import of each of the key variables and analyzing the outcome of alternate search routes in protocols with two or more significant key variables. Table 3.2 shows the results of this analysis. The table lists the 11 key variables in order of their priority

TABLE 3.2
The Comprehensive System Search Strategy:
Key Variables and Cluster Sequences

Schizophrenia Index greater than 3 (*SCZI* > 3)
　Ideation > Mediation > Processing > Controls > Affect > Self-perception > Interpersonal Perception
Depression Index greater than 5 (*DEPI* > 5)
　Affect > Controls > Self-perception > Interpersonal Perception > Processing > Mediation > Ideation
D Score less than Adjusted *D* Score (*D* < *AdjD*)
　Controls > Situation Stress > (The remaining search sequence determined by the next positive key variable or the list of tertiary variables)
Coping Deficit Index greater than 3 (*CDI* > 3)
　Controls > Affect > Self-perception > Interpersonal Perception > Processing > Mediation > Ideation
Adjusted *D* Score less than 0 (*AdjD* < 0)
　Controls > (The remaining search sequence determined by the next positive key variable or the list of tertiary variables)
Lambda greater than .99 (*Lambda* > .99)
　Processing > Mediation > Ideation > Controls > Affect > Self-perception > Interpersonal Perception
Reflections present (*Fr* + *rF* > 0)
　Self-perception > Interpersonal Perception > Controls > (The remaining search sequence determined by the next positive key variable or the list of tertiary variables)
EB style introversive
　Ideation > Processing > Mediation > Controls > Affect > Self-perception > Interpersonal Perception
EB style extratensive
　Affect > Self-perception > Interpersonal Perception > Controls > Processing > Mediation > Ideation
Passive movement exceeds active movement by one or more (*p* > *a* + *1*)
　Ideation > Processing > Mediation > Controls > Self-perception > Interpersonal Perception > Affect
Hypervigilance Index (*HVI*) positive
　Ideation > Processing > Mediation > Controls > Self-perception > Interpersonal Perception > Affect

---

and indicates for each the sequence in which the clusters should be searched if it is positive.

Beginning at the top of the list in Table 3.2 and working down, then, the first positive key variable that is encountered will identify where the search should begin, which can be referred to as the "entry point" into the record, and how the search should proceed. To illustrate this sequential search strategy in practice, guided by Table 3.2, the first key variable to examine is the Schizophrenia Index. If *SCZI* is four or more, the interpretation begins with an examination of the variables in the ideation cluster and then continues with the other two cognitive clusters, mediation and processing. The rest of the interpretation proceeds in order through the control, affect, self-perception, and interpersonal clusters. If *SCZI* is less than four, attention turns to the Depression Index. If *DEPI* is six or seven, the search begins with affect and proceeds through the control, self-perception, interpersonal, and three cognitive clusters, with ideation coming last.

If neither *SCZI* nor *DEPI* is elevated, then the third key variable, which is based on the relationship between the *D* and *AdjD* scores, is examined. If *D* is algebraically less than *AdjD*, the control cluster is searched first and the situation stress array of variables is considered next. At this point there is no universally effective search order dictated solely by an entry point of *D* < *AdjD*. Instead, in this particular search routine, the record itself must indicate where it would be most informative to look after considering the control and situation stress variables. As indicated in Table 3.2, this recourse to the record is accomplished by reading on down the list of key variables and using the next positive finding to guide the remainder of the search. Hence, in a record with *D* < *AdjD*, it might turn out that *CDI* (the fourth key variable) is not more than three and *AdjD* (the fifth key variable) is not less than zero, but *Lambda* (the sixth key variable) is greater than .99. In this case, the search sequence following controls and situation stress would consist in order of the processing, mediation, ideation, affect, self-perception, and interpersonal clusters.

With these examples in hand, the remainder of Table 3.2 should be self-explanatory. Occasionally, however, a record may not contain positive findings on any of the 11 key variables. To address this circumstance, J. E. Exner (1991, p. 151) also provided a supplementary list of nine "tertiary" variables. These tertiary variables, listed in Table 3.3, can be used as necessary in the same manner as the key variables. The examiner continues to go down the list until a positive finding is identified and then uses the search sequence paired with that tertiary variable to guide the interpretation of the record.

Like grouping Rorschach variables into clusters, employing a sequential search strategy for clusters of variables has some important practical and conceptual implications. In particular, this approach to the data promotes a flexible and clinically relevant focus, it facilitates differentiating among symptomatic and characterological patterns of psychopathology and between normal and abnormal adjustment, and it enhances the accessibility of Rorschach protocols to interpretation within multiple theoretical frames of reference.[1]

---

[1]The utility of grouping variables into clusters and employing a sequential search strategy for cluster of variables has become well-established in practice, and the listings in Tables 3.1, 3.2, and 3.3, as noted, have a sound empirical basis. However, Rorschach clinicians and researchers should keep in mind that this approach to interpretation is a tool in development and neither a finished product nor a statement of fact. Additional data and further conceptual refinements may result in modifications of the cluster composition and search orders, while retaining the basic structure and purposes of this interpretive strategy.

TABLE 3.3
The Comprehensive System Search Strategy:
Tertiary Variables and Cluster Sequences

Obsessive Index (*OBS*) positive
  Processing > Mediation > Ideation > Controls > Affect > Self-perception > Interpersonal
  Perception
Depression Index of 5 (*DEPI* = 5)
  Affect > Controls > Self-perception > Interpersonal Perception > Processing > Mediation >
  Ideation
Experience Actual greater than 12 (*EA > 12*)
  Controls > Ideation > Processing > Mediation > Affect > Self-perception > Interpersonal
  Perception
M- > 0, or *Mp* > *Ma*, or *Sum6 Spec Sc* > 5
  Ideation > Mediation > Processing > Controls > Affect > Self-perception > Interpersonal
  Perception
Sum Shading > *FM* + *m*, or *CF* + *C* > *FC* + 1, of *Afr* < .46
  Affect > Controls > Self-perception > Interpersonal Perception > Processing > Mediation >
  Ideation
X – *%* > 20%, or *Zd* > +3.0 or < −3.0
  Processing > Mediation > Ideation > Controls > Affect > Self-perception > Interpersonal
  Perception
Egocentricity Index less than .33 (*3r* + *(2)/R* < .33)
  Self-perception > Interpersonal Perception > Affect > Controls > Processing > Mediation >
  Ideation
MOR > 2, or *AG* > 2
  Self-perception > Interpersonal Perception > Controls > Ideation > Processing > Mediation
  > Affect
Texture more or less than one (*T* = 0, or *T* > 1)
  Self-perception > Interpersonal Perception > Affect > Controls > Processing > Mediation >
  Ideation

Flexibility and Clinical Relevance

The previous description of using key variables to determine where to begin a Rorschach interpretation illustrates the implicit flexibility of the sequential search strategy approach. By allowing the RIM to speak for itself in identifying the most promising entry point into each set of data, this approach eschews preset routines in favor of individual decisions concerning what is most important about a particular protocol. Along with ensuring a thorough interpretation of the available data, then, the sequential search strategy also promotes a flexible and subject-specific interpretive process.

As for clinical relevance, each of the key variables is either a multiply determined index that itself encompasses many features of a protocol (e.g., the *DEPI* is based on 14 different variables) or a finding with numerous well-documented personality and behavioral correlates (such as being a high *Lambda* person). Consequently, the identity of the initial key variable frequently directs examiners not only to the most salient characteristics of a protocol but also to the presently most noteworthy features of the subject's psychological state and coping style. For example, merely finding an *AdjD* < 0 suggests a persistent stress overload in which subjects have been experiencing demands in excess of their coping capacities and, as a result, have probably been subject to chronic or recurring episodes of anxiety, tension, irritability, and impulsivity. In the same way, much can be learned about subjects' core characteristics and potential adjustment difficulties simply from knowing that they have an elevated *CDI* or one or more Reflection responses (see J. E. Exner, 1993, chaps. 15–19).

In addition, the pattern among the clusters with respect to which of them demonstrate personality strengths and which reveal personality weaknesses can contribute directly to differential diagnosis and treatment planning. A cluster containing a preponderance of findings that deviate in a maladaptive direction from normative expectation suggests liabilities in the personality functions associated with that cluster; conversely, a preponderance of normative or notably adaptive findings in a cluster points to assets in whatever personality functions are associated with it.

As noted earlier in introducing the cluster concept, for example, people who display functioning difficulties in the ideation rather than the affective cluster of variables are more likely to have a schizophrenia spectrum disorder than an affective disorder. To illustrate this cluster analysis approach further, subjects with notable liabilities appearing in both the ideation and mediation clusters are particularly likely to have a schizophrenic disorder, whereas those with impaired mediation but adequate ideation are often found to have some other type of psychotic disorder, such as an affective psychosis in the case of both mediational and affective impairments (see Weiner, 1998b). With respect to treatment planning, subjects in whom the ideation, mediation, and affective clusters appear reasonably adaptive, but who show personality impairments in the self-perception cluster or the interpersonal cluster are likely to be individuals whose treatment should be focus primarily on their attitudes toward themselves or toward others (see Weiner, in press). The case presentations in part III elaborate on how implications of many such possible combinations of adaptive strengths and weaknesses associated with each of the seven clusters of variables have specific implications for identifying patterns of psychopathology, forms of maladjustment, and treatment targets.

Differentiating Patterns of Psychopathology

Although deferring until part III further discussion of specific diagnostic and treatment formulations, the present discussion of the Comprehensive System sequential search strategy can nevertheless be used to indicate some implications of the priority sequencing of the key variables for distinguishing three categories of personality dysfunction. Regarding the first of these categories, each of the initial three key variables is typically associated with some type of symptomatic disorder. An elevated *SCZI* raises the possibility of a schizophrenia spectrum disorder, an elevated *DEPI* points to an affective spectrum disorder, and $D < Add$ suggests the presence of an anxiety spectrum disorder.

As the basis for a second category, the next key variable in order, $CDI > 3$, does not refer to any pattern of cognitive, affective, or anxiety-related symptoms that come and go, vary in intensity over fairly short periods of time, and respond fairly well to symptom-oriented treatments. Instead, an elevated *CDI* points to a chronic and persistent impairment in coping capacity due either to developmental arrest or a serious loss of functioning capacity subsequent to some debilitating event. Schizophrenic patients have their good days and bad days when they are more or less interpersonally aversive or out of touch with reality, and patients with mood or anxiety disorders likewise fluctuate from time to time in how much they are impaired by their symptoms. By contrast, seriously impaired coping capacity is a stable handicap that does not get better or worse from day to day; coping deficits remain fixed for the duration of every day, until such time as helpful experiences or successful interventions assist the impaired individual to become more capable. The adjustment difficulties identified by an elevated *CDI* are thus akin to personality or characterological disorders, as these disorders are usually defined.

The next three key variables following $CDI > 3$ also identify persistent personality styles that are frequently associated with potentially maladaptive developmental or characterological orientations (see J. E. Exner & Weiner, 1995, chap. 7). An $AdjD < 0$ indicates relatively chronic and long-standing difficulties in finding sufficient resources to manage stressful situations without becoming unduly upset by them. *Lambda* $> .99$ points to a narrowly focused approach to experience in which situations are characteristically construed in simple and unelaborated ways with little openness to thoughts and feelings concerning them. An $Fr + rF > 0$ identifies people's persistent tendencies to extol their own personality qualities, place their needs ahead of those of others, feel a sense of entitlement to have what they want, and externalize responsibility for their difficulties or shortcomings.

This second group of four key variables ($CDI > 3$, $AdjD < 0$, *Lambda* $> .99$, and $Fr + rF > 0$) thus constitute a second category related primarily to characterological and developmental rather than symptomatic disorders. Like characterological disorders, and as testimony to the early developmental onset associated with such disorders, these four Rorschach features typically appear early in life, if they are going to appear at all, and are rarely acquired following a substantial period of development in which they were not in evidence.

For example, an elevated *CDI* in the record of adult subjects and the persistent deficits in coping capacities it represents are likely to have been present since childhood, except in persons experiencing adolescent or adult onset of personality decompensation or neuropsychological dysfunction. For this reason, an elevated *CDI* shown by a person with a previous history of clearly successful coping often provides a clue to imminent decompensation or dysfunction. On the other hand, neither an elevated *CDI* in a young person nor a long-standing coping deficit in an adult is irreversible. Enriching experiences and constructive interventions may help people overcome such developmental handicaps and, in Rorschach terms, shed a previously existing *CDI* elevation from their record.

Similar considerations apply to minus *AdjD*, *Lambda* > .99, and the presence of Reflection responses. Except in unusual circumstances, life experiences following the childhood years are unlikely to inject such features into a Rorschach protocol. Their presence in records of adolescent and adult subjects typically indicates that they would have been present in these subjects' Rorschachs had they been examined as children. Conversely, although these findings rarely enter older subjects' Rorschachs after having been absent during childhood, they may drop out of their record subsequent to events that have helped them modify some maladaptive trait characteristics.

Proceeding down the priority list of key variables, the next two variables following $Fr + rF > 0$ refer to whether a subject demonstrates an introversive or extratensive *EB* style. Unlike the first three key variables, which are associated with symptomatic disorders, and unlike the next four key variables, which are associated with characterological and developmental difficulties, being introversive or extratensive is not by itself associated with any kind of psychological disorder or adjustment difficulty. Indeed, most people (approximately 80%) are either introversive or extratensive, and preference for one *EB* style or the other identifies nothing more than variations in personality style within the normal range. Although being pervasively either introversive or extratensive (*EBPer*) can contribute to adjustment problems, flexible preference for either ideational (introversive) or expressive (extratensive) ways of dealing with experience has no implications for abnormal personality functioning (J. E. Exner, 1993, chap. 17).

The final two key variables are $p < a + 1$, which identifies tendencies to be passive and deferential in social situations, and a positive *HVI*, which indicates a cautious, distant, and mistrustful orientation to people. Unlike being either introversive or extratensive, being interpersonally passive or distant could be potentially maladaptive. Interestingly, however, persons who elevate on either $p > a + 1$ or *HVI*, without having elevated on any of the first seven key variables, are typically found to be functioning reasonably well, within the normal range, despite showing some mild tendencies to be a bit more deferential or cautious than most people in their interpersonal relationships.

Hence the final four key variables (*EB* introversive, *EB* extratensive, $p > a + 1$, and *HVI* positive) constitute a third category of variables that point neither to symptomatic nor characterological patterns of psychopathology, but rather to normal variations in personality functioning. The tertiary variables listed in Table 3.3 similarly imply distinctive personality characteristics that, in the absence of significant findings on any of the first seven key variables, are more likely to identify aspects of normal rather than deviant personality functioning. Accordingly, in most instances in which a sequential search does not reveal an elevated key variable higher in priority than *EB* style, the subject is likely to be demonstrating relatively normal psychological adaptation.

This three-stage grouping of the key and tertiary variables is by no means discrete, nor does it serve as an absolute basis for distinguishing symptomatic from characterological psychopathology and abnormal from normal personality functioning. Such categorical distinctions run contrary to clinical knowledge that persons with a symptomatic disorder in remission may show primarily characterological problems, that persons with arrested or warped personality development may respond to stressful situations with symptoms of anxiety and depression or even psychotic breakdown, and that the boundaries between normal and abnormal psychological functioning are often blurred and permeable. The key and tertiary variables and other Rorschach indices of these phenomena are similarly likely to identify tendencies, trends, and occasional reasonable certainties rather than precise and invariable categories.

Systematic research to assess the validity of this three-stage grouping of key and tertiary variables has not yet been conducted. Present knowledge goes only so far as to suggest that the preceding clinical conceptualization of what these variables signify provides good reason to believe that the point of entry into a Rorschach protocol, as determined by the Comprehensive System sequential search strategy, contributes substantially to determining a subject's general level of adjustment, distinguishing between symptomatic and characterological disorder, and identifying the salient features of the individual's personality style.

Theoretical Accessibility

Taken together, the clustering of structural and thematic Rorschach variables in relation to personality functions they measure and the examination of these clusters according to a sequential search strategy have important implications for transtheoretical utilization of the Comprehensive System. The Comprehensive System was originally formulated and subsequently refined independently of any particular theory of personality or theoretical perspective on the nature of the inkblot method. Exner's prevailing intent was to codify, systematize, objectify, and standardize Rorschach data and to validate these data against observable behavior. Although his efforts have resulted in an empirically based and psychometrically sound approach to Rorschach assessment, nothing about the system precludes the obtained data from being interpreted within any theoretical frame of reference. The Comprehensive System search strategy calls attention to all of the Rorschach data needed to pursue both perceptual-cognitive and associational-representational approaches to interpretation, as described in chapters 1 and 2, and the composition of the clusters of variables and the guidelines for examining these clusters in sequence lend themselves equally well to formulations couched in trait theories of personality, ego-analytic conceptualizations of impulse and defense, and object relations perspectives on behavior and adaptation. All three frames of reference are utilized in chapters 4 through 8 and are illustrated in the case interpretations presented in part III.

4

Projection and Card Pull in Rorschach Responses

Projection and card pull have long been recognized as complementary influences on the Rorschach response process, in keeping with the widely shared observations noted in chapter 1 that the RIM serves both as a test of perception and a test of association. When subjects respond in terms of their personal associations to the inkblots, the responses they formulate are based largely on projection. When subjects respond in terms of the stimulus characteristics of the inkblots, the responses they articulate are based largely on card pull.

Although decidedly different, the influences of projection and card pull are not mutually exclusive. To the contrary, virtually every Rorschach response combines the processes of perception and association in some proportion. As suggested in chapter 1, even popular and unelaborated responses that are clearly determined by stimulus characteristics of the blots involve some association. Thus, Card V looks like a bat to most people and is commonly seen as one, but very few people would endorse Card V as an exact replica or precise pictorial representation of a bat. Hence, some associational process is necessary to translate an impression of some batlike qualities in this inkblot into a formal response of "bat." Relevant in this regard is the fact that subjects taking the Rorschach are not asked "What is this?" but rather "What might this be?"

Likewise, few if any Rorschach responses emerge solely as a consequence of associations that arise independently of the stimulus properties of the blots. To a greater or lesser extent, responses based primarily on association begin with some feature of the inkblot that triggers certain thoughts or feelings. Consequently, a Card VII response of "Two people who are trying to get away from each other but are stuck together" is rich with projected associations that go well beyond the stimulus properties of the blot, but these associations have assuredly originated in the subject's recognizing that Card VII bears some resemblance to two people. Among Rorschach scholars who have commented on the inherent interaction between projection and card pull in Rorschach responding, Schafer (1954) emphasized that the nature of the instructions causes "responsible reality-testing and free fantasy to interact during the formation of each response" (p. 77).

Accordingly, effective Rorschach interpretation requires examiners to identify the relative contribution of projection and card pull to the manner in which each response is articulated. Responses shaped mainly by projection tend to be unique to each subject and to reveal numerous aspects of the individual's underlying needs, attitudes, conflicts, and concerns. By contrast, responses shaped mainly by card pull are more likely to be similar than different from one person to another and to provide relatively little information about an individual's unique personality dynamics.

Despite their distinctive implications, however, projection and card pull overlap in many respects. Projected material in Rorschach responses appears primarily in thematic imagery rather than perceptual structuring and is identified on an idiographic basis as having specific meaning to the individual who has produced it. As an important exception, however, Color Projection (*CP*) is a structural variable that nevertheless involves the attribution of a stimulus characteristic (chromatic color) that is not present in the card and identifies an aspect of personality dynamics (defensive efforts to deny unpleasant affect). Additionally, there are certain types of thematic imagery that occur with sufficient frequency to demonstrate numerous shared personality characteristics among subjects, and there are also certain images that are more or less likely to be elicited by particular blots and are thus influenced by card pull.

Regarding shared personality characteristics reflected in thematic imagery, the emergence of numerous Rorschach content scales has shown that careful codification of thematic imagery can help to identify dimensions of personality dynamics along which people can be measured and compared on a nomothetic basis. A prominent example of such scales, among others noted in chapter 2, is the Rorschach Oral Dependency Scale (ROD) developed and refined by Masling and his colleagues (Bornstein, 1996; Masling et al., 1967). Other such scales are identified in chapter 6.

As for the role of card pull in thematic imagery, the stimulus characteristics of the inkblots as normatively determined can influence any feature of a response, including the contents of responses and how they are elaborated. Consider a subject who says that Card II "reminds me of violence." The subject is very probably reacting to the red details on Card II, which can readily be seen as blood; Card II may well be the most likely of any card in the entire series to elicit associations to violence. However, suppose that instead of or in addition to articulating violence on Card II, the subject responds to Card VIII by saying, "It reminds me of violence." Card VIII, with its soft pastel colors and unthreatening shapes, has very little card pull for violence, as judged by how infrequently people see violence in it. Hence violence seen on Card VIII is a more dramatic, projective, and revealing response than violence seen on Card II, and Card VIII violence is more likely than Card II violence to identify an unusually intense preoccupation with the instigation and consequences of aggression. This example illustrates how the interpretive significance of a content theme can be judged in part from knowledge of card pull, that is, how people generally tend to respond to the inkblots.

In addition to thus affecting the import of thematic imagery, card pull also bears on the significance of behavioral features of a protocol. Consider, for example, a subject who studies a card carefully for a while and then says, "This is a hard one." A comment of this kind will have considerably more interpretive significance if it is given to an uncomplicated card that most subjects handle with relative ease, such as Card V, than to a complex card that many subjects find relatively difficult, such as Card IX.

Turning to the influence of card pull on the structural variables in a Rorschach protocol, these (as already noted) involve stimulus characteristics of the inkblots that most people recognize. Despite the nomothetic rather than idiographic origins of card pull, however, extensive research has demonstrated vast differences between what people can see in the inkblots and what they choose to report when they are being formally examined. For example, Exner found in his early work on the Rorschach response process that, when nonpatient adult volunteers are asked to report as many things as they can see in each of the 10 inkblots in 1 minute's time, they give an average of 91.9 responses (Exner, Armbruster, & Mittman, 1978). By contrast, nonpatient adults being administered the RIM in the standard way give an average of 22.7 responses (J. E. Exner, 1993, chap. 12). How subjects select the responses they deliver from among the many potential percepts they recognize and which features of the blots they choose to utilize in articulating their responses, as elaborated in J. E. Exner's (1993, chap. 2) analysis of the response process, is a highly variable and idiosyncratic matter.

Accordingly, projected material in Rorschach responses has both idiographic and nomothetic implications, although more of the former, and the influence of card pull in shaping responses has implications both for how they differ from and how they resemble each other, but more of the latter. Distinguishing between the projective and card pull aspects of responses facilitates effective interpretation by providing the following three kinds of information:

1. The more projection there is in a response, the more the response reveals about the subject, especially through its thematic imagery, and the more attention it should receive in the interpretive process.

2. The more a response is determined by card pull, the less projection it involves and the less attention should be paid to its thematic imagery; at the same time, the extent to which subjects' responses are determined by card pull identifies how inclined they are to respond as most people do.

3. Awareness of the types of perceptual structuring, thematic imagery, and test behaviors typically elicited by each of the inkblots proves generally useful in judging the interpretive significance of what subjects do and do not say in responding to them.

MONITORING THE IMPACT OF PROJECTION

Monitoring the impact of projection in Rorschach responses consists of identifying which responses are likely to involve projected material and estimating the extent to which projection has shaped them. As mentioned in chapter 3, J. E. Exner (1989) concluded from his research that responses involving movement, perceptual distortions, and embellishments of various kinds are particularly likely to reveal underlying aspects of personality dynamics. He was, in other words, identifying the kinds of responses in which projection is likely to have occurred, and his formulation can readily be conceptualized in terms of the stimulus characteristics of the blots.

With respect to responses involving movement, the Rorschach stimuli are static blots of ink that do not move. Hence, any attribution of movement to figures or objects seen in them must of necessity come from the inner life of the subject. Perceptual distortions, defined specifically as responses coded with *minus* form level, consist of clearly defined figures or objects that bear little resemblance to the contours of the location where they are seen. Percepts that lack clear definition or that can be easily and readily seen are coded as *ordinary* or *unusual* form, depending on their normative frequency of occurrence. Hence correct coding of minus form level signifies that the subject is seeing something definite in the inkblot that is not close to being there and must therefore be springing from within. Similar considerations apply to any embellishments that go beyond calling attention to the stimulus properties of the blots; because they are not in the blots, they can only constitute projections into the response process of ideas and affects internal to the subject.

With respect to estimating the extent of projection in responses, there are several ways of weighing the unique significance of a particular response for a particular subject and deciding how much interpretive significance to assign its thematic implications. First, as mentioned in the introduction, imagery as well as perception is responsive to card pull, and relatively common movements, distortions, and embellishments are likely to involve less projection and have less interpretive significance than highly unusual ones.

Thus, in the case of movement, as noted by Schachtel (1966, p. 212), the popular M on Card III and the popular FM on Card VIII indicate less about the personal attitudes of subjects than human and animal movement seen elsewhere. Conversely, the thematic imagery of movement responses occurring where movement is seldom seen is likely to be especially revealing. Of similar significance is the commonality or distinctiveness of the type of movement that is projected, even among popular responses. On Card III, for example, "Two women cooking something in a pot" could have implications for the subject's assigning stereotyped gender roles to women or having strong dependency needs; however, the frequency with which Card III is seen in this way lessens the meaningfulness if not the validity of such interpretations. By contrast, Card III as "Two women fighting over something they both want to have" is a relatively infrequent response that probably has substantial idiographic meaning in relation to some aspect of competitive struggle in the subject's life.

Likewise for the popular animal on Card VIII, "Two animals climbing up a mountain" could perhaps be stretched interpretively to suggest concerns with striving and accomplishment, as in "climbing up the ladder of success." Considering how commonly this image is reported, however, such an interpretation would probably stretch the data beyond reason; a more reasonable conclusion would regard the imagery in this response as revealing little of importance about the subject. As an alternative, consider Card VIII seen as "Two animals fleeing for their lives, trying to escape the fires of Hell burning down below." Dramatic and highly idiographic, this latter view of the Card VIII popular animals strongly suggests fears of life-threatening forces over which one has little control, perhaps with an element of guilt over past actions for which the person feels deserving of punishment.

Consideration should also be given in the thematic interpretation of movement to the differing implications of projection onto human and animal figures. Generally speaking, people identify more readily with human or humanlike activities and emotional states than with what animals do or are concerned about. Hence, other things being equal, the material projected into M responses is likely to reveal more about a subject's personality dynamics than the thematic imagery in FM responses. However, as noted by Schachtel (1966, p. 223), there may be taboo activities or personally unacceptable attitudes or strivings that some subjects can more comfortably attribute to an animal, particularly one that is not humanlike, than to people. In such cases, FM themes, particularly in responses as dramatic as

the Card VIII example just given, may be just as revealing as the imagery in
M responses.

In like fashion, *FM* imagery typically says more about a subject's personality dynamics than the themes in *m* responses, but dramatic exceptions
may occur and warrant interpretive emphasis. For example, the *m* response
of "A tree being torn up by the wind and blown away from its roots" has
compelling implications for concerns about being involuntarily separated
from people or places one holds dear, and it is certainly more revealing
than a Card III *M* of "Two women cooking something in a pot" or a Card VIII
FM of "Animals climbing a mountain." These and other considerations in
the interpretation of thematic imagery are elaborated in chapter 6.

Turning to perceptual distortion, *minus* as well as movement responses
vary in how frequently they occur and how dramatic they are. Perhaps the
most common of all minus responses are the several variations of "face"
responses given to *DdS* locations on Card X. All of these responses have
minus form level, because most of their component parts (eyes, nose, mouth,
etc.) are minus and the "face" itself has an arbitrary boundary rather than
a demarcated perimeter. Nevertheless, whereas a minus form quality "face"
would typically suggest concerns about being under the scrutiny of other
people who are looking at you, the Card X "face," because of how frequently
it occurs, should be interpreted very conservatively, if at all, in this vein.

As for differences in the dramatic quality of minus responses, Phillips
and J. G. Smith (1953, chap. 2) proposed categorizing inaccurate forms in
terms of four levels of distortion, ranging from those that approach resembling the inkblot to those that are grossly discrepant from it. They viewed
this categorization as a way of measuring degree of psychopathology, with
the most discrepant responses indicating the most severe disturbance. Although their fourfold classification of minus responses and its relation to
severity of psychopathology have never been adequately examined in research studies, J. E. Exner and Weiner (1995, chap. 3) and Weiner (1966/1997b,
chap. 7) endorsed the clinical utility of distinguishing between more and
less perceptually distorted minus responses. In terms of the present discussion, it follows that the greater the distortion level in a minus response, the
more dramatic it will be, the more it will be based on projection rather than
card pull, and the more it will reveal about a subject's inner life.

Finally, with respect to embellishments, the same considerations of commonality and drama that guide the interpretation of attributed movement
and perceptual distortion help to identify the extent of projection in various
response elaborations and their corresponding import. Two Morbid (*MOR*)
responses can serve to illustrate both considerations. On Card VI, a *MOR*
on the order of "A cat that's been run over" occurs so frequently that it can
almost be called a "popular morbid." In fact, a Card VI *W* of "cat" is coded
as unusual form in the Comprehensive System, whereas "flattened cat" to

the same location is sufficiently common to be coded as ordinary. Accordingly, this particular *MOR* probably involves less projection and is less likely to signify concerns about damage to one's body than uncommon *MOR*s occurring elsewhere in a protocol. As for drama, "wounded bears" on Card II, although another relatively common *MOR* response, gains significance for preoccupation with past or impending harm if it is elaborated into "wounded bears who have been mauled in a fight or shot by hunters, and they're badly hurt and have blood all over them." These same yardsticks of commonality and intensity can be applied to all instances of response embellishment as a way of estimating the interpretive import of whatever thematic imagery the response contains.

Implicit in many of the preceding examples is the fact that the occurrence of projection and the likely significance of thematic imagery may be indicated by more than one feature of a response. Thus, the content of a particular response may be identified as likely to reveal aspects of personality dynamics by virtue of its involving attributed movement and also perceptual distortion. In other instances, a response may combine movement with some embellishment, or embellishments with perceptual distortion, or perhaps all three clues to the presence of projected material. As a general guideline, the thematic imagery of responses containing any two of these three indications of projection—which for handy reference can be called "two-baggers"—can be anticipated to be more personally meaningful to subjects and to provide more information about their inner life than responses with just one of these features. Likewise, "three-baggers" (i.e., embellished and perceptually distorted movement responses) will often prove to be the most revealing responses in a protocol with respect to a subject's underlying needs, attitudes, conflicts, and concerns.

To recap this discussion of monitoring the impact of projection, the purpose of identifying the presence and extent of projection in Rorschach responses is to identify which responses should be read for their thematic imagery and how much interpretive weight to give to likely implications of this imagery. The Comprehensive System search strategy described in chapter 3 incorporates the identification of such responses by indicating where in the interpretive process all movement, minus form, and embellished responses should be read. The present discussion has gone beyond the basic search strategy to present some guidelines for differentiating among responses involving projection with respect to how revealing they are likely to be.

As discussed further in subsequent chapters, the notion of two-baggers and three-baggers can be particularly helpful in this regard. In selecting which responses to read first, examiners are advised to search the Sequence of Scores for responses that combine two or all three of the clues to projection to determine whether there are any that are particularly likely to capture core dynamic elements of a subject's personality. Should a code include, for example, a Morbid *M-* response, the thematic imagery in this three-bagger is likely to make it one of the most significant responses in the record, particularly if it turns out as well that the form level is particularly poor and the morbidity is dramatically elaborated.

To introduce an additional extension of the Comprehensive System, it should be noted that the basic search strategy identifies responses to be read on the basis of their including projected material but does not call for reading any other responses. The rationale in this regard is that the content of responses that do not involve projection has little if any interpretive significance. However, response content that lacks meaning by virtue of being determined by card pull rather than projection can nevertheless contribute important information in a sequence analysis. As elaborated in chapter 8, the point at which thematically bland and unrevealing responses occur, particularly with respect to the cards on which they occur and the responses that have immediately preceded them, often has implications for the nature of a subject's focal concerns and adaptive capacities.

IDENTIFYING THE INFLUENCE OF CARD PULL

Although the importance of the stimulus characteristics of the inkblots is implicit in Hermann Rorschach's original focus on the cognitive-perceptual dimensions of his method, little explicit attention has been paid to the role of card pull in shaping Rorschach responses. Whereas projection was formally incorporated into conceptualizations of the Rorschach beginning with L. K. Frank (1939), card pull appears to have lacked any formal definition in the literature prior to 1950, at which point Ranzoni, Grant, and Ives referred to it as "those properties of the inkblot which seem to predispose the subject to the use of certain aspects of the blot" (p. 108). A few classic texts subsequently mentioned card pull in passing. Beck acknowledged in his third edition that "a few blots or parts of blots have a particular stimulus 'pull' " (S. J. Beck et al., 1961, p. 133), and B. Klopfer et al. (1954) devoted a few pages to "What the cards facilitate" (pp. 320–327). A full chapter on "Stimulus Characteristics of the Rorschach blots" by Aronow and Reznikoff (1976) seems to be the only extended discussion of this topic. In a commentary on the minimal attention paid to such an obvious and potentially important influence on Rorschach responses, Peterson and Schilling (1983) speculated that "like many psychological household words, our proximity to the concept of card pull has allowed it to be taken for granted" (p. 265). Indeed, none of three volumes presenting the Comprehensive System (J. E. Exner, 1991, 1993; J. E. Exner & Weiner, 1995) lists "card pull" in its index.

As for the importance of card pull, attention to the stimulus characteristics of the inkblots and recognition of the perceptual, associational, and behavioral response features they are likely to elicit sharpens decisions concerning the interpretive significance of individual responses. As noted earlier, response features that coincide with expectation based on card pull generally indicate ways in which subjects resemble most other people, whereas features that deviate from expectation identify relatively unique characteristics of the individual.

For example, approximately 80% of nonpatient subjects give one Texture (*T*) response, the vast majority of which occur on Cards IV and VI, the two most heavily shaded cards. Given the implications of *T* for being receptive to and comfortable in close relationships with other people, a subject who gives one *T* and does so in a Card VI popular animal skin response is displaying evidence of normative capacity to form interpersonal attachments. This finding speaks positively to the person's level of adaptation and provides important basic information, but it does not go beyond identifying that the subject resembles most nonpatients in regard to this basic capacity to form attachments.

Suppose, however, that a subject gives one *T*, thereby identifying a normative level of attachment capacity, but does so on Card IX. Suppose further that, in contrast to the popular and hence not very personally meaningful Card VI animal skin, this subject says about the pink detail on Card IX that "the way it's colored and shaded reminds me of sticky cotton candy." Given that this subject was capable of articulating texture where it is seldom noted, as this Card IX response demonstrates, why did this person fail to articulate the more obvious and commonly reported texture on Card VI? This is the kind of question prompted by card pull considerations, and it generates several possible answers that contribute unique information about this person.

For example, perhaps the dark blacks and grays of Card VI, which for many people convey unpleasant or dysphoric feelings, was a more difficult context in which to acknowledge an orientation to interpersonal intimacy than the lighter and more pleasant pastel colors of Card IX. The possibility that this subject is experiencing some dysphoric, or at least ambivalent, affect in relation to attachment issues is increased in this example by the fact that the "sticky cotton candy" would be coded *CF.TF* and thus involves a color-shading blend. As an alternative hypothesis, consider (a) that both "penis" and "vagina" can readily be seen on Card VI (the upper center detail of Card VI is ordinary form for penis, and the lower center detail is unusual for vagina) and (b) that "cotton candy" is a food response with connotations of oral dependency (and would be coded as such in the previously mentioned Rorschach Oral Dependency Scale) and is usually thought of as a child's treat rather than food for an adult. Consequently, perhaps this subject feels more comfortable contemplating interpersonal closeness in the context of childhood dependency than in the context of adult genital sexuality.

Of course, these hypotheses are purely speculative and, in the absence of considerable additional information, should not be assigned the status of reasonable conclusions. Chapter 6 provides detailed criteria for judging the adequacy of inferences based on thematic imagery, and numerous requirements must be met before such inferences can be given serious consideration. Nevertheless, although the hypotheses offered in this example cannot yet be considered reasonable *conclusions*, they are reasonable *speculations*, based on ample knowledge about card pull and about personality dynamics.

Implicit in these examples are some general guidelines for utilizing card pull information to enrich the interpretive yield of Rorschach responses. As previously noted, full utilization of card pull information goes beyond merely identifying the extent to which responses are based on projection rather than stimulus characteristics of the inkblots and involves noting the extent to which response characteristics deviate from normative expectation and hence are likely to be especially meaningful for the individual subject. The general guidelines in this regard can be divided into two categories, one of which pertains to *overt* and the other to *covert* aspects of card pull. Overt card pull refers to characteristics of the blots that subjects in general ordinarily articulate in some way, whereas covert card pull refers to blot characteristics that most subjects can ordinarily recognize but rarely articulate in their responses or comments.

Overt Card Pull

The 10 inkblots that constitute the Rorschach contain numerous stimulus characteristics that almost all subjects respond to directly in selecting, framing, and delivering one or more of their responses. These overt aspects of card pull include (a) whether the blots are relatively simple and "closed" (as are the continuously formed, gray-black Cards I, IV, V, VI, and VII) or relatively complex and "broken" (as are the discontinuous, multicolored Cards II, III, VIII, IX, and X); (b) the actual shape, shading, and color properties of the blots, which J. E. Exner (1996) referred to as the "critical bits" in the Rorschach stimuli, along with their tendency to suggest some kind of movement; and (c) the overall resemblance of the blots to various objects.

As would be expected for Location Choice, *W* responses are normatively more likely to occur on the closed than on the broken blots, and the broken blots are more likely than the closed blots to elicit only *D* responses. As for determinants and content categories, the Comprehensive System normative data indicate that one or more *M, FM, FC, CF, F*, Pair, Human, Animal, and Botany responses are given by 93% to 100% of subjects. In addition, the mode among nonpatient adults is 1.00 or more for *m, C', T, FD*, Art, Clothing, Household, Landscape, and Science responses. Each of these determinants and contents is accordingly expected to occur in a record, whereas those that show a normative mode of zero (which include C, V, Y, Reflections, and the remaining content categories) are ordinarily not expected to occur. The less frequently certain determinants and contents ordinarily occur, the more interpretive significance is likely to attach to their occurring even once in a record. For all of these variables, moreover, their interpretive significance depends not only on how frequently they occur, but also on where they occur in relation to where they are most commonly expected to occur, which is a matter of card pull.

Beginning with the structural data in a Rorschach protocol, the guiding principle in utilizing overt card pull information is the following: Examiners should assign special interpretive significance to deviations from expectation with respect to the locus of perceptual variables and formulate hypotheses concerning why these deviations may have occurred where they did. The previous example concerning the card on which a T appears was an illustration of this facet of interpretation. In similar fashion for other determinants and contents, and for location choices as well, examiners should reflect on where they typically occur, as a way of identifying response patterns that are relatively idiographic and thus likely to be particularly informative. For example, what might it mean if an extratensive subject gives M responses on Cards I, IV, and V but not on Cards III and VII? Among extratensive subjects a total of three M responses demonstrates normative capacity to generate human movement responses, but M are given more frequently to Cards III and VII than to either Cards I, IV, or V. Hence, the subject's response process in this regard must reflect some unusual influence that calls for interpretive attention. Perhaps this subject has sufficient ideational capacity and human interest to generate an expected and thus unremarkable number of M responses but nevertheless has some concerns about interpersonal relationships. If so, could this account for Ms emerging to the single figure characteristics of Cards I, IV, and V but not in response to the pairs of figures typically seen and articulated on Cards III and VII? Although not yet a warranted conclusion, such a speculation would at least seem reasonable and worth pursuing.

In some instances, overt card pull information involving the structural data in a record can warrant conclusions rather than merely speculations. A subject who gives four Popular responses falls within the normative range for demonstrating adequate capacity to recognize conventional reality. Suppose, however, that these four P responses occur on Cards II, IV, VII, and IX. As noted by J. E. Exner (1993, chap. 8), these are the four cards least likely to elicit one of the 13 P responses in the Comprehensive System. What happened in this subject's record to the animals on Card VIII, the people on Card III, the bat or butterfly on Card I, and the animal skin on Card VI, which are the four most frequent Ps, given by 87% to 94% of nonpatients? Perhaps in the course of a thorough sequence analysis some explanation in psychodynamic terms might be found for some of the *P* failures in this example. More likely in such a case, however, this unusual locus of Popular responses indicates less capacity for recognizing conventional reality than first seems the case, and the subject's deviation from expectation, as identified on the basis of card pull information, points to some impairment of reality testing despite the presence of four *P*s.

As also illustrated earlier, the utilization of card pull information is not limited to interpretation of the structural data in a Rorschach protocol but extends as well to thematic and behavioral features of the data. The subject in the previous example who elaborated themes of violence in response to Card VIII but not Card II was responding in a way that deviated from usual expectation based on the kinds of themes typically elicited by the stimulus characteristics of the blots. The same can be said with respect to typically elicited comments in the case of the subject who said "This is a hard one" on being handed Card V but not Card IX. The guiding principle for interpreting structural deviations from expectation applies equally to an unexpected locus of thematic images or test behaviors. The more themes and behaviors differ from those that the inkblots tend to elicit, the more interpretive significance they are likely to have and the more attention examiners should pay to determining this significance.

Covert Card Pull

As previously stated, covert aspects of card pull include characteristics of the inkblots that subjects seldom mention but that nevertheless influence how they respond. In some instances, these unmentioned characteristics consist of perceived objects (e.g., a naked woman) or associated themes (e.g., bloody animals killing each other) of which the individual is fully aware but chooses to censor rather than report to the examiner. In other instances, blot characteristics may convey symbolic meanings to subjects that affect their responses and test behavior without their being consciously aware of them.

As described by J. E. Exner (1993, chap. 2) and mentioned earlier in this chapter, censoring occurs regularly as part of the Rorschach response process. Subjects choosing which responses to give from among the many that occur to them typically weigh the social desirability of what they might report. As in other interpersonal interactions with strangers, especially in formal situations in which they are being evaluated, persons taking the Rorschach tend to suppress impressions they think might strike the examiner as strange, inappropriate, or offensive and thereby reflect badly on them.

Research summarized by J. E. Exner (1993, pp. 41–44) has neatly demonstrated the influence of social desirability on subjects' willingness to report such sexual objects and aggressive themes as naked women and bloody animals. In this research 60 volunteer subjects were shown the Rorschach cards and asked to indicate the relative ease or difficulty with which they could see five possible responses to each blot. As a critical independent variable in the study, half of the subjects were told that the responses they were being asked to rate had been given by successful businesspeople; the other half were told that these responses had been given by hospitalized schizophrenic patients. The responses the subjects were asked to rate included Blood responses to the red areas on Cards II, III, and IX and Sex responses (naked woman, penis, vagina, buttocks) to portions of Cards I, VI, VII, and IX. The majority of those who were given the "businessperson" set rated each of these Blood and Sex responses as being relatively easy to see. In sharp contrast, the majority of those who were given the "hospitalized schizophrenic patients" set rated these responses as relatively difficult to see. As a specific case in point, the response of "penis" to the top central detail of Card VI was rated as quite easy to see by 18 of the 30 "businessperson" set subjects but only 3 of the "schizophrenic" set subjects; conversely, 18 of the 30 "schizophrenic" set but only 4 of the "businessperson" set subjects said this penis response was quite difficult to see.

These latter findings imply that people have little difficulty seeing the top central detail (D6) of Card VI as a penis but may choose not to report this percept, should they have reason to believe that doing so will reflect unfavorably on them or somehow be to their disadvantage. Accordingly, how some people respond to Card VI may be influenced in part by their perceiving D6 as a penis, regardless of whether they report this percept. This is of course a speculation, not a certainty in the way that Card VI is most certainly colored in shades of gray and black. Nevertheless, like other ways in which the inkblots may be seen, the commonly shared impression that D6 on Card VI resembles a penis provides a potential instance of covert card pull in which unstated influences may be at work in shaping how subjects respond.

With further respect to Sex responses, some normative data bear further witness to differences between what most subjects can probably see when they look at the inkblots and what they decide to report. Among the 700 nonpatient adults in J. E. Exner's (1993, chap. 12) Comprehensive System reference sample, just 30 (4.3%) have any Sex responses, and the sample mean is .07. By contrast, among the 320 inpatient schizophrenic subjects referenced by Exner, 146 (45.6%) have one or more Sex responses, and the sample mean is 1.36. Why should schizophrenic subjects be so much more inclined than nonpatient subjects to report Sex responses? One compelling answer to this question is that schizophrenic subjects, because of their frequently poor judgment and inadequate control of thoughts and actions, report impressions that nonpatients may also form but have the good sense and adequate restraint to keep to themselves.

Another possibility, of course, is that schizophrenic persons on the average are more preoccupied with sexual thoughts than people in general and project their concerns in the form of minus form-level Sex responses that most other people do not see. However this may be, the normative data confirm that there are in fact a substantial number of Sex responses in the 10 inkblots that are easy to see. As listed in the form-level tables for the Comprehensive System (J. E. Exner, 1993, chap. 11), there are seven Sex responses coded as ordinary form and an additional 25 Sex responses coded as unusual, meaning they occur infrequently but can easily and readily be seen. These 32 accurately perceived Sex responses include seven locations that resemble a penis and 11 locations that resemble a vagina.

The gap between the presence of 32 clearly recognizable Sex responses in the Rorschach cards and the mean frequency of .07 Sex responses in the records of nonpatient adults provides further evidence that there is much more sex to be seen in the Rorschach than is ordinarily reported. A frequently heard story about the RIM concerns a male psychiatric patient who, after giving a record containing numerous Sex responses, demanded to know why the psychologist had shown him such dirty pictures. As it turns out, the joke may be on us—there is a lot of sex in the inkblots! With respect to covert card pull, the point for examiners to keep in mind is that impressions formed but not reported can nevertheless influence how subjects respond. The more examiners know about the impressions people are likely to form of each of the blots, the more fully they will be able to appreciate and anticipate possible covert card pull and use its apparent influence as a source of information about a subject's personality dynamics.

To take an example of such utilization of covert card pull, consider the contrasting implications of two descriptions by female subjects of the D6 area of Card VI. Keep in mind that this blot detail was easily seen as a penis by subjects with the "businessperson" set in the study just mentioned and is coded as ordinary form quality for "penis." One woman described this location as "an ornately carved nicely polished piece of wood that I'd like to have as a bedpost." The other woman described it as "a big club that would really hurt you if you got whacked by it." In keeping with guidelines for judicious interpretation of thematic imagery to be elaborated in chapter 6, the difference between these two responses could have little meaning. On the other hand, particularly in conjunction with confirmatory data appearing elsewhere in the record or obtained from other sources, these responses could reflect a positive and pleasurable orientation toward heterosexual intercourse in the first case and a negative, fearful orientation in the second case.

In this illustration of covert card pull, these two subjects could have made a conscious decision to refrain from identifying the top center detail of Card VI as a penis and called it something else instead, albeit something influenced by their having identified it as resembling a penis. Additionally in such instances, there is always the possibility that the subject did not identify the location as a penis, or at least was not consciously aware of doing so. However, such lack of conscious awareness would not prevent this blot detail, by virtue of its shape and configuration, from symbolizing phallic properties and stimulating associations to them. When this kind of representation occurs, blot characteristics can generate covert card pull by conveying symbolic meanings that influence how subjects respond without their recognizing either the symbolic meaning or its influence.

Like the influence of recognized but unreported blot characteristics, the influence of unrecognized symbolic meanings can provide valuable information about subjects' underlying attitudes and concerns. As in all instances of using knowledge about the role of projection and card pull in shaping responses, however, examiners can utilize this feature of covert card pull effectively only if they have some sense of what the inkblots are generally likely to symbolize. Unlike blot characteristics that are generally recognizable even if rarely reported—such as the resemblance of the lower center detail (D12) of Card VI to a vagina, which is an unusual form-level percept—the symbolic import of the Rorschach cards is a highly idiographic matter. Like symbols in dreams, the symbolic implications of thematic imagery on the Rorschach can be interpreted and understood only in terms of the individual person's frame of reference.

For example, long cylindrical objects such as the "bedpost" and "club" in the previously cited example may for many people have a phallic significance, but for others they may signify something quite different or perhaps nothing at all. Freud is reputed to have said about his ever-present cigar that it could be a phallic symbol, but then it also could be just his cigar. In the past, some Rorschach clinicians have overlooked the frequently idiographic nature of symbolism and posited universal meaning for certain content categories, such as "fish" representing "a reaction to maternal overprotection" and "bear" being associated with "a benign and sympathetic father figure" (Phillips & J. G. Smith, 1953, pp. 120–121). Others have designated individual cards in terms of specific associations they are believed to generate, as in referring to Card IV as the "father" card, Card VII as the "mother card," and Card VI as the "sex" card (e.g., Brown, 1953; Richards, 1958).

Such assumed universal symbolism of either specific contents or specific cards can be faulted on both conceptual and empirical grounds. Conceptually, appreciation for the frequently idiographic significance of symbols occurring in dreams, as well as extensive experience with the inkblot method, has led leading advocates of psychodynamic thematic interpretation to deny any invariant symbolism in Rorschach responses or cards. Schachtel (1966, chap. 3) explained in detail why assuming that the Rorschach cards regularly have some specific meaning is misleading and "will lead to faulty interpretations" (p. 32). Schafer (1954, chap. 4) likewise expressed serious reservations about assigning invariant meaning to Rorschach symbols. Aronow and Reznikoff (1976) pointed out that, because Rorschach examiners typically do not elicit subject's associations to their responses in the manner that psychotherapists elicit their patients' associations to dream contents, "the Rorschach test is typically far less dependable than the dream in understanding the psychodynamics of test subjects" (p. 230).

Empirically, reviews of the literature have provided little support for the designation of Card IV as the "father" card and Card VII as the "mother" card (G. Frank, 1977; Liaboe & Guy, 1985). As for Card VI being the "sex" card, of the 32 Sex responses coded as ordinary or unusual form level and thus by definition being easily seen, only four occur on Card VI. The cards with the most accurately seen Sex responses listed in the Comprehensive System form-level table are Card II with seven and Card III with five. It may nevertheless be the case that Sex responses are more likely to occur on Card VI than elsewhere. The point, however, is that other blots can also elicit sexualized percepts or associations. In similar fashion, subjects prone to seeing or associating with images reminiscent of their mother can do so just as easily to blot stimuli other than Card VII that are often seen as having feminine qualities, such as the center detail (D4) on Card I and the popular figures on Card III.

Deferring for the moment further illustrations of covert card pull and the possible symbolic significance of blot details, two additional dimensions of blot characteristics must be addressed. First, in addition to unreported or unrecognized impressions of the shape of the inkblots, percepts and associations prompted by the color and shading of the blots can also shape responses in revealing ways. Regarding chromatic and achromatic color, the way people experience various hues and the language in which they are commonly described establish strong connections between color and various emotional states. Most English-speaking people concur that "seeing red" refers to being angry, "feeling blue" to being sad, and "a black deed" to an evil act. Few people would paint a depiction of joy in blacks and grays, which are traditional colors of mourning, and few would paint a funeral in bright shades of yellow, pink, and green (except perhaps when intending to convey some such message as the possibility for happiness even after the death of a loved one).

Without overlooking idiographic perspectives on color and without erring in the direction of universal symbolization, it can still be suggested that the red details in Cards II and III are likely to convey a sense of anger; the blacks and grays in Cards I, IV, V, VI, and VII are likely to arouse depressive affect, especially where they are heavily shaded; and the pastel colors in Cards VIII, IX, and X are likely to stimulate pleasant and lighthearted feelings. These suggestions do not imply that such affective associations are inevitably stimulated by these cards, but only that it is not unreasonable to expect many subjects to be emotionally affected by color and shading characteristics of the blots, even when they do not articulate these characteristics or recognize that they are being affected by them. In these instances, covert card pull is operating, and sensitivity to these possible influences on the responses subjects are giving can contribute to effective interpretation of these responses.

The second additional point to be made about covert card pull concerns a short period of time in the late 1950s and early 1960s when numerous investigators addressed the general as well as the specific meanings of the Rorschach inkblots. Some of these studies consisted simply of asking subjects to divide the blots into those they liked or disliked or to indicate which they considered "masculine" and which "feminine." Other studies employed more sophisticated measures such as the *semantic differential*, in which a composite description of what objects mean to people is derived from examining the adjectives they assign to it in a forced-choice rating paradigm.

In one semantic differential study, for example, Kamano (1960) reported that Card IV was categorized by a sample of college undergraduates as being harder, larger, stronger, stricter, more masculine, and more aggressive than Card VII. Card VII, in turn, was characterized as soft, small, weak, permissive, feminine, and retiring. Despite the potential appeal of these findings, the literature in general, as already noted, does not support the notion of any universal father or mother symbolism associated with Cards IV and VII. As an aspect of idiography, for example, an individual subject could in fact have a big, strong, aggressive mother and a small, weak, permissive father, and for this person Card IV could be the mother card and Card VII the father card. In this vein, Sines (1960) found in another semantic differential study that the meanings a sample of college students attached to Cards IV and VII differed significantly from the meanings they attached to their concepts of father and mother.

Aronow and Reznikoff (1976, chap. 11) provided a detailed review of the semantic differential studies from this past era, and they are not discussed further here. For contemporary purposes, the important point they make is that certain general meanings conveyed by the inkblots—such as Card IV suggesting something big, heavy, large, strong, and in authority—may be stable and pervasive far beyond the limits of specific symbolic referents, such as Card IV symbolizing a subject's father. To the extent that this is the case, how subjects respond to Card IV may not necessarily indicate how they regard their father, but it may regularly say something about how they feel about powerful figures in authority.

In this way, then, an older literature concerned with the general meaning of the inkblots can contribute to present-day understanding of the types of percepts and associations elicited by the blots. This chapter concludes with a review of cumulative knowledge concerning the impact that each of the 10 inkblots is likely to have as subjects proceed through a Rorschach examination. Without repeating previously cited data concerning card pull for various coding categories, this review focuses on meanings that may be conveyed by the blots and reflected in various objects, themes, and affects that each often suggests.

COMMON MEANINGS OF THE 10 INKBLOTS

Appreciation for what the Rorschach blots may frequently signify facilitates the interpretation of projection and card pull influences on how subjects respond in two ways. First, knowing what each of the cards is likely to pull with respect to structural, thematic, and behavioral aspects of responses helps to identify deviations from common expectations. As noted earlier, the more closely responses hew to what the cards ordinarily pull, the more they reveal about ways in which a subject resembles other people. Conversely, the more responses deviate from ordinary expectation concerning the kinds of percepts, associations, and test behavior pulled by each card, the more clearly they point to idiographic and personally meaningful features of a subject's psychological nature.

Second, familiarity with what the blots are likely to signify helps to clarify which aspects of their psychological lives subjects are managing comfortably and which are causing them distress. When subjects deal effectively with particular cards, they are likely to be managing the issues and challenges associated with these cards in an adaptive fashion. Conversely, subjects who respond ineffectively on certain cards may well be having difficulty coping comfortably and constructively with issues and challenges signified by those cards.

Several criteria can help to judge whether subjects are displaying adaptive strengths or coping limitations in how they deal with the individual cards. Generally speaking, dealing effectively with the cards consists of proceeding calmly and with little hesitation to articulate clearly defined, perceptually accurate, and logically organized responses that are free from distressing content. Contrariwise, difficulty dealing with a particular card is suggested (a) when subjects take longer than usual to respond to it, express themselves in a halting manner not characteristic of how they respond to other cards, or make negative comments about the card, such as not liking it or finding it hard to see anything in it; (b) when subjects give vague, minus form, dissociated, or arbitrarily reasoned responses to it; and (c) when subjects report impressions of the card that appear to make them uncomfortable, especially when they state directly that their responses are distasteful or upsetting to them.

As for the issues and challenges signified by the individual cards, each of the 10 Rorschach cards can be considered with specific respect to the perceived objects, associated themes, experienced affects, and evaluative comments it tends to elicit and to the ease or difficulty of formulating responses to it. Available knowledge in this regard ranges from fairly definite information, such as the frequency with which Card VIII elicits the popular animal response, to reasonable but speculative hypotheses, such as the expectation that, at least to some people, D6 on Card VI will resemble a penis or suggest percepts and associations based on such an easily seen resemblance. The comments on the 10 cards that follow are based on a combination of empirical findings concerning Comprehensive System variables and theoretically based psychodynamic speculations, and they also draw on previous analyses of the individual cards by Aronow and Reznikoff (1976, pp. 248–263), Aronow, Reznikoff, and Moreland (1994, pp. 34–38), and B. Klopfer et al. (1954, pp. 320–327).

Card I

As the first card shown, Card I frequently elicits questions from subjects about how they should proceed, especially if they are generally inclined to seek structure and ascertain the rules before they commit themselves in a new situation. Thus such test behaviors as asking how many responses they should give, whether they have to use the whole blot, and if they can turn the card have relatively little import when they occur on Card I, unless they are emphasized in some way, because of the frequency with which they ordinarily occur. On the other hand, requests for structure take on increasing significance for idiographic characteristics or concerns as the administration proceeds. Subjects who are asking in Card VI whether they are allowed to turn the card, or on Card X about how many responses they should give, are probably revealing something noteworthy about themselves, such as discomfort with what they see at the top of Card VI in its upright position and difficulty in dealing simultaneously with as many details as are presented by Card X.

Although Card I does not reveal much about subjects through questions they ask about how to proceed, it does occupy a special place among the 10 cards by virtue of its coming first and presenting subjects with a new and usually unfamiliar task and often a stressful situation as well. Accordingly, the comfort, style, and effectiveness with which people approach Card I can often provide clues to how they tend to deal with new and stressful situations in their lives. In addition, Card I gives subjects their first Rorschach to indicate something about who they are and what is important to them. Initial responses in particular, especially when they contain idiographic elements that go beyond the $W F A$ popular bat, often serve as a "sign in" response: "This is who I am," the subject is saying, "and this is what I want you to know about me." Consider, for example, the possible import as "sign in" responses of "a damaged butterfly" given by a victim of abuse and "an angel" given by a misbehaving child.

Some initial uncertainty or uneasiness not withstanding, Card I usually does not pose a difficult task for subjects. The ready availability of the "bat" and "butterfly" Populars, as well as many other winged or flying creatures seen to the whole card and the easily identifiable human figure in the center detail, provide numerous opportunities for subjects to select bland and simple responses. At the same time, there is some evidence that the shape and darkness of Card I convey to some subjects a negative emotional tone and an impression of something ugly and unattractive. Accordingly, subjects who are depressed and struggling with feelings of dysphoria, guilt, and pessimism may find Card I and the four other gray-black cards relatively discomfiting and difficult with which to deal.

Card II

The most distinctive feature of Card II is its areas of bright red color, which are known to be easily and readily seen as blood and convey to many people an emotional tone of anger and associations to being damaged or harmed. Accordingly, this card may prove difficult for subjects struggling with feelings of hostility and resentment or who are concerned about the vulnerability of their bodies, and whether and how people respond to its red areas often provides information about how they manage such feelings and concerns.

Also noteworthy on Card II is the frequency of ordinary and unusual form-quality Sex responses, which as noted earlier exceeds the number of such responses on any other card. Both male and female sexual anatomy can easily be seen on this card, including a penis in the upper center black detail (D4) and a vagina in either the lower center red detail (D3) or the inner pale red detail in the lower center red (Dd24). How subjects respond to Card II and what if anything they say about these two areas can thus be influenced by what they connote sexually and thus provide clues to subjects' sexual concerns.

Card III

The key import of Card III derives from the extremely common percept on this blot of two people involved in some kind of interaction. Possible implications of the particular kind of interaction that is projected into such responses is picked up in part by the well-validated special scores for Aggressive Movement (AG) and Cooperative Movement (COP). Beyond this specific consideration, however, the interpersonal significance of Card III provides reason to believe that subjects frequently reveal their attitudes and concerns about relating to other people in how they respond to this card, even if they do not attribute movement to the popular figures or fail to report them at all. In fact, the more difficulty subjects have in responding to Card III, the more likely they are to be struggling with negative and aversive attitudes toward social interactions.

Although Card III is less likely than Card II to elicit disembodied Sex responses, its popular human figures include one area (Dd27) that is ordinary form for breast and another area (Dd26) that is ordinary form for a penis. For subjects who are uncertain about their gender-role identity, this feature of the blot may contribute to their being unable to decide whether the people are male or female, to their describing the figures as having both masculine and feminine sexual characteristics, or to their showing signs of difficulty in responding at all to the black details on this card.

Card IV

Although Card IV is not and should not be referred to as the "father card," it has been demonstrated to evoke associations to being big, strong, massive, heavy, powerful, in authority, and sometimes threatening. Such impressions of Card IV are compounded by the frequently mentioned experience of "looking up" at the figure seen, thus placing the observing subject in a weak and inferior position. In this same vein, the figures usually seen on this card comprise giants, monsters, gorillas, and very large people, almost always men and very rarely women. Hence there is good reason to think of Card IV as conveying a sense of authority or an authority figure, usually male but sometimes female as well, to whom one is responsible and subordinate. Moreover, although Card IV is not "*the* father card," because many persons other than a person's father can fill the role of an authority figure and because attitudes toward this father can be expressed on many different cards, Card IV would seem relatively likely to serve on occasion as "*a* father card."

However this may be, the qualities conveyed by Card IV make it likely (a) that the way subjects respond to it provides some clues to their attitudes toward authority and authority figures, and (b) that difficulties in responding to Card IV often reflect concerns in this area. Additionally, because the qualities conveyed by Card IV are also frequently associated with masculinity rather than femininity, it may well be that Card IV responses reveal something about attitudes toward men in general and perhaps toward important, particular men in a subject's life (e.g., including father, husband, and lover).

Card IV is also notable for its dark color and heavy shading, both of which make an impression on most subjects. Like Card I, this card may accordingly pose difficulties for subjects who are depressed or trying to avoid confronting gloomy affects. Because it is even darker than Card I and does not have as readily available a Popular to ease the subject's task, Card IV may prove particularly difficult in this respect. Some subjects may in fact respond with aplomb to each of the first three cards and show their first disturbed approach on Card IV, perhaps because of its implications for dominant authority but possibly also because of its depressive tone.

As for the shading in Card IV, research findings concerning T indicate that articulation of the tactile quality of shading is associated with capacities for forming physically and psychologically intimate attachments to other people—literally being close enough to "touch" each other. For this reason, the percepts and associations people report in response to heavily shaded blot areas often provide information concerning their openness to, attitudes toward, and need for close relationships, and difficulties in dealing with heavily shaded areas speak to aversion, uncertainty, and distress in the context of contemplating such relationships. Although Card IV is a less potent signifier of shading related concerns than Card VI, which is even more heavily shaded and elicits the popular "fur" or "animal skin" response that often involves shading, this card may nevertheless have part of its impact on subjects as a consequence of its shading features.

Card V

Aside from being dark in color and therefore potentially depressing, Card V contains relatively few features that arouse concerns, complicate the response process, or suggest particular percepts, associations, or affects. On the contrary, the solid and unbroken appearance of this blot and its very commonly seen resemblance to the popular "bat" or "butterfly," as well as other winged creatures, make it the easiest blot in the series to which to formulate an adequate response. Because Card V lacks any impact comparable to the newness of Card I, the red of Card II, the interpersonal interaction of Card III, and the dominant authority figure of Card IV, it often provides welcome relief from any distress prompted by Cards I–IV.

Subjects commonly demonstrate that Card V is a "breather" by giving more adequate and less revealing responses than they have on the previous cards, and they may also comment specifically on the ease of their task. Thus, after struggling with uncertainty and upset on the first four cards, subjects may greet Card V with such comments as, "Now this one I *know* is a bat," or "I don't have any trouble seeing this one as a butterfly." When subjects do struggle with Card V, the source of their difficulty is usually less likely to be found in what this blot signifies to them than in some carryover of concerns aroused by their encounter with Card IV.

Card VI

With respect to regularly conveying meaning to persons taking the Rorschach, the dominant characteristic of Card VI is the textural quality suggested by its black and gray shadings. Even more than Card IV, as just noted, Card VI tends to arouse percepts and associations related to interpersonal closeness. The manner in which subjects elaborate responses in which they articulate T, together with what they say about the whole blot or the lower detail of Card VI even without articulating T, often reveal some of their attitudes toward intimate relationships. Similarly, indications of difficulty dealing with this card effectively may help to identify concerns about reaching out to touch other people or anticipating being touched by them, whether physically or psychologically.

Card VI also conveys considerable sexual significance to many subjects. Several previously stated *caveats* regarding covert card pull may bear repeating at this point: Card VI is not "*the* sex card"; it is not always seen as resembling sexual anatomy, it does not always elicit associations to sexual themes, and it is not even first among the 10 cards with respect to the number of ordinary and unusual form Sex contents it contains; and blanket interpretations of Card VI responses based on attributing any universal symbolic sexual significance to it are unwarranted and likely to be misleading.

Despite all this, however, it remains that Card VI is likely to be "*a* sex card" by virtue of the ease with which sexual anatomy can be seen on it and the previously noted frequency with which subjects report doing so when their customary inclination to censor their responses is in abeyance. Like Card II, moreover, Card VI provides clear resemblances to both male and female sexual anatomy, with "penis" to D6 and "vagina" to D12 being accurately perceived responses. Finally, although Cards II and III have more easily seen sexual contents, Card VI appears to elicit reported sexual percepts and themes more frequently than any of the other cards. For these reasons, the interpretive process can be enriched in many cases by the possible sexual significance of how subjects describe Card VI and whether they have difficulty responding to it.

Card VII

The meanings typically associated with Card VII contrast sharply with those usually conveyed by Card IV. Compared to Card IV, Card VII is likely to be seen as attractive rather than threatening, soft rather than hard, weak rather than strong, and passive rather than active. Allowing for individual differences and ever mindful of the pitfalls of gender-role stereotypes, it remains the case that these characterizations of Card VII comprise many features traditionally associated with femininity, just as typical impressions of Card IV consist of traits associated mainly with masculinity. As in the case of Card IV, furthermore, these conjectures fit unequivocal empirical data concerning the types of figures usually seen on Card VII. Whereas Card IV is rarely seen as a female figure, Card VII is hardly ever seen as a male figure, at least not as an adult male. Almost without exception, the partial or whole human figures commonly seen on Card VII are described as being women or children.

Accordingly, subjects' percepts, associations, and test behaviors on Card VII may often have a bearing on their feelings and attitudes toward women. However, no assumptions can be made concerning whether these feelings and attitudes are held toward women in general or toward a subject's mother, grandmother, aunt, sister, teacher, friend, husband, lover, or some other female or feminized figure. In parallel with the interpretation of responses to Card IV, feelings and attitudes expressed in Card VII responses can be tracked to particular people only on the basis of additional information specific to the individual person being examined. Thus, for all of the same reasons discussed with respect to "father" and "sex" cards, Card VII most certainly does not function universally as "*the* mother card," although for some subjects it may serve as "*a* mother card."

Because of the femininity often associated with Card VII, difficulties in responding to it may point to troubling or unresolved concerns subjects have in relation to female figures in their lives. Of further importance in this regard, the lower center detail (Dd26) of Card VII is an ordinary form-level percept for "vagina." Therefore, this card may elicit associations to or concerns not only about femininity but about feminine sexuality. For example, as counterpoint to the earlier illustration of responses by two women to D6 on Card VI, consider the contrasting implications of how two men responded to the D26 of Card VII. One of them said, "It looks inviting, like a nice place to go into"; the other one said, "I don't know what this part is, but I don't want to look at it." These responses would appear to suggest a positive orientation toward heterosexual intercourse in the first case and a negative orientation in the second case.

Card VIII

Card VIII often constitutes a change of pace point during a Rorschach administration, much as Card V does earlier. As already mentioned, Card V is a relatively nonthreatening and easily articulated inkblot that many subjects experience as a welcome relief following the previous four more difficult or challenging blots. Card VIII follows four cards (IV–VII) that are darkly colored in shades of gray and black and presents subjects instead with a softly colored card in pastel hues that is usually experienced as attractive and contains the easily seen popular animal figures in its side details. Like Card V, then, Card VIII often serves as a breathing space in which subjects relax a bit and respond more effectively than they have on Cards IV–VII. Quite commonly, subjects express their relief on being handed Card VIII with such comments as "I like this one," or "Finally a pretty one," or "This one's easy."

On the other hand, for some subjects, Card VIII may present new difficulties. It is more complex than the preceding seven cards with respect to its broken appearance and number of loosely large details, and it is also the first multicolored card in the series. Subjects who generally have difficulty sorting out and integrating the components of complex situations may find Card VIII an unwelcome challenge and have difficulty forming responses other than the obvious Popular. Subjects who become uncomfortable in affect-arousing situations or who prefer to avoid emotional stimulation may also display discomfort and avoidance rather than pleasure and relief in responding to Card VIII.

Card IX

With respect to what it conveys to subjects, Card IX is distinctive mainly for its vague and diffuse quality. Because the colors on Card IX are somewhat muted and the shapes fairly indefinite, the chromatic features of this blot do not appear to be particularly affect arousing, and its form features elicit popular responses less frequently than those of any other card. Consequently, there are few specific concerns regularly suggested to subjects by Card IX, and difficulty responding to it usually reflects a subject's inability or disinclination to come to grips effectively with complex, unstructured situations.

Card X

The broken appearance of Card X and its array of loosely connected but rather sharply defined and colored details give it a close structural resemblance to Card VIII. At the same time, however, the sheer number of variegated shapes and colors that assail a subject's eyes imbue Card X with the type of uncertainty and complexity posed by Card IX. Although Card X is usually seen as a pleasant stimulus and offers subjects many alternative possibilities for easily seen percepts, the challenge of organizing it effectively makes it generally the second most difficult card to manage, after Card IX. Particularly for subjects who feel overwhelmed or overburdened by having to deal too many things at once, responding to Card X, despite its pleasant appearance and bright colors, may be a disconcerting experience that subjects dislike and are happy to complete.

Finally, of note regarding Card X is its position as the final card. Just as the initial response in a record may be a way for subjects to "sign in" and introduce what they feel is important about themselves, the last response may serve as an opportunity to "sign out" by indicating, in effect, "When all is said and done, this is where things stand for me and what I want you to know about me." As a parallel to the examples given earlier of signing-in responses, consider the contrasting implications for the present status of two depressed subjects, one of whom concludes Card X by saying, "And it looks like everything is falling apart" and the other of whom concludes, "And it's brightly colored, like the sun is coming up."

CHAPTER

5

Interpreting Structural Variables

The presentation in this chapter of guidelines for interpreting Rorschach structural variables reflects the previously noted implications of the Comprehensive System search strategy for a personality-oriented rather than a test-centered approach to Rorschach data (see chap. 3). Accordingly, structural interpretation is conceptualized here as a way of describing personality style and assessing personality strengths and weaknesses.

Personality style and personality strengths and weaknesses can be formulated for purposes of clinical assessment in terms of an adaptational model that comprises six dimensions of human behavior: how people attend to experience, how they use ideation, how they modulate affect, how they manage stress, how they view themselves, and how they relate to others. The overall effectiveness with which people can function across these six dimensions of adaptation defines their general level of adjustment. The profile of their relative strengths and weaknesses across these dimensions identifies (a) the kinds of situations in which they are likely to function relatively well or poorly, (b) the types of adjustment difficulty or psychological disorder they are more or less likely to display, and (c) their needs for and prospects of benefiting from various kinds of psychotherapeutic intervention.

These six aspects of adaptation closely resemble the Comprehensive System clusters as described in chapter 3 and previously organized by Weiner and Exner (1991). Attending to experience refers to the personality functions measured by the information-processing and cognitive mediation clusters of variables; using ideation and modulating affect correspond respectively to the ideation and affective features clusters; managing stress pertains to the control and stress tolerance cluster; and viewing oneself and relating to others involve the functions associated with the self-perception and interpersonal perception clusters, respectively.

Along with delineating the interpretive significance of Rorschach structural variables in relation to dimensions of adaptation, the discussion that follows takes account of the well-known but rarely mentioned fact that these variables differ in the directionality of their implications for adjustment. Some structural variables are unidirectional, in that they suggest adjustment difficulties when they are present or abundant but provide little information when they are not. For example, elevated scores on the Schizophrenia Index (*SCZI*), Depression Index (*DEPI*), and Suicide Constellation (*S-CON*) typically point to serious psychological problems, but low scores on these indices do not identify any particular personality strengths and may not even rule out the conditions associated with elevated scores on them. Specifically, *SCZI* < 3, *DEPI* < 5, and S-*CON* < 8 reduce the likelihood of schizophrenia, mood disorder, and suicide risk, respectively, but they do not eliminate the possibility that these conditions are present in some form (see J. E. Exner, 1993, chap. 15).

Unlike unidirectional variables, bidirectional variables on the Rorschach do have adjustment implications for better or worse. In the case of Cooperative Movement (*COP*), for example, which signifies anticipation of collaborative and mutually helpful relationships among people, the more *COP* the better and vice versa. Numerous *COP* tends to characterize socially oriented people whose companionship is sought by others and who are popular among their peers, whereas COP = 0 tends to be associated with feeling uncomfortable in interpersonal situations, operating on the periphery of group interactions,and attracting relatively little peer interest or popularity.

A third group of Rorschach structural variables are tridirectional, in that they identify adequate adaptive capacity when they fall in some intermediate range and adjustment difficulties when they occur either more or less frequently than normal. Dimensionality (*FD*), for example, indicates adaptive awareness of oneself at a normative frequency of one or two *FD*, whereas *FD* = 0 suggests a disinterest in or incapacity for being introspective, which can lead to maladaptively limited self-awareness, and *FD* > 2 raises the possibility of excessive self-awareness or soulsearching, which can produce maladaptive self-consciousness.

The presentation that follows assumes basic familiarity with how structural variables are coded in the Rorschach Comprehensive System and with the nature of their personality and behavioral correlates. Although such basic information may at times be noted, the text does not duplicate fundamental guidelines for coding and interpretation provided elsewhere (J. E. Exner, 1991, 1993; J. E. Exner & Weiner, 1995). Similarly, numerical criteria for assessing the implications of individual structural variables are presented without specification of their source but are based in all cases on reference data provided by J. E. Exner (1993, chap. 2). As a final introductory note, probable and possible personality correlates of structural variables and developmental considerations in their interpretation are stated without specific documentation of their empirical validation, in order to sustain the purpose of this chapter as an interpretive guide rather than a review of research. The empirical basis for these interpretive guidelines can be found in the Exner and Exner and Weiner volumes on the Comprehensive System and in standard texts on personality, abnormal psychology, child and adolescent development, and developmental psychopathology.

Finally, it is helpful to keep in mind the distinction between "codes" and "scores" when discussing structural variables on the Rorschach. The process of assigning codes to Rorschach responses, such as giving a W for location choices involving the whole blot and F for responses determined entirely by form, has traditionally been referred to as "scoring" a record, and the concordance achieved by coders in this process is regularly called "interscorer" agreement. In truth, however, the various ways of designating the location choice, determinants, and other structural features of responses are not scores at all, but instead constitute *codes*. These codes provide shorthand notations for designating the processes involved in developing a response; thus using just the shape of an entire blot in an unsynthesized way to produce a commonly seen percept of an animal figure results in a code of *Wo Fo A P*, and this code then indicate show the subject went about formulating this particular response.

Rorschach codes are thus *qualitative* descriptors of the perceptual and associational processes subjects employ in articulating their responses. As such, codes call attention to the psychological phenomena that they denote, but by themselves they have no direct interpretive significance. For example, *COP* may signify anticipation of collaborative interpersonal relationships, but determining the extent to which subjects are likely to have such anticipations requires knowing how many *COP* they have in their record. Tabulation of the assigned response codes over an entire protocol generates the various frequencies, percentages, ratios, and indices that appear in a Structural Summary and that constitute Rorschach *scores*. Rorschach scores are *quantitative* descriptors of personality functioning, and it is these scores that provide the basis for formulating interpretive hypotheses.

ATTENDING TO EXPERIENCE

Attending to experience consists of the ways in which people focus their attention and perceive their environment. How people attend to their experience involves how much they notice what is going on around them and in themselves, how they go about organizing the information that enters their awareness, and how likely they are to perceive events the way most people do. Successful adaptation is promoted by openness to experience, efficient organization of information, and realistic and conventional perception of events. Conversely, people who have difficulty attending to their experience openly, efficiently, realistically, and conventionally are susceptible to various kinds adjustment difficulties. Each of these personality characteristics is reflected in Rorschach variables that prove helpful in assessing them.

Being Open to Experience (*Lambda*)

Successful adaptation is fostered by a balanced focus of attention that is neither too narrow nor too broad. People who maintain a balanced focus of attention tend to be reasonably aware of internal and external events, able to tolerate ambiguity and uncertainty, interested in a variety of pursuits, and capable of coping with situations in a flexible manner. Flexible people respond to some situations with reflective problem solving and to others with expressive emotionality. They deal with some events in a detached and uninvolved manner, taking them at their face value and not forming many thoughts or feelings about them, and they deal with other events in a concerned and engaged manner, pondering their significance or resonating to their affective tone. Adjustment is served best when these approaches to experience alternate in appropriate relation to the nature of particular situations and events, without oversimplification of those that are truly complex or over complication of those that are in fact quite simple.

Openness to experience is measured on the Rorschach by *Lambda*, and subjects whose *Lambda* ranges between .30 and .99 generally manifest the adaptive characteristics associated with a balanced focus of attention. At all ages, however, *Lambda* > .99 usually identifies lack of adequate openness to experience and tendencies instead to view one's world and oneself with an overly narrow focus of attention. High *Lambda* people lead their lives as if with blinders on, looking straight ahead but rarely to the left or right. As a consequence of their tunnel vision, they notice little more than the bare outlines of events and frequently overlook the subtle nuances of social and interpersonal situations. They tend to make decisions without much thought and to select courses of action without much emotional investment in them. High *Lambda* people are intolerant of ambiguity and uncertainty, have a narrow frame of reference, feel most comfortable in clearly defined and well-structured situations, and favor simple solutions even to complex problems. Their preferences run strongly to an uncomplicated existence in which, located in familiar haunts and surrounded by familiar people, they can manage daily events in a detached, uninvolved, and matter-of-fact way that maximizes closure and minimizes loose ends.

Occasionally high *Lambda* individuals demonstrate a single-minded purposefulness that carries them far along certain paths, such as a career or an avocation to which they become narrowly but intensely devoted. There are also circumstances in which a narrow focus of attention serves adaptive purposes by limiting the awareness of persons who would become upset or disorganized by recognizing fully some unwelcome or threatening circumstances in their lives. For people confronting disaster or tragedy, for example, the wearing of psychological blinders may serve some constructive, self-protective purpose. Whatever its sources, however, such shutting down of awareness exacts the price of a narrowly circumscribed and inflexible lifestyle.

Additionally, the simplistic problem solving and insensitivity to subtlety that accompany narrowly focused attention often result in failure to take adequate account of the kinds of behaviors that are expected or required of people in various situations. Those who notice less than they should are thus at risk for behaving in heavy-handed, insensitive ways that offend others. Like bulls in a china shop, people who are insufficiently open to experience blunder straight ahead to get where they want to go, without recognizing how much breakage they may be causing along the way.

In interpreting these implications of high *Lambda* for a stylistically narrowed focus of attention, examiners should be aware that they apply mainly to records of at least average length. In valid but short records with fewer than 20 responses, an elevated *Lambda* often signifies situational guardedness on the part of the subject and a reluctance to be forthcoming, rather than a characterological commitment to a high *Lambda* style. In either case, whether comprising many or few responses, high *Lambda* records typically consist for the most part of brief and unelaborated responses that reveal relatively little of a subject's inner life. For this reason, as elaborated in chapter 6, there is a fairly reliable direct relationship between the size of *Lambda* and the extent to which examiners must rely primarily on the structural data in forming their inferences. Ordinarily, the thematic imagery in a high *Lambda* record is insufficiently rich to reveal very much about a subject's personality functioning.

When *Lambda* falls below .30 subjects tend to show an excessive openness to experience characterized by an overly broad focus of attention. Unlike narrowly focused people, low *Lambda* individuals are usually highly sensitive to their experience and acutely aware of events in their lives. They welcome and even seek out ambiguous and complex situations, and they typically feel most comfortable in environments that are relatively unstructured and open-ended. They rarely deal with situations in a simple, detached, or objective manner, but are instead likely to become overinvolved in contemplating the underlying significance of events or sorting out their feelings about them. They also tend to have a broad range of interests and to engage in many different pursuits, or at least to contemplate doing so.

As a consequence of these low *Lambda* characteristics, broadly focused people may be lively, interesting, venturesome, and multifaceted individuals who impress others with their verve and sensitivity and have some impressive accomplishments to their credit. However, channeling an unusually broad focus of attention into social charm and impressive accomplishments requires well-developed personality strengths and usually some special talents as well. For people with limited coping capacities and few skills, a broad focus of attention may become a considerable burden to bear. Broadly focused attention and heightened awareness that exceed capacities to channel them adaptively can contribute to people becoming cognitively scattered, easily distractible, and painfully aware of distressing aspects of their lives that they would do better to ignore or overlook.

Specifically, in the absence of sufficient personality strengths and talents to make good use of them, low *Lambda* preference for ambiguity and uncertainty can lead to fuzzy or imprecise impressions of events and difficulty coming to closure when decisions must be made; pleasure in subjectivity can result in excessive contemplation or emotionality in simple and uncomplicated situations, thus impairing capacities for objectivity and leading to the type of behavior commonly described as "making mountains out of molehills"; and endorsement of many different interests can preclude adequate commitment to any of them. Thus, whereas capable and talented high *Lambda* people are likely to achieve on a broad front, those whose attention is too broadly focused for their capacities and talents often display diffuse, short-lived, rapidly shifting, and unsuccessful efforts in many different directions.

Organizing Information Efficiently (*Zd*)

Efficient organization of information consists of an adaptive balance between the amount of information people take in and their capacities to process this amount of information adequately. The amount of information people take in is a function of how carefully and thoroughly they pay attention to objects and events. The longer people look at an object, the more closely they examine an event, and the more extensively they attempt to take account of all aspects of a situation, the more information they acquire. The more capable people are of keeping track of bits of information pertaining to a particular situation and sorting out how these bits of information relate to each other, the more information they will be able to process efficiently.

The efficiency with which subjects organize information is measured on the Rorschach by the Processing Efficiency variable *Zd*, which ranges normatively from -3.0 to +3.0. Subjects whose *Zd* falls within this range are absorbing just about as much information as they can process adequately, and such persons are likely to form conclusions, solve problems, and complete tasks in an efficient manner and with a degree of success consistent with their abilities. Like *Lambda*, however, *Zd* is a tridirectional variable, and people in whom it falls outside of this normative range are taking in more or less information than they can process adequately, and their cognitive efficiency and level of achievement are likely to suffer as a consequence.

Subjects who *overincorporate*, as defined by a *Zd* exceeding +3.0, take in more information than they can organize efficiently and tend to examine their experience more thoroughly than is necessary. They seek out more information than most people would require in order to make a decision; they revise and redo their work products more than most people would find necessary in order to feel satisfied; and, despite having made their best efforts, they are more likely than most people to feel uncertain and unful-filled, as if they have somehow fallen short of their best effort or left some stones unturned.

An overincorporator's pattern of excessive information seeking may nevertheless be adaptive in some circumstances. Persons who attend very conscientiously to their experience often perform admirably when success hinges on being careful and thorough, especially if there is adequate time for them to work in their preferred way. When rapid turnaround is required, however, these individuals struggle mightily with whether to compromise their commitment to thoroughness in order to meet someone else's schedule. Time pressure typically causes them to complete tasks in a state of anxiety and dissatisfaction, or to fail to complete them at all. In this last regard, an overincorporator's excessive intake of information may contribute to underachievement that is attributable not to an aversion to work, but to an accumulation of overdue and unfinished projects.

People who seek more information than they can integrate readily also tend to be handicapped in their decision making. Subjects with *Zd* > +3.0 typically feel they lack sufficient information on which to base choices that need to be made. Overincorporators are consequently likely to be hesitant in making decisions, uncertain about whatever decisions they do make, and easily persuaded to defer and delay rather than come to closure in their opinions and conclusions. Once having made a decision, moreover, they may be reluctant to reconsider it, even when doing so would be advisable, because living with a decision they have made may be less discomfiting to them than reopening the decision-making process. Overincorporators may accordingly show a mixture of indecisiveness and rigidity in how they approach making decisions.

By contrast, subjects who *underincorporate*, as defined by a *Zd* less than −3.0, take in too little information and consequently tend to examine their experience less thoroughly than would be advisable. Instead of weighing decisions carefully, underincorporators come to conclusions hastily, after only cursory attention to relevant considerations; instead of applying themselves to tasks conscientiously, they tend to work carelessly and feel satisfied with final products that do not reflect the full measure of their ability; and, far from being concerned about leaving stones unturned, they are more likely than most people to opt for quick and superficial scanning of situations that barely scratch the surface of what should be taken into account. This pattern of insufficient information seeking rarely serves adaptive purposes. At best, underincorporation promotes rapid decision making and speedy completion of tasks, but often at the expense of ill-considered conclusions and inferior products. Because they take inadequate account of information they could easily process, individuals with $Zd < -3.0$ are generally at risk for errors of oversight in what they choose to think and do, and lack of accomplishment in what they attempt to achieve.

Consistent with the differences in their personality correlates, overincorporation and underincorporation have quite opposite implications for types of psychological disorder and their modifiability. Aside from its previously mentioned possible contribution to underachievement, $Zd > +3.0$ sometimes helps to identify the perfectionism, indecisiveness, and excessive attention to detail associated with obsessive–compulsive disorder, and it may also point to the excessively thorough scanning of the environment seen in people who are hypervigilant to potential sources of danger in their surroundings. It is for these reasons that $Zd > +3.0$ is a criterion score on the Obsessive Style Index (*OBS*), and $Zd> +3.5$ is a criterion score on the Hypervigilance Index (*HVI*).

Whether associated with compulsivity or hypervigilance, overincorporation tends to constitute a relatively fixed and unwavering stylistic preference. Like high *Lambda* individuals, then, people who overincorporate tend to be strongly committed to their preferred ways of attending to experience and equally strongly disinclined to flexibility in this regard. Overincorporation is consequently difficult to extinguish or modify. Psychological disorders in which overincorporation plays a prominent role often prove treatment resistant, and overincorporative persons engaged in psychotherapy usually benefit more from treatment efforts aimed at other features of their personality that may be maladaptive than from efforts to alter their overincorporative style.

A $Zd < -3.0$, on the other hand, helps to identify the patterns of distractibility, inadequately focused attention, and insufficient task persistence usually found in hyperactive young people and sometimes as well in adults with persistent attention deficit hyperactivity disorder (ADHD). Unlike overincorporation or high *Lambda*, however, underincorporation is less a preferred and anxiety-reducing coping style than an unsettling, unwanted, and troublesome inability to function effectively. Underincorporation is consequently much more amenable to change than overincorporation, and most underincorporators, rather than being treatment resistant, are quite eager to receive and well poised to benefit from any help they can get to improve their concentration and work habits. For this reason, the types of cognitive training exercises that typically prove successful in working with ADHD children are very likely to have the effect of bringing a $Zd < -3.0$ up into the normal range, and a finding of $Zd < -3.0$ identifies the need for and likely treatment value of such training exercises.

Perceiving Events Realistically and Conventionally ($X - \%, W:D:Dd, Xu\%, P$)

Realistic perception of events consists of individuals being able to form accurate impressions of themselves and their environment. Being able to see things as they truly are fosters successful adaptation by helping people exercise good judgment. People who appraise themselves and their experiences realistically are likely to comprehend correctly their own capacities and characteristics, the qualities and intentions of other people, the nature and requirements of situations in which they find themselves, and the extent to which alternative responses will satisfy what these situations require. Such exercise of good judgment, as made possible by adequate reality testing, helps people choose appropriate goals and roles for themselves, recognize how they are likely to be perceived by others, assess accurately the implications of interpersonal interactions, appreciate the boundaries of appropriate behavior in various kinds of situations, and anticipate the consequences their actions are likely to have.

People who form accurate impressions of themselves and their environment may nevertheless differ in how conventional they are in perceiving events. Good adjustment is fostered not only by adequate reality testing but also by a modicum of conventionality in choosing which features of one's experience to examine and how to interpret them. Being moderately conventional in these regards leads people to attend both to obvious and ordinary features of everyday life that most people would notice and acknowledge and also to distinctive and unique aspects of situations that most people would ignore or overlook. Similarly, people who are moderately conventional in how they interpret their experience sometimes form common impressions that are widely shared and on other occasions arrive at uncommon impressions that are distinctively their own. These aspects of realistic and conventional perception are measured on the Rorschach by several features of form quality ($X - \%, Xu\%$), location choice ($W:D:Dd$), and use of Populars (P).

$X - \%$. The Distorted Form variable ($X - \%$) provides a good indication of whether subjects are perceiving their experience realistically. The mean for $X - \%$ is .07 among adult nonpatients and ranges from .08 to .10 among young people from age 5 to 16, and subjects with an $X - \%$ no greater than .15 can generally be expected to demonstrate the previously mentioned adaptive characteristics associated with adequate reality testing. On the other hand, the more $X - \%$ exceeds .15, the more likely subjects are to perceive events incorrectly, to form mistaken impressions of themselves, to misinterpret the actions and intentions of others, to fail to anticipate the consequences of their own actions, and to misconstrue what constitutes appropriate behavior. In this way, erroneous conclusions and ill-advised actions stemming from inaccurate perception lead to instances of faulty judgment that undermine adequate adjustment.

The specific implications of $X-$ responses for inaccurate perception depend not only on their frequency but also on the context in which they occur and the extent to which they distort the form qualities of the blots. Thus, when more than 40% of a subject's distorted form responses involve White Space Distortion (i.e., $S - \% > .40$), the person's proclivities to show poor judgment are more likely to represent a problem with anger control rather than a basic impairment of reality testing. Similarly, the pairing of $X-$ responses with certain determinants or content categories may indicate special areas of confusion or concern rather than a global impairment of perceptual accuracy. For example, a record in which all or most of the minus forms occur in M responses may identify a focused difficulty in perceiving people accurately rather than a pervasively compromised capacity to exercise adequate judgment, and a record in which form distortion occurs exclusively in Anatomy (An) responses may point specifically to unrealistic preoccupations with bodily functions rather than generally to poor reality testing.

As for the extent of form distortion in a response, $X-$ responses (as noted in chap. 4) differ with respect to how far short they fall of being considered unusual (Xu). In some instances, an examiner can clearly recognize some part of a distorted perceptor at least see what suggested it, even though the final percept does not meet the criterion for Xu of being easily and readily seen. In other instances, the form of a minus response bears little or no apparent relationship to any part of the blot, and the examiner has no objective clue as to what prompted it. These latter, more extreme distortions of reality have more serious implications for impaired perceptual accuracy and its consequences than do minus responses that border on being unusual. The specific interpretation of $X - \%$ in light of these considerations is incorporated within the Comprehensive System clusters by the steps designated in Table 3.1 as Homogeneity of Minus and Minus Distortion Levels and is discussed further by J. E. Exner and Weiner (1995, pp. 142–144).

As $X - \%$ approaches or exceeds .29, which is a criterion score on $SCZI$, faulty judgment deriving from unrealistic perceptions tends to be associated with increasingly severe kinds of adjustment difficulty. High $X - \%$ subjects are at risk for conduct that is self-defeating, unintentionally harmful to themselves and those around them, and likely to be viewed by others as strange, peculiar, erratic, or incomprehensible. When impaired judgment mounts beyond mild, infrequent, or specifically focused lapses in good sense and progresses to a persistent, pervasive, and severe breakdown in reality testing, the extent of distorted perception on which it is based typically identifies a psychotic degree of disturbance.

W:D:Dd. The locations subjects choose for their Rorschach responses provide a good index of whether they pay attention to situations in a conventional way. With respect to the Economy Index (*W:D:Dd*), nonpatient adults and young people typically give approximately one half of their responses to common details (*D*), from one third to one half of their responses to the whole blot (*W*), and the remaining one sixth or fewer of their responses to unusual details (*Dd*). In younger children the percentage of *W* tends normatively to increase somewhat and the percentage of *D* to decrease somewhat, whereas *Dd* responses remain infrequent. These patterns of balanced Location Choice identify adequate capacity to recognize and respond to specific and ordinary details of everyday life while at the same time being able to appreciate the broader significance of these events and take note of what is unusual as well as what is commonplace.

A marked predominance of *D* responses at the expense of relatively few *W* or *Dd* indicates excessively conventional examination of situations. Subjects with an elevated *D* in their Economy Index tend to be inordinately attentive to ordinary aspects of what they encounter but insufficiently attuned to how events relate to each other or to unusual features of these events. Like high *Lambda* people whose focus of attention is overly narrow, elevated *D* individuals with overly conventional attention tend to function best in relatively limited and undemanding circumstances in which routine is the order of the day and neither careful analysis nor higher level concept formation is required.

In situations calling for flexibility, imagination, creativity, and awareness of more than what immediately meets the eye, on the other hand, these conventionally focused individuals tend to feel uncomfortable and to cope poorly. More often than not, they are insensitive kinds of people who notice mainly what is obvious while remaining oblivious to subtle characteristics and shades of meaning in events to which they respond and in people with whom they interact. In addition, because they lack a global orientation, such high *D* people show little capacity to recognize how individual events relate to each other and combine to produce wholes that may be larger than the sum of their parts. In common parlance, as previously observed in chapter 2, these are people about whom it is said, "They can't see the forest for the trees" or "They never get the big picture."

By contrast, a predominance of either *W* or *Dd* responses at the expense of sufficiently numerous *D* indicates inordinate attention to global or unusual features of experience rather than what is ordinary and commonplace. Attending to experience in a highly global fashion can at times facilitate a grasp of complex relationships between events and lead to creative formulations of such relationships. Carried to excess, however, preoccupation with the big picture can preclude adequate attention to mundane but nevertheless important matters. Thus, scientists contemplating the nature of the cosmos but overlooking to eat lunch may advance knowledge while damaging their health.

Paying special attention to unusual aspects of experience can similarly result in creative deviations from conventionality, and imaginative nonconformists may be regarded by others as interesting and stimulating people. However, when an excessive focus on what is unusual causes people to overlook what is obvious, being unconventional can cease to be adaptive, and individual idiosyncracies may contribute to a person's being viewed by others as eccentric and strange. Specifically, $Dd > 3$ occurs in only 5% of nonpatient adults, and young people are generally no more likely than adults to use Dd locations. Hence, $Dd > 3$ usually indicates a maladaptive preoccupation with unusual aspects of experience, and it serves as a criterion variable in the OBS index.

At the same time, however, the point at which unconventionality becomes maladaptive in this or other ways depends on the context in which it is displayed. People who are only mildly nonconforming in their outlook may have difficulty adjusting comfortably and being well-received in highly structured settings governed by strict rules and fixed expectations. Conversely, even fairly determined nonconformists may function happily and effectively and be most welcome in loosely structured settings defined by flexible standards, individual self-determination, and a laissez faire attitude toward authority.

Xu% and P. Whether persons interpret their experience in a conventional way is indicated by the $Xu\%$ in their record and by their number of P responses. Nonpatient adults average an $Xu\%$ of approximately 15%, and an $Xu\%$ in the 10% to 20% range indicates typical and adaptive tendencies to perceive people and events in an accurate but sometimes idiosyncratic manner. Subjects with an $Xu\%$ below 10% are likely to be more conventional than most people in the impressions they form and less likely to venture down paths not frequently taken by others. Such conventionality is especially likely to be marked when a record contains only a few minus responses and the $Xu\% < 10\%$ is accordingly accompanied by an $X + \% > 90\%$.

In the opposite instance, subjects whose $Xu\%$ exceeds 20% are inclined to be more individualistic than most people in how they view the world and more venturesome in the paths they choose to follow. Not uncommonly, an elevated $Xu\%$ is associated with a degree of sensation-seeking behavior rarely seen in low $Xu\%$ people. In a record with an $Xu\%$ of from 20% to 30% but no minus responses, the resulting $X + \%$ of 70% to 80% may temper somewhat the implications of high $Xu\%$ for idiosyncracy. Generally speaking, however, the further $Xu\%$ falls below 10% or rises above 20%, the more likely it is to be associated with maladaptive manifestations of excessive or insufficient conventionality, respectively.

The number of Popular responses ranges normatively from four to seven, with children under age 10 normatively giving slightly fewer P than older people. At all ages, however, a finding of $P < 4$ suggests an unusual degree of idiosyncracy, whereas $P > 7$ identifies more than average endorsement of conformity. Although P and $Xu\%$ are thus both measures of conventionality in perception, they may at times diverge. Some people who have little inclination to think or act conventionally may nevertheless be quite capable of recognizing conventionality, especially if they are asked directly to identify conventional modes of response. Such people may even give considerable lip service to conventionality, especially when they believe it would be in their best interest to do so, while remaining strongly committed to being unique and different. In this circumstance, the Rorschach is likely to show an average or above average number of Populars, by which these subjects display their awareness of conventionality, and a high $Xu\%$, by which they affirm their preference, given freedom of choice, to eschew conformity and do things their own way.

It is also possible for a low frequency of P to derive not from subjects being averse to giving common responses, but from their being unable to see what is obvious to most people. In the latter circumstance, failure to give Populars may have implications for impaired reality testing as well as unconventionality. The possibility that $P < 4$ identifies inaccurate rather than merely unconventional attention to experience becomes likely when it occurs in conjunction with an elevated $X - \%$. In this combination, the low P accentuates the reality testing impairment demonstrated by the high $X - \%$. Contrariwise, an adequate number of P often attenuates the maladaptive implications of an elevated $X - \%$ by identifying some retained capacity to recognize conventional reality. For this reason, a substantial number of Populars helps to account for instances in which disturbed subjects with numerous minus responses have nevertheless managed to avoid being hospitalized or even coming to mental health attention.

Finally of note with respect to matters of conformity, $Xu\%$ and P can combine with $W:D:Dd$ to provide a particularly powerful clue to whether a person is more or less likely than most people to attend to experience in a conventional manner. High $Xu\%$ and low P together with a low $D\%$ and an elevated $Dd\%$ are especially likely to identify nonconformity, whereas low $Xu\%$ and high P occurring along with a high $D\%$ usually identify a strong commitment to conventionality.

USING IDEATION

Using ideation refers to how people think about the experiences they have and the impressions they form. People adapt best when they are able to think logically, coherently, flexibly, constructively, and to a moderate extent. Conversely, tendencies toward illogical, incoherent, inflexible, overly fanciful, and excessively preoccupying ways of thinking constitute personality liabilities that interfere with psychological adjustment.

Thinking Logically and Coherently (WSum6)

Logical thinking consists of forming reasonable conclusions about relationships between events. People who are thinking logically come to reasonable conclusions on the basis of sufficient evidence and with adequate appreciation for how certain they can be about their conclusions. When people lose this capacity to think logically, whether momentarily or for some extended period of time, they tend to reason in an arbitrary fashion, derive unwarranted conclusions from limited or circumstantial evidence, and fail to distinguish between conclusions that are relatively reasonable, or at least plausible, and conclusions that are at most tentative, if not improbable or impossible.

Coherent thinking involves maintaining a connected flow of associations in which ideas follow each other in a manner comprehensible to oneself and to others. Being able to think coherently allows people to sustain a continuously relevant train of thought that facilitates solving problems, making decisions, and communicating clearly to other people. When the capacity to think coherently becomes impaired, people tend to formulate and express their ideas in a dissociated or loosely connected manner that derails goal-directed thought, causes wandering off into irrelevance, and undermines efforts to make oneself understood. Incoherent thinking thus leads to confusion in those who have it and perplexity in those who observe it.

Illogical and incoherent thinking is reflected on the Rorschach in the weighted sum of the six Critical Special Scores (WSum6). Four of these Critical Special Scores—Incongruous Combination (INCOM), Fabulized Combination (FABCOM), Autistic Logic (ALOG), and Contamination (CONTAM)—are coded for instances of arbitrary thinking in which various objects, ideas, and impressions are integrated, combined, or assumed to interrelate in unlikely or bizarre ways. The other two Critical Special Scores—Deviant Verbalization (DV) and Deviant Response (DR)—are coded for instances of dissociated thinking in which ideas fall out of sequence or intrude on each other to produce strange, rambling, tangential, and sometimes unintelligible verbalizations. The nature of these Critical Special Scores is elaborated and illustrated by J. E. Exner and Weiner (1995, pp. 136–142).

The Comprehensive System reference data show a clear developmental trend in the normative frequency of the *WSum6* variable, decreasing from a median ranging from 10.0 to 14.0 in 5- to 9-year-olds to medians of from 6.0 to 8.0 in 10- to 14-year-olds, 4.0 in young people age 15 and 16, and 3.0 in adults. A *WSum6* of 12 or less in adults and adolescents and 15 or less in younger children usually signifies good capacities to think logically and coherently, whereas *WSum6* > 15 in adults and adolescents and a *WSum6* > 18 in younger children begin to suggest problems in thinking clearly and rationally. These normative data are congruent with general expectation that early adolescents will think less clearly and rationally than older adolescents and adults, and children even less than early adolescents.

The larger their *WSum6* becomes, the more likely people at any age are to display instances of arbitrary and circumstantial reasoning and to have moments in which loose and scattered ideation confuses them and is confusing to others. They may be quick to conclude that chance events have some special significance related to them alone, for example, or that events occurring at the same time and objects located in the same place must necessarily bear some relationship to each other. They may have difficulty keeping their mind focused on what they are saying in a conversation and lose their train of thought right in the middle of a sentence, or they may express a rambling sequence of ideas that others find difficult to follow and that they themselves would be hard-pressed to reconstruct.

Should *WSum6* exceed 17 in subjects age 13 or older, 18 in 10- to 12-year-olds, or 20 in children less than age 10, a formal thought disorder is likely to be in evidence, and a point is scored on the Schizophrenia Index (*SCZI*). Additionally, as elaborated by J. E. Exner and Weiner (1995, pp. 136–142), the implications of an elevated *WSum6* for thought disorder are moderated when the Critical Special Scores that indicate mild cognitive slippage (*DV* and *INCOM*) outnumber those that indicate more serious ideational impairment (*DR*, *FABCOM*, *ALOG*, and *CONTAM*), and when the Special Scores are of the relatively mild variety coded as Level 1 and do not include any of the more bizarre verbalizations coded as Level 2 Critical Special Scores. Conversely, the more *WSum6* exceeds the minimum criterion for a point on *SCZI*, is dominated by the more serious Special Scores, and includes Level 2 Special Scores, the more likely a subject is to have the type of thought disorder typically observed in schizophrenia, schizoaffective disorder, delusional disorder, and paranoid and schizotypal personality disorder (see Weiner, 1998b).

Thinking Flexibly (*a:p*)

Flexible thinking promotes good adjustment in many ways. Most importantly, people who think flexibly can contemplate alternative perspectives on their experiences and consider changing their point of view. They keep their mind open to new information and previously unfamiliar ideas, no matter how long or firmly they have held their present opinions and beliefs. Being able to think flexibly in this way helps people learn more than they knew before and make informed decisions that guide them in adaptive directions. Such flexibility is especially helpful when people must confront changing circumstances in which their old ways of doing things no longer work very well and only a fresh frame of reference will serve their purposes.

Flexible thinking is indicated on the Rorschach by a balanced tendency to attribute active and passive movements to figures seen in motion, as reflected in the Active:Passive Ratio ($a{:}p$). The attribution of movement to the inkblots is an ideational activity, and subjects who give approximately equal numbers of active and passive movement responses tend to demonstrate ideational flexibility in making decisions and adapting to new situations and unfamiliar demands. However, if the sum of the $a{:}p$ values exceeds four and either of these values is more than twice as large as the other, the data indicate an imbalance that usually identifies cognitive inflexibility.

Unlike people who think flexibly, persons who show an unbalanced $a{:}p$ in their Rorschach tend to cling rigidly to their previously held convictions and resist reevaluating their beliefs on the basis of new information. They consequently tend to be closed-minded people who rarely change their opinions and seldom entertain the possibility of modifying their perspectives on themselves and external events. Not surprisingly, this type of inflexibility frequently impedes progress in forms of psychotherapy aimed at helping people modify their frame of reference (Weiner, in press), and it also interferes with adaptation to new situations and unfamiliar demands. Consistently with what has previously been said about *Lambda* in this latter regard, the implications of an unbalanced $a{:}p$ ratio for inflexibility are usually intensified by a high *Lambda* and moderated by a low *Lambda*.

Thinking Constructively (*Ma:Mp*)

Constructive thinking consists of using ideation in a realistic and task-oriented fashion to solve problems and plan deliberate courses of action. Being able to confront challenging situations directly and think purposefully about how best to deal with them helps people master their fate, rather than exist at its mercy, and move through their lives by intent, rather than by accident. Human movement (*M*) responses in the Rorschach provide a good index of capacity to use ideation effectively in this way, especially when the movements attributed to human figures are active in nature. However, when the number of passive human movements (*Mp*) in a record exceeds the number of active human movements (*Ma*), subjects are likely to be using fantasy excessively as an alternative to constructive problem solving.

Specifically, with respect to the *M* Active:Passive Ratio (*Ma:Mp*), *Mp* > *Ma* identifies a predilection for escapist fantasy or what has aptly been called an "abuse of fantasy." People who abuse fantasy attempt to deal with situations in their lives not by thinking through what they could or should do about them, but instead by imagining how other people or fortuitous events will make their decisions and solve their problems for them. There is a Walter Mitty quality about Mp people, and not infrequently they will be described by others as daydreamers who often seem lost in their own reveries and inattentive to what is going on around them. For Mp people, theirs is not to take arms against a sea of troubles, but to fantasize how fate will make everything right. Hence, whereas $Ma \geq Mp$ indicates normative capacity to think constructively, $Mp > Ma$ signifies an excessive reliance on fantasy that interferes with good adjustment.

Thinking in Moderation (EBPer, INTELL, FM + m)

Although being able to think logically, coherently, flexibly, and constructively are personality strengths that promote good adjustment, there can sometimes be too much of a good thing. People function best when they can use ideation effectively without allowing thoughts to dominate their psychological lives at the expense of feelings or their peace of mind. Being open to emotional as well as ideational experience contributes to good adjustment by providing people with a broad repertoire of coping skills, and being in control of the contents of their minds helps people avoid becoming preoccupied with disturbing thoughts. People who think excessively rather than to a moderate extent often lack sufficient capacity to experience and express feelings, tend to impose an intellectual framework on their emotions, and are susceptible to becoming preoccupied and distracted by intrusive ideation. Three Rorschach variables that help to distinguish between moderate and excessive thinking are the Pervasive Experience Balance ($EBPer$), the Intellectualization Index ($INTELL$), and the sum of the animal and inanimate movement responses ($FM + m$).

EBPer. Capacities for using ideation effectively without undue sacrifice of emotionality are reflected on the Rorschach in a moderately introversive EB style in which M exceeds the weighted sum of the chromatic color responses ($WSumC$) by more than 1.5 (or more than 2.0 in records in which $EA > 10$), but is not more than 2.5 times the value of $WSumC$. Moderately introversive people rely primarily on thoughtful deliberation in making decisions and solving problems, but they remain flexibly open to experiencing and being influenced by feelings as well. Pervasive introversiveness, however, in which M exceeds $WSumC$ by a ratio of more than 2.5:1, indicates a maladaptively excessive preference for dealing with experience primarily through ideational rather than affective channels. Ordinarily, M responses speak to personality strength and good adjustment, especially when they involve accurately perceived whole human figures engaged in active movement, and it may seem that there can never be too many of such responses. However, when *M* exceeds *SumC* to the extent of an *EBPer*, subjects are failing to give the emotional side of their life its just due.

Pervasively introversive people tend to be heavy thinkers who have difficulty being doers as well. Contemplation comes much easier to them than expressing themselves, and their decisions are made on the basis of rational deliberations in which feelings and intuition are seldom allowed to participate. Because adaptation is facilitated by taking steps as well as pondering them, and by being open to the influence of flashes of insight as well as extensively analyzed information, the excessively ruminative style of such individuals often prevents them from functioning as effectively as they otherwise might. Because of their limited channels for affective expression, moreover, pervasively introversive people have considerable difficulty dealing comfortably and effectively with emotionally arousing situations. Consequently, despite their preference to avoid emotionality altogether, they are more vulnerable than most people to becoming overwhelmed and disorganized when confronted with intense emotional stimulation, especially when their *WSumC* is particularly low, because they have few skills and little experience to bring to bear in resonating and responding to affectively charged situations.

INTELL. The three response characteristics that contribute to *INTELL*—Art (*Art*) and Anthropology (*Ay*) contents and the Abstract (*AB*) special score—share in common an ideational effort by subjects to interpose some distance between themselves and a real encounter with whatever feelings may have been elicited by their percepts or associations. The contents of a work of art have no actual existence in the subject's world; contents coded *Ay* are by definition remote from the subject's time, place, and sociocultural context; and abstract themes and events are by definition only symbolic or representative of what is really likely to occur. Accordingly, when subjects give *Art*, *Ay*, and *AB* responses, they are usually attempting to deal with feelings by incorporating them within an intellectual frame of reference that keeps emotions at a distance and minimizes their impact.

An *INTELL* of four or five indicates a prominent inclination to use intellectualization as a way of coping with unpleasant or otherwise unmanageable affects. When $(2AB + Art + Ay) > 5$, intellectualization is usually serving as a cornerstone among a subject's defensive operations. Although being an intellectualizer can help people mute the intensity of their emotions and thus safeguard them against distress, relying excessively on intellectualization constitutes an immoderate use of ideation that has maladaptive consequences. People who minimize or take distance from affect in this way sacrifice being able to deal with feelings in a candid, genuine, and forthright manner.

In interpersonal situations that by most people's standards call for direct and undisguised expression of love, pleasure, anger, or dismay, for example, intellectualizers are likely to respond with fancily phrased but bland, contrived, and artificially sounding allusions to affect that convey an impression of not caring, not wanting to get involved, and not wanting to reveal oneself. In addition to thus sacrificing the quality of their interpersonal relationships, intellectualizers can fall victim to intense emotional experience. Like being pervasively introversive and having few skills for dealing directly with feelings, heavy dependence on intellectualization leaves people vulnerable to becoming extremely upset in the face of affective stimulation that breeches their lines of defense. Moreover, an elevated *INTELL* typically indicates the presence of underlying distressing affects against which vigorous defenses have been erected, which accounts for its having emerged as a *DEPI* criterion variable.

FM + m. Animal movement (*FM*) and inanimate movement (*m*) responses, which taken together constitute the left side of the experience base (*eb*), signify intrusive ideation that resists conscious control. *FM* is typically associated with disconcerting awareness of needs that are not being met, and *m* indicates worrisome thoughts about being helpless to prevent other people or events from determining one's destiny. *FM + m* represent ideas that come unbidden into one's mind and that, unlike the intentional ideation associated with *M* responses, cannot be removed from conscious awareness simply by wishing to do so. *M* ideation is illustrated by a person's deciding to think for a while about where to go on vacation, becoming satisfied with having thought sufficiently about this matter, and then by conscious intent beginning to think about something else. *FM + m* ideation, by contrast, is occurring when people would prefer to stop thinking about whatever is on their mind and think about some other topic instead, but find themselves unable to do so.

Individual experience typically includes a modest amount of intrusive ideation that is present from time to time, and *FM* and *m* are both tridirectional variables that normatively show some frequency. *FM* ordinarily ranges from three to five and identifies the kind of motivation associated with needs that are pressing to be met. Subjects in whom *FM* < 3 are usually less aware than most people of having unmet needs. Such low *FM* people are often found to be psychologically drab, unmotivated, undemanding, and easily satisfied individuals who seldom experience needs or wants, rarely entertain hopes and dreams, and often lead empty and uneventful lives. In some instances, however, low *FM* reflects neither limited need arousal nor self-denial, but instead an orientation toward gratifying needs as soon as they arise, without allowing them to linger unmet as a source of intrusive ideational concerns. Low *FM* people of this type may regularly opt for getting their needs met rather than worrying about them and accordingly engage in self-gratifying behaviors without sufficient delay or restraint. In these instances, low *FM*, like high *Lambda*, can contribute to various kinds of conduct problems and to behavior that is unwelcome or offensive to others.

The typical frequency of *m* is one at all ages, and it maybe that subjects who give no *m* at all are less concerned than they should be about everyday events in their lives over which they have little control. There is often an indifferent or unworried quality about $m = 0$ people that is especially striking when they are in fact involved in situations that impose distasteful requirements on them, such as having to do a job they dislike or sit in jail, or in which important decisions are being made about them by others, such as whether they will be expelled from school, involuntarily hospitalized, granted custody of their children, placed on probation, or hired for a job. People being constrained or evaluated in such circumstances who do not give any *m* responses may be relatively unconcerned about what they are undergoing, even when for various reasons they state otherwise. More commonly, however, psychological circumstances in which people are being compelled to behave contrary to their wishes, or are being evaluated for administrative purposes that will lead to some judgment being made about them, produce elevations in *m*, as do any kinds of events that threaten a person's sense of physical safety and well-being. The more *m* that subjects give, the more concerns they are likely to be experiencing about being helplessly at the mercy of forces outside their control.

In light of normative expectations, then, subjects whose *FM* + *m* does not exceed six are probably not unusually preoccupied with intrusive ideation. An *FM* + *m* > 6, on the other hand, typically identifies maladaptively excessive thinking involving inability to prevent conscious awareness of disconcerting and worrisome ideas that serve no apparent purpose. This level of intrusive ideation often contributes in turn to impaired concentration. Distracted by thoughts they would prefer to banish from their minds but cannot, people with an elevated *FM* + *m* are typically at risk for adjustment difficulties in work and educational situations that call for sustained attention. An elevation in *FM* + *m* may also occur in connection with sleep disorders (especially among people who complain of having difficulty falling asleep because they have too much on their minds) and posttraumatic stress disorder (especially in persons who complain of intrusive ideation).

MODULATING AFFECT

Modulating affect refers to the manner and comfort with which people process emotional experience. As such, affect modulation consists both of how people deal with feelings arising from within themselves and how they respond to the feelings of others and to emotionally charged situations in general. Good psychological adaptation is fostered by well-developed capacities to modulate affect sufficiently, pleasurably, and in moderation. Should such capacities be deficient or become impaired, affect frequently becomes processed in a constricted, dysphoric, or overly intense manner that leads to adjustment difficulties.

Modulating Affect Sufficiently (*Afr, WSumC:SumC'*)

Sufficient modulation of affect consists of being able to engage in emotionally toned situations and exchange feelings with others. This capacity for involvement with affect allows people to feel comfortable in situations in which moderate levels of emotion are being aroused or expressed. Being thus comfortable, they can tolerate becoming emotionally stimulated in such situations, they can recognize and respond to feelings being expressed by others, and they can let their own feelings emerge and become known to people around them. In situations of unusual emotional intensity, such as confrontation with a person who is extremely upset or irrationally angry, even well-adjusted individuals may prefer to withdraw or keep their feelings to themselves. Absent such extremes, however, people who can modulate affect sufficiently seldom avoid emotional interchange with their environment. The capacity for sufficient modulation of affect is reflected on the Rorschach by an adequate Affective Ratio (*Afr*) and a large enough *WSumC* that equals or exceeds the number of achromatic color (*SumC'*) responses in the record.

Afr. Nonpatient adults show a mean *Afr* of .69, and subjects in whom *Afr* > .49 are usually as willing as most people to process emotional stimulation. An *Afr* < .50, on the other hand, normatively occurs in only 7% of adults and is likely to indicate an aversion to situations involving expressions of feelings and, consequently, to maladaptive emotional withdrawal. In nonpatient young people *Afr* < .50 occurs more frequently than in adults and must accordingly be interpreted more conservatively. Specifically, in the reference samples, *Afr* < .50 ranges from 8% to 24% among the 5- to 11-year-olds and from 15% to 38% among 12- to 16-year-olds.

Because expression of feelings is particularly likely to occur in interpersonal situations, and because close relationships between people usually involve exchanging feelings as well as ideas, low *Afr* individuals are at risk for being socially as well as emotionally withdrawn. Not infrequently, the emergence of strong feelings will lead them to break off an interpersonal interaction, even when they are in the company of friends and loved ones. For example, low *Afr* people are often made uncomfortable by displays of affection and would prefer them not to occur, particularly if they are expected to respond in kind. Should people around them become involved in hugging and kissing, such emotionally avoidant individuals would like to see the group disperse, or at least its emotional exuberance subside. Should voices be raised in anger, they prefer to leave the room rather than enter the fray; for them an argument that most people would welcome as a way to clear the air holds little appeal and is not available as an adaptive maneuver. Such aversion to emotionality often limits the social attractiveness of low *Afr* people, because others correctly perceive them as being distant or reserved individuals who rarely reveal their feelings and resist becoming engaged on an emotional level.

Finally, with respect to the interpretive significance of a low *Afr*, the particular composition of a record may sometimes yield an *Afr* < .50 that is misleading with respect to the subject's receptivity to emotional stimulation. This possibility for misinterpretation arises when a record involves complex and well-integrated percepts on Cards VIII, IX, and X that indicate considerable interest in being involved with these multicolored cards but result in only a few discrete responses to them. Consider, for example, a low *Afr* subject with just one response on Card X who gives a synthesized *W* percept of "A bouquet of pretty flowers, all different colors." This subject is less likely to be withdrawn from emotionally charged situations than a low *Afr* person whose only response to Card X is "Two crabs on the side, and that's all I see." With this illustration in mind, examiners should be prepared to temper the implications of *Afr* < .50 in subjects who appear to become quite involved inproducing their responses to Cards VIII–X, even though these responses are few in number.

WSumC:SumC'. Normative expectancy for *WSumC* varies in relation to whether subjects' *EB* style indicates primarily ideational or primarily affective ways of dealing with experience. Among adult nonpatients, those with an introversive *EB* show a mean *WSumC* of 3.16, whereas those with an extratensive *EB* show a mean *WSumC* of 6.07. Independently of *EB* style, however, and at all ages, a *WSumC* of 2.5 or more indicates basically adequate capacity to experience and express affect in adaptive ways. At times, a sufficient but relatively modest *WSumC* may be overshadowed by a weight of *M* that inhibits affectivity, as in the case of the pervasive introversiveness previously described. In such instances, however, the sufficient capacity for processing affect reflected by *WSumC* > 2.0 remains in place as a coping resource on which even pervasively introversive people can draw when they choose to relax their ideational stance.

On the other hand, for all types of persons a *WSumC* falling below 2.5 indicates maladaptively insufficient capacity to experience and express feelings. Regardless of how many *M* they have, individuals with a low *WSumC* have a functioning disability that limits their ability to recognize how they feel and describe their feelings to others. Faced with interpersonal situations that call for sharing one's emotions, they feel uncomfortable and unsure of themselves, unable to put their feelings into words, and uncertain about how else to go about letting their feelings be known. Such difficulties in processing affect often lead people to avoid emotional situations altogether, and, for this reason, a *WSumC* < 2.5 is often found in conjunction with a low *Afr* and may identify one of its sources.

Low *WSumC* becomes particularly problematic for adjustment when its value is exceeded by the level of *SumC'* in a record. Level of *SumC'* usually indicates the extent to which a person's affective experience is being internalized rather than expressed. Additionally, as is discussed in the next section, *C'* also has implications for the kinds of unpleasant internalized affects associated with feelings of gloom, sadness, and dysphoria. Aside from the emotional tone suggested by *SumC'*, a finding of *SumC'* > *WSumC* indicates a maladaptive constriction of capacity to express affect. Although a low *Afr* and a low *WSumC* also speak in part to insufficient capacity to express affect, it is *SumC':WSumC* that is specifically designated in the Comprehensive System as the *Constriction Ratio*.

Persons with an unbalanced Constriction Ratio in which *SumC'* > *WSumC* frequently struggle with bottled up emotions they are unable to express directly. People with this type of emotional blockage are often painfully aware of having many more strong feelings than they can get off their chest and make known to others. At times the dammed up feelings of emotionally constricted individuals escape their conscious awareness and become channeled instead into somatic equivalents. Tension headaches and gastrointestinal distress are two examples of physical complaints that commonly result from or are exacerbated by affects for which people cannot find avenues of direct expression. This is not to say that *SumC'* > *WSumC* is diagnostic of somatoform disorder, but only that the emotional blockage signified by an unbalanced Constriction Ratio may play a role in susceptibility to psychophysiological dysfunction.

Modulating Affect Pleasurably
(*SumC'*, *Col-Shd Bld*, *SumShd*, *S*)

Sufficient capacity to experience and express affect makes a *quantitative* contribution to good adjustment, but it does not ensure that affect will be processed in a *qualitatively* adaptive manner as well. Qualitative aspects of emotionality comprise the tone and intensity with which people experience and express affect, and people function most comfortably and effectively when they can process affect not only in sufficient quantity, but also pleasurably and in moderation.

Pleasurable modulation of affect consists of being able to sustain a positive emotional tone that promotes feeling happy and enjoying oneself. Capacities for happiness and enjoyment provide the foundation for being able to take pleasure in oneself and one's activities. These personality assets are reflected on the Rorschach in an emphasis on the bright and chromatic features of the inkblots rather than the dark, shaded, and empty features of the cards. The likelihood of a positively toned affective life is enhanced when the structural data combine an adequate level of *WSumC* with a low frequency of determinants and Location Choices that typically identify dysphoria, anhedonia, ambivalence, and anger. Specifically, the records of people who have developed and retained adaptive capacities for pleasurable processing of affect will ordinarily show few *C'*, no Color Shading Blends (*Col-Shd Bld*), a Sum Shading (*SumShd*) equal to or less than *FM + m*, and infrequent White Space (*S*) answers.

SumC'.   Use of *C'* has a median frequency of one among adult nonpatients and at every age from 5 to 16 except age 7, for which the median frequency is two in the nonpatient reference sample. With few exceptions, *C' > 2* indicates a maladaptive extent of painful internalized affect, and it serves as a criterion score on the *DEPI* index. The unpleasurable affective tone signified by *C'* responses closely resembles common associations to the meaning of black and gray. There is little doubt in most people's minds, for example, concerning the negative, undesirable, and unpleasant emotional quality of "being in a black mood" or "suffering through a gray day." Accordingly, an elevated *SumC'* typically points to feelings of sadness, gloom, unhappiness, and psychological misery.

Col-Shd Bld.   Responses involving a *Col-Shd Bld* have a median frequency of zero in nonpatients of all ages, and even one such response suggests dysphoric tendencies associated with ambivalent emotionality. People whose records show *Col-Shd Bld > 0* tend to be confused and uncertain about how they feel, and they often imbue people and events in their lives with both positive (the color) and negative (the shading) emotional characteristics at the same time. As a consequence, subjects who give *Col-Shd Bld* frequently have difficulty sorting out their feelings, and their proclivity to attach both pleasant and unpleasant connotations to experiences in their lives curtails their chances for being able to enjoy themselves. Their pleasurable moments are made bittersweet by anticipations that the other shoe will drop, a sunny day turn stormy, and rain fall on their parade, and even the best of times are spoiled for them by concerns that moments of joy are too good to last.

Although a subject's *EB* style ordinarily does not alter the clinical significance of other indices of modulating affect pleasurably that are discussed in this section, the implications of *Col-ShdBld* = 1 constitutes an exception in this regard. The nonpatient reference data indicate that extratensive adults are twice as likely as introversive adults (51% vs. 23%) to give a *Col-Shd Bld* response. Accordingly, although the meaning of *Col-Shd Bld* responses for ambivalent emotionality remain the same for both types of people, it may be that extratensive individuals accommodate a modest degree of emotional uncertainty more easily than introversive persons, without having it interfere substantially with their adaptation.

Hence *Col-Shd Bld* > 0 serves generally as an index of the type of anhedonia that prevents people from feeling happy or enjoying themselves, but for some extratensive individuals a more conservative index of *Col-Shd Bld* > 1 may be necessary to identify a maladaptive elevation on this variable. Nevertheless, *Col-Shd Bld* > 0 is a criterion score on *DEPI* and combines with *SumC'* > 2 to constitute what can be called a "dysphoric duo." As indicated next, the implications of this dysphoric duo for an unpleasurable emotional tone grow even stronger in the presence of an excessive *SumShd*.

SumShd. This variable, which constitutes the right side of the *eb*, shows a median frequency of three in both introversive and extratensive nonpatient adults. Young people in the age groups from 5 to 11 show median frequencies of two or three for *SumShd*, and among 12- to 16-year-olds the median for *SumShd* is four. In comparison, the left side of the *eb* (*FM* + *m*) has a normative frequency of five in adults, ranges from five to eight in 5- to 8-year-olds, and is either six or seven for 9- to 16-year-olds. A divergence from these expected frequencies such that *SumShd* exceeds *FM* + *m* suggests that a person is experiencing an unusual amount of emotional stress.

With respect to the types of stress suggested by the four components of *SumShd*, the implications of elevated *C'* for dysphoria have already been noted. Diffuse Shading (*Y*), like *C'*, involves articulation of the dark and shaded features of the blots, and *Y* > 1 is often associated with stress-related feelings of paralysis or hopelessness. Texture (*T*) > 1, as is elaborated in discussing structural indices of interpersonal perception, identifies individuals' disturbing concerns about not having as much close contact with other people as they would like to have. Vista (*V*) > 0, as is discussed in the section on variables concerned with examining oneself, identifies negative affective experience associated with self-critical attitudes.

The presence of some combination of these four variables to an extent that *SumShd* > *FM* + *m* constitutes an emotional stress flag and bears witness to maladaptive unpleasurable affect. Subjects with this stress flag in their records may not always be fully aware of their unpleasant affects, especially if they are using intellectual defenses to blunt the impact of their emotions or mechanisms of denial to conceal the existence of these feelings. Likewise, people with *SumShd* > *FM* + *m* may not necessarily display negatively toned affect, especially if they are introversive individuals who are oriented to keeping their feelings to themselves. Whether or not consciously recognized and directly expressed, however, the excessive level of emotional stress indicated by an elevated *SumShd* acts as an impediment to pleasurable modulation of affect, and *SumShd* > *FM* + *m* is another of the *DEPI* criterion scores.

S. Subjects who give White Space responses on the Rorschach are doing just the opposite of what has been asked of them. The standard instructions ask people to look at some inkblots and say what they might be. If subjects respond to the empty space on a card instead of the blot of ink, they are in effect countermanding the instructions and defining the task in their own terms. Showing some autonomy and self-determination in this way may indicate adaptive capacity to be one's own person. However, an excessive frequency of space responses is likely to reflect generalized oppositional tendencies that go beyond adaptive autonomy and are associated with underlying feelings of anger or resentment.

The median *S* is one for nonpatient adults and either one or two among all age groups from 5 to 16. A finding of *S* > 2 is uncommon at all ages and usually identifies a personality liability that interferes with pleasurable affective experience. Individuals with an elevation in *S* typically harbor more than ordinary amounts of anger and resentment toward people and situations in their lives that they regard as unfairly failing to meet their needs or posing obstacles to their goals. The manner in which high *S* people are likely to express their anger and resentment depends on their general inclinations toward assertiveness or passivity, both of which are interpersonal dimensions of adaptation discussed in the last section of this chapter. However channeled, excess anger and resentment as shown by *S* > 2 constitute an unpleasant affective state with considerable potential to foster problematic behavior.

Finally of note in completing this discussion of four indices of pleasurable modulation of affect is the fact that each of them functions primarily in a unidirectional fashion. When elevated, they identify the tendencies to dysphoria, anhedonia, ambivalence, and anger that have been noted. When normative, they suggest relative freedom from these affective impediments to good adjustment, but they do not necessarily indicate that subjects are living their lives happily, enjoyably, and without emotional uncertainty or rancor.

Modulating Affect in Moderation (*EBPer, FC:CF* + *C, CP*)

Modulating affect in moderation consists of maintaining an adaptive balance between emotional and ideational channels of expression, between reserved and expansive patterns of emotional discharge, and between modest and strained efforts to process affective experience in a positive manner. People who modulate affect in moderation can experience and express feelings without becoming excessively emotional; they can deal with feelings in either a formal or casual manner, depending on the circumstances; and they can take and appreciate positively toned situations where they find them, without having to force pleasantness and enjoyment into situations that do not in reality afford much of either. These capacities for modulating affect in moderation are reflected on the Rorschach in sufficient but not preoccupying attention to the chromatic features of the blots, an age-appropriate Form–Color Ratio (*FC:CF + C*), and avoidance of Color Projection (*CP*) responses.

EBPer. With specific respect to articulating the chromatic features of the blots, a moderate but not pervasively extratensive *EB* style has implications for good adjustment in the same manner as was previously discussed for a moderately introversive *EB* style. Moderately extratensive people are ordinarily capable of recognizing and responding to their feelings and the feelings of others without losing sight of the constructive purposes to which thoughtful reflection can be put. However, an *EBPer* in which *WSumC* exceeds *M* by a ratio of more than 2.5:1 indicates a maladaptive preference for dealing with experience primarily through affective channels at the expense of adequate ideational channels. Whereas a sufficient *WSumC* reflects good adaptive resources, especially when *FC:CF + C* is in normative balance, extratensive subjects with *EBPer* typically give short shrift to the ideational side of their life.

Pervasively extratensive people tend to be highly expressive and action-oriented individuals who rarely contemplate their decisions. They typically solve problems with practically oriented trial-and-error methods, rather than with reflection and conceptualization, and they are more likely to make decisions intuitively on the basis of what their "instincts" tell them than on the basis of thoughtful planning and analysis. Because adaptive behavior frequently requires deliberate planning as well as reactive affect, the overly emotional style of pervasively extratensive individuals often detracts from the effectiveness of their problem solving, the quality of their decisions, and the adequacy of their adjustment. Particularly when they are notably lacking in *M*, these individuals are likely to have considerable difficulty dealing constructively with situations that call for imposing some delay between their having feelings and their acting on these feelings.

FC:CF + C. An age-appropriate balance of *FC*, *CF*, and *C* responses identifies a broad and potentially adaptive repertoire of styles for experiencing and expressing affect. *FC* responses are associated with relatively well-modulated and reserved processing of emotion in which feelings emerge and dissipate slowly and are deeply felt but mild to moderate in their intensity. *CF* and *C* responses, by contrast, are associated with relatively unmodulated and spontaneous processing of emotion in which feelings come and go quickly and tend to be superficial but often quite intense while they last. In all persons' lives there are some situations in which good psychological adjustment is best served by formal and restrained expression of relatively stable affects, and there are other situations in which casual and expansive expression of relatively transitory affects contributes to coping effectively, having a good time, and giving pleasure to others. A balanced Form–Color Ratio thus identifies good capacity to mesh one's emotional style in these respects with the nature of one's circumstances.

As anticipated in discussing age differences in chapter 2, developmental changes in how affect is typically expressed call for age-based criteria for defining a balanced $FC:CF + C$. Reserved and well-modulated expression of affect is by and large an adult characteristic associated with emotional maturity, whereas spontaneous and unmodulated affective expression typifies the behavior of children rather than adults. The normal tendency of children to become affectively more stable and restrained during their developmental years is generally regarded as an index of their emotional maturation. Consistent with these developmental facts, the Form–Color Ratio shows a predictable progression from childhood into adolescence. In young children, FC responses are few in number and less frequent than $CF + C$ responses; over time, FC gradually become numerous, whereas the frequency of $CF + C$ remains fairly constant; and by midadolescence FC exceeds $CF + C$ on the average and continues to do so into and during adulthood.

Specifically, the adult reference sample data indicate median frequencies for $FC:CF:C$ of 5:3:0 among extratensive persons and 3:2:0 among introversive persons. Extratensive subjects thus give more color responses than introversive subjects, as would be expected, but for both adult groups a somewhat larger FC than $CF + C$ defines the average. Among adults, an age-appropriate balance in the Form–Color Ratio accordingly ranges from a slight preponderance of $CF + C$ responses to a substantial preponderance of FC responses. An adult's Form–Color Ratio falls outside of this normative range when $CF + C$ exceeds FC by more than one, or when FC exceeds $CF + C$ by more than three. Although this numerical range provides only a rough interpretive guideline, subjects with $CF + C > FC + 1$ or $FC > (CF + C) + 3$ are likely to be having difficulty modulating their affect at an adaptive level of moderation, and the extent of this difficulty will be proportional to how far their Form–Color Ratio deviates from this normally expected range.

Adults whose records contain an age-inappropriate emphasis on $CF + C$ tend to be emotionally immature individuals who experience and express affect dramatically and with intensity, but whose affects are also shallow and superficial. More like children than most other adults, they are quick to develop strong feelings and equally quick to let them pass. They may suddenly become very angry at someone or something, only to forgive, forget, and calm down in short order. They may be emotionally reactive people known to others for their ready laughter or the ease with which they become tearful, but in whom neither gaiety nor tearfulness ordinarily lasts very long. They may develop strong feelings of friendship and love rapidly, following only brief acquaintance with the objects of their interest and affection, but they also grow disenchanted with friendships more rapidly than most people and more quickly fall out of love.

For this reason, individuals with an excessive $CF + C$ are more likely than most people to have a wide circle of acquaintances they have known casually for a relatively short period of time, as opposed to a small group of friends they have known intimately for a long period of time. Excessively $CF + C$ individuals tend to be viewed by emotionally mature adults as lively and engaging people who are refreshingly open about their feelings, easy to get to know, and someone they might enjoy being with at a party. At the same time, however, adults with this personality liability are likely to be seen as overly excitable, childishly naive in their willingness to expose their feelings to people they hardly know, and unlikely or disingenuous participants in a serious conversation.

Like the other descriptions in this chapter of behavior patterns likely to be associated with various structural patterns, the preceding capsule of people in whom $CF + C > FC + 1$ is overdrawn. Not all subjects with this finding in their Rorschach show all of the characteristics just mentioned, nor do they necessarily show any of them to the extent described. Nevertheless, this description does give the flavor of the types of adaptive limitations that often mark the lives of emotionally immature people whose affective intensity exceeds ordinary limits of moderation. The more this index of emotional immaturity deviates from the normative range, the more likely subjects are to display maladaptively shallow, labile, unstable, and intense patterns of affective behavior. Because C responses represent an even more intense form of affective discharge than CF, a substantially excessive $CF + C$ takes on increased interpretive significance for emotional volatility whenever it includes C as well as CF responses.

Contrary to persistent belief, however, the maladaptively unrestrained emotionality that is associated with $CF + C > FC + 1$ and intensified by the presence of C does not necessarily imply impulsivity. Strictly defined, *impulsivity* refers to episodes of loss of control consisting of emotional outbursts or ill-conceived actions that are uncharacteristic of how the person ordinarily behaves. People who are being impulsive usually recognize that they are expressing themselves or acting in ways atypical for them, that feel unnatural, and that they will probably have reason to regret. By contrast, the lack of restraint reflected in excessive $CF + C$ constitutes a personal preference and an abiding disposition to let one's affects and actions flow freely. Overly expressive and overly active $CF + C$ people are merely behaving in ways that typify how they conduct their lives and that help them feel comfortable.

Accordingly, when *CF* + *C* individuals display relatively unrestrained behavior, their actions rarely surprise people who know them, because they are behaving as they usually do. By contrast, individuals displaying episodes of impulsivity are imposing less restraint on their behavior than they customarily do, and their lapses in self-control lead to actions that stun, perplex, and catch others off guard. An instance of problematic behavior committed by an excessively *CF* + *C* person might lead friends and associates to say, "There you go again" or "You're carrying on as usual today," whereas the same behavior committed by someone acting impulsively might be more likely to evoke such responses as, "What's got into you today?" or "This isn't like you." Rorschach findings that do identify susceptibility to episodes of impulsivity are discussed in the next section in relation to resources for managing stress.

Although unrelated to impulsivity as strictly defined, the overly intense and labile affectivity indicated by excessive *CF* + *C* has significant implications for mood disorder. In particular, the rapidly fluctuating emotions of *CF* + *C* people raise the possibility of mood swings associated with bipolar or cyclothymic conditions. Especially when an excessive *CF* + *C* appears in conjunction with many of the previously noted indices of unpleasurable affect, subjects giving such records are likely to show alternating episodes of dysphoria and euphoria that, if sufficiently marked or prolonged, will have diagnostic significance.

Additionally, as suggested previously, the expansive affective style associated with excessive *CF* + *C* may contribute to the kind of social and emotional withdrawal reflected in a low *Afr*. Being comfortable with expressing themselves freely does not prevent *CF* + *C* people from recognizing that their characteristic lability and expansiveness can prove a handicap in certain kinds of interpersonal situations. In particular, adults who have difficulty modulating affect in moderation often become aware that most other adults do not respond favorably to their childlike intensity and excitability, except perhaps on festive occasions. To minimize their involvement in situations in which matters often go poorly for them, excessively *CF* + *C* people may avoid or withdraw from affective interchange. Should this occur, the depressive quality of a low *Afr* may emerge as counterpoint to the usually positive emotional tone of elevation in *CF* + *C*.

All of these implications of an excessive *CF* + *C* apply to children and adolescents as well as adults, provided that the criterion for defining an unbalanced Form–Color Ratio is modified in light of age-specific reference data. Like adults, children and adolescents with *CF* + *C* > *FC* + *1* will show dramatic, intense, shallow, and superficial affect, at least by adult standards. However, because young people ordinarily show more such behavior than adults, as already noted, a different standard is required to identify when they lack ufficient capacity to modulate affect in moderation and when their emotional intensity has implications for adjustment difficulties or psychological disorder. The reference data indicate that a cutting score of $CF + C > FC + 2$ is necessary to identify an unusually unbalanced Form–Color Ratio in young people from age 11 to 16; for children age 10 and under, a finding of at least $CF + C > FC + 3$ is required to exceed the normative range.

Turning next to the implications of an age-inappropriate emphasis on FC, adults whose records show $FC > (CF + C) + 3$ tend to be emotionally reserved individuals whose affects run deep and long but who typically experience and express feelings in a very low key. Only gradually, over an extended period of time and after substantial accumulation of good reason, do they become angry, happy, sad, friendly, or loving. Typically, they are known to others for their emotional calm and for how unlikely they are to become excited or upset or to develop strong passions. Once formed, however, their emotions are deeply felt and highly stable. Whereas anger easily aroused tends to pass quickly, the slowly emerging anger of people with excessive FC tends to persist for long periods of time, and those who arouse their displeasure may find it difficult to dispel. Similarly, whereas rapidly waxing affection tends to wane with equal speed, the gradually developing affection of people with excessive FC diminishes slowly, and those who gain their love often continue to receive it indefinitely. The interpersonal relationships as well as the affects of these individuals are very stable over time, and they are much more likely than most people to value a small number of close friendships over a large circle of casual acquaintances.

This caricatured description of subjects in whom $FC > (CF + C) + 3$ includes many seemingly desirable features of emotional maturity (e.g., depth, restraint, and stability). However, it is modulation of affect in moderation that holds the key to good adjustment, and excessive FC, like excessive CF, defines an unbalanced Form–Color Ratio and creates a risk of adjustment difficulties. Whereas excessively CF individuals process affect with too much spontaneity, excessively FC individuals experience and express affect with too much reserve. Typically they deal with emotional interactions in a formal, tepid, and understated fashion and have limited capacities to relax emotionally, show their feelings, and relate to others on a casual and informal basis.

As a consequence, people with $FC > (CF + C) + 3$ often impress others being cold, remote, disinterested, difficult to get to know, and not very much fun to be around. Although their emotional calm may be welcome in serious situations, their inability to replace their usual sobriety with some exuberance in lighthearted situations often results in their being regarded as stuffy, dull, and emotionally inhibited individuals. Their friends and loved ones may recognize and appreciate the depth and dependability of the excessively FC person's feelings toward them. However, they are also likely to regret that these feelings of love and affection are rarely expressed by this type of person, at least not in any way that approaches being effusive or demonstrative.

People whose Rorschach contains excessive *FC* may often feel uncomfortable or function poorly in emotionally involved situations as a consequence of their inability to relax and express their feelings freely. Hence, like people with excessive *CF*, they may develop a preference to avoid such situations, which usually means avoiding interpersonal interactions that are not strictly formal. Their excessive *FC* can lead in this way to their becoming socially or emotionally withdrawn individuals whose aversion to affect is reflected in a low *Afr*. Generally speaking, examiners finding a low *Afr* during the interpretive process have good reason to consider whether the aversion it indicates originates in a deficient capacity to modulate affect in moderation, as indicated when either *FC* or *CF* is excessive.

Like excessive *CF*, excessive *FC* implies maladaptive affective modulation for children and adolescents as well as adults. Young people who are more likely than their peers to experience and express affect in a formal and reserved manner and who lack normative capacity for spontaneous and unrestrained emotional displays are at risk for adjustment difficulties. Like adults whose color use is excessively well-modulated, children and adolescents with this Rorschach pattern are likely to be emotionally inhibited individuals who cannot engage comfortably in the emotionally high-pitched give-and-take of youthful peer relationships. Although these emotionally inhibited young people may be viewed positively by parents, teachers, and other adults as commendably mature, they are likely to be regarded by their agemates as different and strange and to be faced with problems of social isolation.

Age-appropriate translation of an unbalanced Form–Color Ratio into these implications for emotional inhibition requires modifying the criterion for an excessive *FC* in light of the reference data. Consistent with the normative tendency of young people to show less modulation of affect than adults, the Form–Color Ratio becomes interpretively significant for subjects age 14 or less when $FC > (CF + C) + 1$, and for adolescents age 15 and 16 when $FC > (CF + C) + 2$. Like the adult criterion of $FC > (CF + C) + 3$, these age-adjusted criterion scores rarely occur in nonpatient samples.

CP.   By insisting that a black and gray inkblot is chromatically colored, subjects giving Color Projection (*CP*) responses are straining to transform a potentially dysphoric stimulus feature of the card into a bright and appealing characteristic. Such responses accordingly identify tendencies to deny unpleasant affect by attributing attractive qualities to situations and events that are in fact quite otherwise. Consistent with this formulation of the process underlying the interpretive significance of *CP*, Color Projection responses almost always involve pleasant percepts, such as "a pretty flower" or "a colorful butterfly." Only very rarely do subjects report a *CP* with unpleasant connotations, such as seeing an achromatic card as looking "bloody" or "diseased" because of chromatic colors projected onto it.

CP occurs in fewer than 2% of the Rorschach records of nonpatients at all ages, and $CP > 0$ is thus a dramatic finding with considerable import. Subjects with one or more CP in their records are usually individuals who keep themselves in more or less constant good spirits by using denial to ward off any potentially depressing feelings and concerns. Ever cheerful and optimistic, CP people look at life through rose-colored glasses. By ignoring the existence of threatening and distasteful events, they sustain their ebullience and high hopes even in times of turmoil and travail. By refusing to acknowledge the negative aspects of any situation in which they find themselves, they remain at least superficially content. In sharp contrast to Col-Shd Bld people, who see gloomy portents even in pleasant experiences, people with CP find silver linings in every dark cloud.

The euphoria thus usually associated with CP constitutes in some respects an intensification of the expansive and positively toned emotionality observed in individuals with excessive $CF + C$. There is an important difference between these two variables, however. Numerous $CF + C$ identifies a characterological style of processing affect that comes naturally to the person and is ordinarily stable over time, even though it may alternate in cyclothymic individuals with manifestations of dysphoria. CP, on the other hand, identifies a primitive defensive maneuver involving contrived avoidance of reality and forced gaiety, rather than any natural mode of expressing or enjoying oneself. People who use denial in the manner captured by CP responses are in effect telling themselves, "If I don't see it, it's not there," just as young children often cope with threatening situations by closing their eyes, in the belief that not seeing what is there will make it go away. Because it is so strained and contrived, the defensiveness indicated by CP is very fragile and likely to crumble quickly when challenged, which is a vulnerability important to keep in mind in the treatment of CP people. Because individuals with $CP > 0$ are at considerable risk for rapid mood swings, the co-occurrence of CP with indices of depression frequently raises the possibility of bipolar disorder or cyclothymic tendencies.

MANAGING STRESS

Except when they are asleep or totally at their leisure, people are almost constantly immersed in circumstances that require them to make decisions concerning what they should think and how they should express themselves; likewise, the vicissitudes of doing one's work and conducting one's personal life call for almost constant problem solving. The necessity of making decisions and solving problems constitute demands that people regularly experience in their everyday lives. These demands can derive either internally, from thoughts and feelings, and sometimes from external events, including what other people say and do. Whatever their source, such demands constitute a stress in the sense that they must be met in some way in order for people to feel comfortable and function effectively. The more adequately people can meet the demands they experience, the more likely they are to manage stress successfully and to reap the rewards of good psychological adjustment. Conversely, difficulties in meeting life's demands in some satisfactory fashion constitute failures in stress management that lead to numerous maladaptive consequences.

The extent of the psychological resources people can bring to bear in managing stress thus determines in large part how well they adapt to themselves and their environment. Adequate resources to minimize subjectively felt distress and maintain a consistent coping style promote psychological well-being and successful adaptation to life demands. Conversely, the triumvirate of insufficient resources, a high level of experienced stress, and inconsistent coping efforts typically eventuates in lives marked by distress, disappointment, and limited accomplishment. Each of these potential assets or limitations in stress management can be measured on the RIM (as presented next).

Mustering Adequate Resources (*EA, CDI*)

Being able to muster adequate resources for meeting the demands of everyday living consists of having at one's disposal effective ways of thinking about these demands and appropriate channels for experiencing and expressing feelings about them. Hence, capacities for using ideation effectively and modulating affect sufficiently and pleasurably, as discussed in the preceding two sections of this chapter, capture the essential components of being a psychologically competent and resourceful person. In addition to what can be learned from ideational and affective variables considered separately, the Experience Actual (*EA*) variable on the Rorschach provides a combined ideational/affective index of adaptive capacities that serves as a useful barometer of psychological competence. As a companion variable, the Coping Deficit Index (*CDI*) measures several aspects of the amount and kind of adaptive resources on which subjects can draw in meeting their experienced demands.

EA. The interpretive significance of *EA* derives from the fact that it represents the sum of those variables that reflect subjects' preferred and self-selected ways of dealing with experience, whether in an ideational and contemplative manner (*M*) or in an emotional, expressive manner (*WSumC*). With respect to the self-selected nature of *M* and *WSumC* behavior patterns, people may at times disavow responsibility for conducting themselves in an introversive or extratensive fashion, as by saying, "Don't blame me; that's just the way I am." Observers may similarly make allowances for the conduct of excessively ideational or emotional people by saying, "It's just in their nature, and they can't help it." Consistent with these "excuses," abiding dispositions such as being an introversive or extratensive person do in fact exert a powerful influence on how people typically behave.

Nevertheless, it is characteristic of M-type and $WSumC$-type behaviors that people have considerable control over them and can initiate and discontinue them as they choose. Contemplative people engaged in thinking about a problem can decide to stop thinking about it and to think about something else instead. Expressive people engaged in displaying some affect can elect to stop emoting and instead keep their feelings to themselves. Should ideation escape such conscious control, it becomes the type of intrusive ideation associated with the left side of the eb ($FM + m$) rather than with M-type activity; should emotions make their presence felt despite a preference to avoid them, they constitute the type of unpleasant affective experience associated with the right side of the eb ($SumShd$) rather than with $WSumC$-type activity. These specific corollaries of $FM + m$ and $SumShd$ have already been discussed, and their general implications for adequate capacity to meet psychological demands are elaborated later.

As for the implications of EA, the nature of M-type and $WSumC$-type activities makes the sum of M and $WSumC$ a useful index of how much resource people have available for planning and implementing deliberate strategies of coping with decision-making and problem-solving situations. Generally speaking, the more EA subjects have in their record, the more adaptive capacity they have at their disposal and the more competence they are likely to display in pursuing their aims and objectives. In fact, people who show an abundance of EA on the RIM but a life pattern of spotty accomplishment, whether measured in achievement-related or interpersonal terms, are usually people who for some reason have not lived up to their potential and could be functioning substantially better than they are.

In this regard, the positive implications of abundant EA for adaptive capacity may be compromised by a marked imbalance in its two components. Just as being pervasively introversive or extratensive can limit the range of situations with which a person can deal comfortably and effectively, being deficient in either M or $WSumC$ can undermine the adaptive capacity usually indicated by an adequate EA. Whether people are introversive or extratensive, they should ordinarily have at least two M responses and a $WSumC$ of at least 2.5 in their records to indicate minimally adequate capacities to reflect on their experiences and to process affect. Regardless of the size of EA, a finding of $M < 2$ indicates maladaptively limited ability to deal with situations by thinking them through; correspondingly, even when EA is large, $WSumC < 2.5$ identifies maladaptively limited ability to experience and express emotions. This means that adequate *EA* can be taken as an indication of adequate psychological resources only when *M* and *WSumC* are both sufficiently large to rule out specific deficiencies in either ideational or affective coping capacities.

EA has a mean frequency of 8.83 in nonpatient adults and, with $M > 1$ and $WSumC > 2.0$, should reach at least six in order to indicate adaptive capacity within the broad average range. Individuals in whom $EA < 6$ usually have limited coping resources and are more likely than most people to meet life's demands in an inept and ineffective manner that provides them little gratification and earns them limited success. For this reason, noticeably low *EA* in adults who have a prior history of substantial accomplishment often helps to identify loss of functioning capacity from some previously higher level. Although exceptions may occur, low *EA* in a previously achieving person may therefore reflect deterioration associated with the onset of serious psychological disorder or neuropsychological dysfunction.

The most important exception to the implications of low *EA* for limited competence or loss of function involves short records with a high *Lambda*. The high *Lambda* style discussed previously does not necessarily lead to a low *EA*, because an average length record can be 50% pure form and still allow opportunity for enough human movement and chromatic color response to generate an adequate *EA*. Hence, low *EA* in a high *Lambda* record of average length has the same implications for insufficient resources as it does in average length records with $Lambda < 1.00$.

On the other hand, a short but valid record with fewer than 20 responses in which $Lambda > .99$ is less likely to indicate a high *Lambda* style than a guarded approach by the subject. Not uncommonly, especially when they are being evaluated for administrative rather than clinical purposes, psychologically competent subjects with a history of accomplishment will produce a guarded record with relatively few responses, a high *Lambda*, and a low *EA*. In these instances, a low *M* and/or *WSumC* probably represent what subjects are choosing to withhold, rather than what they are unable to produce. It is reasonable to expect that such subjects would give a longer and fuller record with adequate *EA* if they were being examined under circumstances to which they were less resistant. At any rate, care should be taken not to overinterpret or be misled by a low *EA* in this circumstance.

Finally, consistent with its implications for coping skills, *EA* is a developmental variable. Adults ordinarily possess greater psychological competence than children, and normative maturation is defined in part by the gradual acquisition of an expanding repertoire of adaptive capacities. As would be expected, then, nonpatient adolescents at age 15 and 16 show the same mean level of *EA* as adults; in youngsters from age 9 to 14, *EA* is somewhat lower than in adults but retains a mean above 8.00 at each age; and among younger children, mean *EA* ranges from 7.51 at age 8 down to

5.08 at age 5. Thus, the criterion of *EA* < 6 identifies normatively insufficient coping resource for most adolescents as well as for adults but must be scaled down somewhat for early adolescents and younger children.

Young people whose *EA* falls below the normative range for their age are typically handicapped by developmental arrest. In some instances, this developmental arrest reflects constitutionally determined developmental disorders that are impeding the normal maturation of coping skills. In other instances, low *EA* youngsters are constitutionally sound individuals who have lacked the kinds of nurturing and instructive developmental experiences from which children learn how to think about their experiences and deal with their emotions. In either case, a low *EA* and its implications for adjustment difficulties frequently respond well to interventions emphasizing coping skill training. As time passes, however, poor coping skills become entrenched, and the problems to which they lead become increasingly resistant to modification. By adulthood, a persistently low *EA* often signifies a chronic limitation in adaptive capacities that is unlikely to change very much and to which people must accommodate as best they can.

CDI. By combining a low *EA* with several other variables associated with difficulties in coping adequately with stress, affect, and interpersonal relationships, the Coping Deficit Index (*CDI*) provides a broadly based measure of adaptive resources that has specific implications for differential diagnosis and treatment planning as well as personality description. The vast majority of nonpatients at all ages show a *CDI* of three or less, and a *CDI* > 3, unlike *EA* < 6, is only slightly more common among 5-year-olds (12%) than among adults (3%). *CDI* also differs from *EA* in being a unidirectional rather than a bidirectional variable. As previously noted, low *EA* signifies a personality liability and abundant *EA* a personality asset, and the more the better, as long as its *M* and *WSumC* components remain in good balance. *CDI*, by contrast, is noteworthy only when it is elevated and has little meaning when it is not elevated.

To elaborate this last point, a *CDI* < 4 is often associated with adequate resources for functioning in a reasonably competent manner, but a low *CDI* does not indicate any special personality assets, nor does it preclude the possibility of adjustment difficulties related to liabilities in using ideation, modulating affect, or conducting interpersonal relationships. On the other hand, an elevated *CDI* is a definite indicator of adjustment difficulties, and subjects with *CDI* > 3 typically show inept and ineffective ways of attempting to cope with ordinary experiences of daily living.

The specific implications of an elevated *CDI* also depend on the level of a subject's *EA*, and the relationship between *CDI* and *EA* helps to distinguish two different patterns of coping inadequacy. In one of these patterns, an elevated *CDI* occurs in conjunction with a low *EA*. This *CDI/EA* pattern characterizes individuals with limited psychological competence whose coping difficulties cut broadly across many aspects of their lives and who are likely to have enjoyed little educational, occupational, or interpersonal success. Among children and adolescents the combination of elevated *CDI* and low *EA* identifies urgent needs for skill training and a good likelihood of its proving beneficial. Young people with developmental arrest are particularly likely to benefit from being helped to learn basic ways of dealing with problems by thinking about them and of responding to situations by expressing feelings about them. The amenability to such basic training in social skills tends to diminish with age, however, and by adulthood the prospects of modifying a pattern of elevated *CDI* with low *EA* are limited.

The other pattern of coping inadequacy identified by an elevated *CDI* involves the seemingly paradoxical presence of an adequate or even substantial level of *EA*. This second combination usually occurs in people who are not generally incompetent and may even have significant accomplishments to their credit, but who have pronounced difficulty managing their interpersonal relationships in a comfortable and rewarding manner. This pattern of coping deficit coexisting with an adequate *EA* helps to account for circumstances in which well-educated, high-achieving, and personable individuals surprisingly produce a Rorschach protocol with *CDI* > 3. More often than not, such individuals will be found to be struggling in their lives with the consequences of inadequate social skills that are not immediately apparent in how they present themselves. Such individuals can frequently benefit from treatment focused on interpersonal anxiety reduction and social skills training. Offsetting the impediment to skill training ordinarily posed by an elevated *CDI* in an adult, the competence reflected by an adequate *EA* offers promise for a favorable response to socially focused intervention in persons whose coping difficulties are largely restricted to their interpersonal encounters. The interpersonal variables included in the *CDI* are discussed in their own right in the last section of this chapter.

With respect to specific diagnostic implications of an elevated *CDI*, its implications for limited competence make it sensitive to forms of depression that are marked not so much by dysphoric affect or negative cognitions as by pervasive helplessness. As elaborated in the Comprehensive System volumes (J. E. Exner, 1991, 1993; J. E. Exner & Weiner, 1995), an elevated *CDI* should not by itself be considered diagnostic of a mood disorder; however, almost 80% of subjects with independently diagnosed mood disorders who fail to show an elevation on *DEPI* are likely to elevate on *CDI* (J. E. Exner, 1993, chap. 15). Elevations in *CDI* are also commonly found among persons with other disorders characterized by manifestations of helplessness and spotty success in contending with life's challenges. These include people who succumb to alcohol and substance abuse; persons with characterological disorders, especially those who become involved with the criminal justice system; and individuals who in earlier versions of the *Diagnostic and Statistical Manual of Mental Disorders* would have met criteria for being diagnosed "Inadequate Personality" (American Psychiatric Association, 1968).

Minimizing Subjectively Felt Distress (*D, AdjD*)

By virtue of the goals they pursue, the responsibilities they assume, and the relationships they form, some people lead relatively stressful lives in which they deal frequently with demands to make decisions, solve problems, handle feelings, and take action. Other people encounter relatively little stress by virtue of leading a comparatively restricted life in which neither the expectations they have of themselves nor the external requirements they confront on a daily basis place many psychological demands on them. However, the apparent level of stress people face, as measured by some objective standard or the consensus impression of others, bears no necessary relationship to their subjective sense of well-being. Some people manage what seem to be highly stressful and demanding situations with aplomb, without feeling or manifesting any undue distress, whereas others have difficulty managing seemingly simple and only mildly stressful situations without becoming markedly upset. Which of these responses to stress is more likely to occur depends on the extent to which individuals' coping capacities are sufficient to meet the demands they are facing.

Having sufficient adaptive resources to manage the stresses in their lives allows individuals to minimize their experiences of subjectively felt distress and maintain a sense of comfort, composure, and satisfaction. Being able to meet the demands in one's life without becoming unduly upset by them contributes further to good adjustment by fostering peace of mind, a psychological equilibrium that is stable over time, and the abilities to tolerate frustration and maintain self-control. The adequacy of coping capacities in relation to the level of demand people are experiencing is measured on the Rorschach by two closely related indices, the D-Score (*D*) and the Adjusted D-Score (*AdjD*).

D. Because it derives from conjoint consideration of all of the determinants coded in the Comprehensive System except Dimensionality and Reflections, *D* is one of the most broadly based, dependable, and interpretively meaningful summary scores that can be calculated from Rorschach data. One of its two components, the *EA*, provides a good index of available resources for formulating and implementing deliberate strategies of coping with experienced demands. Its other component, the Experienced Stimulation (*es*) variable, monitors in similar fashion the level of ideational and emotional demands being imposed on people by internal and external events in their lives. As mentioned previously in discussing the left side *eb* and right side *eb* portions of *es*, the combined total of the animal and inanimate movement responses and the shading and achromatic color responses in a record captures psychological experiences that operate outside of a person's conscious control and thus constitute imposed stresses that require being managed.

A D of zero, indicating a modest difference of no more than 2.5 between *EA* and *es*, defines the normative range for this variable and has numerous positive implications for adjustment. Persons with $D = 0$ are usually relatively free from overt anxiety, tension, nervousness, and irritability. They tend to be satisfied individuals who feel no particular need to change the way they are or the circumstances they are in, and they tend to be fairly stable individuals who, other things being equal, present a psychological picture today that closely resembles the picture they presented yesterday and will present tomorrow. They have at least average capacities to tolerate frustration and to persevere in the face of obstacles, and they ordinarily are as capable as most people of controlling their behavior and avoiding impulsive episodes of intense emotionality or ill-advised actions.

Nevertheless, $D = 0$ may in some circumstances identify a vulnerability to certain adjustment problems. In some instances, for example, $D = 0$ may be achieved at the expense of a "hunkered-down" lifestyle in which people are maintaining their psychological equilibrium and stability not by virtue of good coping resources, but by determined efforts to keep stressful experiences at a minimum and disturbing thoughts and feelings out of their conscious awareness. Like high *Lambda* people, and especially when they also have a high *Lambda*, $D = 0$ people whose *EA* and *es* are both low typically lead very restricted lives in which they avoid new or challenging circumstances that would impose psychological demands on them.

As long as it can be maintained, a hunkered-down approach to life can insulate people against becoming psychologically distressed. However, this type of insulation is thin and the stability it provides quite fragile. The psychological equilibrium of $D = 0$ people with low *EA* and low *es* survives on the basis of restriction and avoidance. Should such people be forced to confront even ordinary levels of stress of the kind that most other people deal with daily, their limited adaptive capacities prove inadequate and they quickly become overwhelmed. In RIM terms, the low *EA* of hunkered-down people allows them to function in a $D = 0$ fashion as long as they maintain a low *es*, but it does not give them any coping resources in reserve on which to draw when circumstances change suddenly and burden them with an average or higher *es*; should this occur, the mounting *es* of these hunkered-down individuals soon outstrips their limited *EA*, and they become precipitated from their $D = 0$ status into a maladaptive *D-minus* position.

Secondly, with respect to potential disadvantages of $D = 0$, the stability and satisfaction it identifies can impede personality and behavior change that would be desirable. Whereas stability is an asset for people who are functioning relatively well, it is a liability for people who are having psychological difficulties. In patient populations in particular, $D = 0$ is likely to be associated with chronic and characterological conditions that are relatively resistant to change, rather than with acute and symptomatic conditions that are relatively responsive to interventions. Accordingly, the distinction between a $D = 0$ and a *D-minus* Rorschach record often proves helpful in differentiating between symptomatic and characterological forms of psychopathology and between acute and chronic forms of a disorder. In addition, because individuals' satisfaction with themselves and their life are known to minimize motivation for psychotherapy, $D = 0$ people who might benefit from treatment aimed at personality or behavior change tend to be relatively disinterested in receiving or being influenced by it.

Resistance to change is especially characteristic of individuals who show a *D-plus* pattern in their Rorschach responses. Having an abundance of coping capacities and considerable resource in reserve on which to call when they need it, *D-plus* people usually display very good stress tolerance and admirable talent for remaining calm, cool, and collected no matter what is happening around them. *D-plus* people are typically unflappable individuals whose presence is welcome at times of emergency or crisis, because they keep their heads while most others are losing theirs.

On the other hand, otherwise capable *D-plus* people commonly lack sufficient sensitivity to deal with people and situations effectively. Able to remain calm and unflustered because they do not let events trouble them, they sometimes ignore or minimize the implications of events that should capture their attention and cause them concern. Able to avoid overreaction to the danger of circumstances and the distress of others, they frequently fail to notice subtle signals of impending difficulty or interpersonal strain. Moreover, because the personality style of *D-plus* people is even more entrenched and stabilized than that of people with $D = 0$, they are even less likely to entertain the notion that there is anything about themselves that they should change. Hence they are particularly unlikely to consider psychotherapy should they need it or to respond positively should they receive it.

Turning next to the maladaptive implications of a *D-minus* status, this summary score indicates the extent to which people are likely to be feeling anxious, tense, nervous, and irritable, and it is typically associated with limited tolerance for frustration and a resulting proclivity for impulsiveness. As anticipated in the earlier discussion of affect modulation, the impulsivity associated with *D-minus* differs from the expansive emotionality and action orientation seen in subjects with excessive $CF + C$ in their records. Whereas excessive $CF + C$ indicates a comfortable, enjoyable, and persistent preference to express oneself with little restraint, *D-minus* identifies a susceptibility to unwelcome, unpleasant, and episodic losses of self-control.

The specific implications of *D-minus* vary with its magnitude. A *D-minus* of one identifies a mild degree of subjectively felt distress that may be annoying and perhaps of concern to individuals but usually does not seriously compromise their adaptation. In the context of fairly structured and predictable circumstances, in fact, people with $D = -1$ tend to function in a reasonably untroubled fashion that seldom attracts the attention of others. When *D-minus* exceeds one, however, structure alone no longer suffices to ward off the consequences of experiencing more stress than one can find ways to manage, and subjectively felt distress begins to become preoccupying, disorganizing, and overtly manifest. As matters get worse and *D-minus* rises beyond two, people grow increasingly likely to be incapacitated by stress, to describe themselves as being "stressed out" or "too upset to think straight," to lose self-control in ways that shame and embarrass them, and to appear to others as being noticeably agitated and distraught.

Although psychologically painful and disruptive, *D-minus* has some positive implications for treatment opposite to those associated with $D = 0$ and *D-plus*. Because *D-minus* identifies an unwelcome and unpleasant psychological state, it contributes to people being dissatisfied with themselves, being motivated to change, and being receptive to interventions designed to reduce their level of subjectively felt distress and its maladaptive consequences. The positive treatment implications of *D-minus* are conceptually consistent with generally established knowledge concerning prognosis in therapy: People who feel upset and want to change derive more benefit from psychotherapy than those who do not (see Weiner, 1998a, chap 2).

With further respect to psychotherapy, *D-minus* Rorschach data can also provide some useful guidelines in treatment planning. In some instances, *D-minus* results from an unusually large *es* in the presence of at least average *EA*. People who show this pattern typically have adequate coping resources but a life filled with an inordinate amount of stress, from whatever sources. Such individuals are likely to profit most from a treatment approach focused on reducing the amount of stress they experience, whether by resolving anxiety-producing conflicts, restructuring their perspectives on events in their lives, or modifying the kind of life they are attempting to lead.

In other cases, *D-minus* people display no more than an average amount of *es* but a low *EA*. For these individuals stress reduction would be accomplished only at the expense of inducing the hunkered-down lifestyle described earlier. Unless hunkering down appears to be the only available avenue for reducing their subjectively felt distress, *D-minus* people with low *EA* benefit instead from a treatment approach focused on imparting coping skills and promoting improved stress management. In RIM language, successful treatment in this second instance elevates *EA* without closing off *es* and achieves a $D = 0$.

AdjD.   Generally speaking, the stress that people experience in their lives comes in two forms. Some forms of experienced stress persist over time and respond only gradually, if at all, to changing circumstances, whereas other forms of experienced stress wax and wane quickly in response even to momentary fluctuations in the demands people are facing. Stress related to dysphoric mood, for example, tends to linger and make its presence felt over an extended period of time. The level of dysphoria experienced by depressed persons may fluctuate periodically, particular events may contribute to their feeling better or worse on different occasions, and an accumulation of positively experienced events may eventually extinguish their gloomy affect. Such fluctuations and eventual remission take time, however, and dysphoria neither appears nor disappears at a moment's notice.

As a contrasting example, stress related to concerns about one's safety and well-being ordinarily arises as soon as threatening circumstances appear and dissipates when they cease to exist. Thus students worried about the outcome of an examination stop worrying on learning that they did well, and people who immediately become fearful on being confronted with a snarling dog instantly feel much better if the dog is restrained and led away by its owner. Such situationally related stress can interfere with adaptation and contribute to subjectively felt distress in the same manner as persistently experienced stress. Obviously, however, subjectively felt distress attributable largely to situational determinants is more easily overcome or alleviated than subjectively felt distress caused mainly by persistent sources of stress. As quickly as one can avoid, escape, or alter the precipitating circumstances, the subjectively felt distress will disappear.

The *AdjD* variable on the Rorschach helps to distinguish between relatively persistent and relatively situational experienced stress. Of the six determinants that compose *es*, four are reasonably stable over time. In the 3-year retest data discussed in chapter 1, *FM*, *T*, *C'*, and *V* showed respective stability coefficients of .72, .87, .67, and .81. By contrast, the other two determinants in *es*, *m* and *Y*, are highly unstable over time, with 3-year retest correlations respectively of .31 and .23 (J. E. Exner & Weiner, 1995, p. 22). Research has confirmed, furthermore, that the *m* and *Y* components of *es* can be quickly and dramatically driven up and down by environmental manipulations (J. E. Exner, 1993, chaps. 2 & 16). Accordingly, as prescribed by the Comprehensive System scoring guidelines, an *Adjusted es* is produced by reducing *es* by the number of *m* and *Y* greater than one each (the normative expectation), and comparison of this *Adjusted es* with *EA* yields the *AdjD* score, which indicates the extent of subjective distress a subject is feeling beyond what appears attributable to situational stress.

In this way, $D < AdjD$ becomes the Rorschach index of situational distress, and people showing $D < 0$ but an $AdjD = 0$ are likely to be basically stable and psychologically comfortable individuals who are presently experiencing the ill effects of more situational stress than they can manage adequately but who will return to a customary state of psychological equilibrium as soon as the situational demands on them abate. Like $D = 0$, then, $AdjD = 0$, especially in the company of at least average EA, generally points to good adaptive capacities, as reflected in having sufficient psychological resources to cope adequately with the ongoing demands in one's life.

At the same time, however, $AdjD = 0$ may have some of the same implications as $D = 0$ for resistance to change and a limited response to psychotherapy, even in the presence of $D < 0$. Not unusually, $AdjD = 0$ people with $D < 0$ are motivated to receive help and participate in a treatment program for as long as their situational distress continues to be fueled by events outside of their control. Should their circumstances improve and their situational distress be alleviated, then their motivation to change or remain in therapy may quickly evaporate. Enthusiastic beginnings and rapid disengagement consequently characterize the treatment course of many such individuals, especially when psychotherapy or pharmacotherapy is focused primarily on symptom reduction.

An $AdjD < 0$ has implications for persistent stress overload related to long-standing inability to muster sufficient coping resources to minimize subjectively felt distress. The larger the $AdjD$-minus, the more incapacitating this personality liability is likely to have been, and the more likely the individual is to show a history of limited or declining accomplishment and chronic psychological malaise. Thus, the correlates of $Adjd < -1$ often include either a lifelong pattern of ineffective efforts at mastery or a collapse of coping effectiveness subsequent to the onset of a chronic stress disorder.

Maintaining Consistency (EB Style)

In addition to being able to muster adequate psychological resources and minimize their experiences of subjectively felt distress, people manage stress most adaptively when they can employ consistent patterns of dealing with decision-making and problem-solving situations in their lives. In many respects, consistency functions as counterpoint to flexibility in promoting good adjustment. Flexibility allows people to shift their ideational perspective and alter their emotional tone in response to the varying demands of changing circumstances, and being flexible is what allows people to respond differently in different types of situations. Consistency, on the other hand, defines a cohesive personality style in which persistent preferences for certain basic ways of coping with experience contributes to people responding similarly in similar situations as they recur.

Flexibility and consistency in preferred patterns of coping are indicated on the RIM by the nature of the EB style. EB style indicators of flexibility have already been discussed in this chapter in relation to aspects of using ideation and modulating affect; specifically, the *EBPer* variable, whether identifying the subject as being pervasively introversive or pervasively extratensive, was identified as indicating a maladaptive lack of flexibility in coping style. From a positive perspective, adaptive flexibility is indicated in Rorschach data by a balanced *EB* style in which neither *M* nor *WSumC* is more than 2.5 times larger than the other. Consistency as well as flexibility is demonstrated when subjects avoid *EBPer* but still maintain sufficient preference for either ideational (*M*) or expressive (*WSumC*) modes to satisfy the criterion for being introversive or extratensive (i.e., a difference between *M* and *WSumC* greater than 1.5, or greater than 2.0 in records with *EA* > 10). Failure to show an introversive or extratensive pattern identifies the ambitent *EB* style, which is characterized not by adaptive flexibility but by maladaptive inconsistency.

Persons with a clearly defined but not pervasive introversive or extratensive *EB* style are typically capable of modifying their behavior as circumstances change. At times they make decisions by contemplating alternative possibilities in a deliberate manner, whereas at other times they allow their actions to be guided by how they feel rather than what they think. Sometimes they solve problems conceptually, by mulling over possible solutions in their minds, whereas at other times they seek solutions by trying out various courses of action. In being thus flexible, introversive and extratensive individuals employ a preference for either a primarily ideational or primarily expressive coping style and fairly consistently approach similar kinds of situations in similar ways. As a result, they tend to be reasonably predictable and dependable in how they conduct themselves. People who know them well generally know what to expect of them and how they are likely to respond to particular kinds of events, and introversive or extratensive individuals tend themselves to have a fairly clear sense of what kind of people they are, how various types of situations affect them, and how they are likely to behave from one situation to another.

By contrast, the lives of individuals with an ambitent *EB* style tend to be marked by inconsistent coping efforts, unpredictable behavior, and an uncertain self-image. They have difficulty making decisions, because they vacillate at length between following the dictates of their minds and the murmurings of their hearts. They solve problems neither by concerted efforts to conceptualize them nor by sustained trial-and-error experimentation, but rather by a hodgepodge of both methods that typically proves less efficient than either method used singly. They conduct themselves in highly variable and unpredictable ways, even in similar circumstances, and even those closest to them have difficulty anticipating what they are likely to say, do, think, or feel from one moment to the next. As for their self-image, ambitent people are often painfully aware of lacking clear commitment to any preferred coping style or set of values, and they may at times voice concerns about not knowing what kind of person they are or how they are likely to respond in various situations.

As would be expected, an ambitent *EB* style occurs more frequently in nonpatient young people, who are in the process of developing their preferred coping styles, than in nonpatient adults, who would ordinarily be expected to have theirs in place. Specifically, ambitent records occur in from 25% to 40% of nonpatient young people in the age groups from 5 to 14. By ages 15 and 16, however, the normative frequency of ambitence is down to approximately 20%, which is its frequency in nonpatient adults as well. Accordingly, the implications of an ambitent *EB* style for inconsistent coping style are less likely to be associated with adjustment difficulties in children and young adolescents than in older adolescents and adults. As for the maladaptive correlates of ambitence among adults, the Comprehensive System reference data indicate a 44% frequency of ambitence among outpatients and a 56% frequency among patients hospitalized with depression.

VIEWING ONESELF

Psychological adjustment is enhanced by individuals' capacities to view themselves in favorable ways that maintain adequate self-esteem and promote positive self-regard. Feeling satisfied with the characteristics they recognize in themselves gives people a sense of well-being and brings pleasure into their lives. People also benefit from being able to view themselves in thorough ways that enhance self-awareness and contribute to a stable sense of their identity. The more fully individuals' self-perceptions capture their nature, the more likely they are to feel familiar and comfortable with themselves. Limited or impaired capacities to view themselves favorably and thoroughly, on the other hand, make people susceptible to adjustment difficulties associated with negative self-attitudes and an insufficient grasp of the kind of person they are.

Maintaining Adequate Self-Esteem (*Fr + rF, 3r + (2)/R*)

Self-esteem consists of the attitudes people form toward their personal qualities and capabilities. The level of an individual's self-esteem derives largely from comparative judgments: The more favorably people compare themselves to others with respect to their qualities and capabilities, the higher their level of self-esteem; conversely, the more inclined people are to regard themselves as being less able, accomplished, or attractive than others, the lower their level of self-esteem. On the other hand, being beautiful, bright, or talented does not make a person intrinsically more worthy than anyone else or any more entitled to prosper and enjoy the good life. Likewise, being only moderately endowed with intelligence, good looks, and other enviable attributes does not diminish a person's worth or entitlement. Whether people think well or poorly of themselves is thus determined not so much by the quality of their attributes and accomplishments as it is by whether they perceive their attributes and accomplishments accurately and regard themselves as having made respectable use of their endowments and opportunities.

Consistent with this formulation, the purposes of good adjustment are served when people can maintain an adequate level of self-esteem that steers a broad middle ground between self-denigration and self-glorification. Adequate self-esteem promotes self-acceptance, self-respect, and self-confidence based on realistic appraisal of individuals' capabilities, and it contributes to their feeling generally satisfied with themselves and their actions. Individuals with adequate self-esteem do not underrate their attractiveness to other people or their abilities to succeed in various undertakings, and thereby become displeased with themselves and their efforts; and they do not overrate how appealing and talented they are, and thereby become enchanted with themselves and what they have done.

People with adequate self-esteem can also typically strike an adaptive balance between preoccupation with themselves at the expense of adequate attention to the needs and interests of others, on one hand, and total absorption in what other people want and enjoy at the cost of sufficient regard for their own preferences and individuality, on the other hand. This adaptive balance allows people with adequate self-esteem to avoid acting either as if they were the center around which all else revolves (a hallmark of inflated self-esteem), or as if their worthiness resided only in the importance of persons around whom they were able to revolve (a corollary of deficient self-esteem). Balanced attention to self and others and seeing oneself as being a worthy person are measured on the Rorschach by Reflections $(Fr + rF)$ and the Egocentricity Index $(3r + (2)/R)$.

$Fr + rF$. Reflection responses are associated with marked tendencies to overvalue personal worth and for individuals to become preoccupied with their own needs at the expense of concern about the needs of others. Only 7% of nonpatient adults give Reflection answers, which bears witness to an expectable association of $Fr + rF > 0$ with problematic rather than normative adjustment. Like features of color use, however, the occurrence of Reflections is an age-related phenomenon. Consistent with the fact that young people tend to be more self-centered than adults, children and adolescents give Reflections more frequently than their elders. Even so, $Fr + rF > 0$ remains normatively infrequent during the developmental years, with a rate ranging from 13% to 37% of nonpatients in the age groups from 5 to 16.

With few exceptions, people with $Fr + rF > 0$ in their records are self-centered individuals who have an inflated sense of their importance and an exalted estimate of their attributes. They tend to be selfish, self-serving, arrogant persons who assign higher priority to their own needs and interests than to those of others and are rarely drawn to acts of helpfulness and generosity that entail self-sacrifice. They characteristically externalize responsibility for their failures, deny shortcomings in themselves, and blame any difficulties they encounter on the actions of others or on events outside of their control. They approach life situations with an air of superiority and a sense of entitlement, as if whatever they want to have should be theirs for the asking and whatever they wish to enjoy should be placed at their disposal. Ordinarily they prefer to be in the limelight rather in the shadows, to be the focus of others' attention rather than a person invisible in the ranks, and to receive acclaim rather than go unnoticed. In these respects, then, subjects with Reflections in their Rorschach records usually show many characteristics commonly regarded as constituting narcissistic personality traits.

Counterintuitively, however, there does not appear to be any direct relation between the number of Reflection responses subjects give and how narcissistic they are likely to be. Giving any Reflections at all is a very stable phenomenon, and $Fr + rF > 0$ constitutes a trait variable that rarely changes over time. The number of Reflections in a record with $Fr + rF > 0$ is not particularly stable, however, and subjects who give one Reflection today may well give four tomorrow and two the next day. In other words, whether a subject gives Reflections at all is unlikely to vary over time, but the number of Reflections in the records of subjects who give them may change from one testing to another.

With respect to adjustment difficulties, the selfishness, self-admiration, sense of entitlement, and externalization of responsibility associated with $Fr + rF > 0$ often contribute to problematic interpersonal relationships and to unrealistic perspectives on success and failure. At a minimum, these characteristics may elicit negative reactions from people who find the narcissist's lack of humility and infrequent altruism objectionable or offensive, and they may lead to repetitive pursuit of goals beyond the narcissist's capacities—that is, biting off more than one can chew—and failure to learn anything from being unable to achieve these goals. In more extreme forms, the self-glorification associated with Reflection responses may participate in the unbridled optimism characteristic of hypomania, and the insensitivity to the needs of others typically shown by subjects who give Reflections may contribute to the flagrant callousness characteristic of psychopathy.

On the other hand, despite its frequent association with adjustment difficulties and forms of psychopathology, $Fr + rF > 0$ is not necessarily maladaptive, at least with respect to two kinds of circumstances. The first of these circumstances concerns people engaged in occupations or avocations in which chasing the spotlight and thriving on the adulation of others are not only appropriate and adaptive but also necessary for success. Among persons who perform for a living, for example, whether as showpeople or in other lines of work in which accomplishment depends on attracting the attention of others, enthusiasm for showing themselves off and being noticed is essential for enjoying their job and doing it well. Accordingly, $Fr + rF > 0$ and the narcissism it indicates is likely to foster comfortable adaptation among people whose work or hobbies call for putting themselves front and center and striving to bask in the admiration of others; conversely, the absence of Reflections in the records of those who are called on to perform may identify a potential source of uneasiness or dissatisfaction in their jobs or forms of recreation.

The second circumstance that may limit the maladaptive implications of $Fr + rF > 0$ involves a distinction between two groups of people who give Reflections: some who can be described as relatively "nice narcissists" and others who qualify for being labeled relatively "nasty narcissists." Nice narcissists are people who despite their self-centeredness show considerable genuine interest in others. Even while placing their own priorities first, nice narcissists enjoy being around other people and often work hard at being informative, entertaining, and ingratiating, as a way of ensuring an appreciative audience of listeners and observers who will gratify their needs for attention and admiration. Likewise, even though primarily concerned with getting their own needs met, these individuals may reach out and attach themselves to other people in a spirit of collaboration, as a way of sustaining interpersonal relationships on which they can depend for help and support. Most people have among their acquaintances nice narcissists of this type who are charming, likable, and entertaining but who can be expected to direct conversations to what they want to say about themselves and their experiences and to become restless and disinterested when other people are holding forth about matters of concern to them.

Nasty narcissists, by contrast, tend to be angry and avoidant individuals who have little genuine interest in other people and neither seek nor wish to have them as an audience or source of support. The interpersonal life of nasty narcissists is characterized by interpersonal distance, lack of close attachments, a competitive rather than collaborative orientation, and hostile intent to exploit and manipulate others to their own ends, without regret or remorse. This type of narcissism among people who give Reflections often has a distinctly psychopathic flavor. Although nasty narcissism may be disguised under a veneer of social conformity or even a pretense of altruistic motives, its psychopathic nature usually contributes to individuals being disliked or at least not socially sought after, and to various kinds of callous antisocial conduct that disregard the rights and feelings of others. The

Rorschach indices of interpersonal adaptation discussed in the final section of this chapter provide a good basis for distinguishing between nice and nasty patterns of narcissism.

3r + (2)/R. The Egocentricity Index provides a measure of the balance people strike between focusing on themselves and paying attention to others. In nonpatient adults $3r + (2)/R$ has a mean value of .40 and ordinarily ranges from .33 to .44. Scores in this middle range indicate people's adaptive inclination to attend to themselves sufficiently but not excessively. People with a moderate Egocentricity Index do not avoid focusing on themselves, nor do they become so self-absorbed as to ignore what is going on in the lives of other people. Consistent with developmental knowledge concerning the greater egocentricity of children than older people and the gradual diminution of egocentricity with maturation, $3r + (2)/R$ shows distinct age level differences. From a mean value of .69 among nonpatient 5-year-olds, $3r + (2)/R$ decreases in a steady linear fashion to a mean of .43 at age 16. Accordingly, the normative middle range for this variable among young people must be determined individually for each age by utilizing the mean and standard deviation values in the Comprehensive System reference data.

Adults in whom $3r + (2)/R < .33$, and young people in whom it falls more than one standard deviation below the mean for their age, are usually not paying sufficient attention to themselves and may even be purposefully avoiding self-focusing. More often than not, individuals' motivation for ignoring themselves in this way derives from a low estimate of their personal worth, or just the opposite of the inflated self-estimate associated with $Fr + rF > 0$. In the more specific terms used earlier, low Egocentricity subjects tend to compare themselves unfavorably to other people, whom they regard as being more able, more attractive, more talented, and generally more worthwhile than they are. For this reason, a low Egocentricity Index frequently identifies people's failure or inability to maintain adequate self-esteem and, because of the typically depressive impact of thinking poorly of themselves, serves as a *DEPI* criterion variable.

Of further importance with respect to the implications of low Egocentricity for adjustment difficulties is the fact that the level of $3r + (2)/R$ is highly stable over time, with retest correlations in adults of .90 over 3 weeks, .89 over 1 year, and .87 over 3 years. Consistent with what is known in general about the development and continuity of self-esteem as a personality trait characteristic, then, a low Egocentricity Ratio in the record of older adolescents and adults is unlikely to have emerged recently or in reaction to any current experiences of failure or inadequacy. Instead, low Egocentricity tends to be associated with chronically low self-esteem that dates back to childhood and ordinarily shows little situational fluctuation.

When $3r + (2)/R > .44$ in adults, or in young people exceeds their age-group mean by more than one standard deviation, Reflection responses are usually present. In this combination an elevated Egocentricity Index embellishes the narcissistic features suggested by $Fr + rF > 0$ by providing companion evidence of an unusual degree of preoccupation with oneself and a high level of self-esteem. Occasionally, however, subjects may produce a high Egocentricity Index in the absence of any Reflection responses. Whereas the high Egocentricity in such instances continues to point to inordinate preoccupation with oneself, the lack of Reflections signifies that individuals are not taking any special pleasure in their self-focusing. High Egocentricity without Reflections may thus be the Rorschach equivalent of paying a lot of attention to oneself but not enjoying it very much. It is as if high Egocentricity people with Reflections will frequently look at themselves in the mirror and like what they see there, whereas high Egocentricity people without Reflections will not like what they see when they look in the mirror but will nevertheless keep coming back to look some more. For this reason, the combination of high Egocentricity with $Fr + rF = 0$ appears to have the same implications as a low Egocentricity Index for unfavorable self-perception and is also a *DEPI* criterion variable.

Another possible combination of these two self-perception variables consists of an Egocentricity Index that is low despite the presence of Reflection responses. This apparent contradiction raises the possibility that the narcissism demonstrated by the subject's $Fr + rF > 0$ does not constitute a primary personality characteristic but instead has emerged secondarily as an effort to compensate for the limited self-esteem indicated by the low Egocentricity. In other terminology, this Rorschach pattern may be identifying how a "superiority complex" can arise as a way of denying, disguising, or defending against underlying feelings of inferiority. Accurate identification of such compensatory narcissism has important treatment implications, particularly with respect to avoiding challenges to narcissistic defenses that, if undermined, would leave the patient vulnerable to severe self-denigrating depression.

Promoting Positive Self-Regard (V, MOR)

Self-regard has many features in common with self-esteem, and the terms are often used synonymously. However, there is a subtle shade of difference in their meaning that has implications for the manner in which some personality characteristics foster good adjustment and others contribute to adjustment difficulties. Self-esteem, as just discussed, consists of the general value people place on themselves and is typically a stable trait characteristic that persists unchanged over time. Self-regard, on the other hand, can be usefully conceived as comprising numerous specific attitudes that people have toward themselves, some more favorable than others. Unlike level of self-esteem, which is a unitary characteristic with a single value, self-regard from this perspective is thus a composite of relatively positive and negative self-attitudes. Moreover, in contrast to the stable value judgment that defines the level of a person's self-esteem, the attitudes that constitute an individual's self-regard often fluctuate in response to changing circumstances.

In more specific terms, self-regard can be considered to embrace the varying attitudes that people form toward specific aspects of themselves and their actions. If asked, "What do you like and dislike about yourself?" most people will respond with a list of self-regard statements pertaining to their various physical, mental, or psychological characteristics: "I like my face;" "I wish I were taller"; "I'm pretty smart"; "I get embarrassed too easily'; "I'm a kind person." Similarly, if asked their opinion of things they have done, most people will present a range of positive and negative attitudes toward specific features of their conduct, past and present: "I'm proud of what I have accomplished in my work"; "I feel bad that I wasn't around more for my children"; "I played a great game yesterday"; "I did a stupid thing this morning."

Whether individuals' self-attitudes at a particular point in time are primarily favorable or unfavorable determines their overall level of self-regard, and positive self-regard, like adequate self-esteem, fosters good adjustment by helping people feel good about themselves. Primarily negative self-regard, on the other hand, contributes to adjustment problems associated with self-critical, self-denigrating, and self-loathing attitudes and with depression and suicidality. For purposes of differential diagnosis and treatment planning, personality descriptions of psychologically troubled people should go beyond indicating an overall level of self-regard to specify as much as possible the particular kinds of positive and negative attitudes that troubled people hold toward themselves and their actions.

Distinguishing between self-esteem and self-regard in this way helps to account for instances in which people who generally view themselves favorably nevertheless form specific negative attitudes toward something about themselves or what they have done. Even highly narcissistic people may at times regret a decision they made or some action they took that turned out not to have been in their best interests. Unlike people with chronically low self-esteem, however, narcissistic individuals who are berating themselves for having made a mistake do not allow such transient self-critical attitudes to diminish their overall sense of being superior and entitled individuals.

As a further illustration, people who view themselves as being worthwhile compared to others typically retain an adaptive level of self-esteem even when faced with changes in their bodies that generate negative attitudes toward their physical characteristics. Most persons have occasion to experience unwelcome alterations in how their bodies look and function. These bodily changes sometimes involve normal age-related developments, such as pubescent growth in a young person or thinning hair in an older one;

sometimes they result from accidents or illnesses producing malaise, inca-
pacitation, or disfigurement, such as visible scarring from a burn; and sometimes they emerge from traumatic experiences that cause concern about
the vulnerability of one's body to damage or dysfunction. Like negative
attitudes toward things people have done, concerns about the adequacy
and attractiveness of parts of their body can lead to painful affect and
various kinds of maladaptive behavior, such as shame and withdrawal,
without detracting from their general sense of comparing favorably to others as an able, decent, and worthwhile person.

It is because self-regard is more reactive to ongoing events and changing
circumstances than self-esteem and thus more likely to fluctuate over time
that the distinction between them facilitates understanding complex patterns of self-attitudes that comprise both favorable and unfavorable elements. For use in concert with Reflections and the Egocentricity Index as
measures of self-esteem, the Rorschach Vista (V) and Morbid (MOR) variables monitor aspects of self-regard.

V. Vista responses occur in just 19.5% of the records of nonpatient adults
and are even less frequent in young people. Nonpatients from age 5 to 11
hardly ever give V, and from age 12 to 16 the normative frequency of records
with $V > 0$ increases only gradually from 3.3% to 14.3%. V is a unidirectional
variable, and the normatively prevalent finding of $V = 0$ has no particular
significance as an index of high self-regard or good adjustment. However, V
> 0 is typically associated with self-critical attitudes that become increasingly
negative as V grows larger. The more V in a record, the more likely it is that
subjects' attitudes toward some aspects themselves or their actions have
progressed from displeasure and dissatisfaction to disgust and loathing.

Reliability data indicate a 1-year retest correlation of .87 for V, suggesting
that it is a highly stable determinant (J. E. Exner, 1997a). For purposes of
clinical interpretation, however, this large stability coefficient can be misleading. Because few adults and almost no young people normatively give
any V responses, the high frequency of $V = 0$ in both the first and second
records of subjects being retested guarantees a substantial correlation over
time. Moreover, there is reason to believe that $V > 0$ is neither stable nor
as trait-related as $Fr + rF > 0$. In particular, experiences in which people feel
regret or remorse have been found to increase the likelihood of V appearing
in their Rorschach. A case in point is the discovery of a notable frequency
of $V > 0$ in the records of clearly narcissistic, psychopathic prison inmates,
whose externalizing and self-righteous style would ordinarily be expected
to insulate them against self-criticism. Further investigation suggested that
these psychopaths with *Vista* had not retreated from their narcissistic stance
but were nevertheless upset with themselves for having been caught, con-

victed, and imprisoned for their offense. Hence, there may be instances when *V* responses occur on a reactive and transient basis in persons who are not ordinarily self-critical and may even continue to regard themselves as superior and entitled individuals.

With this in mind, the adjustment implications of $V > 0$ should be weighed in light of the Reflections and Egocentricity Index in subjects' records and their recent history. $Fr + rF = 0$ and either a low or high Egocentricity Index accompanying the presence of Vista points to chronic self-criticism and persistently poor self-regard as well as low self-esteem. Needless to say, such a combination contributes to susceptibility to dysthymia and recurrent depressive episodes, especially when there are no recent events in the person's recent life that can be identified as likely precipitants of remorse or regret. Conversely, the clearer the evidence for recent events that could have led to reactive self-recriminations, especially when $Fr + rF > 0$ and Egocentricity is elevated, the more likely it is that $V > 0$ is a clue to situationally related self-critical attitudes.

MOR. The presence of an inordinate number of *MOR* responses typically identifies individuals' negative and unfavorable attitudes held specifically toward their body and its functions. Like *V*, *MOR* is a unidirectional variable; a low frequency of *MOR* responses has no implications for personality strengths or assets other than freedom from the negative self-attitudes indicated when *MOR* are frequent. Among nonpatients, *MOR* shows a median frequency of zero in adults and in young people from age 11 to 16. From ages 5 to 10, the median frequency of *MOR* ranges from 0 to 2, and records in which $MOR > 2$ are infrequent at all ages. Accordingly, the presence of three or more *MOR* responses in a record indicates individuals' significant difficulty maintaining an adaptive level of self-regard, particularly as a consequence of viewing their body as damaged or dysfunctional.

Accurate interpretation of *MOR* responses requires more than tallying their frequency, however, for two reasons. First, even when they are infrequent, *MOR* responses (as noted in chap. 4) always involve some projected elements, and even a single *MOR* in a record may by virtue of its thematic content have implications for some specific negative self-attitude. Second, even when *MOR* are numerous, their implications for negative self-attitudes varies with their thematic content. Hence the discussion in this chapter of interpreting Rorschach structural variables shades at this point into the consideration of content themes, which is the topic of chapter 6. Proceeding for the moment in relatively structural terms, however, it is possible to differentiate two types of *MOR* responses that have somewhat different implications for negative body image.

One type of *MOR* conveys a clear sense of identification with the object seen and suggests that subjects see themselves in a similarly negative light.

Thus, contents described as damaged, diseased, dead, deformed, decrepit, broken, torn, tattered, or dysfunctional in some way give good reason to believe that subjects regard their own bodies either as having such undesirable characteristics or as being vulnerable to them. In the other type of *MOR*, subjects appear to be identifying not only with a damaged or dysfunctional object that has been the victim of some aggression, but at least in part with the perpetrator of the aggression as well.

Consider, for example, the common response to Card II of "Two animals who have been wounded and they are bleeding." This Morbid response suggests self-identification as a person who has been damaged or is vulnerable to being harmed. By contrast, seeing Card II as "Two animals bleeding, the way they look after I've shot 'em when I go hunting" suggests identification with the hunter rather than the hunted and with the aggressor rather than the victim. To be sure, identification with the aggressor is a complex psychological phenomenon, and, as a defensive maneuver, it may be more or less successful in eliminating self-perceptions of being damaged, dysfunctional, or vulnerable. Thus, a subject who reports "A squashed bug like I just stepped on it" may be identifying both with the bug and the squasher. Generally speaking, however, subjects who report just "A squashed bug," without any reference to a perpetrator, are likely to be less defended against negative self-attitudes and to feel more intensely concerned about the adequacy and integrity of their bodies than those who qualify their *MOR* responses with apparent identification with the aggressor as well.

Enhancing Self-Awareness (FD)

Viewing oneself adaptively involves maintaining a moderate level of self-awareness. As mentioned previously in using *FD* as an example of a tridirectional variable on the Rorschach, subjects' being sufficiently introspective to recognize their personal characteristics contributes to good psychological adjustment. Adequately introspective people tend to be cognizant of how best to meet their own needs, sensitive to how their behavior affects other people, and relatively amenable to reconsidering their image and impressions of themselves. When present, such capacity for introspection and self-awareness typically contributes to effective participation and positive personality change in psychotherapy (see Weiner, 1998a).

People who lack self-awareness, on the other hand, are at risk for adjustment difficulties involving inadequate understanding of themselves, insufficient appreciation of the impact they are likely to have on other people, and limited capacity to examine themselves in a critical fashion and modify their behavior accordingly. Excessive enthusiasm for introspection can also lead to adjustment difficulties, however. People who are overly aware of themselves are inclined to be self-conscious to a fault. Constantly examining themselves and ever alert to how they may look or sound to others, they have difficulty relaxing and just being themselves in a natural, unstudied, and unconcerned manner. Whereas the conversation of persons lacking in self-awareness rarely contains any statements of self-reflection (e.g., "I wonder why I said that?") or self-observation ("I notice that I'm drumming my fingers; I must be nervous"), the conversation of persons who are excessively introspective is often so peppered with such asides as to interfere with communication and make listeners uncomfortable.

The *FD* variable provides a Rorschach index of interest in and capacity for introspection. Consistent with developmental expectation, children from age 5 to 9 are not inclined to be introspective and rarely give *FD* responses; the median *FD* is zero at each of these ages. However, approximately 66% of 10- to 11-year-olds, 75% of 11- to 16-year-olds, and 79% of adults give *FD* responses, and the median frequency for adolescents and adults ranges from one to two. Accordingly, as noted earlier, $FD = 0$ in adolescents and adults suggests a maladaptive disinterest in or incapacity for being introspective, and $FD > 2$ is likely to be associated with an unusual degree of self-consciousness and soul-searching.

Forming a Stable Sense of Identity [*H:Hd + (H) + (Hd)*]

A stable sense of identity fosters good psychological adjustment by providing people a clear and consistent impression of the kind of individual they are, what they believe in, and where they have been and where they are going in their lives. Knowing oneself, being comfortable with oneself, having commitments to a set of values and purposes, and experiencing continuity between past, present, and future personal events define the essence of a stable sense of identity. Adequate self-esteem, positive self-regard, and sufficient self-awareness all contribute to people being able to form a sense of identity, which is a developmental process that typically culminates in the late adolescent and early adult years. The process of identity formation is facilitated when people have had opportunities to form identifications with real people in their lives after whom they could model themselves in some appropriate fashion. Beginning with Erikson's (1963) original conceptualization of identity formation, people's identities have in fact frequently been defined as the sum of all of their prior identifications.

The capacity to identify with real people and the likelihood of having done so are reflected in the Rorschach by the Interpersonal Interest variable in the Comprehensive System, which is the ratio of the number of whole and real human figures (*H*) seen to the number of partial or imaginary human figures [*Hd + (H) + (Hd)*]. Adaptive identifications are indicated on this variable by the presence of at least two *H* responses and a total number of *H* that equals or exceeds the number of [*Hd + (H) + (Hd)*]. Subjects with a sufficient frequency of H to meet these criteria typically have adequate capacity to identify comfortably with people who are a real part of their lives and have had opportunities to form such identifications. This combination of identificatory capacity and opportunity provides the foundations for developing a clear and stable sense of personal identity.

Consistent with developmental expectations concerning identity formation, the frequency of H shows some age-related trends. Although almost all subjects at all ages give at least one H, the occurrence of $H < 2$ increases from just 10% among nonpatient adults and 16-year-olds to 17% to 25% among 11- to 15-year-olds and exceeds 25% among children below age 11. On the other hand, the mean number of H equals or exceeds the mean number of $[Hd + (H) + Hd)]$ for every age group in the reference samples except 7-year-olds. Accordingly, $H < 2$ is likely among adults to indicate insufficient identifications on which to base a stable sense of self but should be interpreted more conservatively in this regard among young people. At all ages, however, an adequately established or normally forming identity may be lacking when H, whatever its frequency, is less numerous than $[Hd + (H) + (Hd)]$.

This interpretive significance of $H < [Hd + (H) + (Hd)]$ derives from the likelihood that a Rorschach protocol containing more partial and imaginary human figures than whole and real human figures suggests maladaptive tendencies to identify with partial objects or with people who do not participate in the subject's everyday real world. In the case of partial figures, it may well be that subjects who give an inordinate number of human detail responses are correspondingly inclined to identify selectively with some but not other characteristics of people to whom they become close, much in the manner of individuals who engage excessively in object splitting. As for imaginary figures, subjects with many such percepts may for various reasons be finding it more difficult or uncomfortable to identify with people with whom they actually have regular interaction than with fictitious or remote characters, such as famous figures from the past, heroes in novels and soap operas, and celebrities from the world of sports or entertainment. Modeling oneself after such fictitious or remote characters could have the benefit of resulting in emulation of positive characteristics they display, but doing so contributes much less to a stable sense of identity than modeling oneself after a parent, sibling, teacher, or good friend with whom one has a close, enduring, and regularly interactive relationship.

RELATING TO OTHERS

The way in which people relate to others is determined by the attitudes they have toward other people, the degree of interaction they have with them, and the manner in which they approach and manage interpersonal attachments. Adaptive interpersonal relationships are characterized by the abilities (a) to sustain a reasonable level of interest, involvement, and comfort in interacting with other people; (b) to anticipate intimacy and security in these interpersonal interactions; (c) to balance collaboration and acquiescence with competitiveness and assertiveness in relating to other people; and (d) to perceive people and social situations in an accurate and empathic manner. Psychological adjustment accordingly suffers when people become disinterested, disengaged, or uncomfortable in social situations; when they prefer distance over closeness to others and come to regard interpersonal closeness as threatening rather than supportive; when they become subservient or domineering to an extent that precludes comfort and mutuality in interpersonal relations and casts the individual as either a psychologically abused or psychologically abusive person; and when they misinterpret the motives and others and the implications of interpersonal events.

Sustaining Interpersonal Interest, Involvement, and Comfort (*SumH, [H:Hd + (H) + (Hd)], ISOL*)

People live in an interpersonal world, and the common experience of all people attests the vital role of company and companionship in keeping one's peace of mind and sense of well-being. Few punishments are more harsh than solitary confinement, few characters are more sympathetic than Robinson Crusoe before he found Friday, and few individuals are more removed from living the good life than those who by design or misfortune must pass their days in seclusion. To adjust adequately to their circumstances and find satisfaction in their lives, people need to be interested in being around other people and comfortable in interacting with others in a variety of situations and pursuits.

The Interpersonal Interest variable on the RIM, which was discussed in the previous section in relation to its implications for identity formation, also provides information concerning the extent to which people are attentive to and feel comfortable in relationships with others. Subjects indicate their level of attentiveness to others by the total number of human contents they give (*SumH*), including whole, partial, real, and imaginary figures. Nonpatient adults and young people beginning at age 9 average between five and six human contents in their records, and mean *SumH* is just slightly under five among 5- to 8-year-olds. Generally speaking, then, a *SumH* > 3 identifies average or more than average interpersonal interest and constitutes a personality asset, whereas a *SumH* < 4 indicates limited interest in people and constitutes a personality liability.

As for comfort in interpersonal relationships, a surplus of [*Hd* + *(H)* + *(Hd)*] over *H* responses suggests not only the deficiencies in identification noted in the previous section, but also a maladaptive extent of social discomfort. Persons with this imbalance in their human contents typically experience uneasiness in dealing with people who are real, live, and fully functional, that is, who literally have all of their parts in place and in working order. At a fantasy level, such individuals may well be attempting to minimize feelings of threat or inadequacy in interpersonal situations by limiting the capabilities they perceive in them, which they can do by seeing them as being not really human or all there. It is as if by saying, "You're a fictitious person," or "You're dead," or "You don't have any feet to stand on or arms to do anything with" the interpersonally uncomfortable person can conclude, "So you can't do anything to harm me or embarrass me."

In the absence of adequate capacities to sustain interest and comfort in interpersonal relationships, people are at substantial risk for maladaptive patterns of withdrawn and avoidant behavior that may culminate in interpersonal isolation as well as social disinterest and discomfort. The Isolation Index (*ISOL*), being based on the frequency of five contents that are devoid of people (Botany, Clouds, Geography, Landscape, and Nature), provides a useful measure of interpersonal isolation. *ISOL* is a unidirectional variable that has no particular implications for personality strengths when it is low; when elevated, on the other hand, *ISOL* is typically associated with limited interpersonal interest and minimal social interaction.

ISOL as a percentage of *R* has a mean of .20 among nonpatient adults and averages .20 or less among young people from age 9 to 16. Among the 5- to 8-year-old groups in the reference sample, mean *ISOL* ranges from .17 to .25. Generally speaking, a weighted sum of the *ISOL* contents ($Bt + 2Cl + Ge + Ls + 2Na$) greater than one fourth of *R*, especially in adolescents and adults, indicates maladaptive social withdrawal and interpersonal isolation. At all ages, $ISOL > .33$ should be taken as an index of either marked avoidance of social interaction or of markedly deficient opportunities for interpersonal contact. In this latter regard, subjects with an elevated *ISOL* are not infrequently found to be individuals who, even while in the company of an apparently ample number of acquaintances or family members, have very few people who play an important part in their lives.

Anticipating Interpersonal Intimacy and Security (*SumT, HVI*)

People who are well-adjusted typically expect to form close relationships with other people and relish opportunities for doing so. Close interpersonal relationships define the nature of *intimacy*, which can occur on either a physical or psychological basis. People who hold and touch each other in a fond, caressing manner are involved in an intimate relationship, as are those who feel spiritually at one with each other and share their innermost secrets. The basic capacity to establish intimate relationships ordinarily emerges early in life, in the form of bonds of attachment between young children and their primary caretakers, and the capacity to attach oneself to significant others in close and mutually supportive relationships continues throughout the life cycle to foster successful adaptation and a sense of well-being.

Looking forward to opportunities for intimacy defines the nature of *security* in interpersonal relationships. Like the capacity for attachment, feeling secure in close relationships develops early in life, as a consequence of consistently nurturing experiences that promote a child's sense of trust in other people. Individuals who have developed the capacity for trust feel secure in the expectation that close relationships will add pleasure and richness to their lives without posing any threat to their safety and peace of mind. Security in interpersonal relatedness accordingly leads people to reach out for interpersonal relationships, to prefer engaging others close up rather than at a distance, and to regard intimacy as an opportunity to be cherished rather than as a danger to be avoided.[1] Two Rorschach variables that can often provide useful information concerning interpersonal intimacy and security are *T* and *HVI*.

T. Apparently because of its being coded for responses involving a tactual sensation (i.e., some property of an object that people can touch and feel), the Texture (*T*) determinant has implications literally for interest in reaching out and touching someone, whether physically or psychologically. Consistent with the expectation that normally functioning people have the capacity to form attachments to other people, almost all nonpatient subjects have some *T* in their record. In the reference data for nonpatients, the frequency of records with $T = 0$ is just 11% in adults; less than 10% at ages 7, 8, 15, and 16; and between 12% and 18% for all other ages except 5-year-olds, of whom 37% have *T*-less records. The presence of *T* provides a good indication of adaptive capacity to anticipate and establish close, intimate, and mutually supportive relationships with other people. Generally speaking, people who give *T* responses are likely not only to enjoy but to need, want, and reach out for physical and/or emotional closeness to others.

T is a complex variable, however, and its interpretive significance is tridirectional. Most nonpatients give just one Texture, and both $T = 0$ and $T > 1$ are unusual findings that have implications for adjustment problems. The absence of *T* typically indicates basic impairment in the capacity to form close attachments to other people. *T*-less individuals do not necessarily avoid interpersonal relationships, and, if their level of interpersonal interest is at least average, they may be as likely as people in general to have friends

---

[1] These comments on attachment, intimacy, security, and trust reflect the formulations of Erikson (1963) and Sullivan (1953), whose seminal contributions on the dynamics of interpersonal relatedness are acknowledged with appreciation.

and acquaintances and even to fall in love and marry. However, their relationships tend to be distant and detached, rather than close and intimate; their friendships tend to develop with people who share their preference for relating at arms' length rather than up close; and their marriages, if successful, are typically to spouses who are comfortable with companionship, mutual respect, and shared interests but for whom neither love nor marriage involves much personal intimacy.

Individuals with no T in their records typically feel uncomfortable in proximity to those who give Texture, because they experience them as intrusive kinds of people who encroach on their privacy and personal space and have excessive expectations of physical and psychological closeness. T-less persons themselves neither anticipate nor seek out intimate interpersonal relationships; even while sometimes giving lip service to or actually deluding themselves into believing that they would really like to have such relationships, they remain aversive to and unable to enjoy being in them. From the perspective of $T > 0$ people who befriend or marry T-less persons, these friends and spouses are likely to be experienced as cold, distant, remote, and undemonstrative people, even though they may be loyal friends and loving spouses.

The likelihood that limited capacity to form attachments and aversion to intimacy will be associated with adjustment difficulties is reflected in the available reference data for nonpatient and patient adults. Whereas $T = 0$ occurs in just 11% of nonpatient records, the frequency of T-less records increases to 57% in inpatient depressives, 64% in outpatients, 70% in inpatient schizophrenics, and 72% in character disorders. Not surprisingly, absence of T is particularly common, indeed characteristic, of patients with paranoid and antisocial disorders, both of which are defined in large part by distrust or disavowal of close attachments to other people (see Gacono & Meloy, 1994).

As for elevations in T, a finding of $T > 1$ typically indicates that individuals are experiencing more needs for closeness to other people than are being met in their present circumstances. Elevated T has at times been described as signifying an "affect hunger," and $T > 1$ can indeed be taken as a clue to a person's feeling emotionally deprived and interpersonally needy. In addition to identifying a painful emotional state of loneliness, having more than one Texture response sometimes motivates maladaptive behaviors that arise as efforts to alleviate the psychological pain associated with $T > 1$. In particular, $T > 1$ people are at risk for reaching out desperately and indiscriminantly for close relationships, and their interpersonal neediness may transcend their better judgment. Should this happen, they may become involved in embarrassing, unrewarding, exploitative, or promiscuous entanglements that bring new difficulties into their lives as the price of their finding some fleeting surcease of loneliness.

T is additionally a complex variable in the sense that, in the same manner as *V*, it has both trait and state features. *T* is a very stable variable, with a 1-year retest correlation of .91, and whether or not people have *T* in their records rarely changes over time. Texture, like the capacity to form attachments that it represents, rarely disappears once it has been established, regardless of whatever disappointing or unpleasant interpersonal circumstances a person may encounter. The absence of Texture may sometimes give way to an intensive encounter with a compelling figure of identification with whom previously unattached persons form their first intimate relationship, as for example with a therapist. By and large, however, such a major change in interpersonal orientation becomes increasingly unlikely to occur spontaneously and increasingly difficult to promote psychotherapeutically as children grow into adolescents and then adults. Accordingly, both $T = 0$ and $T > 0$ constitute trait variables.

On the other hand, among persons who give Texture ($T > 0$), the number of *T* they give is responsive to situational events. Most importantly in this regard, persons who are attached to other people ordinarily experience emotional deprivation and a temporary increase in their needs for closeness and affection when they suffer an object loss, as through death of or separation from a loved one or some other interruption of a valued relationship, and such experiences of loss often produce a corresponding elevation of *T* in their Rorschach. *T*-less people do not show *T* in reaction to such events, apparently because such people do not experience object loss in the same psychologically painful and needy way as do people who have Texture to begin with.

Accordingly, $T > 1$ is very likely to identify a distressing state of experienced deprivation and need for closeness that has arisen in response to some actual, fantasied, or threatened loss of a valued relationship. Reactive depressions frequently emerge in this way, and an elevated *T* may often help to identify a situationally determined depressive disorder in subjects who do not elevate on *DEPI*, which consists mainly of trait variables and is more sensitive to endogenous than to reactive depression. Occasionally, persons with $T > 1$ will be chronically needy individuals who show a lifelong pattern of always feeling interpersonally deprived and never getting enough intimacy into their lives, no matter how many close relationships they actually have formed. In most instances, however, elevated *T* should be interpreted as a sign of emotional distress secondary to object loss within recent months and should prompt inquiry into the nature of this loss if it is not already known.

HVI. The Hypervigilance Index (*HVI*) is a unidirectional variable that has no particular implications for successful adaptation when it is absent but strongly suggests problematic interpersonal relatedness when it occurs. Like

EB style and an elevated *Lambda*, a positive *HVI* identifies not merely some individual personality state or trait, but instead bears witness to a pervasive frame of reference that colors many different facets of a person's behavior. In persons who are hypervigilant, this frame of reference revolves around being inordinately alert to potential sources of danger or threat in their environment, usually as a consequence of feeling unable to trust the motives of others and depend on the safety of their surroundings.

More specifically, *HVI* is associated with an approach to the world in which people's close interpersonal relationships are discomfiting, viewed with alarm, and avoided in favor of keeping their distance from others, carefully guarding the boundaries of their personal space, and taking pains to preserve their privacy. In addition, because they view the world as dangerous and other people as duplicitous, individuals who are hypervigilant approach and assess people and situations cautiously, often suspiciously, before making any commitments to them. Usually concerned about needing to protect themselves, they typically conduct their lives in a guarded fashion, taking few risks and keeping their thoughts and feelings largely to themselves.

Consistently with these corollaries and its broad stylistic implications, *HVI* is a multifaceted variable that cuts across three dimensions of personality functioning. The most important of these is the dimension of relating to others that is discussed here. The centrality of interpersonal insecurity in being hypervigilant is reflected in the fact that $T = 0$ is a requisite variable for coding *HVI*. Of the seven other *HVI* variables, at least four of which in addition to $T = 0$ must be present to demonstrate a positive *HVI*, four are also related to interpersonal functioning. These include $[H + (H) + Hd + (Hd)] > 6$, which indicates paying considerable attention to people; $[(H) + (A) + (Hd) + (Ad)] > 3$, which indicates strong need to protect or distance oneself from figures by seeing them as imaginary rather than real; $H + A{:}Hd + Ad < 4{:}1$, which indicates a protective or perhaps hypercritical focus on parts of figures rather wholes; and $Cg > 3$, which, depending on the context of the response, can indicate concerns about protecting oneself (e.g., "A man wearing a helmet and a suit of armor") or concerns about not being able to see people clearly and thus discern their motives (e.g., "They're wearing cloaks, so I can't see what kind of people they are").

Two other *HVI* variables relate to the previously discussed dimension of adaptation that concerns how people pay attention to their world. These variables are a *Z*-frequency $(Zf) > 12$ and a $Zd > +3.5$. This type of organizational activity in the Rorschach identifies unusually strong inclinations to attend to how events relate to each other and to search out the environment carefully and thoroughly before coming to closure about what it may contain. Attending to experience in this overincorporative way has obvious implications for a hypervigilant style of confronting the world.

The remaining *HVI* variable is $S > 3$, which was discussed previously in the context of the affective dimension of adaptation. As noted then, elevated *S* identifies underlying anger or resentment that is usually being channeled in some maladaptive way. Anger plays a role in hypervigilance by virtue of projection, in the classical psychodynamic sense of projective defense. When people project, feelings of anger and the hostility they breed are likely to be disavowed by attributing them to other people, who are then regarded as angry or hostile individuals whose motives cannot be trusted and who constitute a potential threat to one's security.

Consistently with the implications of hypervigilance for substantial adjustment difficulties, *HVI* rarely occurs in nonpatients of any age. Only 2% of the adults in the normative reference sample are positive for *HVI*, the age groups from 11 to 16 show a 0% to 3% frequency of this variable, and positive *HVI* is completely absent from the records of 5- to 10-year-olds. *HVI* is also relatively infrequent among the patient groups in the reference data: 18% in inpatient schizophrenics, 10% in inpatient depressives, 7% in character disorders, and 4% in outpatients. On the other hand, J. E. Exner (1993, p. 439) reported finding a positive *HVI* in 88% of a sample of subjects diagnosed as paranoid schizophrenic and in 90% of a sample of patients with paranoid personality disorder. Hence, although *HVI* is not necessarily indicative of paranoia, it does capture the type of interpersonal insecurity and hyper-alertness to danger that typify paranoid tendencies, and paranoid persons can be expected with few exceptions to show this Rorschach variable.

Balancing Interpersonal Collaboration and Acquiescence With Competitiveness and Assertiveness (*COP, AG, a:p*)

A repetitive theme in this chapter's presentation of dimensions of adaptation has been the centrality of balance in promoting good psychological adjustment. This final part concludes on this note with respect to the balance people strike between being cooperative and acquiescent in their relationships with others or being competitive and assertive. Clearly a broad range of normality exists in this regard. Among happy and successful people there are many who are relatively easygoing and subservient in their interpersonal relationships and many others who are relatively hard-driving and domineering. Only when one of these preferred styles of relating becomes exaggerated at the expense of the other are people likely to conduct their lives in maladaptive ways. Various aspects of this personality characteristic are measured on the Rorschach by the *COP, AG,* and *a:p* variables.

COP. Cooperative Movement (*COP*) responses signal an interest in collaborative engagements with others. As would be expected from the normality of such interest, *COP* has a mean frequency of 2.07 in nonpatient adults, almost 80% of whom have at least one *COP* in their record. *COP* is even more common in young people, among whom *COP* > 0 characterizes from 84% to 97% of nonpatient records for the age groups from 5 to 16. Generally speaking, subjects with one or two *COP* responses tend to view interactions among people in positive ways and to participate in them willingly. Because their words and deeds typically communicate to others their positive interpersonal orientation and openness to collaboration, such people usually enjoy an at least average extent of social acceptance and popularity.

COP functions as a bidirectional variable, and persons with more than an average number of *COP* responses tend to be notably successful in their social lives, other things being equal. Thus, *COP* > 2 is commonly associated with being regarded as likable and outgoing and being sought after as a friend or companion. The considerable popularity frequently enjoyed by high *COP* people appears to derive from their strong commitment to being agreeable and cooperative, their customary anticipation of friendly interactions, and their high level of interest in seeking out harmonious relationships with others.

The absence of *COP*, by contrast, identifies a maladaptive deficiency in the capacity to anticipate and engage in collaborative activities with others. Unlike the positive interpersonal messages communicated by people who give *COP*, subjects in whom *COP* = 0 typically convey to others a disinterest in or even a distaste for doing things together in mutually cooperative ways. As a consequence, no-*COP* individuals tend to impress others as being distant or aloof, and, although they may not be actively disliked, they are unlikely to be popular or enthusiastically received members of their social group. The personality characteristics indicated by *COP* = 0 do not necessarily prevent people from forming close interpersonal relationships, especially if they have a *T* in their record. However, in combination with an elevated *ISOL* and a low *SumH*, lack of *COP* often indicates interpersonal avoidance and withdrawal.

AG.   Responses containing Aggressive Movement (*AG*) identify an expectation that interactions in the real world are likely to be assertive or at least competitive, rather than collaborative and acquiescent. Although *AG* responses often involve anger and hostility, as when they are coded for "Two angry bears fighting," they may also invoke struggle without rancor, as in "Two guys arm wrestling to see who is stronger." This diversity in the coding of *AG* reflects the fact that people can and do act aggressively without being angry. Because aggression is often taken to imply anger, however, there is some advantage to referring more generally to the assertive than to the aggressive implications of *AG* responses. Thus, the preferred way to interpret *AG* responses is as an indication of inclinations to display either verbal or nonverbal assertive behavior.

Like some anticipation of collaboration in interpersonal interactions, some inclination to be assertive is normally to be expected in people. Consistent with this expectation, *AG* shows a median frequency of 1.0 in nonpatient adults and at every age from 5 to 16, with the exception of median frequencies of 0 at age 6, 2.0 at age 9, and 1.5 and age 10. Absence of *AG* is found in just one third of nonpatient adults and even less frequently in children and adolescents. With respect to interpretive significance, a finding of *AG* > 2 falls beyond the normal range and indicates for persons at all ages substantially more than usual likelihood of behaving in an assertive fashion. Only 14% of nonpatient adults show *AG* > 2, whereas its frequency ranges from 7% to 16% among 8- to 16-year-old nonpatients, and from just 3% to 5% of 5- to 7-year-old nonpatients.

An elevation in *AG* can participate in a variety of adjustment problems in which possibilities for pleasant interpersonal relationships are undermined by seeing the world as a dog-eat-dog place, anticipating adversarial and antagonistic interactions when people get together, and behaving in an inordinately aggressive, belligerent, or domineering manner. As one extreme case in point, antisocial criminals convicted of violent crimes not uncommonly have numerous *AG* responses in their records. On the other hand, being a high *AG* person is not always or necessarily maladaptive. Just as being an overincorporator may foster success in people whose work involves keeping careful records, and just as having Reflections can increase the pleasure of people who perform for a living or as a hobby, numerous *AG* contents sometimes identify a personality asset among people whose daily responsibilities call for them to take charge, be in control, and tell other people what to do. Interesting in this regard is the fact that *AG* > 2 has been found more frequently than would be expected in nonpatients among such vocational groups as surgeons, police officers, professional football players, and clergy (J. E. Exner, 1993, p. 528).

In addition, the usual implications of *AG* > 2 for problematic interpersonal relationships can be offset by two other features of the data. First, high *AG* individuals who also give *COP* are demonstrating capacity to envision cooperative as well as competitive exchanges among people. Second, when people with *AG* > 2 do not show any elevation in *S*, the likelihood is minimized that their assertiveness is fueled by anger. In these circumstances, high *AG* people may be comfortable in their interpersonal relationships as well as satisfied with their work. On the other hand, little is known at present about the adaptive capacities of subjects who give no *AG* responses at all. Whereas high *AG* people with no *COP* may be too competitive for their own good and too lacking in a cooperative and acquiescent spirit to form enjoyable interpersonal relationships, people with *AG* = 0 may lack sufficient assertiveness to stand up for themselves when they should and to avoid being exploited and manipulated by others. In the absence of data to validate this hypothesis concerning $AG = 0$, maladaptive passivity can be inferred with confidence from the $a{:}p$ ratio discussed next.

$a{:}p$. The ratio of active to passive movement responses ($a{:}p$) in a protocol was discussed previously with respect to the implications for cognitive inflexibility when either a or p is more than twice as large as the other. The $a{:}p$ ratio also has implications for social relatedness, especially with respect to identifying people who are likely to be inordinately acquiescent in their interpersonal relationships.

Active movement responses are normatively much more frequent than passive movement responses. The mean value for a is almost three times the mean value for p in nonpatient adults (6.48:2.69), and mean a ranges from two to five times larger than mean p in the 5-year-old to 16-year-old age groups. Accordingly, a surplus of active over passive movements constitutes normative expectation, and $a > p$ does not have any positive interpretive significance. Even when a responses are many times more numerous than p responses, there is no basis for inferring that subjects are any more active, assertive, or energetic in their interpersonal relationships than people in general. The $a{:}p$ ratio is thus a unidirectional variable, and records in which active movements are as numerous as passive movements or no more than one fewer do not identify any particular personality characteristic or asset except the absence of passivity. However, when passive movements outnumber active movements by more than one, the data indicate maladaptive tendencies to be subservient and dependent in relating to others.

Specifically, $p > a + 1$ is an unusual finding that occurs in just 1% of nonpatient adults. Children and adolescents are slightly more likely than adults to show this result, but the frequency of $p > a + 1$ ranges only from 6% to 14% among the age groups from 5 to 16. Generally speaking, then, people at all ages who give this preponderance of passive movements are likely to be behaviorally passive in their interpersonal relationships. Such people are inclined to subjugate their needs and wishes to those of others, to defer in their choices to what others prefer, and to accommodate their actions to satisfy the requests of those around them. High p individuals frequently lead their lives at the pleasure of others on whom they depend. They are more comfortable being followers than leaders, they shrink from taking initiative, and they feel most comfortable when other people make their decisions for them and also remove from their shoulders the responsibility for these decisions.

Remaining Interpersonally Empathic (Accurate M)

Adequate empathic capacity makes an important contribution to good social and interpersonal adjustment. Accurate empathy, defined as being able to put oneself into other peoples' shoes and appreciate how they feel, helps individuals understand the nature and actions of people with whom they interact. This understanding in turn increases the likelihood of a person's interpreting social situations accurately and responding appropriately to them. Conversely, people who are prone to misjudge the attitudes and intentions of others and to forming inaccurate impressions of situations in which they are involved are at risk for feeling uncomfortable and responding inappropriately in the company of others.

With respect to its manifestations on the Rorschach, empathic capacity is a subset of the form-level indices of perceptual accuracy discussed earlier in this chapter. Specifically, the form level of responses involving human movement (M) typically provide information about the accuracy of subjects' social perception and their ability to form realistic impressions of people and interpersonal events. Accurately seen M responses ($M+$, Mo, and Mu) identify empathic capacity, whereas perceptually distorted M responses ($M-$) indicate deficient empathy.

As would be expected, the frequency with which subjects give M responses varies with their EB style. Among nonpatient adults in the reference samples, introversives have a mean M of 6.40 and extratensives a mean M of 2.89. Introversive people are not necessarily any more empathic than extratensive people, however, and what is critical in the reference data is just a 3.2% frequency of giving $M-$ responses among the introversives and a 0% frequency among the extratensives. Young people are somewhat more likely to give $M-$ responses than adults, but the percentage of those doing so remains small: 5.0% to 21.7% among 5- to 12-year-olds and 9.3% to 11.8% among 13- to 16-year-olds. As for the total number of M in their records, the mean is just under two in 5- and 6-year-olds, increases to above three among 7- to 10-year-olds, and exceeds four among 11- to 16-year-olds.

Accordingly, there is reason to believe that two or more accurately perceived M identifies adequate capacity for empathy at all ages, whereas $M- > 1$, which constitutes a criterion score on $SCZI$, indicates a maladaptive impairment of social perception. The frequencies of giving $M-$ responses among the patient sample in the reference data are 28.1% in outpatients, 31.7% in the character disorder group, 40.3% in the inpatient depressives, and 80.0% in the inpatient schizophrenics. The more $M-$ responses there are in a record, the more likely and more severely the subject is likely to be having adjustment difficulties attributable in part to faulty perception of people and social interactions.

In concluding this chapter, it is finally important to comment further on the numerous distinctions that have been drawn between stable, persistent, and trait aspects of the Rorschach structural data, such as a low Egocentricity Ratio and an elevated *Lambda*, and situational, reactive, and state features of the data, such as m and elevations in T and V. Although trait variables are by definition and as indicated by their stability coefficients unlikely to change over time, almost any Rorschach indicator of maladaptive personality characteristics can be modified by psychotherapeutic intervention. As cases in point, Weiner and Exner (1991) found that dynamic psychotherapy reduced the frequency with which a group of patients showed $3r + 2/R < .33$, *Lambda* $> .99$, *Afr* $< .50$, and $p > a + 1$, all of which are highly stable variables.

6

Interpreting Content Themes

As elaborated in chapter 1, the Rorschach Inkblot Method (RIM) is best conceived as a measure of perception and association in which the way people structure their response process provides information about structural features of their personality functioning and the thematic imagery they produce reveals aspects of their underlying personality dynamics. The discussion in chapter 4 of the complementary roles of projection and card pull in shaping Rorschach responses speaks further to the utility of distinguishing perceptual and associational aspects of the response process. However, as noted in chapter 2, there is no mutually exclusive relation between perceptual structuring and personality structure, on the one hand, and between thematic imagery and personality dynamics, on the other hand. Thus, for example, a large number of *An* responses, which is a structural variable, is likely to identify people's underlying concerns about the functioning of their body, which is a personality dynamic; repetitive thematic imagery involving aggressive interactions suggests a generally assertive nature, which is a structural personality feature.

As these examples indicate, the content of Rorschach responses provides a bridge between structural and thematic aspects of the data, particularly as the focus of interpretation shifts from content categories to content themes. The discussion of structural variables in the preceding chapter addresses the interpretive significance of several content categories, including the number of *H* in a record, the ratio of *H* to *Hd + (H) + (Hd)*, and the presence of three indices based entirely or in part on content categories— *ISOL (Bt, Cl, Ge, Ls, Na)*, *INTELL (Art, Ay)*, and *HVI (Cg)*. As informative as it may be, attention to these content categories only begins to tap the richness of Rorschach data with respect to delineating the personality dynamics that constitute subjects' inner life—that is, the nature of their underlying needs, attitudes, conflicts, and concerns.

In the first place, whatever the significance of the frequency with which a content category occurs, uncoded specifications of the particular content can provide important additional information. As was suggested in chapter 5, for example, a *Cg* response involving "fancy dresses" (which serve a decorative purpose) is likely to differ in dynamic significance from a *Cg* response of "helmets" (which serve a protective purpose). Second, unelaborated contents that do not generate a noteworthy structural score may nevertheless have considerable dynamic import. Consider the implications for feelings of isolation in a subject who does not have an elevated *ISOL* but who nevertheless gives three *Ge* responses, each of which is "an island." Similarly, subjects who are in fact given to aggressive behavior may show little elevation in *AG* as a result of giving a high *Lambda* or a pervasively extratensive record containing few movement responses.

Third, even though several of the structural variables discussed in chapter 5 are coded on the basis of thematic imagery (i.e., *MOR*, *COP*, *AG*, the *a:p* and *Ma:Mp* ratios, and the Critical Special Scores), the tabulation of their frequency does not identify the specific content of the elaborations they contain. Fourth and finally, although complex coding schemes can be devised to capture aspects of the ways in which responses are embellished with thematic imagery (as noted in chap. 4), idiographic and psychodynamically significant features of the manner in which subjects elaborate their Rorschach responses may defy being easily or profitably reduced to structural codes.

With these considerations in mind, the present chapter moves on from the tabulation of content categories to interpretive utilization of content themes. Useful interpretation of content themes consists of the following four procedures: (a) identifying the responses in a record most likely to be rich in thematic imagery; (b) reading these responses and generating associations to them; (c) drawing on these associations to formulate hypotheses concerning a subject's personality characteristics; and (d) determining the plausibility of these hypotheses on the basis of general considerations for judging the adequacy of thematic interpretations. This chapter discusses each of these steps in interpreting content themes and concludes with some guidelines for assigning meaning to specific types of thematic imagery.

IDENTIFYING RESPONSES RICH IN THEMATIC IMAGERY

With respect to the richness of their thematic imagery for generating hypotheses about personality dynamics, all responses are not created equal. Some responses reveal numerous facets of a subject's inner life, some warrant modest speculation concerning a few aspects of the person's moti-vational makeup, and some say little or nothing about the individual's un-derlying characteristics. As indicated in chapter 4, the responses in a record that are most likely to be dynamically revealing and are accordingly most fruitful to examine for their thematic imagery are those that involve projec-tion. The more projected elements there are in a response, and the less the response is determined by card pull, the more information the thematic content of the response is likely to provide concerning an individual subject's underlying needs, attitudes, conflicts, and concerns.

The benefits of focusing on selected responses for the interpretation of thematic imagery is consistent with the point made previously that the RIM is not solely a projective instrument. Responses can be formulated on the basis of card pull and delivered without projection, that is, without attrib-uting any characteristics to the inkblots that are not already in them; an entire record produced in this way, although unusual and perhaps some-what sterile, can be valid and interpretable. Typically, however, protocols contain a mix of responses, some of which involve no projection, some a little projection, and some a great deal of projection. In interpreting content themes, examiners need accordingly to determine how much attention and how much weight to give to the thematic implications of particular re-sponses on the basis of the extent to which these responses appear deter-mined by projection rather than card pull.

Selective attention and differential emphasis in Rorschach content inter-pretation of individual responses has much in common with guidelines for interpretation in dynamic psychotherapy. In psychotherapy, everything pa-tients say has *some* meaning, but much of it has *little* meaning. The thera-pist's task is to recognize and respond appropriately to those patient state-ments that have the *most* meaning. Therapists can err by making a big deal out of everything patients say or too big a deal out of anything they say. Likewise, the Rorschacher's challenge is to give each response its just due, neither too much nor too little, in deciding how much significance to attach to its content themes. As previously indicated in chapters 3 and 4, projection is most likely to have occurred in Rorschach responses that involve form distortion, movement, or embellishments that go beyond the stimulus char-acteristics of the blots. Form distortion, movement, and embellishment thus provide three important indications that a response is likely to be rich in thematic imagery and should be read for this reason.

This guide to identifying content-rich responses does not mean that accurate form responses without movement or embellishment should go unread, however. Responses that involve little or no projected material may nevertheless contain features of note, such as comments and other inter-pretively significant test behaviors (the subject of chap. 7). Additionally, the sequence within which relatively unrevealing responses occur may be helpful in understanding the significance of content-rich responses that precede or follow them. As mentioned in chapter 3 and elaborated in chapter 8, some responses take on sequential importance precisely because they are intrinsically bland and less interesting than the responses surrounding them.

GENERATING ASSOCIATIONS
AND FORMULATING INTERPRETIVE HYPOTHESES

As demonstrated by the use of *MOR*, *COP*, and *AG* as structural variables in chapter 5, content themes can be codified to produce quantitative scores on which to base interpretive statements. Numerous formal content scales have been developed along these lines, some of which will be noted in due course. However, the essence of Rorschach content interpretation consists not of coding responses, but of reading them word for word, generating qualitative associations to what these words might signify, and using these associations as a basis for formulating interpretive hypotheses about a subject's personality characteristics.

The number and utility of the associations generated by reading the content-rich responses in a record usually depend on three factors: (a) the frequency of such responses and the clarity of the symbolism they contain, both of which are in the subject's hands to determine; (b) the familiarity of the examiner with personality dynamics and ways of interpreting symbolic material, which are didactic matters that can be learned and taught; and (c) the examiner's interpersonal sensitivity and capacity for symbolic association, which are personal qualities people possess and that can be enhanced by experience, training, and psychotherapy. As a consequence of these three factors, some records are thematically more revealing than others, some examiners know more than others about how to interpret thematic imagery, and some examiners, by virtue of their empathic and imaginative capacities, are better able than others to associate to possible meanings of content themes.

Before turning to didactic guidelines for interpreting thematic imagery, some further observations are indicated concerning the role of theory in this aspect of the interpretive process. As elaborated in chapter 1, data generated by the RIM can be interpreted from many different theoretical perspectives, and no particular theory is necessary to account for the utility of these data. The discussion in chapter 1 pointed out that Rorschach data provide useful information about personality functioning because the inkblots confront subjects with a representative problem-solving task and an associational situation that fosters personalized attributions. However, although the RIM does not need a single overarching theory to explain how and why it works, its transtheoretical nature does not render personality theory irrelevant to effective interpretation. To the contrary, thorough familiarity with some cohesive theoretical frame of reference concerning personality functioning plays a very important role in translating the implications of Rorschach data into sensible, informative, and useful descriptions of personality structure and dynamics.

Personality dynamics was defined in chapter 1 as referring to the manner in which personality states and traits interact to influence each other and to the ways in which underlying needs, attitudes, conflicts, and concerns influence people to think, feel, and act. Implicit in this definition is a psychodynamic formulation of personality in which human behavior is explained in part by thoughts and feelings that lie outside of conscious awareness. The notion of a dynamic unconscious that influences what people say and do, without their being fully aware of this influence, is of course a cornerstone of psychoanalytic approaches to understanding human behavior, and psychoanalytic theories provide a rich source of hypotheses concerning the latent meaning of what people say and do when taking the Rorschach.

The discussion that follows in this chapter and the case illustrations in chapters 10 through 14 reflect the author's psychodynamic orientation to the interpretation of thematic imagery and the formulation of personality dynamics. However, note must also be taken that neither psychoanalytic theory nor psychodynamic interpretation is monolithic. Contemporary diversity among dynamically oriented theorists and clinicians is ably summarized by Pine (1990) in *Drive, Ego, Object, and Self*. In this very important contribution, Pine described and contrasted what he called the "four psychologies": a *drive psychology* addressed primarily to urges; an *ego psychology* concerned mainly with modes of defense and adaptation; an *object relations psychology* focused on relationships and their internalization, distortion, and repetition; and a *self psychology* dealing with phenomena of differentiation and boundary formation, personal agency and authenticity, and self-esteem.

Writing primarily from the perspective of psychotherapy, Pine illustrated the differences between these psychologies by indicating how the same patient comment could be interpreted in four different ways, depending on whether the therapist chose to focus on its instinctual, defensive, object-related, or self-referential implications. Similar diversity can easily characterize psychodynamic interpretation of Rorschach imagery. Consider, for example, a Card II response of "Two bears fighting, they're cartoon characters, and there's blood all over where they're wounded." Does this response signify underlying aggressive urges, defensive distancing from expressions of anger, anticipation of interpersonal hostility, or concerns about being or becoming a damaged object? Perhaps all four elements are present in this fairly transparent example. However, influenced by which features of a response appear most emphasized, the implications of other available data, and their theoretical preferences, examiners looking at complex content themes may derive equally warranted but contextually different inferences from them.

With this in mind, and anticipating a diversity in emphasis likely to characterize content interpretation, this chapter describes an approach to generating associations and formulating hypotheses based on the content themes in the distorted form, movement, and embellished responses that are selected for close reading on the basis of their projected elements.

Distorted Form Responses

People normally tend to perceive their experience accurately. Human adaptation and survival depend on being able to form accurate impressions of objects and events, and the consequences of mistaken perceptions and faulty judgment can be fatal, not merely psychologically maladaptive. Consequently, examiners should ponder in every instance of inaccurate perception why it has occurred at a particular moment in certain circumstances. Even psychotically disturbed or brain-damaged persons with seriously impaired reality testing do not misperceive all of their experience all of the time. Why, then, does a particular subject do so here and now?

This question should be asked about all distorted form responses in the course of interpreting thematic imagery. Specifically, why does the subject give a minus form on this response and at this point in the record, and what is suggested about the subject's underlying dynamics by possible answers to this question? Given the fact that a minus response constitutes, by definition, a failure in adaptive functioning, four possible reasons for such a breakdown can be identified.

1. The source of difficulty or distress that unnerves subjects and for the moment undermines their contact with reality may reside in the content of the response being given. Suppose a man's very first response is a minus "battleship" to all of Card I. Something about the significance to him of a battleship and his need to sign in with it as his first response would appear to be upsetting to him. Could a battleship signify to him a big, powerful, indestructible object that wins wars and defeats the enemy? Or, in his eyes is a battleship an oversized, slow-moving craft that is easily outflanked by smaller and swifter vessels, has outlasted its usefulness, and should be put in mothballs? Or, is it possible that being a battleship has both meanings to a man who is experiencing strong needs to see and portray himself as strong and capable because he has underlying concerns about becoming inept and outmoded and being put out to pasture?

Like interpretations in psychotherapy, these and other associations to "battleship" are hypotheses to be investigated and modified in light of what meaning a battleship actually has for this man. What is important about the illustration with respect to doing thematic interpretation is that the minus form of the response appears attributable to its content, the significance of which to this man was sufficiently distressing to undermine for the moment his ability to distinguish fact from fantasy, that is, what the blot does and does not resemble. In some instances subjects may erase any doubt concerning whether a form distortion has originated in the content of a response by commenting on it in a negative fashion, as for example if this man had said to Card I, "I don't like the looks of this one; it's like a battleship."

2. As a second possible source of distress leading to a minus percept, the structural characteristics of a response instead of its content may be responsible for a temporary breakdown in reality testing. Just as *M-* responses may have particular implications for interpersonal insensitivity and poor social judgment, as discussed in chapter 5, the pairing of minus form quality with determinants other than *M* may also help to identify types of concerns subjects have and kinds of situations likely to cause them difficulty. Thus, a notably frequent occurrence of distorted form in responses involving Texture, Vista, or chromatic or achromatic color may respectively indicate disruptive underlying concerns about forming close relationships with others, maintaining self-regard, being able to express feelings, or being unhappy.

3. Instead of occurring as a consequence of some disturbing feature of either the articulated content or the structure of a response, minus responses may constitute a reaction to some latent thematic or structural stimulus impact of the card that is not directly expressed. This source of ineffective responding harks back to the discussion in chapter 4 of what the individual blots commonly suggest, and a temporary breakdown in reality testing may reflect difficulty in coping with issues signified by a particular inkblot.

Consider, for example, a woman who gives a *WF-* response of "mountain" on Card VI. Although "mountain" can generate some associations, such as being imposing if one is looking up at it or dangerous should one attempt to climb it, it does not seem particularly obvious or compelling as a symbolic clue to distress severe enough to disrupt this woman's contact with reality (certainly less so, for example, than the previous example of "island," which has some fairly compelling implications for concerns about being isolated, alone, or cut off from others). Similarly, the use of the whole blot and a pure form determinant for this response do not offer much basis for speculating about the origins of its poor form quality.

However, attention to what Card VI commonly signifies, whether or not articulated by the subject, generates two possibilities worth considering. With respect to structural considerations, this is the card most likely to pull Texture. If this is a woman without any *T* in her record, could her difficulty in responding effectively to Card VI be attributable to its textural qualities and accordingly to disruptive concerns she has about interpersonal intimacy? With respect to thematic content, could her difficulty be attributable to the frequency and ease with which sexual anatomy is seen on Card VI (as noted in chap. 4) and thereby provide a clue to underlying distress concerning sexual matters?

4. Finally, minus responses may arise for none of these first three reasons, but instead as a reaction to the response or card that preceded it. Consider a subject who sees the black part of Card III as "Two people doing something together" and follows this Popular response with a *DF-* "trees" to the center red detail (D3). Surely something could be said about the possible symbolic significance of "trees"; like "mountains," however, "trees" does not readily compel associations that would seem likely to account for this response being a minus. Moreover, the structural coding of the response is bland, except for the distorted form, and very little special significance attaches to this Rorschach detail, except for its being red. Would it make sense to hypothesize, then, that the perceptual distortion in this "trees" response represents a carryover from the response of "Two people doing something together" and represents a disruptive result of distress experienced in relation to having seen this Popular response? If so, it might be that this subject, on forming and reporting an impression of two people engaged in a collaborative endeavor, became upset because of underlying concerns about not being able or having insufficient opportunity to participate in such collaborative activities with others, and, as a result of being distressed, was temporarily unable to function effectively in proceeding to give the next ("trees") response.

To illustrate potentially revealing distress carried over from a previous card, suppose a subject sees Card IV as "a big monster" and then gives a minus response of "bug" to Card V. The Card IV response of "big monster" clearly has some thematic significance, but its implications are limited by its being an ordinary form-level response and perhaps a Popular as well. As for the minus on Card V, "bug" does not have much compelling symbolic significance, and, as noted in chapter 4, Card V is a relatively bland and unthreatening card that offers an easy Popular. A possibility to keep in mind in this and similar instances is that the minus is unrelated to either "bug" or Card V, but instead represents the disruptive result of distress carried over from Card IV. If so, this carried over distress provides more reason than was apparent from the Card IV response alone to think that the subject has some underlying concerns about relating to large and powerful figures.

Movement

The content themes in movement responses often provide valuable clues to how people view themselves, how they regard others, and how they feel about interpersonal relationships. As noted in chapter 4, *M* responses are likely to be more informative in these respects than *FM* responses, because projections onto human figures are more directly representative of subjects' inner lives than projections onto animal figures. The contents of *M* responses involving animal rather than human figures, such as "Two bears giving each other high-fives" on Card II, probably fall in between human *M*s and *FM*s in the directness with which they signify some underlying attitude or concern; as *INCOM* or *FABCOM* responses, however, animals in human movement involve an embellishment (the Special Score) that, as discussed in the next section, adds interpretive weight to such responses. As for content themes in *m* responses, these are also important to utilize as a basis for generating associations, but they are less likely than either *M* or *FM* contents to have interpersonal significance.

The particular value of *M* responses as a source of information about personality dynamics has long been recognized among Rorschach clinicians. In the opinion of Mayman (1977), *M* responses are the "richest, most revealing, consistently most interesting responses which occur on the Rorschach test" (p. 230). Piotrowski (1977) argued that "human movement responses elicited by the Rorschach plates . . . provide, more than any other single test component, specific and significant information about the individual's role in interhuman relationships that matter to him" (p. 189).

For the purposes of tapping the potential utility of *M* response content in suggesting interpretive hypotheses, it is helpful to generate associations to each of three aspects of such responses: who the figure is, what type of activity the figure is engaged in, and what kind of interaction, if any, is taking place between figures. Ordinarily, who the figures are and what they are doing reflects many of the subject's self-perceptions and attitudes toward others; how figures are interacting reflects aspects of the individual's interpersonal orientation and conceptions of how people in general relate to each other.

To illustrate these three potential *M* content characteristics, consider three subjects whose first responses to Card I are "An angel with her wings extended" (whole), "A bosomy woman with her arms stretched out" (center detail-D4), and "Two people beating up a person in the middle" (whole). In the first example, the type of figure is of particular interest. The concept of "angel" commonly elicits associations of goodness, innocence, and purity; certainly there is little doubt in most people's minds that "being a perfect angel" signifies being extremely well behaved. Hence, persons giving this content may well perceive themselves as being highly virtuous or aspire to achieving such status. Among people who in fact have displayed conduct problems, such responses as "angel" may represent protestations of their innocence. Of course, these are not yet conclusions. As is always the case in interpreting thematic imagery, such associations to response content are only reasonable hypotheses worthy of being explored further.

In the second example not only the type of figure ("bosomy woman") but also the activity attributed to it ("arms stretched out") seem significant. A "bosomy woman" could be an erotic object with an appealing figure, or she could be a maternal object whose breasts offer nurturance. In the latter case, her outstretched arms may represent a gesture of willingness to provide such nurturance, and the subject giving this response may have unmet needs to be nurtured and taken care of by a maternal figure. Once more, these are hypotheses rather than conclusions, and the point of the example is to illustrate how the process of generating associations can translate content themes into interpretive possibilities.

The third example contains two types of figures, perpetrators of aggression who are administering a beating and a victim who is being beaten. This complex response suggests interpretive possibilities involving not only the figures and what they are doing but also the interactions among them. Do subjects identify with the aggressors in the response and see themselves as people who contend with others by exerting physical dominance over them? Do subjects instead identify with the person being beaten and have either concerns about being abused by specific people in their life or a general view of the world as a place where they are constantly at risk for being victimized or beaten down? Or, does an uncertain and perplexing fusion of both identifications cloud subjects' inner life? With respect to the interaction depicted in this response, the aggression it portrays includes a cooperative element as well, in that two of the people are apparently working in concert to abuse the third person. Do subjects view the world as a confusing place in which they can never be sure whether people are more likely to collaborate or compete with each other? In this example, as in the previous two, associations to thematic elements provide the basis for formulating alternative possibilities that can then be explored further, both in the Rorschach protocol and in other sources of data concerning an individual's personality functioning.

Note, however, that the angel, the bosomy woman, and the aggressors/victim examples involve percepts with ordinary form quality. Suppose instead the response to be interpreted for its content theme is "Two people fighting" seen in the upper center black details on Card X (D8), which is a minus form percept. Reprising the discussion in chapter 4 of two-baggers, this is a response that suggests not only some concerns about unfriendly interactions between people (the aggressive M), but also sufficient distress at the prospect of interpersonal hostilities to cause the subject a temporary breakdown in reality testing (the minus form) on associating to it. As a general principle, distorted form in an M response intensifies the significance to the subject of whatever the content theme of the response suggests and warrants inferring that the person is experiencing considerable distress in relation to it.

As mentioned previously, numerous aspects of how human figures are described and how they are seen as acting, whether individually or in tandem, have been codified independently of the Comprehensive System to yield quantifiable guidelines for interpretation. Best known among these are the Concept of the Object Scale developed by Blatt et al. (1976), the Mutuality of Autonomy Scale developed by Urist (1977), the Primitive Defenses Scale of P. M. Lerner and H. Lerner (1980), and the Separation–Individuation Themes Scale constructed by Coonerty (1986). Although conceptually sound and in some instances adequately validated (see P. M. Lerner, 1993; Stricker & Healey, 1990), these scales have been used mainly in research studies rather than as an integral feature of interpreting Rorschach protocols in clinical practice. For the most part, the attention called by these content scales to interpretively significant aspects of *M* responses will be reflected in a careful and thorough process of associating to the type, activity, and interaction of human figures in Rorschach responses, as just discussed.

Regarding content themes in *FM* responses, the same considerations in generating associations and interpretive hypotheses apply as in the case of *M* responses: What types of animal figures are seen, what are they doing, and how are they interacting with each other? Keeping in mind some caution that these responses may be less clearly and directly indicative of subjects' personality dynamics than their *M* responses, the same kind of reflection on their meaning serves as a source of potentially useful speculation concerning how people view themselves, others, and the interpersonal world.

The content of *m* responses rarely reveals very much about a subject's interpersonal orientation, but inanimate movements can at times provide critical information about how people view themselves and their current level of functioning. Consider, for example, the implications of signing off on Card X with a final response of "It looks like something that is disintegrating, just falling apart"; or repetitively describing objects as "drooping," "sagging," or "falling down"; or frequently reporting such percepts as "explosion" or "volcano erupting." In the first instance, some compelling associations to the content theme could well suggest that the person is concerned about falling apart or is on the verge of some decompensation. In the second instance, the possibility of some depressive preoccupations with aging or loss of function, especially in an older person, suggests itself. In the third instance, usual meanings associated with these concepts point to possible concerns about loss of self-control and perhaps some risk of inappropriate or destructive behavior.

Like *M*, *m* can also combine with distorted form to enhance the thematic significance of a response and lend weight to its implications for underlying personality dynamics. To resurrect the "battleship" example used at the beginning of this section, suppose that this *FQ-* response to Card I is given as "A battleship ponderously plying its way through the waves." This version of the response clarifies somewhat the uncertainty about whether the self-image of battleship has positive or negative connotations for the subject, in that ponderosity is not usually a desired characteristic. Moreover, as a further illustration of a two-bagger, the negative self-percept identified by the content of the *m* in this response is indicated by the minus form to be a distressing source of concern for the subject.

Embellishments

As indicated in chapter 4, embellished Rorschach responses involve several respects other than distortion of form and attribution of movement in which subjects, as a manifestation of projection, attribute characteristics to their percepts that go beyond the stimulus properties of the inkblots. These include unusual ways of thinking and reasoning about percepts that result in coding one or more of the Critical Special Scores; other features of thematic elaboration or distinctive response style that are coded for one of the other Special Scores; and ways of describing percepts that do not result in any distinctive coding, such as in the previous example of seeing a woman who is "bosomy."

Like minus form responses, Critical Special Scores represent an instance of cognitive slippage. Whereas an *FQ-* indicates inaccurate perception, a Critical Special Score (*DV, INCOM, DR, FABCOM, ALOG,* or *CONTAM*) identifies illogical or incoherent thinking. Accordingly, responses containing Critical Special Scores should be approached with respect to their content themes in the same manner as responses with distorted form, by asking, "Why does this instance of disordered thinking occur at this point in the record?" Then, depending on how this question is answered, associations should be generated as already illustrated to either the content of the response, the structural coding of the response, the stimulus impact of the card, or the preceding response or card.

Of the other Special Scores coded for various kinds of response embellishments, those most likely to contain interpretively significant content themes are *MOR, COP,* and *AG.* The *COP* and *AG* responses always receive attention in the course of reading the movement responses in a record and have already been the subject of examples in this discussion. As for *MOR* responses, the process of generating associations to their content themes is both especially revealing and particularly challenging. Responses with morbid content are usually a rich source of hypotheses concerning subjects' self-image, mainly with respect to how they view their bodies and bodily functioning. At the same time, however, *MOR* responses often suggest a wide range of alternative possibilities from which to choose.

The challenge of interpreting *MOR* responses was discussed in chapter 5 in relation to deciding whether a subject who gives a response such as "a squashed insect" is identifying primarily with the victim (the insect) or with the victimizer (whoever did the squashing). The ambiguity in this instance is analogous to the situation depicted in the previous example of two people beating up a third person, in which the identification of the subject may be unclear. Sometimes *MOR* responses are delivered or elaborated in a manner that helps to establish whether the subject feels more closely allied with the perpetrator or with the victim of aggression. Thus a subject who says, "It looks like a squashed bug, like I just put my foot on it" is probably leaning toward self-identification as the one who does the damage (although such a self-percept may originate in part as a defense against fears of being weak and defenseless). By contrast, the identity of a subject who says, "It looks like a poor little bug who was minding its own business when somebody stepped on it" probably involves concerns about being the one who gets damaged (although such concerns may also occur in people who are basically victim-izers but also face life with a "Live by the sword, die by the sword" mentality that leads them to expect becoming a victim themselves at any moment).

The various kinds of embellishments for which *MOR* is coded generate some additional uncertainties in the associational process, beyond the vic-tim/victimizer distinction. Thus, some *MOR* responses involve damage or disease, as in the "squashed bug" example or in responses in which figures are seen as bleeding, wounded, sickly, or ill. Other *MOR* responses involve figures that are essentially intact, but whose natural and undamaged state involves some deformity or malfunction. Examples of this type of *MOR* are adjectival descriptions of people as being "deformed" or "having shriveled arms" and the use of nouns that convey as much, as in "Looks like a couple of cripples." Inanimate objects can similarly be described not as being damaged or broken, but as not functioning they way they should, as in "Some kind of machine, but it's not working properly." These two types of *MOR* response content have somewhat different implications for how sub-jects may perceive themselves and accordingly for the associations gener-ated during the interpretive process.

In similar fashion, other response embellishments that are not formally coded in the Comprehensive System should nevertheless be identified and used as a basis for generating associations, as in the example of the "bosomy woman." To continue with this example, the previous comments on "bosomy" addressed only its possible implications for women being viewed as erotic or maternal objects. As another distinct possibility, especially when given by a female subject, "bosomy woman" could reflect an image of being either a sexually attractive or nurturant person.

Generally speaking, in fact, because distorted form, movement, and em-bellished responses all involve some projection onto the inkblot, all of them reflect some representation of a subject's inner life. Miale (1977) observed that projective material is usually self-referential, and Mindess (1970) rec-ommended imagining that Rorschach subjects share characteristics in common with what they report seeing in the inkblots. In this vein, a potentially fruitful way of generating associations to responses containing projection consists of regarding them as possible self-representative figures, which has been formalized in the Comprehensive System as the "I am" technique. The "I am" technique consists of prefacing projected responses with the words "I am" and then considering whether the resulting statement says anything that might offer a glimpse of the subject's self-image. Thus, to draw on previous examples, the statements "I am a ponderous battleship," "I am a bosomy woman," and "I am someone getting beaten" say a good deal about how subjects probably view themselves. As a companion technique to "I am," which reveals aspects of subjects' actual self-image, the prefaces "I wish I were" or "I'm sorry I am" can be used in addition to provide clues to subjects' aspirational or negative self-image.

As a final consideration in deriving interpretive hypotheses from content themes, suppose that an embellished response also involves distorted form and contains movement. For example, to continue with the illustration of the ponderously moving battleship on Card I, say that the subject added, "and it looks like its superstructure got shot off" or "it's got some holes amidships" (reference to the inner white spaces). It is now a three-bagger, which is a response for which there are three reasons to believe that it includes content-rich and dynamically significant projected elements. The interpretation of this response can now be extended to hypothesize a self-image as being not only lumbering, ungainly, and vulnerable, but as already having been damaged in some way. In what particular way subjects might feel damaged would depend on the particular meaning to them of "super-structure" or "holes amidships."

Just as the content of two-baggers is likely to be more personally revealing and point more clearly to specific kinds of underlying concerns than the content of responses that involve only distorted form, movement, or embellishments, three-baggers frequently turn out to be the most informative and reliable responses in a record on which to base hypotheses concerning a subject's inner life. To take this line of reasoning one step further, a three-bagger involving human movement, grossly distorted perception, and a particularly dramatic embellishment, should such a response exist in a record, probably holds the key to unlocking the essence of how subjects feel about themselves and/or the interpersonal world.

DETERMINING THE PLAUSIBILITY OF THEMATIC INTERPRETATIONS

Once associations to content themes have been generated and translated into descriptions of personality characteristics, the next step in the interpretive process consists of judging the likely accuracy of these descriptions.

How plausible are the thematic interpretations derived from associating to content-rich responses, in other words, and how much confidence can be placed in their validity? Under no circumstances should examiners take as true their impressions of the symbolic significance of content themes without first subjecting these impressions to close scrutiny based on well-conceived criteria for judging the adequacy of such impressions.

For purposes of clinical work, criteria for judging the adequacy of content interpretations can be translated into guidelines for conducting effective thematic analysis. Several such guidelines have been mentioned previously. At this point, to aid in determining the plausibility of thematic interpretations, these guidelines can be reviewed and extended to form of a set of practice principles that comprise (a) identifying significant responses, (b) employing conservative inferences, and (c) focusing on compelling themes.

Identifying Significant Responses

Considerable attention has already been paid in this and the preceding chapters to the value of focusing content analysis on those responses most likely to contain projected elements, namely those involving form distortion, movement, or embellishments. The themes of such "content-rich" responses ordinarily produce a greater yield of interpretive hypotheses than whatever themes may appear in other responses. As a corollary of this finding, whether responses appear determined primarily by projection or primarily by card pull provides a useful criterion for evaluating thematic interpretations based on them. Specifically, the more projected elements there are in a response, the more likely it is that personality characteristics suggested by its thematic content are truly characteristic of the subject.

This structural guideline for determining the weight or probability that should be assigned to a thematic interpretation can be extended in several ways. With respect to form distortion, the further minus responses deviate from accurate perception, the more projection they involve and the more likely it is that their thematic implications will provide dependable descriptions of the subject. Among movement responses, as already noted, themes involving M generally are more revealing and thus yield more reliable inferences about a person than themes involving FM or m. Regarding embellishments, the more numerous or elaborated they are in a response, the greater is the likelihood that the theme of the response says something reliable about the subject.

Also serving as a criterion for the adequacy of a content interpretation is the previously noted concept of two-bagger and three-bagger responses. In more formal terms, the confluence of indices of projection in a single response increases the likelihood that inferences based on the thematic imagery in the response will prove valid. Thus, content interpretations of responses that combine distorted form (especially when grossly distorted), movement (especially involving human figures), and embellishments (particularly when numerous and extensive) merit considerable credence. Correspondingly, the certainty accorded to content interpretations diminishes as each of the manifestations of projection becomes less pronounced.

Finally, this group of structural considerations in judging the adequacy of content interpretations includes the previously noted potential significance of the first ("sign in") and last ("sign out") responses in a record. Should these responses contain projected elements, they should be identified by virtue of their placement as significant responses with respect to their likelihood of generating accurate inferences about a subject's personality dynamics.

Employing Conservative Inferences

Being conservative in drawing inferences from content themes consists of giving greatest credence to those symbolic meanings that show the most clarity, involve the least ambiguity, possess the readiest rationale, and encompass the least scope. Remote, uncertain, vague, and overly encompassing associations to the possible significance of content themes run considerable risk of suggesting personality features that do not in fact characterize a particular subject, blurring features that do characterize the subject, and generally proving embarrassing to psychologists who base conclusions on them. On the other hand, inferred symbolic meanings that are compelling by virtue of their seeming transparency, relative certainty, sound logical basis, and appropriately narrow focus satisfy criteria for adequacy and have considerable promise for providing accurate and sharply focused descriptions of personality characteristics.

To elaborate on these elements of respectable symbolic interpretation, some response contents are more clearly and less ambiguously suggestive of a particular meaning than others. A percept of a "spear" is very likely to have some significance related to spears being weapons, for example, with spear falling very obviously within the class of objects called "weapons." Although spears could be conceived as being something other than weapons or as being used for nonweaponry purposes, these would be remote possibilities compared to the transparent significance of "spear" as a weapon. The special importance to a subject of this attention to a weapon, if any, would depend on other features of the response, such as its form quality and how it is embellished. However, the basic associative link between "spear" and "weapon" is not only fairly obvious but also relatively unambiguous in that there are few, if any, reasonable alternatives.

By contrast, consider a suggestion by Phillips and J. G. Smith (1953, p. 128) that the content "teeth" symbolizes concerns about masturbation, especially when given by children and adolescents. Whatever link may exist between teeth and masturbation, it is certainly less apparent than the link between spear and weapon. According to Phillips and Smith, masturbation is a defense employed against frustrated dependency needs, "teeth" represent unsatisfied dependency needs, and seeing teeth on the Rorschach consequently identifies underlying conflicts concerning masturbation. Along with still lacking clarity and being far from obvious, this symbolic explanation does not take into account some equally possible alternatives that make it ambiguous as well as murky.

As a response relating to functions of the mouth, for example, teeth could have implications either for gaining nurturance, as in chewing, or for expressing aggression, as in biting. Moreover, for many people, especially in the first half of life, teeth may be especially important with respect to making an attractive appearance; in the latter half of life, attention to teeth may signify concerns not so much about appearance but about health and the aging process. Thus an adolescent who sees "crooked teeth" may be a lot more concerned about orthodontia than about masturbation, and a middle-aged or elderly person who sees "loose teeth" may be much more concerned about periodontia than about oral dependence or oral aggression. The point is not to affirm these latter hypotheses as necessarily being more accurate than the equation of teeth with masturbation, although they are more readily apparent. What is critical in this example with respect to judging the adequacy of symbolic interpretations is the fact that "teeth" is more ambiguous as a symbol and generates more alternative associations than "spear."

To illustrate the concepts of clarity and ambiguity further in thematic interpretation involving human movement, the previous Card I example of two people beating up a third person leaves little doubt that aggressive action is being represented by the beaters and victimization by the person being beaten. What other possibilities could be anything but remote? But consider the center detail of Card I (D4) seen as "A woman with her arms up." What does having her arms up signify? Is she waving hello, waving goodbye, gesturing in supplication ("Help me"), gesturing in despair ("I give up"), or doing something else entirely? In some instances, responses are elaborated in ways that help answer such questions and clarify the symbolic representation in the imagery (e.g., "A woman with her arms up praying to God to help her"). Without such response elaboration, there is no easy way to choose among these possible alternative meanings of seeing a woman with her arms up. Hence selecting any one of them as a reliable clue to the subject's underlying needs or attitudes would fail to satisfy criteria for adequate content interpretation and therefore be unwarranted.

Turning from the clarity and certainty required for adequate content interpretations to criteria concerning their rationale and scope, inferred symbolic meanings should be taken seriously only when they are relatively easy to justify with a few steps of logical reasoning. To reprise an example from chapter 4, a percept of "club" could have phallic significance, but it could just as well signify a weapon, or perhaps both a phallus and a weapon, or some other cylindrical object that is greater in length than circumference. Although there is consequently some uncertainty concerning the meaning of this response, there is little difficulty in providing a rationale for these possibilities. "Club," like "spear," falls in the class of "weapons," and its association with phallus or any other long cylindrical object derives from their being similarly shaped, which is a simple, logical rationale involving few levels of inference.

For contrast, consider the assertion that a response of "fish," by itself and without any elaboration, "reflects a relinquishment of striving for independence from an overwhelmingly possessive mother figure and is associated with a profound passivity and inertia and with a clinging dependency" (Phillips & J. G. Smith, 1953, p. 121). How, it might be asked, does one get from a fish to passivity, inertia, clinging dependency, and the attitudes and conduct of the subject's mother? If there is a logical rationale for these symbolic inferences, it does not come readily to mind. In the earlier example of equating teeth with masturbatory concerns, a logical rationale was provided but required making several rather large inferential leaps, such as assuming that masturbation serves defensive purposes. Generally speaking, the less tortuous the logic and the fewer levels of inference that are necessary to translate a content theme into a symbolic association, the more likely it is that the association will lead to a valid and useful personality description.

As for the scope of content interpretations, conservatism calls for a narrow focus limited primarily to contemporaneous personality dynamics. That is, inferences based on thematic imagery are most likely to be accurate when they address underlying needs, attitudes, conflicts, and concerns of the individual at the present time. A firm grasp of a subject's personality dynamics as gleaned from Rorschach responses allows knowledgeable clinicians to formulate many reasonable hypotheses concerning past events in individuals' lives that have shaped their nature and how they responded to those events when they occurred. Likewise, dynamic as well as structural aspects of personality functioning have implications for how people are likely to think, feel, and act in various kinds of future situations. In terms of criteria for judging the adequacy of content interpretations, however, those that focus most narrowly on current personality dynamics merit most credence. The more extensively content interpretations are elaborated, on the other hand, and the farther they look into the past or future, the more speculative and less reliable they become.

Schafer (1954, chap. 5) wrote a chapter about judging the adequacy of interpretations that remains a model of psychodynamic sophistication and scientific discipline in the interpretive utilization of content themes. With respect to the advisable scope of interpretations, Schafer's following "rule of evidence" should continue to guide examiners in their work:

> Since at present there seems to be no evidence in Rorschach test records to support or refute genetic reconstructions concerning specific, important, early experiences and relationships, and since current representations of the remote past are historically unreliable even though revealing of current pathology, interpretation can and should pertain only to the present personality structure and dynamics of the patient or to changes in these in the relatively recent past. (p. 145)

Identifying Compelling Themes

Content interpretation yields the most dependable information when it proceeds on the basis of particularly compelling thematic imagery. The compelling themes in a record are those that are most repetitive, most dramatic, most original, and most spontaneous. The more response content combines repetitiveness, drama, originality, and spontaneity, the more likely it is to contain imagery that is representative of a subject's inner life. Conversely, themes that appear infrequently and emerge belatedly in the context of bland and ordinary kinds of responses should not be relied on heavily, if at all, in formulating hypotheses concerning personality dynamics.

Of these markers for compelling themes, repetition is perhaps most obvious in importance and the one most frequently noted in traditional Rorschach literature. B. Klopfer et al. (1954, chap. 13), Mindess (1970), Phillips and J. G. Smith (1993, chap. 6), and Schafer (1954, chap. 5) are among those who have stressed the considerable likelihood that the recurrent themes in subjects' records say more about them than the occasional themes. The adage "One swallow doesn't make a summer," familiar to all assessment psychologists, is most definitely applicable to the interpretive significance of a content theme occurring only once in a record. On the other hand, the repetition marker does not preclude the drama, originality, and spontaneity markers of a content theme, giving it interpretive weight despite its occurring in just a single instance.

Whereas repetitiveness of a content theme can be determined objectively by counting its frequency, assessing whether imagery is dramatic requires a more subjective approach to the data. Drama as a marker of compelling content themes typically must be inferred from the ways in which responses are embellished, the quality of the language they contain, and the emotional intensity with which they are expressed. Consider, for example, the qualitative difference between Card III seen as "Two people picking up a basket" and a structurally similar response of "Two big guys struggling with all their might to pick up some heavy object, and I think they're succeeding." Seeing "big guys" rather than two people and seeing them as "struggling with all their might" rather than merely "picking up" lend drama to the second response, as does the subject's opinion that their effort is bearing fruit.

Originality in content themes is akin to drama, and being original rather than commonplace contributes to thematic imagery being dramatic. In its own right, however, originality is important to consider in weighing the import of a content theme because, like repetition, it can be judged against some fairly objective benchmarks. Specifically, the normative expectations for response content, ranging from the frequency standards for ordinary form level (responses given by at least 2% of subjects) and Popular content (given by at least one third of subjects) to the generally expected thematic imagery of responses to each card (see chap. 4) provide standards for what is commonplace. The more response content diverges from these expectations, the more original it is and the more credence it merits as a reflection of a subject's inner life.

The weighting of thematic interpretations according to how much projection they appear to contain and how little they correspond to common stimulus-determined impressions of the inkblots has a long tradition in Rorschach assessment that should be acknowledged. Hertzman and Pearce (1947) pointed out that the more responses depart from conventional modes of perception and expression, the more likely they are to reveal significant dynamic aspects of personality functioning. Subsequent contributors who emphasized that validity and information value of content interpretations depends on how much they deviate from commonly reported percepts, how little they are stimulus determined, and how fanciful and imaginative they are include Brown (1953), Phillips and J. G. Smith (1953, chap. 6), Schafer (1954, chap. 4), and Mindess (1970). Aronow, Reznikoff, and Moreland (1994) similarly recommended that examiners "should be most reluctant to accord dynamic meaning to responses that are in keeping with the stimulus qualities of the blots and should conversely give greater weight to responses that seem out of step with the blot stimulus characteristics" (p. 38). Aronow et al. (1994, chap. 10) also provided a concise overview of the guidelines formulated by earlier authors for conducting valid content interpretation.

Finally, with respect to spontaneity, the significance of content themes is usually reflected in how early in the response process they are elaborated. For example, consider a response to the upper side details in Card IX (D3) of "Two sorcerers casting spells at each other." Assuming this response has some implications for concerns about aggressive interpersonal reactions or perhaps for an underlying wish to possess the magical powers of a sorcerer, these implications are more compelling if this imagery is reported during the free association phase of the administration than during the inquiry. Should a subject initially describe this Rorschach detail as "Some kind of human figures" and elaborate the "sorcerers casting spells" only when shown the card for the second time, then it is reasonable to infer that the needs and concerns driving the projected elements of the response are less pressing and urgent than if they had emerged more spontaneously at the first viewing.

Similarly, thematic imagery emerging immediately after the examiner has begun the inquiry by reading back the subject's free association should be regarded as more compelling than imagery that does not appear until late in the inquiry, after the examiner has invited further comment (e.g., as by saying, "I'm not sure how you're seeing it"). Generally speaking, the more an examiner has to pull for thematic imagery, even while keeping within the boundaries of standardized guidelines for conducting the inquiry, the less compelling the content theme will be as clue to the subject's personality dynamics.

ASSIGNING MEANING TO SPECIFIC CONTENT THEMES

Having addressed the identification of content-rich responses and the process of generating and evaluating the plausibility of interpretive associations to them, it remains in the final section of this chapter to address the meaning of various specific content themes. The discussion that follows identifies aspects of content to which examiners should pay special attention and certain questions they should address to aspects of the imagery they contain. Given the innumerable forms that Rorschach associations can take, no attempt is made to compile exhaustive lists of either content themes or response contents. However, by suggesting possible meanings for imagery involving certain kinds of people, animals, objects, activities, and anatomy, the text provides illustrative guidelines that examiners can apply in attempting to elucidate the symbolic or representational significance of whatever specific images they encounter.

Types of People

The types of people seen on the Rorschach usually reveal aspects of the way subjects view themselves and others. The characteristics of a particular human figure can indicate an actual self-image, an image of how individuals would like to be or fear being, an attitude toward people in general or some person in particular, or wishful thinking about how people should be. Which of these meanings is most likely is a matter for examiners to contemplate after they have generated some associations to a human figure response. Parameters of human figure responses to consider in this process include their age, gender, size, special characteristics, particular roles, specific identity, and missing parts.

Regarding age, is there a notable focus on younger people (which might suggest some regressive tendencies or at least some longing for earlier times when life was less complicated or more rewarding), or does there seem to be a preoccupation with older people (which could suggest concerns about growing older and losing vitality)? Concerning gender, is there an unusual frequency of males or females, especially involving such deviations from normative expectation as seeing a woman on Card IV or men on Card VII? If so, the subject may be experiencing discomfort in relation to the gender being ignored or perhaps some gender-role identity conflicts. The latter is especially relevant to consider when human figures are of indeterminate gender or have sexual characteristics of both genders (e.g., "A person with breasts and a penis" on Card III). As for size, are the figures repetitively emphasized as being large or small? Stressing size one way or the other may say something about regarding oneself as being too big or too little, or other people as being larger or smaller than oneself (which could lead to experiencing oneself as being dominated by bigger and more powerful people or as being or wishing to be big and powerful enough to dominate others).

As for special characteristics, do the figures have any qualities that may signify particular preoccupations or concerns related to self or others, such as "a big head" (perhaps an index of being intelligent, intellectually oriented, or conceited), "a shapely figure" (possibly indicative of physical attractiveness or erotic appeal), or "withered arms" (probably representative of being weak or powerless)? Are the figures of a class of persons, real or imaginary, that have fairly common connotations for better or worse, such as "angel," "saint," "witch," "devil," "dwarf," or "robot"? "Robot" provides a particularly rich array of associations. Does being a robot mean being a humanoid object lacking self-determination and manipulated by others, or a detached object without feelings who is immune to the taunts of others, or a superior object possessed of superhuman physical capacities and faultless logic?

Regarding particular roles of human figures, are there dramatic responses involving people who serve in such functions as being a "king," "judge," "preacher," "showgirl," "ballerina," "magician," "model," "cowboy," "wrestler," or "clown"? Like personal characteristics, these and other ascribed roles typically suggest associations that may lead to insights about aspects of a subject's inner life. What does it mean to be a "clown," for example? Clowns are entertainers skillful at making people laugh and beloved by people of all ages. Yet clowns are also tragic figures and buffoons who look foolish, act ridiculously, and are objects of pity and scorn. Who would relish being "the class clown" in a schoolroom or the operatic clown Pagliacci, a loser in love who laughs bitter tears? Clowns are also personas rather than real people; their true nature and actual feelings are hidden beneath their layers of makeup and costuming. Could a smiling clown be showing a brave face to the world, for example, laughing on the outside while crying on the inside?

As in all of these illustrative content themes, the actual meaning of "clown" to a subject depends on what that person associates with being a clown. After formulating various alternative possibilities suggested by a content theme, examiners must then choose among them as best they can on the basis of (a) response elaborations that clarify a subject's underlying feelings (e.g., "It's a clown's face, painted up to look happy, but it looks like he's crying and his makeup is running"); (b) other sources of information in the test data that support a particular hypothesis (such as prominent evidence of underlying depression being defended against by trying to keep true feelings hidden); or (c) what subjects may say in a posttesting feedback session when "clown" responses are brought up for discussion and they are asked directly what being a clown signifies to them. At all times, in the spirit of conservatism advocated in this chapter, examiners attempting to sort out the possible meanings of symbolic representations should heed an admonition by Klopfer that these are "hazardous procedures" (B. Klopfer et al., 1954, p. 385).

In terms of any specific identity given to human contents, subjects not infrequently report seeing figures that resemble specific real or fictional people, such as "Jesus," "Buddha," "Queen Elizabeth," "Tinkerbell," "Tarzan," "Satan," "Wonder Woman," "Genghis Kahn," "Teddy Roosevelt," "the Virgin Mary," or "George Washington." The personal characteristics associated with such figures may represent aspects of subjects' actual or idealized self-image or attitudes they have toward other people. In the case of George Washington, for example, associations flow easily to his being the father of his country, a courageous and determined soldier, a powerful and respected president, a stern but just leader, and a person who could not tell a lie. Does a male subject giving a George Washington response identify himself as having these qualities (whether or not with justification), does he aspire to becoming such an admirable person, could he regard his father as being such an admirable man, or is it possible that he sees men in general as having such qualities, perhaps more so than he does?

Finally, with respect to missing parts, human detail responses should be noted for possible implications of what is excluded. Subjects who tend to see only heads may be excessively intellectual in their orientation and have difficulty dealing with the physical and sexual aspects of their existence. People who see bodies only from the waist up may also have some underlying concerns about sexuality, especially if they add such comments as "I don't see the rest of it" or "The bottom part doesn't look like anything." Contrariwise, subjects may focus on bodies that have no heads or on just the lower halves of bodies, in which case it is reasonable to pursue the hypothesis that they are oversexualizing their existence and demeaning their intellectual capacities or generally disavowing the importance of the mind in their lives. As further examples, subjects who see people without hands may be expressing concerns about not being capable of doing things with their hands or perhaps guilt about doing things with their hands that they should not have done, and those who see people without legs may be expressing concerns about not being able to stand on their own two feet or to ambulate themselves out of dangerous or unpleasant situations.

Types of Animals

Like the types of human figures in Rorschach responses, the types of animals subjects see can have implications for their self-image and their opinions of other people. Notice should be taken in particular of the size of animal figures, of any special characteristics ascribed or intrinsic to them, and of any specific connotations they often convey. Regarding size, the question to ask is whether the animal contents in a record show an unusual emphasis on large and powerful animals (bear, bull, eagle, elephant, gorilla) or small and not very powerful creatures (ant, frog, insect, mouse, robin, worm). In keeping with the previously discussed guidelines for identifying compelling content themes, an unusual emphasis on large or small animals can be monitored by how frequently they occur, whether they occur in unexpected places (such as seeing the black details on Card II as "insects"), and how dramatically they are expressed.

As in the case of human figures, an emphasis on large or small animals raises the possibility that subjects see themselves or others in similar fashion and with similar implications, especially when the animal contents are embellished in ways that point in certain interpretive directions. Thus, "great big bears that are dangerous" could signify a self-image or aspiration as someone large and strong and not to be messed with, or a concern that there are people as well as animals out there who are larger and stronger than oneself and must be approached with caution, if at all. By contrast, "tiny little worms" could signify identifying oneself as a lowly, insignificant, unworthy creature who could easily be stepped on, or an attitude that most people are no more capable or important than worms and deserve to be stepped on, at least figuratively. With these two illustrative responses (as with the "clown" example just discussed), using the "I am" technique can help to generate interpretive hypotheses: What are the implications for subjects' personality dynamics of saying to themselves "I am a great big bear" or "I am a tiny little worm"?

Animal figures may be embellished not only with certain qualities, such as the dangerousness of the aforementioned bear, but also with additional physical characteristics that enhance their interpretive significance. Is a "gorilla" on Card IV elaborated as having "a massive body" or possessing "enormous strength," for example, or, to make matters more complicated, does the subject say, "A big gorilla, but he's got these little arms"? Could the big gorilla with little arms represent a self-image of being big and apparently strong but being in fact unable to do very much, or could it represent an attempt to deny the power of other people whose dominance is feared or resented, by means of using fantasy to handicap them with weak arms?

In addition to special qualities or characteristics that might be ascribed to them, some animals have distinctive inherent features that can generate useful associations even if the subject does not call attention to them. For example, "armadillos" have armored bodies, "turtles" have shells that provide protection as long as they stay inside them, and "porcupines" have a prickly exterior that can cause pain to anyone who approaches them too closely. Hence an emphasis on these contents may have implications for concerns about protecting oneself, even at the expense of staying inside one's shell. Similarly by nature, "sharks," "barracudas," and "piranhas" are predators, and "vultures" and "hyenas" are scavengers. These and similarly suggestive implications of certain animals for certain behavioral qualities should be noted in the course of analyzing content themes.

Finally, with respect to specific connotations that animal figures may have, there are numerous animals that rightfully or by virtue of myth and common language usage have come to symbolize various personality characteristics. Thus lions are brave, lambs are meek, donkeys are stubborn, and peacocks are proud. With an eye to value judgments, who would like to be identified as a weasel or a skunk or be in a position of having to trust or befriend people thus identified? By asking what specific animal figures might connote, examiners can often add some interesting hypotheses to their interpretive process. In doing so, however, they should be careful never to lose sight of the tentative nature of symbolic equivalence and the conservative guidelines for content interpretation spelled out earlier in this chapter.

Types of Objects

An almost infinite number of different objects can appear in the content of Rorschach responses. Whatever their number and variety, however, most object contents fall into certain classes or types of objects that have interpretive significance by virtue of some shared characteristics. Two such groupings of content categories that are coded in Comprehensive System indices have been discussed in chapter 5. One of these is the Isolation Index, which takes account of the Botany, Cloud, Geography, Landscape, and Nature contents in a record, all of which represent an unpopulated environment and have implications for social isolation. Aside from contributing to the Isolation Index and thus having significance for interpersonal adjustment difficulties, each of these contents may have special interpretive significance by virtue of embellishments that may or may not generate any additional code.

For example, "a decayed leaf" and "a rotting tree trunk" are Botany contents that are also Morbid and consequently (as discussed in chap. 5) suggest not only social isolation but also pessimistic thinking and depressing concerns about losing one's bodily integrity and functioning capacities. On the other hand, "a safe harbor" and "a high bluff that would be difficult to climb up" are Geography and Landscape responses, respectively, that have no other coded features but include some content-rich embellishments. "Safe harbor" might well indicate concerns about finding protection or perhaps satisfaction that one has found a protected situation. The high bluff that is difficult to climb might also be a protected place, if one is ensconced on top of the bluff; among other possibilities, however, this response might signify concern about facing insurmountable obstacles in one's life or some eager anticipation of taking on a challenging task.

The other grouping of content categories coded in the Comprehensive System involves the Intellectualization Index, which takes account of the Art and Anthropology responses in a record. Also, as discussed in chapter 5, both Art and Anthropology contents identify an intellectualized way of thinking about experience. However, like the components of the Isolation Index, Art and Anthropology contents may be elaborated in very revealing ways. "A painting" can be "smudged," "torn," "beautiful," or "a testimony to the skill of the artist," for example; "It looks like an old relic from an Indian burial place, all cracked and covered with dirt" prompts associations that go well beyond the implications of its being an Anthropology content.

Human and animal figures and the content components of the Isolation Index and the Intellectualization Index usually constitute more than three fourths of the responses in a record. Most of the remaining contents in the majority of records involve objects that can be usefully categorized on the basis of the purposes they serve. Thus it is helpful in the interpretive process to determine whether the objects depicted cluster together in any meaningful way with respect to how they typically are used. The previous example of "spear" as belonging to the class of "weapons" provides a case in point. Suppose a record includes an emphasis on spears, clubs, and arrows (primitive weaponry), or on airplanes, tanks, and cannons (contemporary weaponry), or on phasers and ray guns (futuristic weaponry)? Beyond the implications of some of these responses being coded as Anthropology and others as Science content, their common theme raises the possibility that the subject is preoccupied with employing or being victimized by instruments of aggression.

As testimony to the complexity of interpreting thematic imagery, however, this list of weapons is not symbolically homogenous. "Cannon" is
strictly an attack weapon, for example, whereas "tank" also offers protection, at least from small arms fire, and being "built like a tank" usually
conveys a sense of invulnerability. Moreover, some but not all of these
weapons, being long and cylindrical in shape, may have significance as
phallic symbols rather than weapons, or for some subjects they may signify
both phallus and weapon. In this last instance, a fantasied equation between
phallus and weapon would conjure up in turn numerous potentially revealing hypotheses concerning how a male subject views what he can do with
this organ of his body or how a female subject views what can be done to
her by it. The purpose in this and all of the examples being used in this
discussion, as already noted, is not to provide any exhaustive or definitive
list of interpretations warranted by specific content themes, but rather to
illustrate the complexity as well as the richness of symbolic interpretation
and the typically speculative and tentative nature of each of the many
alternative hypotheses an individual response can generate.

Turning to another type of object that regularly appears in Rorschach
responses, Clothing contents are coded for the class to which they belong
but often have more interpretive significance than is reflected merely by
their frequency of occurrence. The question to consider about an item of
clothing is what it might be used for. Discussions in previous chapters have
identified two categories of clothing on the basis of purposes they can serve:
Some items of clothing are protective, such as "helmet," "suit of armor,"
and "bullet-proof vest"; other items of clothing are decorative, such as
"tuxedo" and "pretty hat." A third category of clothing is noteworthy for
being concealing, such as "cloak," "hood," and other overgarments that
obscure a person's facial features or bodily characteristics.

Protective clothing responses suggest subjects' concerns about needing
to insulate themselves against danger or threats to their physical safety.
Concealing clothing suggests related but qualitatively different concerns
about having difficulty determining what people are like and how they are
likely to act, and consequently feeling uncertain of their motives and unsure
whether to trust them. These implications of concealing clothing are sometimes dramatized by subjects who embellish cloaked or hooded figures with
such comments as, "I can't tell what kind of people they are" or "It's not
clear what they are doing." The nature of the concerns suggested by protective and concealing items of clothing account for the loading of Clothing
content on the Hypervigilance Index.

As an additional possibility, the interpretive significance of concealing
clothing may at times derive from the fact that it serves to obscure secondary sexual characteristics that identify people as male or female and may
be erotically stimulating. Like the earlier illustration of figures of indetermi-

nate gender or possessing sexual characteristics of both genders, seeing figures whose gender is obscured by their clothing may reflect confusion in gender-role identity. It may also be informative to consider whether clothing responses involve primarily masculine or feminine attire. Exclusively masculine garments are relatively few in contemporary dress, although "athletic supporter" and "biker's motorcycle jacket" would qualify as examples. Exclusively feminine garments not uncommonly given in Rorschach responses include "dress," "skirt," "corset," and "brassiere."

To illustrate once more the translation of content associations into interpretive hypotheses, what might it signify for a male subject to report several feminine undergarments, especially in the context of dramatic responses containing many projected elements? Does this man have an uncertain gender-role identity and find himself uncomfortably attracted to feminine ways and accoutrements? As a reaction to such uncertainty or for various other reasons, could he have strong needs to present himself in a hyper-masculine way, as a man who knows about women and how to have his way with them sexually? If he is being examined by a woman, is it possible that such responses as "lacy silk panties" or "a G-string like the nude dancers wear" are intended not only to show off his macho but also to have a seductive or shocking impact?

Finally, it is important to note in considering Clothing responses whether they involve decorative items of dress that neither protect nor conceal the body but instead adorn or reveal it. How people dress frequently constitutes a statement they are making about themselves, a statement that says, "This is who I am," or "This is how I would like to look," or "This is how I want to be seen." Clothing that makes a statement may also be saying something about how a subject views other people. Thus, responses of "a man wearing a nice suit" and "a man in rumpled clothes" could reflect a male subject's inclination to see either himself or some other man or men as careful or as careless about their dress and other personal habits as well. A female subject seeing a woman in "a low cut gown" or "a skimpy bathing suit" could among other possibilities pride herself on being physically attractive, be expressing some exhibitionistic tendencies, long for the kinds of enjoyable recreation associated with wearing either garment, or be preoccupied with concerns that other women are more attractive than she is and that they lack the decency to keep their bodies properly covered.

Types of Activity

Whether response contents involve human figures, animal figures, or various types of objects, content analysis should include attention to the types of activity in which they are engaged. Because all types of activity are coded for movement, responses involving activity contribute to the Comprehensive

System interpretive process by virtue of their coding for *M*, *FM*, or *m*. In addition, the codes for active, passive, cooperative, and aggressive movement discussed in chapter 5 represent aspects of the thematic imagery contained in movement responses. As in previous illustrations involving other coded response characteristics, however, qualitative aspects of what people, animals, and objects are depicted as doing provide more information about subjects' personality characteristics than can be gleaned from Comprehensive System codes alone.

With respect to activity in which a human figure is involved, for example, movements such as "resting," "crying," "falling" and "curling up in a ball" are all passive, but each has unique implications for how subjects may be feeling or seeing themselves. Thus, "resting" suggests a sense of comfort and relaxation, "crying" usually identifies sadness, "falling" brings to mind the possibility of something bad happening (as in "heading for a fall"), and "curling up in a ball" conveys withdrawal or an attempt to protect oneself. Similarly, such active movements as "running," "hiding," "yelling," and "playing" differ in the associations they prompt concerning a subject's underlying attitudes or concerns.

As for animal activity, suppose one passively moving animal figure is seen as "gliding along in the breeze" and another as "sinking into the mud," or suppose one actively moving animal is seen as "looking for food" and another as "baring its teeth." Types of activity also vary considerably among inanimate objects that are moving, as for example when they are "drooping," "exploding," "blowing in the wind," or "zooming along." In each instance, interpretive hypotheses should be generated by speculating about what the type of activity attributed to the animal or object might signify to the subject. What might it mean, for example, to see oneself as "sinking into the mud," and, drawing on the "I am" technique mentioned earlier, what different implications might there be for "I am drooping" as opposed to "I am zooming along"?

All of the preceding examples address solitary activities of just one figure or object. Also revealing, especially with respect to a subject's interpersonal attitudes and orientation, are the implications of how two or more figures or objects are interacting. Most interactive movement responses can be coded as Aggressive or Cooperative, but, like active and passive, these categories do not fully reflect the shades of meaning that many such responses contain. Aggressively interacting people may be "glaring at," "shouting at," "hitting," or "killing" each other, for example, which suggests different levels of angry and aggressive action, or they may be engaged in socially sanctioned competition that may not even be unfriendly, such as "arm wrestling." Cooperatively interacting people may be rather blandly "shaking hands" or "dancing together," or they may more intensely be "having a real good time together" or "saying they love each other." Interacting animals and objects can similarly exemplify a broad range of interpretive meanings. As some common examples, actively moving bears on Card II can be "fighting" or "playing patty-cake," and jet airplanes on Card II can be seen as "flying in formation" or as "being in a dogfight."

Types of Anatomy

After identifying and pursuing the implications of the types of humans, animals, objects, and activities involved in thematic imagery, examiners will have pretty much exhausted the interpretive possibilities of content analysis. Also worthy of special attention, however, are any Anatomy contents that occur in a record. In structural terms, an accumulation of Anatomy responses suggests concerns about bodily functioning, and content embellishments may provide additional insights into the nature or extent of these concerns. Morbidity in specified organs, as in "sick looking lungs" or "a diseased liver" increases the likely intensity level of a somatic preoccupation and may even relate to specific problems in subjects' lives, such as heavy smokers being particularly worried about their lungs and heavy drinkers being especially concerned about their livers.

Sex responses should also receive special attention for their possible dynamic significance. Sex contents include not only Anatomy contents (for internal organs), but also responses in which the sexual content is a human or animal detail (for external organs) or sexual activity (as in "people having intercourse"). Taken together, however, and analyzed for the implications of the imagery they contain, Sex responses can provide many clues as to how people regard their own sexuality, their sexual functioning, and their sexual interactions with others.

Another organ that is often embellished in ways that are revealing by virtue of its symbolic significance is the heart. Hearts for most people symbolize love and compassion. One whose "heart is full" has found true love, people can suffer and even die from a "broken heart," almost nobody wants to be considered "cold-hearted," people who seem excessively compassionate are called "bleeding hearts," and pleas for kindness and mercy may include "Have a heart!" Anatomy responses involving hearts should accordingly be examined for any embellishments that might reflect on the nature of a subject's interpersonal attitudes.

7

Interpreting Test Behaviors

On an equal footing with structural variables and content themes, test behaviors provide a third source of data on which to base Rorschach interpretations. As people go about the process of reporting what the ink-blots might be, their basic behavioral style and interpersonal orientation influence many aspects of how they conduct themselves during the examination. In addition, subjects' current attitudinal and emotional state at the time of the examination typically have an impact on their manner of dealing with the testing situation. Accordingly, examiners can enrich their Rorschach assessments by utilizing subjects' test behaviors along with the structure and content of their responses as bases for formulating hypotheses about their personality functioning.

Three different kinds of Rorschach test behaviors can be distinguished. One kind of behavior relates specifically to the process of being administered the Rorschach, such as how a subject handles the cards. A second kind of test behavior relates to the process of being examined, as illustrated by an expression of concern about what test results might show. The third kind of test behavior arises as an aspect of being in a two-person professional situation, as in the case of an unusually deferential subject who repetitively addresses the examiner as "doctor," "sir," or "ma'am." Of these three kinds of test behaviors, only the first is specific to a Rorschach examination. The second type of behavior reflects an attitude toward being examined that would probably exist without there being a Rorschach in the test battery, and the third type represents an orientation toward people in authority that would probably be present without there being a psychological examination.

Hence specific knowledge about the Rorschach plays a greater role in grasping the interpretive significance of some kinds of test behaviors than others, and clinical sensitivity in general contributes to understanding the interpersonal implications of certain test behaviors independently of the Rorschach method itself. For purposes of discussion, test behaviors that contribute to Rorschach interpretation can be characterized as involving (a) ways in which subjects turn and handle the cards, (b) comments or personalized remarks that subjects make during the response process, and (c) the expressive and interpersonal style subjects manifest while taking the RIM.

CARD **TURNING AND HANDLING**

Like all test behaviors, card turning and handling are representative samples of behavior that indicate how people are generally inclined to act in problem-solving and decision-making situations and also how they may be feeling at the moment. In addition to being informative, the manner in which subjects turn and handle the cards is, except in unusual circumstances, an ever-present feature of all Rorschach examinations. Standardized administration procedures require subjects to hold the cards, each of which they will either turn or not turn. Examiners who do not ask or, if necessary, insist that subjects take the cards in hand are not only violating standardization but also sacrificing useful data.

In 10 inkblots representing 10 separate samples of behavior, then, personality traits and states of individuals taking the Rorschach are likely to influence whether and how they turn the cards. With respect to personality traits, for example, subjects who are rigid and authoritarian by nature may hold the cards in the position in which they are handed to them and not even consider turning them. Among subjects who are sufficiently flexible to consider turning the cards, those who are relatively autonomous and self-assured may just go ahead and do so, whereas those who are relatively submissive or concerned about staying within the rules may first ask for permission ("Can I turn the card?").

After being given permission to turn the card with the standard response of "If you like" or "It's up to you," subjects who are particularly deficient in self-determination and self-confidence or who are unusually fearful of doing the wrong thing may ask for further clarification of the rules ("Is it alright to look at it from any direction?"). Such subjects may also continue on subsequent cards to ask for permission ("Can I turn this one?"). They may also express their timidity or anxiety in the manner as well as the frequency of their requests for permission; thus, instead of casually asking, "Can I turn the card?", they may inquire in a formal and concerned manner, "Is it permitted to turn the card?" or "Does the test allow me to look at it from a different perspective?" As a further example of the influence of personality traits on card-turning behavior, subjects who are compulsive may be inclined to examine the cards carefully in each of the four possible positions, whereas those who generally attend to their experience superficially may be likely to limit their card turning to an occasional casual glance at one or two of the blots in a different position without undertaking any careful examination of multiple cards in multiple alternate positions.

Turning to subjects' attitudinal and emotional states at the time they are being examined, those who take the examination seriously and feel positively toward the examiner and the evaluation process tend, unless their personality traits dictate otherwise, to become sufficiently involved in the response process to wish to look at the cards in various positions. Conversely, subjects who are disinterested in being examined or skeptical about the purpose of the examination may not bother to turn the cards as a way of seeing more in them. On the other hand, subjects who are not merely disinterested or skeptical but overtly hostile and defiant may show an oppositional pattern of test behavior in which they turn each card upside down as soon as it is handed to them. In these last instances, the card turning is usually not an understated gesture, but instead a very pointed and emphatic action that communicates, "You want me to look at it this way, but I'm going to do it in just the opposite way."

The experience of anxiety is also likely to influence card-turning behavior, although not in such a clearly defined manner as being compulsive (as reflected in looking at all or most cards carefully in each position) or feeling defiant at the moment (as reflected in turning each card upside down immediately on being handed it). Feeling anxious about being examined may lead to guardedness and minimal involvement in the Rorschach, which would be manifest in no card turning at all, or concerns about doing well, which might lead to a conscientious search for percepts involving considerable card turning.

In addition, as elaborated in chapters 5 and 6, specific percepts and associations that subjects form while looking at the inkblots can be upsetting to them and cause them to become situationally anxious. Subjects can sometimes reduce their distress in such situations by turning the card after giving a response that upsets them. From a sideways or inverted position the disturbing percept may be less visible or may even disappear, and from the new perspective subjects may even be able to articulate a relatively benign response in its stead. In giving such replacement responses subjects may at times verbalize the role of the card turning in reducing their distress. Consider, for example, a subject who first sees Card V as "a vampire bat, looking for someone to bite," which is an accurately perceived Popular that nevertheless connotes concerns about being victimized by a dangerous creature. After giving this response the subject turns the blot over and says, "It's better this way, just a butterfly." This sequence of responses lends strength to the inference that the "vampire" response was distressing, while at the same time it shows the utility of turning the card in taking distance from an anxiety-provoking response and replacing it with a bland impression of the blot.

The influence of situational test-related anxiety on card turning may also appear without any obviously disturbing percept being articulated. Suppose a subject studies Card VI carefully for a while, says, "I'm not sure what this is," and then inverts the card and describes it as "a bearskin rug." If the Popular "bearskin rug" was available as a response, why did the subject not give it in the upright position without having to turn the card first? Could it be that something about the inkblot in its upright position triggered some disturbing associations that suffused the Popular and motivated the subject to invert the card? If so, could the disturbing element have been the phallic-like projection sticking up at the top of the blot? Although this line of reasoning requires confirmation before being considered valid, as emphasized in chapter 6, it serves to illustrate how response-determined anxiety can lead to inverting a card. Unlike card turning motivated by defiance, which is typically an immediate and automatic act performed before the subject has even glanced at the card, card turning motivated by anxiety usually occurs only after a subject has looked at an inkblot and formed some impression of it.

Numerous other personality traits and states could be added to this brief illustrative list of characteristics that influence card-turning behavior. What needs to be kept in mind, however, is that none of these personality characteristics necessarily or inevitably leads to particular patterns of card turning, nor do the ways in which subjects turn the cards or ask about doing so always identify any specific personality trait or state. For example, the links suggested in previous examples between authoritarianism and the absence of card turning, and between compulsivity and extensive card turning, can easily be reversed. Thus, a subject with an authoritarian personality who is concerned about following the rules and gaining the examiner's approval, and who sees the Rorschach situation as calling for a high *quantity* of production, might turn the cards frequently in the process of giving a long record. Conversely, a cooperative but compulsive individual who sees good performance on the Rorschach as measured by a high *quality* of production might strive to develop the best possible response to each card in its original position, and not turn the cards at all in the process of producing a short record composed of the kinds of responses aptly referred to by Schachtel (1966, p. 292) as "definite masterpieces."

Despite allowances that must constantly be made for such alternative possibilities, subjects' personal dispositions and current attitudes and affects are nevertheless likely to influence whether and how they turn the cards, and card-turning behavior can accordingly provide clues to these personality characteristics. As in the case of interpreting content themes, examiners need to ponder what particular patterns of card turning might signify and then formulate reasonable hypotheses concerning the personality characteristics that contribute to and are therefore likely to be revealed by card-turning behavior. To assist in formulating such hypotheses, card-turning behavior can be distinguished as occurring in two varieties. As already implied, some card turning represents a style of searching for percepts and includes behaviors that can be categorized as *curious turning*, *systematic turning*, *haphazard turning*, and *oppositional turning*. Other instances of turning the cards serve as signals of distress and can be categorized as *avoidant turning*.

Curious Turning

Although specific categories of card-turning behavior have yet to be codified and monitored for their frequency in research studies, a curious search for percepts probably accounts for most instances of looking at the inkblots in various positions. This is not to say that finding percepts in the inkblots is difficult. To the contrary, research on the Rorschach response process has revealed that almost everyone can see many more potential responses than they actually report; J. E. Exner (1993, p. 34) estimated in this regard that subjects typically deliver fewer than one fourth of the answers available to them. Hence subjects' difficulties in responding are typically not a matter of finding responses, but of deciding which and how many of their impressions to share with the examiner. The search for a manageable number of responses with which subjects can feel comfortable often leads them to turn the cards out of curiosity.

Whether or not with permission, curious card turning usually consists of looking briefly at some but not all of the cards in various positions, turning these cards casually into some but not all possible positions, and giving responses in some but not all of the positions in which the card is viewed. Consistent with its brief and casual nature, the act of looking at a particular blot in a particular position may often be nothing more than a quick glance, after which the card is returned to the original upright position. Hence curious card turning is unsystematic and gives little indication that the subject attaches much importance to the process of examining the blots from different perspectives.

There is a possibility that some of the plates are more likely than others to pull card-turning behavior. For example, the position of the popular animal details on Card VIII (D1) appears to lead fairly frequently to curious card turning, as if to get a clearer view of the figure. As just mentioned, there has been no research on card-turning behavior to identify any such nomothetic patterns. From an idiographic perspective, however, curious card turning has few implications for personality functioning, other than representing a normative approach to the Rorschach task that stands in contrast to the other categories of card turning discussed next. Whereas curious card turning suggests that a subject is reasonably relaxed and at least moderately involved in the examination situation, these other categories provide clues to inflexibility, defensiveness, and distress.

Systematic Turning

As distinct from curious turning of the inkblots, systematic card turning represents a purposeful and determined effort to examine the inkblots in a thorough and regularized fashion. In its most extreme form, systematic turning consists of (a) looking at each and every card first in its upright position and then in each of the other three possible positions, in the same sequence; (b) not merely glancing at but studying each card carefully for some period of time in each position; and (c) either giving responses in each position or, by some comment, indicating that consideration was given to articulating a response in that position (e.g., "On this one I'm not able to see anything when I hold it sideways" or "It still looks like the same thing from this angle"). The closer subjects come to this pattern, the more systematic they are being in their card-turning behavior and the more likely they are to display personality characteristics associated with this type of behavior.

Specifically, systematic card turning suggests a compulsive personality style marked by rigidity, inflexibility, and a penchant for orderliness. People who turn the cards systematically are likely to be conscientious, dedicated, and disciplined individuals who follow strict sets of rules and take their lives and their responsibilities seriously. In addition, subjects who take the trouble to turn the cards systematically are usually very much involved in the test-taking process. Except for rare instances in which a person gives a short, high *Lambda* record despite systematic card turning, this test behavior increases the likelihood that the obtained Rorschach data are broadly and accurately reflective of the subject's personality functioning.

Haphazard Turning

In haphazard card turning, subjects turn more of the cards more frequently than in curious turning but without the orderliness and consistent sequence seen in systematic card turning. The cards move round and round in the subject's hands and back and forth between different positions, many of which are held for only a few seconds. This seemingly aimless turning of the cards rarely eventuates in much productivity, however. Whether of long or short duration, haphazard card turning serves no productive purpose. Instead, this pattern typically generates only a few brief and grudgingly delivered responses and is often a prelude to attempts at rejection (e.g., "I don't see anything in this one," or "This one doesn't look like anything").

Subjects who display haphazard card turning usually have only a minimal investment in the Rorschach task. Especially when they give just a single response or attempt rejection after just a brief period of haphazard card turning, they are likely to have little interest in being examined or to be making a determined effort to avoid becoming involved in it. Subjects taking the Rorschach in this way may even seem to be bored or to have their mind elsewhere, and they may go so far as to yawn frequently, drum their fingers impatiently, or look around the room or out the window after finishing with a card, rather than keeping their attention focused on the examiner and showing some anticipation of viewing the next card. Some may compound their limited search for percepts with such comments as, "I hope this doesn't last too long, because I've got something important to do after I'm done here"—thus implying that what is being done here is not very important.

Subjects who extend haphazard card turning over some period of time do not necessarily give more responses than those who give the cards extremely short shrift, but the way in which they are limiting their involvement in the examination at least suggests some motivation to give the appearance of being cooperative. Unlike short-shrift haphazard card turners, who have little compunction and show no embarrassment about treating the examination as a waste of their time, those who go more fully through the motions of complying with the procedures often make comments intended to placate rather than put off the examiner, such as, "I'm sorry I can't tell you anymore, but I'm doing my best." Despite such pleasantries as may occur, however, neither seemingly diligent nor overtly detached subjects who display haphazard card turning are in fact doing their best, except with reference to minimizing their engagement in the response process. Accordingly, haphazard card turning often gives reason to be concerned that the obtained Rorschach data provide only a similarly fleeting glimpse of the subject's personality characteristics.

Oppositional Turning

The hallmark of oppositional card turning, as previously noted, is a pointed and emphatic reversal of the position of the cards when taking them in hand. Oppositional card turning is characterized further by a subject's turning many or most of the cards in this way and inverting them immediately, with barely a glance at the inkblot. The more frequently cards are inverted in such a preemptory and automatic fashion, without there having been any opportunity for card pull influence on the subject's behavior, the more likely it is that oppositional card turning is being manifested.

As a fairly transparent representative sample of behavior, oppositional card turning provides good evidence of a general inclination to favor defiance over compliance and resistance over capitulation. Although there are circumstances in which compliance and capitulation represent maladaptive coping strategies while defiance and resistance would serve constructive purposes, oppositional card turning rarely signifies an adaptive balance between doing and refusing to do what one is asked or expected to do. Instead, this particular test behavior usually identifies subjects' predilection for constant strained efforts to assert their autonomy, even at the expense of being perceived as difficult, uncooperative, or intransigent. Some oppositional card turners may assert their autonomy in a relatively hostile and overtly belligerent manner, and others in a relatively deceptive and passive–aggressive fashion; which manner is more likely is often suggested by the subject's content themes and such structural variables as the $a{:}p$ ratio.

Unlike haphazard card turning, however, oppositional card turning does not necessarily limit the length or richness of a Rorschach protocol. For some generally oppositional subjects the situation of being examined by a person they perceive as an authoritarian and intrusive figure may exacerbate their usual recalcitrance and result in their giving a short, sketchy, and uninformative record. For others, however, the act of beginning to examine the cards in exactly the opposite position from the one shown to them may prove sufficient to demonstrate their autonomy. Having done so, they may proceed to respond fully and openly and even revert to a pattern of curious or systematic card turning.

Avoidant Turning

In contrast to card turning that represents curious, systematic, haphazard, or oppositional styles of searching for percepts, avoidant turning constitutes an effort to deny or take distance from percepts rather than find them. Unlike these other patterns of card turning, then, avoidant turning is not a persistent feature of how people deal with many or most of the cards, nor does it provide information about a subject's test-taking attitudes or general personality characteristics. Rather, avoidant turning occurs as a specific negative reaction to a particular response or blot characteristic and reveals distress associated with the subject's impressions and associations at the moment.

Avoidant card turning contributes to the interpretive process by helping to highlight responses or blot characteristics that should receive special attention for their possible dynamic significance. Every change in the position of a card that does not appear determined by a stylistic pattern of card turning gives good reason to examine the response preceding it for potentially interpretable indications of the origins of the subject's distress. Interpretively significant clues to distress often appear in the thematic content of a response that has precipitated inversion of a card, as in the instance of a person struggling with concerns about hostility who turns Card II immediately after reporting, "Two bears fighting and hurting each other." A less direct but still pertinent clue to the underlying concerns in this example could also emerge in a comment about the blot, such as "I don't like the red in this one."

There are also times when subjects turn a card in avoidance without reporting a response or giving any other manifest clue to the impression or association that disturbed them. In these instances, the common expectations for each card, as presented in chapter 4, sometimes provide useful basis for speculation about what is causing the subject's distress. For example, Card III is frequently seen as two people engaged in some joint venture. People who are unhappy and depressed about lacking opportunities for close and collaborative interpersonal relationships may perceive a cooperative M in Card III, even without being consciously aware of doing so, then become upset at contemplating pleasant interactions being enjoyed by others but not being available to them, and then, without delivering a response, turn the card over to make the upsetting confrontation go away. In this instance, the subject's inversion of Card III after looking at it for a while, particularly if not followed by any good human responses and if accompanied by other behavioral signs of distress, suggests the possibility that the subject is troubled by an unsatisfying interpersonal life. In this manner, then, whenever it occurs, avoidant card turning, as distinguished from other card-turning patterns that reflect general attitudes and coping styles, signals that aspects of a response or card, whether or not articulated, have some special meaning for the subject and should be given careful attention for their interpretive significance.

Avoidant card turning may occur once or many times during a Rorschach administration, depending on how frequently subjects form an impression or association that troubles them and how inclined they are to use card turning as a way of escaping or taking distance from a troubling percept or blot characteristic. Subjects who resort frequently to avoidant turning are usually finding the Rorschach task very difficult and are struggling to find answers they can feel comfortable giving. Such desperate searching is typically bred of reluctance to be forthcoming, not inability to see things in the blots. Particularly when relatively few responses emerge despite lengthy examination of many or all of the blots involving considerable card turning, it is usually the case that subjects who would like to cooperate and do what the examiner wants can nevertheless not bring themselves to share their impressions freely.

Card Handling

Along with noting how subjects turn the cards in their search for percepts, examiners can learn a good deal about their attitudes toward the examination and their interpersonal style by observing how they handle the Rorschach cards. Ways of handling the cards are more varied and less readily categorized than patterns of card turning. Nevertheless, it is possible to illustrate some common and revealing ways in which subjects take, hold, and return the cards.

How do subjects take each card from the examiner, for example? As the examiner takes each card off the stack, do subjects lean forward and reach out to take it and thus spare the examiner from even having to extend an arm? Or do subjects instead sit back motionless and wait for the examiner to lean forward, reach out, and literally place each card in their hands? It is reasonable to infer that the subject in the first instance is positively motivated to participate in the examination and respectful of and eager to please the examiner. The subject in the second instance, unless seriously depressed or extraordinarily passive, is probably trying to avoid becoming involved in the examination process and is also making a point of not being subservient to the examiner—the examiner is in effect being treated as a lackey who must do all of the work.

Once subjects have the cards in their hands, they may reflect various attitudes in how they hold them. Subjects who are trying to keep disengaged from the examination may treat the cards with disdain, as objects not worth holding. After taking a card in hand at the examiner's insistence, for example, they may drop it on the table with a show of distaste as if it were some foul-smelling object and then give their responses without picking it up again. Subjects responding in this way who wish to turn the card may just poke at it with one finger to move it into another position. Such disrespect for the cards strongly suggests disrespect for the examination and for the examiner as well. Generally speaking, how subjects handle an examiner's cards speaks to how they regard and plan to treat the examiners themselves.

As another example of distancing in card holding, subjects who intend no disrespect but are troubled by what they see in the cards may also prefer not to keep holding them, at least not close. Such subjects may stretch out their arms and hold the cards as far away as possible, presumably in order to see them better this way. At times, subjects may even prop up the cards in some way so that they can step back and look at them from afar. Except when such behavior is attributable to farsightedness, it is likely to reveal test-determined distress.

Most subjects continue to hold the cards until they are through with them and do so in an unremarkable fashion that does not convey much information about their attitudes and personality style. In some instances, however, they may hold the card especially carefully and gently, as people hold something both valuable and fragile. Possible sources of such behavior include an unusual degree of timidity, fearfulness of doing the wrong thing, extremely high regard for the examiner's status and property, and strong needs to please the examiner and be given a good report. On other occasions, subjects may grasp the cards roughly, as if unconcerned about or perhaps intent on doing them some harm. They may go so far as to flick the cards with their fingers or "accidentally" drop one or more on the floor. Behaviors of this type suggest hostility toward the examination, disrespect for the examiner, and denigration of the test results, all being taken out on the cards. Whatever other forms they may take, such unusual ways of holding the cards typically have fairly transparent implications for the manner in which subjects are structuring in their own minds the nature and purposes of the examination and their relationship with the examiner.

After subjects are finished with a card, they need to return it to the examiner. Characteristic features of how subjects took the cards often recur when they give them back, thus confirming inferences based on their card-handling behavior. Those that reached out to take the cards now reach out to give them back. In some cases, this courtesy and apparent wish to comply, cooperate, and make a good impression extends to direct assistance: Having seen the examiner place returned cards in a pile, subjects begin themselves to put each card on the pile after their last response to it. Those who are orderly or compulsive by nature may even take care to keep the cards neatly stacked. By contrast, subjects involved in a covert power struggle with the examiner, who are determined not be subservient and who initially waited for the examiner to place the cards in their hands, now move nary a muscle to return it. Instead, they make it necessary for the examiner once more to reach out and do all of the work necessary to retrieve the card.

Subjects who feel negatively toward the examination process may at times show their feelings in other pointed ways when they are through looking at the cards. Whereas subjects who care about the examiner's good will may stack the cards neatly, those who are attempting to demean the importance of the examination may just toss the cards more or less in the examiner's direction after they have finished their responses. As in all of these examples and others that could be generated, the interpretive significance of card-handling behaviors is to be found in the motivations that appear to have caused them.

COMMENTS AND PERSONALS

As already indicated in many previous examples, the interpretive significance of Rorschach responses is often enriched by comments and personalized remarks that accompany them. Personalized remarks that have a direct bearing on why the blots look as they do—as in "It looks like a piece of machinery that I use in my work" or "My mother used to have a brooch with this same kind of design on it"—are formally coded as Personal (*PER*) in the Comprehensive System. *PER* thus constitutes a structural variable and, as shown in Table 3.1, loads on the interpersonal cluster. For purposes of discussion, however, there is some benefit to considering Personals along with other kinds of comments as aspects of subjects' test behavior.

Comments

People responding to the Rorschach frequently make comments that are not an integral part of reporting what certain parts of the inkblots might be and why. These extra-test comments can be categorized by distinguishing among those that are *response-referential*, those that are *self-referential*, and those that are *examiner-referential*. As elaborated next, all three kinds of comments typically reveal either certain generally characteristic attitudes of the subject or subjects' specific thoughts and feelings about the examination situation. Hence, attending to these comments and speculating about their possible meaning can provide useful information about these attitudes, thoughts, and feelings.

Response-Referential Comments. Comments of this type consist mainly of evaluative statements about responses or about the inkblot stimuli and running explanations of how subjects are approaching their task. In making evaluative comments about their responses, subjects often give some indication that a response pleases or displeases them ("I like that response"; "I don't think that's a very good response"). Responses that elicit expressions of pleasure may contain elements bearing on aspects of their lives in which subjects correspondingly take pleasure, whereas expressly displeasing responses may furnish clues to the nature or extent of distressing concerns.

For example, subjects who say to Card III, "Two people helping each other; I like that response," are giving a good form cooperative *M* and also indicating that they are probably quite comfortable with the type of interpersonal interaction it represents and likely to be involved in such interactions. By contrast, consider this response to Card V: "It looks like a black umbrella, with the edges tattered like it got caught in a storm; that's probably not a very good response." Now we have a minus form, Morbid, *FC'* response with a strong depressive flavor, along with expressed displeasure to lend emphasis to how distressing it is for this subject to deal with experiences that connote dysphoria or bodily damage.

In addition to helping to identify specific sources of pleasure or distress in subjects' lives, evaluative comments on responses may have more general implications for subjects' attitudes toward themselves if they become pervasive. Frequent positive comments about their responses suggests that subjects are generally inclined to be pleased with themselves and their products, even to regularly letting other people know what a good job they think they are doing, as in, "That's a good response, isn't it?" Conversely, repeated negative comments about responses constitute a form of bad-mouthing that may generally characterize how subjects view their own efforts, as in, "I guess I've given another poor response there, haven't I?"

Instead of revealing self-attitudes in repetitive evaluative comments about their responses, subjects may offer opinions and value judgments that reflect characteristic ways of viewing others. For example, consider Card I as "A statue in the middle, a figurine, very nicely carved" and Card X as "An example of modern art, but it's not very well done." Aesthetic considerations aside, these two responses illustrate very different attitudes toward other people and what they produce. The first example carries a tone of admiration and respect, whereas the second smacks of scorn and denigration. Remaining always careful to avoid overgeneralization from a single instance, examiners may nevertheless learn from repetitive comments of this kind that one person is generally of a generous nature and inclined to look for and extol the good in people, whereas another person tends generally to view people cynically and unsympathetically as deserving to be put down rather than lifted up.

Evaluative comments about the inkblots can have implications for what causes subjects pleasure or distress and can reveal generally benevolent or malevolent attitudes. Thus, saying Card VIII "is a pretty one" may indicate comfort and enjoyment in dealing with affectively stimulating situations; repetitive comments of this kind, especially when addressed to cards that people rarely describe in glowing evaluative terms (such as IV and VI), may identify a persistent need or orientation to seeing the world in positive terms and/or a positive attitude toward being examined and a wish to curry favor with examiners by praising their materials. Contrariwise, "I don't like this one" can be a clue to difficulties in processing commonly noted stimulus characteristics of the blots (such as the textural qualities of Card VI) or common associations to them (such as the aggressive interactions frequently attributed to Card II); repetitive negative comments about the blots can reflect a generally sour disposition and/or negative attitudes toward being examined and a wish to demean examiners by demeaning the quality of their materials.

At times, evaluative comments about particular blot details can suggest specific interpretive hypotheses concerning subjects' underlying concerns. Consider, for example, a subject who gives a popular animal skin response to the lower portion of Card VI (D1) and then says about the upper center portion (D6) such things as "What's that ugly thing?", "I wouldn't want to go near that, whatever it is," or "That part doesn't belong." In the spirit of conservative symbolic interpretation, these comments could be interpreted as meaning nothing at all, just as Freud's cigar was simply his cigar. As another possibility, however, such comments could indicate some troubling concerns about dealing with male sexuality. Similarly, suppose a subject reports a popular "two women from the waist up" to the upper details of Card VII (D2), but then says the lower part (D4) "has nothing to do with it" and, pointing specifically at the lower center detail (D6), adds "and this in particular means nothing to me." A male subject commenting in this way could be fearful of or disinterested in physical heterosexual intimacy, and a female subject saying this might be revealing needs to minimize or deny the importance of her own sexuality in her life.

Finally, with respect to response-referential comments, subjects may provide some clues to aspects of their personality functioning by describing their own response process. Thus, subjects who are giving an unusual frequency of W responses make it a point to say, "I prefer to use the whole blot each time," thereby adding emphasis to their apparently global orientation and insufficient attention to the details of their experience. Similarly, pervasively introversive subjects may go out of their way on Cards VIII–X to say, "I didn't use the color" or "The color has no significance," even when they have given such responses as "a bouquet of flowers" or "an underwater scene," and thereby make all the more clear their difficulty in recognizing or expressing their feelings. In terms of thematic implications, subjects giving a popular human figure to the upper and side parts of Card IV (D7) may state emphatically about the lower center part (D1) that "I didn't use this part" or "This down here is not part of it." Like the disavowal of D6 on Card VI, this pointed exclusion of D1 on Card IV provides reason to consider the possibility of—but not definitely to infer—some phallic aversion.

Self-Referential Comments. Comments that are self-referential but not Personals occur most commonly in the form of expressed opinions or concerns about performance. In a positive vein, subjects may compliment themselves by saying such things as "I did pretty well on that one, didn't I" or "I guess I gave you plenty of responses." This kind of self-congratulation may indicate general narcissistic tendencies to applaud oneself without embarrassment, or compensatory needs for self-reassurance to ward off concerns about not performing well, or an attempt to elicit praise or reassurance from the examiner. As in other instances of multiple interpretive possibilities, examiners need to sort out which among the alternatives seems most consistent with other available data.

By contrast, subjects may be self-critical and self-depreciatory in commenting on their performance, as by saying, "I don't think I did very well on that one" or "I probably didn't give you enough responses" or "I'm not very good at this sort of thing." Opposite to self-congratulation, self-abnegation may reflect chronic low self-esteem, and the apology contained in confessions of inadequacy may be motivated by hopes of eliciting sympathy and forgiveness from the examiner. In addition, apparently self-critical comments such as "This is not my cup of tea" may also constitute subtle ways of taking distance from the examination and minimizing the significance of the Rorschach findings. That is, by saying that they have little talent for complying with the instructions, they are saying that the RIM is not a suitable measure for assessing them and that little stock should be taken in whatever their responses appear to suggest.

Along with evaluative comments, another frequent kind of self-referential comment consists of asides and off-task revelations that often approach but do not meet criteria for being coded as a Deviant Response (*DR*). Typical examples of this kind of comment include the following: "It's a bug; I don't like bugs"; "It looks like a lake; fishing is my favorite hobby"; "I've always liked pretty colors, and I've sometimes thought about taking up painting myself"; "It looks like they're fighting, and that's something I don't believe in." Although not Personals, by virtue of not being advanced as a basis for seeing what has been reported, comments of this type can provide information about subjects' actual lives, such as their favorite hobby.

In addition, self-referential asides often have implications for underlying motivations that prompt them. As one possibility, they may indicate subjects' needs to reach out to the examiner and have the examiner become more fully aware of and more favorably disposed to the kind of person they are. As a second possibility, they are often employed as a subtle effort to divert attention from the Rorschach task. It is as if subjects are attempting to say with these asides, "Let's put these blots away and just talk about me, and I'll tell you whatever you want to know." This latter possibility should be considered in particular when asides follow responses that appear to have been upsetting in some way to a subject; conversely, the appearance of asides may be a clue to distress having been experienced in relation to the response that preceded them.

Examiner-Referential Comments. Like response-referential and self-referential comments, remarks about or addressed to the examiner (e.g., "Do you do a lot of this kind of testing?") often represent an effort to take some distance from the Rorschach task. In addition to interrupting the free association or inquiry process, these comments often serve as an indirect way of suggesting that there are other more interesting matters that could be discussed—usually matters less distressing and revealing than formulating Rorschach responses—if only the examiner would put the inkblots away. As in the case of other kinds of comments, then, those involving the examiner may provide clues to the particular impact of aspects of the response process that have immediately preceded them.

In addition, examiner-referential comments can be useful in identifying how subjects feel about the testing situation and toward people in general. Like patients in psychotherapy manifesting positive transference, subjects whose attitudes toward being examined are primarily positive and who wish to curry the examiner's favor often say so in various direct or indirect ways. Directly, they may intersperse their responses with expressions of appreciation for the examiner's availability to see them and spend so much time with them; with compliments on the examiner's style ("You have a very gentle approach") or appearance ("That's a nice outfit you're wearing"); or with praise for the examiner's abilities ("I was told you have an excellent reputation"). Indirectly, positively inclined subjects may show their feelings with comments about the examiner's possessions ("This is a comfortable office"), profession ("I think I'd enjoy your line of work"), or measures ("From what I've heard, these inkblots are supposed to be a pretty good test").

In opposite fashion, subjects who dislike or resent being examined and hold the examiner at least partly responsible may reveal their displeasure in a variety of negative comments. Directly, they complain about the examination ("I don't see any purpose in this"), question the usefulness of the procedures ("I read somewhere that these inkblots are not a valid measure of anything"), or challenge the competence of the examiner ("How many evaluations like this have you done?"). Indirectly, they may find fault with the examiner's location ("How come you have your office in such an out-of-the-way place?"), activities ("It must be pretty dull doing what you do all day long"), and procedures ("I don't think the way your secretary answers the telephone is very courteous").

When positive and negative examiner-referential comments of these kinds occur repeatedly, they begin to suggest not just specific reactions to the examination situation, but also more general dispositions to approach people and situations in either a salubrious or dyspeptic frame of mind. The types of interpersonal attitudes subjects reveal in their comments can take many specific forms beyond simply having a positive or negative flavor. Many aspects of subjects' test behavior in addition to their comments contribute to inferences about their interpersonal style, and these are discussed further in the final section of this chapter concerned with expressive and interpersonal style.

Personals

As previously noted, responses coded as Personals (*PER*) consist of comments in which subjects explain or justify a response on the basis of their past experience or prior knowledge. Personals accordingly constitute on-task behavior and share with determinants the role of accounting for why the inkblots looked as they did to a subject. For interpretive purposes it is helpful to categorize Personals into three types—*self-justifying, self-aggrandizing*, and *self-revealing*—with somewhat different implications.

Self-Justifying Personals. Self-justifying Personals consist of straightforward and unelaborated statements of resemblance between a blot or blot detail and something the subject has seen elsewhere. Common examples of this type of Personal would be a bat that "looks just like ones I've seen"; cartoon figures that "I see on the television"; and organs of the body that "are like pictures I've seen in an anatomy book." Such unelaborated Personals serve primarily defensive purposes for subjects who utilize them. That is, by justifying a Rorschach percept on the basis of actual perceptions in their lives, subjects attempt to minimize any possibility of their reporting an inaccurate impression or appearing to lack a good reason for having reported it. Subjects who frequently resort to such self-justifying Personals are likely to be insecure people who lack confidence in their capacities and judgment and are inclined to defend against the anxiety of uncertainty by going to great lengths to let others know the basis of their actions and conclusions.

Self-Aggrandizing Personals. Self-aggrandizing Personals go beyond mere mention of prior knowledge or experience that justify a percept to elaborate in proud fashion how much the subject knows or has done. In this type of Personal, for example, a totem pole on Card VI becomes "the kind of native symbol I remember from my travels to the South Seas"; Card IX "reminds me of the impressionist paintings I've seen hanging in the Louvre"; and a jet airplane on Card II evokes the comment, "I used to fly one of those suckers, and I know all about them." People who give numerous self-aggrandizing Personals may be basically insecure, just as those who give numerous self-justifying Personals, but they are inclined to defend against their insecurity quite differently. Instead of apologetically attempting to prove themselves adequate and respectable, they immodestly tout their talents and accomplishments to prove themselves superior and admirable. They are accordingly likely to conduct their interpersonal relationships in a narcissistic fashion intended to impress others, including the examiner. Their narcissism is typically serving compensatory purposes, however, and others may find their overbearing, self-focused, know-it-all manner difficult to tolerate.

Self-Revealing Personals. Self-revealing Personals resemble self-aggrandizing Personals in providing elaborations beyond minimal justification of a response, but they have a flavor more of sharing information than of showing off. Illustrative Personals of this type would be "It looks just like my dog at home; I've had a lot of pets, but I like dogs best"; "It's a rose arbor, like my grandmother used to have when I was young and lived with her"; "An animal skin rug, something like one we have in our family room."

Self-revealing Personals often indicate an effort by subjects to reach out to the examiner, as if to say, "I want you to know more about me as a person." Not infrequently, this kind of Personal has an appealing quality, even if it momentarily interrupts the response process. Unlike the other two types of Personals, moreover, self-revealing Personals are likely to have positive rather than negative implications for interpersonal adaptation, particularly with respect to a genuine interest in sharing personal experiences with others. As a possible corollary of such interest, informative and relatively nondefensive Personals may predict openness and a strong commitment to the treatment alliance in patients entering psychotherapy.

EXPRESSIVE AND INTERPERSONAL STYLE

The manner in which subjects express themselves in delivering Rorschach responses and the interpersonal style with which they relate to the examiner in so doing constitute the final aspects of test behavior that contribute information to the interpretive process. Key aspects of expressive style include ways of engaging in or avoiding the Rorschach task, ways of using language, and ways of showing affect. Interpersonal style in Rorschach testing consists of the manner in which subjects present themselves as parties to a two-person situation in which one person is evaluating the other.

Engaging in or Avoiding the Rorschach Task

Most subjects, most of the time, respond to the Rorschach task by taking the cards as handed to them, looking at them, saying what they might be, handing them back, and subsequently responding to the examiner's inquiry questions in a task-oriented manner. These behaviors define engagement in the Rorschach task, and they demonstrate both subjects' cooperation with the examination procedures and their general capacity to respond appropriately and responsibly in necessary, even if unwelcome, problem-solving situations. By contrast, some subjects, even when giving an adequate number of responses, sometimes reveal in their test behavior efforts to disengage from the Rorschach task. The appearance of such momentary avoidance in subtle aspects of how subjects turn and handle the cards and intersperse their responses with comments has already been discussed in this chapter. Subjects' expressive style may in addition provide fairly direct indications of task avoidance that take the form of changing the subject, disavowing responsibility, or refraining from responding at all.

Changing the Subject. Subjects who change the subject while taking the Rorschach typically produce the kinds of off-task comments previously noted. However, some further characterization of these comments is helpful in identifying and assigning appropriate significance to them. Subjects may change the subject directly, as by starting to talk about their symptoms instead of looking at a card that has just been handed to them. Less directly, they may begin by talking about the blots instead of responding to them, as with "It's colorful," "This one is quite symmetrical, with a distinct line down the middle," or "A lot of these look the same." Descriptions of this type help subjects maintain the pretense of being engaged in the Rorschach task, but in fact they serve as ways of avoiding giving responses. Examiners should never accept such comments about the inkblots in lieu of responses indicating what they might be; in every such case, unless responses subsequently emerge, examiners should respond to card descriptions by saying, "Yes, but what might it be?"

Disavowing Responsibility. As in other instances in which the response process becomes disrupted in some way, attempts to change the topic call for attention to possible features of the inkblots or the associations they are stimulating that are causing the subject some distress. The presence of distressing concerns can similarly be inferred from efforts to disavow responses either before giving them ("It doesn't really look one, but it could be a . . ."; "If I really stretch my imagination, I could say it's . . .") or after the fact (". . . but it's not a good likeness"; ". . . although, to tell you the truth, it's not anything at all, just a blob of ink").

This last example in particular has many earmarks of attempts to avoid or deny by disavowal what a response has signified to a subject. As a form of expression, "To tell you the truth" often gives reason to wonder whether what will be said or was just said has some grains of untruth; why else would it be necessary for individuals to make a point of pledging their truthfulness when no one has questioned it? By saying, "It's not anything at all," subjects instruct the examiner to pay no attention to what the response may in fact suggest; by adding for good measure that it is "just a blob of ink," subjects reassure themselves that there is no reality to whatever the blot has made them think or feel.

Refraining From Responding. The most obvious way in which subjects attempt to avoid engagement in the Rorschach task is by refraining from responding at all. Short of stating an unwillingness to be examined, subjects can be unresponsive either by attempting to reject one or more cards or by a long delay in their reaction time. Examiners who follow closely the Comprehensive System guidelines for administration will rarely encounter rejections. Informing reluctant subjects that "You can take your time, we've got as long as we need, and you'll see some things sooner or later" almost always proves sufficient to elicit responses that presumably were being withheld. In fact, rejections occur so rarely in properly conducted administrations that their presence gives good reason to question the validity of the obtained data, even if the total number of responses is adequate (i.e., $R > 13$). For interpretive purposes, efforts to reject ("I don't see anything in this one"; "This one doesn't look like anything"; "Nothing but a bunch of colors") convey the same information as do other indices of avoidance. Specifically, attempted rejection of a card means that (a) something is troubling the subject, (b) the source of the trouble lies somewhere in the characteristics of the blot or the impressions it has conveyed, and (c) identifying this source will contribute to understanding the subject as a person.

Delayed responding, particularly when subjects are apparently looking intently at a card, has the same interpretive implications as attempts at rejection. Normatively, most subjects give their first response to most cards within several seconds. Reaction times longer than 10 seconds begin to suggest that subjects are having some difficulty with a card, the nature of which can be revealing. As reaction times grow longer, the likelihood of difficulty increases and the interpretive significance of this difficulty becomes greater. Similar considerations may apply when subjects give a first response quickly and then study the card at length before giving a second response. In this instance, some structural or thematic feature of this second response may relate to underlying concerns that would be helpful to identify.

To illustrate the use of inordinately long reaction times as a clue to psychological problems, suppose a subject responds promptly on each of the five colored cards but very slowly on each of the gray-black cards. It may well be that this person's delayed reaction time on the achromatic cards represents difficulty dealing with gloomy situations and reflects a depressive affective state. Long reaction times preceding responses containing certain kinds of thematic imagery may similarly be a clue to distress related to this imagery, and efforts to refrain from responding to certain cards may reveal concerns about themes usually associated with them, even if the subject does not articulate these themes. Why, for example, should a subject take a very long time to describe Card II as "Two bears playing"? Could it be that this easy and benign Popular emerged only after the subject struggled with aggressive or morbid connotations of the red color on the blot, and furthermore that the playful tone of the eventual response served particularly as a way of denying or warding off the discomfiting aggression or morbidity first associated to the card? There is no certain answer to this question in the absence of additional data; the point, however, is that this is the type of question that should be asked of patterns of test behavior that suggest avoidance of engagement in the Rorschach task.

Attempts at rejection and prolonged initial reaction times are of particular interest in this regard, because historically they served as the two main grounds for inferring "shock" on the Rorschach. The concept of "shock" was introduced by Hermann Rorschach as a way of referring to discrepant performance on the color cards. Along with "shading shock," which was later used to describe difficulties in dealing effectively with the gray-black cards, "color shock" was used for many years as an index of neurosis or maladjustment (see Goldfried et al., 1971, chap. 9). Shock also became interpreted in terms of its thematic as well as structural implications. In an extensive discussion of the concept of shock, Phillips and J. G. Smith (1953, chap. 8) assigned specific meaning to the appearance of shock on each of the 10 cards: for example, "Shock on Card I is evidence for an unresolved and intense relationship with a mother or nurturing figure" (p. 201) and "Shock on Card II is characteristic of persons who appear to be driven by intense, often uncontrolled, destructive impulses" (p. 205).

Over time it became clear that the proposed structural interpretations of shock lacked precision and the suggested symbolic significance of shock on each card lacked the necessary interpretive conservatism discussed previously in chapter 6. Neither color shock nor shading shock has demonstrated validity as an index of overall maladjustment, and the possible dynamic meanings of shock are always multiple rather than isomorphic. Regarding multiple dynamic meanings, the suggestion in the previous illustration of Card II seen as "Bears playing" following a long reaction time (i.e., that the subject was struggling with and defending against aggressive and morbid connotations of the blot) is consistent with the Phillips and Smith guideline for interpreting shock on this card. As an alternative possibility, however, suppose this subject's attention was captured not by the red on Card II, but by associations to two figures interacting pleasantly and enjoying themselves, and suppose further that this person feels distressed by a lack of pleasurable interpersonal interactions in life. Then actually seeing Card II as bears playing could be what is upsetting the subject and causing the delayed reaction time, which in turn provides the clue that something about Card II is upsetting.

As discussed in chapter 6, only with additional information from a subject's response elaborations, from other test data, or from posttesting discussion of the subject's associations can uncertainty involving such alternative possibilities be resolved. Nevertheless, despite the shortcomings of classical notions of shock, the likelihood remains that attempts at rejection and delayed reaction times combine with other indices of subject distress—including form distortion, critical special scores, avoidant card turning, off-task comments, and direct expressions of dismay—to guide examiners in formulating potentially fruitful questions concerning why they have occurred here and now.

Using Language

The language that people use in expressing themselves usually reveals a great deal about their intelligence, level of education, personality style, and present frame of mind. Much can be inferred about these characteristics by attending to such language features as a subject's vocabulary knowledge, verbal fluency, grammatical correctness, and penchant for pedantic, informal, profane, or other kinds of word usage. However useful it may be, on the other hand, learning about people from the language they use in giving Rorschach responses involves general clinical skills rather than any types of data or psychodiagnostic acumen specific to the RIM. Consistent with the emphasis throughout this chapter, the discussion here focuses on three types of linguistic data specific to the Rorschach task: wordiness, qualifiers, and sign-offs.

Wordiness. Wordiness in Rorschach responses refers simply to how many words subjects use in framing their responses. Examiners are typically aware without having to do a word count of whether a record comprises mainly responses of ordinary length, contains many unusually long and elaborated responses, or consists primarily of brief, "bare bones" responses. The difference between garrulous and terse responses can be especially meaningful in the free association period, before the examiner has begun any inquiry. For example, suppose a subject gives the following response to Card I: "It looks to me like some sort of a bat, like it's flying, because here's the body in the middle, and these outer parts look like wings stretched out, big wings, and they're all black, and bats are black, of course, and the head is up here and the tail is down here, and is there anything else I should tell you about it, except that I don't care much for bats?" By contrast, another subject says to Card I, "A black bat flying around." These two illustrative responses would be coded identically, as *Wo FMa.FC'o A P 1.0*. Clearly, however, their verbiage speaks to different characteristics in the two subjects.

Unusually long or short responses raise three interpretive possibilities. First, with regard to test-taking attitudes, garrulity and terseness may indicate, respectively, engagement and cooperation with the Rorschach task or avoidance and minimization of the response process. Second, with respect to personality style, being long-winded or cryptic during an examination may reflect a subject's general disposition to communicate with others in an expansive and forthcoming manner or to be a circumspect person of few words. Third, in terms of differential diagnosis, giving examiners a great many or a limited number of words to write down can provide clues to a subject's being hypomanic and energized in the first instance or depressed and lethargic in the second.

Qualifiers. Qualifiers consist of ways of introducing responses that indicate a subject's commitment to them. Most commonly people begin their Rorschach responses with such relatively noncommittal phrases as "It looks like . . . ," "It might be . . . ," "It resembles . . . ," or "It reminds me of . . ." In some instances, however, subjects load up on qualifying phrases in a way that goes beyond being normally noncommittal. To take some extreme examples, consider a subject who regularly begins response with such statements as, "Well, I suppose it might possibly could be . . ." or "If I really have to say something, and if I stretch my imagination, recognizing that it's not really anything, I could say . . ." Like the previously noted comments that involve disavowal of responsibility for responses, repeated use of such noncommittal qualifiers in introducing responses indicates some need to deny in advance the validity of any conclusions suggested by the test results. In addition, pervasive tentativeness in delivering responses may reflect a general personality style characterized by limited self-assurance, reluctance to take a definite stand on anything, and fearfulness of commitment.

Instead of being tentative, subjects may at times deviate from normative ways of qualifying their responses by expressing an unusual degree of certainty about them. Thus, they may say, "That's definitely . . . ," "No doubt about this one, it's . . . ," or "I'm sure this is . . ." Such certainty may be an indication that subjects generally have an assertive nature or strong needs to minimize ambiguity in their life. As another possibility, the sequence in which such definitive qualifiers occur may say something particular about subjects' underlying concerns. Say, for example, that a subject shows a long reaction time and considerable difficulty formulating an adequate response to Card IV and then, on being handed Card V, says emphatically, "Now I know what that is!" When firm commitment to a response or card follows a previous response or card that seemed troubling to subjects, this sequence lends emphasis to just how troubling the previous response; to anticipate chapter 8, this sequence also helps to identify one way in which people tend to deal with upsetting circumstances, that is, by a compensatory overemphasis on what is safe and certain.

Sign-offs. Sign-offs refer to phrases that subjects may use to end their responses to each card. Normatively, most people after giving their last response to a card hand it back or put it down without comment or make a matter-of-fact comment on the order of "That's all I see" or "I can't think of anything else on this one." Consistent with the guidelines for conservative interpretation presented earlier, little or no significance should be attached to sign-offs that approximate normative expectations. Occasionally, however, subjects handing back or putting down a card make conclusory statements that do convey some special meaning, depending on their content.

For example, consider the following sign-offs, each delivered emphatically: "There's nothing more on this card!"; "That's all I'm going to tell you about this one!"; "I have no idea what else it could be!" As in other instances when individuals protest too much, conclusory statements of this kind suggest that in fact there is something more on this card, that subjects have some idea of what it might be, and that, if willing, they could tell the examiner all about it. Such statements also convey a tone of assertiveness, certainty, and self-assurance that provides clues to similar characteristics in the subjects' general personality style.

As a further example involving a different shade of meaning, suppose a subject frequently signs off with statements such as "I'm afraid that's all I see," "I'm sorry I can't tell you more about it," or "I wish I could do a better job for you." Although perhaps serving as excuses for not being fully responsive, these comments differ sharply from those in the previous paragraph in their implications for the subject's personality style. Here there are suggestions of an apologetic, self-denigrating, self-effacing way of presenting oneself to others, even to the point of being concerned about performing well for the examiner's benefit.

Showing Affect

The affect that subjects display while taking the Rorschach has obvious implications for their emotional state at the time of the examination and for more enduring features of their affective style. Whether apparent in their overt emotions (laughing or crying), facial expressions (smiling or scowling), or tone of voice (plaintive or shrill), behaviorally observed affect constitutes an important source of information about a subject's personality functioning. Comparing the kinds of affect subjects show while taking the Rorschach with the affective implications of the structural and thematic features of their responses may be particularly revealing. In doing so, however, examiners should be attuned to learning from, rather than explaining away, any apparent discrepancies.

This latter point was well made by Schafer (1954), who pointed out that "observations of behavior should never be construed so as to negate certain general implications of the test responses proper, and vice versa" (p. 72). Thus, if subjects appear angry, anxious, elated, or depressed and give numerous Rorschach indications of these same affects, then inferences concerning their presence and pervasiveness are strengthened. Subjects who complain of and display apparently distressing affects but do not show them on the Rorschach, especially in the context of a rich protocol, may well be less distressed than they complain of being. On the contrary, subjects who appear emotionally calm but produce numerous Rorschach indices of emotional upset may well be heavily defended people who are more disturbed than they appear to be and have little awareness of their own problems.

Interpersonal Style

People taking the Rorschach bring to the testing situation and their relationship with the examiner the same personality traits and interpersonal attitudes that characterize how they generally conduct themselves. Consequently, the interpersonal style subjects manifest while taking the Rorschach always provide clues to what they are like as people. Aspects of interpersonal style are woven into the thread of virtually all of the test behaviors previously discussed in this chapter. For example, when subjects are gentle or rough in handling the cards (which belong to the examiner), when they show willingness or reluctance to participate in the testing (which is being conducted by the examiner), and when they comment positively or negatively on what they have heard about the Rorschach (which is being used by the examiner), they are behaving interpersonally, just as much as when they are being overtly hostile, surly, deferential, or ingratiating.

Drawing diagnostic inferences from the interpersonal style manifest during a Rorschach examination consists largely of applying observational skills and psychodynamic sensitivity to subjects' behavior. As noted in the introduction to this chapter, then, the subject–examiner interaction is less a matter of Rorschach data than of general clinical phenomena. For this reason, having already discussed a broad range of Rorschach-specific subject–examiner interactions, this chapter does not pursue this topic further. On the other hand, attention should be called again to some classic contributions in the literature concerned with the interpersonal meaning of the Rorschach situation (Schachtel, 1966, chap. 12), the influence of situational and interpersonal variables in projective testing (Masling, 1960), and the interpersonal dynamics of the testing situation (Schafer, 1954, chap. 2).

Finally of note, aspects of a subject's interpersonal style can sometimes facilitate the important distinction between the two types of high *Lambda* records mentioned in chapter 5. As previously noted, some records with *Lambda* > .99 are the product of guardedness and should be interpreted cautiously, as in not being misled by a low *EA* or a *D* = 0 that does not signify what such findings usually signify. Other high *Lambda* records reflect a stylistic commitment to narrowing a person's frame of reference and can be interpreted as fully as the data allow. The response total provides the most reliable way of distinguishing between these two types of records: a valid but short high *Lambda* record is likely to be guarded, whereas a high *Lambda* record with at least an average number of responses is likely to be stylistic. Additionally, it may well be that a person giving a high *Lambda* record who does so in an unfriendly, tight-lipped, grudging, and dismissive manner and who responds with few words after long reaction times is giving a guarded record. Conversely, the likelihood of a stylistic high *Lambda* record is increased when subjects seem friendly and cooperative and respond promptly and at length. Often, in the latter instance, examiners are not even aware until they have completed their coding that they have taken a high *Lambda* record, because the subject's responses seemed so full when they were being given.

8

Conducting a Sequence Analysis

As stated in chapter 2, sequence analysis consists of examining conjointly the structural, thematic, and behavioral features of Rorschach responses and noting the succession in which these response characteristics occur. Sequence analysis has long been recognized as the only adequate way of integrating all of the data provided by a Rorschach examination into a cohesive interpretation of the findings. Surprisingly little attention has been paid in the literature to systematic procedures for conducting a sequence analysis, however. Brief discussions in B. Klopfer et al. (1954, chap. 11), P. M. Lerner (1991, chap. 9), Phillips and J. G. Smith (1953, chap. 9), and Schafer (1954, chap. 6) constitute most of what has been available for Rorschach examiners to read on this subject. Clinicians attempting to illustrate sequence analysis in published or presented case studies have more often than not merely begun with the first response to Card I and generated interpretive hypotheses while reading through the rest of the responses in order.

As elaborated in chapter 3, however, interpreting a Rorschach protocol by reading it through from beginning to end, although unquestionably thorough, constitutes an inefficient and potentially misleading procedure. Considering responses in their numerical order does not assign priority to those responses that may bear most critically on identifying a subject's personality strengths and weaknesses and does not discriminate among features of the data that are likely to carry more or less interpretive weight. Examiners can avoid these shortcomings of traditional approaches to sequence analysis by embedding sequential interpretation in the Comprehensive System search strategy. Preceding in this way involves identifying the most critical responses in a record, examining the sequences surrounding them, and then moving systematically from more to less significant sequences of responses. Eventually all of the meaningful sequences in the record are considered, but they are examined in approximate order of which seem most and which least salient to describing the subject's personality functioning.

The preceding chapters have presented five building blocks of efficient sequence analysis, beginning with discussion in chapters 3 and 4 of how the Comprehensive System search strategy can be used as a roadmap to guide the interpretive process and of how distinguishing between projection and card pull can help identify which responses should receive most attention. Chapters 5, 6, and 7 then elaborated how the structural, thematic, and behavioral dimensions of Rorschach responses can be translated into inferences and hypotheses concerning personality processes. Hence, most of what examiners need to know in order to conduct a sequence analysis has already been discussed. This chapter amplifies this interpretive approach in two ways that set the stage for the case material that follows in part III. The first involves clarifying specific procedures for implementing a sequence analysis within the Comprehensive System search strategy. The second consists of presenting a model for sequential interpretation in which successive changes in response quality are used as a basis for identifying what subjects are concerned about, how their concerns affect them, the manner in which they cope with or attempt to resolve their concerns, and how successful they are in these coping efforts.

IMPLEMENTING A SEQUENCE ANALYSIS

As is illustrated in the case examples that follow in chapters 10 through 14, effective sequence analysis in Rorschach interpretation can begin by applying the Comprehensive System guidelines summarized in Tables 3.1 and 3.2. Using these tables, examiners can identify the first key variable in a record and use it to lay out the order in which they will examine each of the seven clusters of variables, supplemented by the situation stress array as indicated. Two of the clusters, self-perception and interpersonal perception, identify specific responses that should be read for their thematic imagery, namely, all minus, Morbid, movement, embellished, and human responses. Each of the other clusters calls attention to certain kinds of responses that should be examined carefully for their qualitative or sequential features, such as the extent of cognitive slippage in a Critical Special Score (ideation) and the level and homogeneity of form distortion in minus responses (mediation).

In each instance in which the search strategy goes beyond the quantitative data in the Structural Summary to address some feature of the Sequence of Scores or the verbal content of certain types of responses, the targeted feature or response should be examined in context to answer two questions that define the essence of sequence analysis: First, what can be learned from the total package of structural features, thematic images, and test behaviors that characterize this particular response? Second, what can be learned from individual or combined structural, thematic, or behavioral characteristics of responses that precede or follow this response? Proceeding in this way entails a series of minisequence analyses, each cued during the interpretive process by one of the "steps" in Table 3.1 that calls attention to the Sequence of Scores or to qualitative aspects of response content.

Thus, examining the context in which targeted features of the data occur makes sequence analysis an integral aspect of Rorschach interpretation utilizing the Comprehensive System. As a way of organizing the information that emerges from sequence analyses conducted in this way, a model can be proposed for utilizing changes in the quality of subjects' responses to infer the nature of their concerns, defensive style, and coping adequacy.

A MODEL FOR SEQUENTIAL INTERPRETATION

Inferences from Rorschach data about personality functioning can be conceptualized within any theoretical framework and formulated in any terminology with which examiners are familiar. Provided that a theoretical orientation and its preferred terminology are reasonably coherent and lend themselves well to describing personality processes, the Rorschach will serve the interpretive purposes of informed examiners whatever their persuasion and language. As elaborated in chapter 5, the present book is oriented around conceiving of the Rorschach as a measure of personality processes that identifies adaptive strengths and weaknesses in six dimensions of personality functioning: attending to experience, using ideation, modulating affect, managing stress, viewing oneself, and relating to others. To provide a framework for delineating assets and liabilities in coping styles and capacities, sequential interpretation can be approached as a search for indications of *concern*, *defense*, and *recovery*.

Concern in this model refers broadly to whatever may be a particular focus of interest or source of distress in a person's life, that is, what the individual is concerned about. Some concerns are pleasantly preoccupying or positively motivating, such as growing orchids as a hobby or being intent on succeeding as a stockbroker. Other concerns can be anxiety provoking or functionally disruptive, as when people are inordinately fearful of failure or cannot allow themselves to fall asleep without first performing some elaborate ritual. Rorschach data, particularly the content of responses, usually provide considerable information, more or less directly, about the matters that occupy people's minds, both consciously and unconsciously. Concurrently, structural and behavioral features of responses, together with how subjects elaborate their content themes, usually indicate whether what people have on their minds is mainly a source of satisfaction or dismay in their lives.

Previous chapters have identified numerous Rorschach indices of distress in relation to concerns suggested by a response and have discussed ways of attempting to ferret out the origins of these concerns. Applied in the context of a sequence analysis, these interpretive guidelines make possible a simple but fairly encompassing rule of thumb: Whatever subjects are handling well on the Rorschach represents aspects of their lives that are not problematic for them and that constitute areas of personality strength, whereas whatever they are handling poorly signifies troublesome aspects of their lives that constitute personality liabilities and interfere with their adaptation. Thus, after the starting point for a minisequence analysis has been localized in a particular response, the interpretive process begins with determining whether or not any features of the response appear to suggest distressing or disruptive concerns and, if so, what the nature of these concerns might be.

Defense in the present context refers generally to whatever means a person characteristically employs to reduce or escape from painful and unwelcome thoughts and feelings generated by troubling concerns. The particular defensive or coping style on which people rely usually says a great deal about the kind of people they are, whether they are well or poorly adjusted, the types of psychological disorder to which they may be prone, and the forms of psychotherapy to which they may be more or less responsive. There is reason to believe, for example, that Rorschach indications of reliance on defenses involving object splitting and projective identification increases susceptibility to borderline personality disorder (P. M. Lerner, 1993; P. M. Lerner & H. Lerner, 1980) and that Rorschach evidence of an ideational coping style (i.e., being introversive) predicts more favorable response to psychodynamic and cognitive therapy than to behavioral therapy (Weiner, in press).

Accordingly, after identifying an apparent emergence of distressing or disruptive concerns, the next step in sequential analysis consists of assessing how subjects attempt to regain their psychological equilibrium. Efforts to cope with aroused distress can appear in either structural, thematic, or behavioral aspects of the data. With respect to structure, for example, three common examples of defensive reactions to anxiety-provoking situations and experiences can readily be described. As one example, subjects can cope by leaving the field, which in Rorschach terms consists of directing their attention elsewhere by ignoring the part of the card where they have seen a distressing response and giving their next response to a location that excludes this detail. As a second example, subjects in Rorschach-induced distress can constrict their frame of reference and seek safety in bland conventionality, by turning next to a Popular response involving pure form only. As the third example, a subject can use intellectualization to strip an upsetting response of its emotional impact, for example, by making it into a painting or statue.

To continue with examples of defense reflected in thematic imagery, subjects can employ denial by turning a threatening image into one that is benign as well as intellectualized: "It's a couple of witches casting a spell, but they're the good kind of witches, like the Witch of the North in the Dorothy story" (reference to *The Wizard of Oz*). They can use repression to blot out disturbing connotations of that they are reporting: "That looks like a dangerous character doing something, but I really have no idea what he might be up to." They can use reaction formation to cancel out negative imagery with a completely opposite kind of imagery: "The first thing I see is a couple of science fiction guys shooting death rays at each other, but, as I look at it some more, I can also see it as a couple of kids playing together and shooting water pistols."

In their test behaviors, subjects can utilize externalization of responsibility for a percept as a way of minimizing its impact, as when an adult comments, "It's something a child would draw" (implying that whatever subjects saw in it has no relevance to their thoughts and feelings). They may go further into projective attribution of blame, as by saying after a disturbing Morbid response, "Whoever made these must be a sick person." They may resort to isolation of affect by choosing to describe rather than respond to chromatic features of the blots, as in saying, "The red here is quite bright, but it doesn't mean anything" or "These colors serve to demarcate the different countries in the map I see."

Paralleling the discussions of content themes and test behaviors in chapters 6 and 7, these illustrations provide common examples of coping efforts encountered in Rorschach data, but they do not begin to constitute an exhaustive list of the defensive maneuvers with which people combat anxiety or how these defensive operations are manifest on the Rorschach. Attempts to compile such exhaustive lists would strain present knowledge and be incomplete at best. The present discussion is intended merely to call examiner's attention to the importance of exploring Rorschach sequences for clues to subjects' defensive styles and to encourage them to draw on their general knowledge of personality processes to identify what kinds of coping maneuvers appear to be in evidence. For additional information on Rorschach assessment of specific defensive operations, readers will benefit from familiarity with the contributions of Schafer (1954), Cooper, Perry, and Arnow (1988), and Cooper, Perry, and O'Connell (1991).

Recovery in a Rorschach sequence has to do with how successful subjects are in overcoming the disruption produced by a distressing response and reestablishing an effective level of functioning. The key questions in assessing recovery can be simply put: How adequate are the responses subjects produce following anxiety-provoking Rorschach experiences, and how long does it take them to reestablish adequate responding? By and large, the coping efforts in the preceding examples of structural and thematic indications of defensive operations are adaptive in their own right. An ordinary detail, good form Populars, and works of art, unless elaborated in some inappropriate way, are all components of normative responses that identify personality strengths. Likewise, assuming adequate form, good witches casting a spell, a "character" doing something, and children playing contribute structural data indicative of good ego strength and a positive interpersonal orientation (three *Mao* and two *COP*). Subjects giving such responses at times of distress are accordingly demonstrating reasonably good utilization of defensive operations defenses in the service of recovery.

By contrast, suppose that "witches casting spells" to the side details on Card I (D2) is followed by a minus form "bird" to the center detail (D4). Given that there is nothing especially dramatic about a static and unelaborated bird seen here, it is reasonable to infer that the temporary breakdown in reality testing indicated by the distorted form perception is attributable to anxiety caused by associations to "witches casting spells." Moreover, in this example, it would appear that the defensive effort to escape anxiety by redirecting attention to a different detail has been unsuccessful: The distressing response has been followed by a maladaptive one, no recovery has occurred, and preliminary indications are that leaving the field is not proving to be an effective defensive maneuver for this subject and the subject's defenses against anxiety are limited. Both of these inferences could of course be modified in light of additional data. As one data point, however, this illustrative sequence warrants the concerns just noted about the subject's adaptive capacities.

What about a "Dangerous character doing something, but I don't know what" given to Card IV? Suppose that following this response the subject gives back the card, takes Card V in hand, studies it at length, and says, "This is a hard one, I'm not sure what it is, maybe the head of an alligator on the side, getting ready to bite someone." Card V is an easy card, not a hard one, and it offers a readily seen and usually nonthreatening Popular that many subjects who have struggled with Card IV seize on with relief (e.g., "Now this one is no problem, it's a butterfly for sure"). In this example, the repression with which the subject attempted to avoid the danger suggested by Card IV has not worked very well. The person is still upset, as is apparent in the "hard one" comment and the delayed reaction time; in the individual's inability to give the Popular or even attend to the whole blot, as most people do on Card V; and in the fact that the person ends up with a structurally adequate response (*Do FMo Ad*), but one in which the concerns about dangerousness repressed on Card IV break through in the form of an alligator "getting ready to bite someone." Once again, then, the sequence has identified ineffective coping and raises questions about how well repression works for this subject and how capable the person is of coping with anxiety.

To complete this series of examples, consider the "Science fiction guys shooting death rays at each other" given to the upper side details of Card IX (D3). Suppose the subject next says the following: "The more I look at it, it looks more like a couple of fish just swimming around, but maybe they're the poisonous variety." Now the response has deteriorated in form, from ordinary to minus, which provides some clue to how distressing it was in its first version, and there is a concerted effort to reverse its initial impact, by turning the "science fiction guys" into fish and having them "just swimming around" rather than "shooting death rays." However, the inadequacy of this defense effort is revealed not only by the form distortion but also by the eventual reemergence of concerns about aggression in the fish being described as poisonous. In addition, being of "the poisonous variety" seems a rather stilted form of expression for someone who began talking about "science fiction guys," and it also begins to smack of an INCOM—are there poisonous fish? Hence, the effort at reaction formation breaks down, there is perhaps some last gasp effort at intellectualization, and the subject is demonstrating limited capacity to recover from the distressing impact of the original response.

Thus far these examples of poor recovery have concerned the adequacy of subjects' responses immediately following anxiety-producing Rorschach experiences. Also important is the second question initially posed in this regard, namely, how long does it take for subjects to regain their equilibrium when it becomes disrupted? Subjects may assert adequate defensiveness fairly promptly, either within the context of a single response that was initially distressing, in the next response or two, or at least on the next card. At other times a distressing response may set off a series of disturbed, inadequately defended responses that continues throughout a card or extends over several cards. Rapid restitution suggests some combination of relatively mild upset and relatively good defenses. By contrast, the longer the series of poor quality responses that follow an upsetting Rorschach experience, the more severe was the initial upset, the less adequate are the subject's defensive capacities, or both.

MONITORING RESPONSE QUALITY

The use of sequence analysis to aid in identifying what concerns people find troubling and how successful they are in coping with the anxiety that troubling concerns generate requires careful monitoring of response quality.

Deterioration in response quality is a certain indicator that some aspect of the Rorschach situation has proved distressing and that the nature of this Rorschach event will shed light on aspects of subjects' personality functioning, especially with respect to their liabilities and unresolved problems. Maintenance of good response quality indicates aspects of the Rorschach situation that are within the capacities of individuals to manage effectively, and the manner in which people display effective management of their perceptions and associations identifies their personality strengths. Improvement in response quality following some decay provides information concerning the means people ordinarily employ to cope with anxiety and how successful these maneuvers are; as was discussed, the longer and more seriously deterioration persists in a Rorschach record before improvement occurs, the more troubled people are likely to be and the less adequate their defensive capabilities.

Numerous previous examples have illustrated that deterioration and improvement in response quality can occur across various segments of a record. Taking the 10 blots as a whole, some subjects may begin poorly and improve as they go along, possibly indicating initially disorganizing anxiety that they are able to overcome as they warm to their task and become more comfortable with the examiner and the examination situation. Other subjects may perform adequately on the first few cards and then sink into gradually deteriorating performance as the examination wears on, which may indicate a person who puts up a brave front and starts out reasonably well in a new situation, only to become increasingly upset and fall apart as the situation wears on. Such individuals are likely to be functioning less well psychologically than first impressions suggest and less well than is thought by people who know them only slightly and spend just brief periods of time with them. Such people are also likely to be at risk for clinical deterioration in their psychological condition.

Taking the cards individually, subjects may show an overall pattern of improvement or deterioration within cards rather than across all 10 cards. Repetitive patterns of beginning well and finishing poorly on many cards, or vice versa, also have implications for how subjects' behavior is likely to change for better or worse as they become increasingly involved in situations. Additionally, as noted previously, some subjects may perform adequately on the gray-black cards but relatively poorly on the chromatic cards, or vice versa, thus identifying difficulties they are having in dealing either with dysphoric or euphoric kinds of emotions. As a further possibility, some subjects may perform relatively well or poorly on those cards that are most likely to elicit impressions of two figures interacting in some way, thus indicating either interpersonal uneasiness and a likelihood of doing their best work when working alone, or interpersonal contentment and a tendency to function best when being sociable rather than solitary.

At the level of individual responses, subjects reveal many features of their underlying concerns, coping style, and defensive adequacy by changes in the quality of their responses from one to the next. Such changes have already been amply illustrated, as have changes at a fourth level that occurs within a single response. Responses that start out poorly and end well have been *rescued*, as in this response by a female subject to Card VI: "I don't know what that is . . . I don't like this one . . . something sexual perhaps . . . well, let's say this part (upper middle-D6) is a penis, like a drawing of it in an anatomy book." The subject in this instance was clearly distressed by the sexual connotations of what she saw, was on the verge of attempting a rejection or opting for a vague impression, but, before finishing, pulled herself together psychologically and delivered a good form, intellectualized sex response, coded *Do Fo Hd, Sx, Art*. By contrast, responses that start out well and end poorly have been *spoiled*, as in an initial response to Card III of "Two people talking to each other" (a good form, human movement Popular) elaborated with "and this red spot in the middle is their hearts" (thus adding a minus form element and a *FABCOM* to the response). To complete this cycle, this spoiled response could in turn be rescued if the subject said, "It's not really their hearts; what I mean is that the red is like on a Valentine showing hearts, and it symbolizes that they love each other").

As indicated by the examples here and in previous chapters, the quality of responses can be monitored primarily on the basis of whether they contain any undesirable elements with respect to evidence of adaptive capacities. All of the structural indices of personality assets discussed in chapter 5 contribute to good response quality; conversely, indices of personality liabilities contribute to poor response quality. Of all of these structural variables, form level is the easiest to recognize and may in fact carry the most weight in deciding whether a response should be considered of good or poor quality. In addition, such considerations as whether responses involve ordinary or unusual details, differentiated or vague developmental quality, *EA* or *es* determinants, and indications of cognitive control or slippage can help to categorize responses as good or poor in quality. Finally, content elaborations that range from being unremarkable to containing blatant aggressive or sexual imagery, together with test behaviors that suggest comfortable self-assurance or overt dismay and loss of self-control, also provide clues to whether responses represent good or poor quality efforts to comply with the requirements of giving a valid Rorschach protocol. Examiners attending to these features of Rorschach responses will be able to monitor their quality in ways that facilitate drawing inferences from sequential analyses.

IDENTIFYING ADAPTIVE STRENGTHS AND WEAKNESSES: CASE ILLUSTRATIONS

9

Introduction to Case Illustrations

Chapters 10 through 14 consist of case material in which Rorschach protocols are used to illustrate the principles of interpretation delineated in chapters 3 through 8. As illustrations, the case presentations that follow are not intended to constitute case studies or psychodiagnostic evaluations, nor are they used to demonstrate the validity of Rorschach inferences. Adequate case studies require detailed information concerning an individual's presenting problems, developmental history, family background, and current personal and social context. Thorough psychodiagnostic evaluations call for a battery of assessment instruments selected on the basis of the referral questions to be addressed and comprised of both relatively structured and relatively unstructured instruments, all of which are interpreted fully. Convincing demonstrations of the validity of Rorschach inferences necessitate comparing them systematically with data from other tests, known events in a subject's life, and reliable reports of the person's behavior in various kinds of situations.

Given these requirements, an adequate case study involving a thorough psychodiagnostic evaluation and convincingly demonstrating the validity of the Rorschach inferences must entail long and elaborate discussion. Including such extensive discussions here would have severely restricted the number and variety of protocols that could be presented and the types of people and problems they exemplify. For this reason, the decision was made to utilize an illustrative approach to the case material, rather than a case study, psychodiagnostic, or validating approach. Chapters 10 through 14 accordingly contain 10 complete Rorschach protocols, each preceded by some brief identifying data and background information concerning the subject and followed by discussion of the most prominent implications of the data for personality assets and liabilities. Without presuming to be thorough or definitive, the discussions also address implications of the Rorschach findings for differential diagnosis and treatment planning and for the underlying dynamics of subjects' past and present behavior.

The interpretive approach used in presenting these 10 cases illustrates how personality processes can be elucidated by an integrated examination of Rorschach structural variables, content themes, test behaviors, and sequential processes employing the Comprehensive System interpretive search strategy reviewed in chapter 3. The clusters of variables listed in Table 3.1, as elaborated with respect to dimensions of adaptation in chapter 5, guide the interpretive process. The order for searching clusters of variables shown in Tables 3.2 and 3.3 directs the sequence of this process, and inferences are drawn according to the principles previously outlined for distinguishing between card pull and projected aspects of responses (chap. 4) and working with structural variables (chap. 5), content themes (chap. 6), test behaviors (chap. 7), and sequence analysis (chap. 8).

The case discussions in chapters 10 through 14 organize the dimensions of adaptation into four categories of issues that correspond to cluster groupings apparent in Tables 3.2 and 3.3. As these tables show, the processing, mediation, and ideation clusters constitute a "cognitive triad" of clusters that are always examined together in some order, regardless of which sequence is dictated by the first positive key variable in a record. Likewise, the self-perception and interpersonal clusters, both of which pertain to object relationships and include many overlapping variables, are examined together in each of the search sequences listed in Tables 3.2 and 3.3. The affect and control clusters stand alone and have no fixed sequential relation to the others. With this in mind, the Rorschach findings concerning personality assets and liabilities are presented in the cases that follow under the four headings of cognitive issues, personal and interpersonal issues, affective issues, and stress management issues, with the order in which these issues are discussed being determined by the nature of the record. Figure 9.1 shows the relations between the seven clusters of variables in the Comprehensive System as developed by J. E. Exner (1993, chap. 13) and shown in Table 3.1; the six dimensions of adaptation described by Weiner and Exner (1991) and elaborated in chapter 5 of this book; and the four categories of issues in assessing personality functioning that are used to organize the case discussions in chapters 10 through 14.

The various principles of Rorschach interpretation that guide the inferential process are for the most part not repeated in the course of the case discussions in the following chapters. Readers unsure of the basis for relating certain features of the Rorschach data to particular personality characteristics should consult the elaboration of these relations provided in chap-

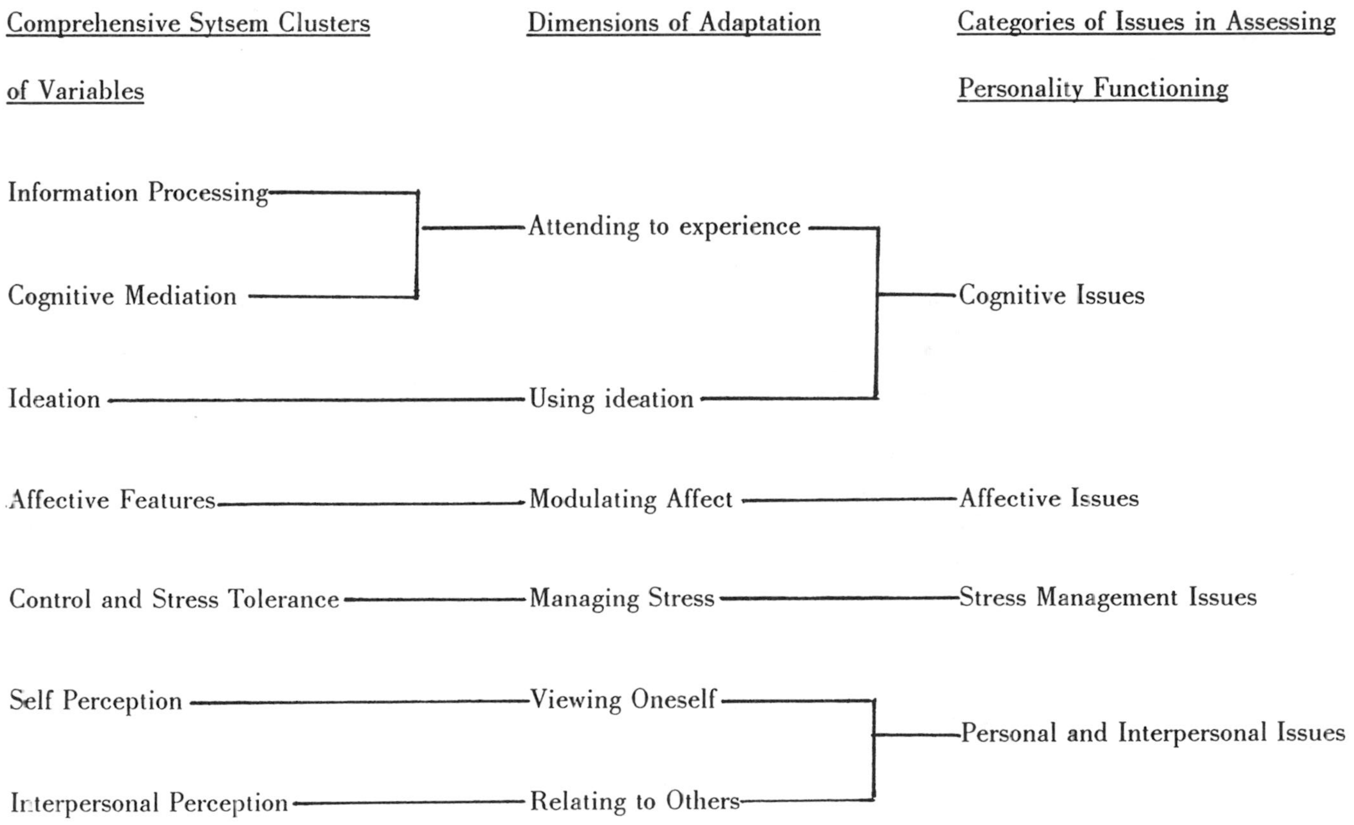

FIG. 9.1. Relationships between comprehensive system clusters of variables, dimensions of adaptation, and categories of issues in assessing personality functioning.

ters 3 through 8. Likewise, mention of similarity to or deviation from normative expectation does not always include review of the relevant reference data. Normative expectations are discussed in chapter 5 and are available in detail in the Comprehensive System texts (J. E. Exner, 1993, chap. 12; J. E. Exner & Weiner, 1995, chap. 3). As illustrations of interpretation, moreover, these case discussions do not attempt to provide complete personality descriptions of the subjects or to document the accuracy of the interpretations offered, although in some instances note is taken of particularly obvious and significant links between the Rorschach data and events in a subject's life.

With further respect to completeness, let it be acknowledged that the case discussions do not address every meaningful aspect of the structural, thematic, and behavioral data contained in the records, but rather involve some selective focusing. Experienced and sensitive Rorschach clinicians may see in these 10 protocols implications for personality functioning that are not mentioned. These may be implications that I chose not to mention, for one reason or another, or perhaps failed to appreciate fully. Such is the diversity and richness of the RIM, especially with respect to the interpretive significance of content themes. As discussed in chapter 6, thematic imagery frequently provides a basis for multiple or alternative inferences, and readers may with good reason see symbolic meanings in these protocols in addition to or different from those suggested here. Transcending these possibilities for divergence in focus or emphasis, the interpretations offered in the text demonstrate how Rorschach data can be used to generate a substantial number and range of conclusions and hypotheses that paint a vivid portrait of a subject's personality style and adaptive capacities and limitations, a portrait that in turn has important implications for differential diagnosis and treatment planning.

As a final *caveat*, addressed to readers who would have preferred fewer cases presented in more detail, opting for a broad range of cases presented in brief was also influenced by Schafer's (1954) similar choice. Schafer stated in this regard that, in the context of a textbook as opposed to an actual assessment in clinical practice, what mattered was not being "right" or "wrong" in what he inferred from the protocols he presented, but was instead being able "to illustrate *a way of thinking* about Rorschach test records and to demonstrate that this way of thinking leads to personality descriptions of individual patients" (p. 191).

Schafer pointed out further that using individual case histories to validate Rorschach inferences runs considerable risk of "unwitting opportunistic selection or editing of clinical material" that may be adduced to "prove" something but is likely to create an illusion of understanding. Speaking as a scientist as well as a clinician, Schafer observed that validation requires systematic rather than anecdotal coordination of clinical and test data, and he accordingly chose to avoid detailed clinical summaries in his case illustrations. The case presentations in chapters 10 through 14 are written in this tradition.

The following chapters are designed to address the six dimensions of adaptation identified in chapter 5 and include protocols illustrating common types of records in which these aspects of personality functioning guide the interpretive process.

Chapter 10 addresses the dimension of attending to experience and includes a high *Lambda* guarded record in a subject undergoing an administrative evaluation and a low *Lambda* ambitent record in a person with substance abuse problems.

Chapter 11 addresses the dimension of attending to experience and includes two introversive records, one involving a hospitalized paranoid schizophrenic and the other an anorexic adolescent with many obsessive-compulsive features.

Chapter 12 addresses the dimension of modulating affect and includes the records of two depressed subjects, one a court-referred nonpatient with previously undiagnosed and untreated emotional problems and the other a person hospitalized with a history of suicide attempts and showing probable bipolar disorder.

Chapter 13 addresses the dimension of managing stress and includes records of two subjects with $D < AdjD$, one a delinquent teenager with generally limited coping skills and the other an academically dysfunctional dental student with specific problems in handling work-related tasks, interpersonal relationships, and variable moods.

Chapter 14 addresses the dimensions of viewing oneself and relating to others. Illustrating self-perception and interpersonal perception in a single chapter does not signify that these two dimensions of adaptation are any less important to psychological adjustment than the previous four dimensions, each of which is given a separate chapter. However, interpretive hypotheses concerning adaptive strengths and weaknesses in these two dimensions will by this point in the text have been fairly thoroughly elaborated in discussing the cases in chapters 10 through 13. For completeness, however, two cases involving narcissistic self-centeredness are presented in chapter 14 to illustrate different patterns that such records may take. One of these cases involves an angry and action-oriented psychopathic man about whom there were questions of dangerousness, and the other case concerns an introversive and emotionally reserved woman without diagnosable psychological disorder but with maladaptive patterns of interpersonal relatedness.

Taken together these 10 cases touch on a fairly broad range of clinical issues, illustrate a variety of personality styles, and include some varied demography as well. There are five male and five female subjects; eight adults and two adolescents; and eight Caucasian subjects, one African American, and one Hispanic. Four of the subjects were outpatients when examined, four were hospitalized, and two were in prison awaiting trial. The records were obtained over many years' time in different parts of the country, and, except where a matter of public record, the identifying data have been disguised but not in any ways that affect the clinical significance of the findings.

10

Attending to Experience

Attending to experience refers to the manner in which people focus their attention and perceive their environment. As elaborated in chapter 5, good psychological adjustment is facilitated by openness to experience, efficient organization of information, and realistic and conventional perception of events. Conversely, people whose frames of reference are excessively broad or narrow, who process too much or too little information, or who are unwilling or unable to see the world as most people do are at risk for adjustment difficulties. Among Rorschach indices of how people attend to their experience, *Lambda* stands out as being perhaps the single most important structural variable in the RIM. *Lambda* sets the tone in many ways for the rest of a protocol, especially when it is unusually high or low, and the level of *Lambda* has particular implications for how much confidence can be placed in various features of the Structural Summary and for how much can be learned from the thematic imagery in a record.

The following cases illustrate opposite poles of this critical variable. The first exemplifies a valid but guarded high *Lambda* protocol in which several aspects of the subject's current psychological status can be identified and some clues to her underlying concerns suggested, but in which many important indices cannot be taken to mean what they usually mean and the overall information yield is relatively meager. Especially notable in this latter regard are a deceptively low *EA*, an unreliable $D = 0$, and the extent to which the subject's test behaviors assume prominence in identifying her guardedness and other features of her coping style.

The second case is a low *Lambda* record in which it can be expected that the subject's openness will result in a structurally revealing and thematically rich set of responses. In this instance, the low *Lambda* has been maladaptive and has apparently contributed to numerous difficulties with stress management, affect modulation, self-perception, and interpersonal relatedness.

CASE 1: GUARDEDNESS IN A WOMAN BEING EVALUATED FOR ADMINISTRATIVE PURPOSES

Ms. Anderson is a 40-year-old, married, Caucasian, professional woman with no children who has moved with her husband to a different state and applied for licensing in the new location. Although she passed the necessary examinations without difficulty, a routine background check suggested that she has a drinking problem. She admits to drinking fairly heavily on social occasions, but she denies having any problem with alcohol. Her licensing has been deferred pending evaluation of her psychological status. She is unhappy about having to undergo this evaluation and concerned about the results, and she indicates that she has generally been tearful and anxious for the past few weeks. However, she has not been in treatment, has not been taking any psychotropic medication, and has not previously had any contact with a mental health professional. Ms. Anderson's Rorschach protocol follows in Tables 10.1, 10.2, and 10.3 and Fig. 10.1.

TABLE 10.1
Rorschach Protocol of Ms. Anderson

Responses	*Inquiry*
Card I	
1. My first reaction is a butterfly.	E: (*Repeats response*) S: It's got the wings of a butterfly.
2. But maybe it's more of a moth.	E: (*Repeats response*) S: Yes, it's also a moth; appendages here (D1), a mouth here (Dd22), tail, and body shape. They have a fuzzy little mouth.
	E: What made it look fuzzy? S: No, I know that moths have a fuzzy mouth, but this does not look fuzzy.
3. (*pause*) I can't get anything else out of it, but it's definitely insect oriented.	E: (*Repeats response*) S: It just looks like a bug, with the wings and body shape.

(Continued)

TABLE 10.1
(Continued)

Responses	Inquiry
Card II	
4. Geez, I'm seeing butterflies everywhere.	E: *(Repeats response)* S: It's right here (D3), with little gossamer wings. E: What suggests gossamer wings? S: The different shades of paint on it makes it look silky, like there are different layers of tissue.
5. And lobster claws.	E: *(Repeats response)* S: These here (D2), I guess because where I used to live they were popular.
6. Insects again—the feeler part, the mouth, of a gnawing insect.	E: *(Repeats response)* S: Just the mouth and the lips (D4), the way they protrude.
7. And I see a fish head.	E: *(Repeats response)* S: The eyes and mouth, the shape of a fish head. I just see it here in this part (Dd31).
Card III	
8. Two dancers, Oriental I think. (*puts card down*)	E: *(Repeats response)* S: The feet, the posture, the shape of the head; it could be men as well as women, but it has an Oriental feeling, maybe because of the black and reds. They could be bowing to each other after the dance, as well as dancing. E: You mentioned the black and reds. S: The colors made me think of Oriental colors.
Card IV	
9. (*pause*) Geez (*pause*) I see two feet; I think of it as a caricature of a person, with little arms, a strange-looking head. Let's call him a creature, how about that? (*puts card down*)	E: *(Repeats response)* S: Or a beast, I don't know what. I see boots, weird arms; I'd call it a person from outer space, as depicted on TV. E: You said it had a strange-looking head? S: It's hard to think of it as a head. It's just a blob, but the hair gives it some definition. Maybe it's some sort of cap he has on.

(Continued)

TABLE 10.1
(Continued)

Responses	Inquiry

Card V

10. Back to butterflies and moths. These are inkblots, right? (Yes) Right, it's the inkblot test, and that's a moth. That's where I come from on that one.

E: (Repeats response)
S: There are wings, and butterflies have those things at the bottom, and antennae or feelers at the top.

E: Is it more like a butterfly or a moth?
S: Butterfly wings are usually more perfect, the wings look more like a moth; but the body section looks more like a butterfly.

Card VI

11. Only thing that comes to mind is a totem pole. I don't know what it's rising from, the eagle symbol or something. This one isn't as perfectly side by side as the others; it ran a little. (puts card down)

E: (Repeats response)
S: A reptile, or like an eagle-type symbol on top of a blob (D3).

E: You said you don't know what it's rising from.
S: Yes, the rest of it (D1) doesn't bring anything to mind.

Card VII

12. (long pause) I can imagine the top two figures as young girls, the pony tails I guess.

E: (Repeats response)
S: Two girls faces with pony tails is what it is (D1).

13. And then there's a pig-like figure in the second level. (puts card down)

E: (Repeats response)
S: I thought of a play, not a pig in real life. It's a caricature of a pig.

E: I'm not sure what you're seeing.
S: It's here (D3), here's the snout, the mouth, eyes; it has the characteristics of a mask in a play.

Card VIII

14. A dog or wolf-like animal.

E: (Repeats response)
S: Just a dog here (D1)

E: What made it look like a dog?
S: A head, four legs, the overall shape, and the running.

(Continued)

TABLE 10.1
(*Continued*)

Responses	Inquiry
	E: Running?
	S: It looks like he's running. He's slim and looks sleek.
	E: What suggests sleek?
	S: The shape, he doesn't look pudgy.
15. And the other part of it is crab-like. (*puts card down and looks out window*)	E: (*Repeats response*)
	S: You have little appendages all over the place; it's just this part (D4).
Card IX	
16. (*long pause*) All I can think of is some kind of eruption, a volcanic eruption. If I turn it this way (V)—is there any upside down? (Any way you like) That's it. (*puts card down*)	E: (*Repeats response*)
	S: I see it this way (>). It looks like an eruption.
	E: What gives it that look?
	S: The tree line is here, and it's reflected, and there's a big cloud-like mass.
	E: It's reflected?
	S: Yes, that's what it looks like.
	E: What suggests clouds?
	S: It could also be smoke from a forest fire and rising like that, to tie in the colors, but the pink and the peach are easier to tie in as an eruption.
Card X	
17. v Seahorses.	E: (*Repeats response*)
	S: It's this part here (D4).
	E: What made it look like seahorses?
	S: It helps that they're green, and they have little noses.
18. > (*pause*) < Medusa (*laughs*)	E: (*Repeats response*)
	S: Something snake-like. All these different things coming out of it (D1). They don't look like snakes coming out of a head, but they could be.
19. Crab-like (*puts card down*)	E: (*Repeats response*)
	S: This is the crab-like thing, these two globs (D1)

TABLE 10.2
Sequence of Scores for Ms. Anderson

Card No.		Loc.	No.	Determinant(s)	(2)	Content(s)	POP	Z	Special Scores
I	1	Wo	1	Fo		A	P	1.0	
	2	Wo	1	Fo		A		1.0	INC,PSV
	3	Wo	1	Fo		A		1.0	PSV
II	4	Do	3	FVo		A			
	5	Do	2	F-	2	Ad			
	6	Do	4	F-		Ad			INC
	7	Ddo	31	Fu		Ad			
III	8	W+	1	Ma.C'.Co	2	H,Ay	P	5.5	COP
IV	9	W+	1	Fo		(H),Cg	P	4.0	
V	10	Wo	1	Fo		A		1.0	
VI	11	Do	3	Fo		Ay			AB
VII	12	Do	1	Fo	2	Hd	P		
	13	Do	3	Fo		(Ad)			
VIII	14	Do	1	FMao		A	P		
	15	Do	4	Fu		A			
IX	16	W/	1	ma.rF.CFo		Na		5.5	
X	17	Do	4	FCo	2	A			
	18	Do	1	Fu		(Hd)			
	19	Do	1	Fo	2	A	P		

Cognitive Issues

Ms. Anderson's Structural Summary indicates a valid record of 19 responses, no elevation of the *S-CON*, and a first positive key variable of *Lambda* > .99. Accordingly, following Table 3.2, the search order for the variable clusters is processing, mediation, ideation, controls, affect, self-perception, and interpersonal perception.

The fact that this is a high *Lambda* (2.80) record with fewer than 20 responses raises the possibility of its being a guarded record. As frequently occurs in such records, this possibility is confirmed in Ms. Anderson's case by her test behavior, which is notable for her efforts to take distance from and avoid involvement in the Rorschach task. She does not turn the cards at all until Card IX, when she finally gets sufficiently involved to ask, "Is there any upside down?" She then does some turning on Cards IX and X,

TABLE 10.3
Structural Summary for Ms. Anderson

Location Features	Determinants		Contents	S-Constellation
	Blends	Single		
Zf = 7	M.C′.C	M = 0	H = 1, 0	NO . . FV+VF+V+FD>2
ZSum = 19.0	m.rF.CF	FM = 1	(H) = 1, 0	YES . . Col-Shd Bl>0
ZEst = 20.5		m = 0	Hd = 1, 0	NO . . Ego<.31,>.44
		FC = 1	(Hd) = 1, 0	NO . . MOR > 3
W = 7		CF = 0	Hx = 0, 0	NO . . Zd > +- 3.5
(Wv = 0)		C = 0	A = 9, 0	NO . . es > EA
D = 11		Cn = 0	(A) = 0, 0	YES . . CF+C > FC
Dd = 1		FC′ = 0	Ad = 3, 0	NO . . X+% < .70
S = 0		C′F = 0	(Ad) = 1, 0	NO . . S > 3
		C′ = 0	An = 0, 0	NO . . P < 3 or > 8
		FT = 0	Art = 0, 0	YES . . Pure H < 2
DQ		TF = 0	Ay = 1, 1	NO . . R < 17
. . . . . . (FQ-)		T = 0	Bl = 0, 0	3 . . . . . TOTAL
+ = 2 (0)		FV = 1	Bt = 0, 0	
o = 16 (2)		VF = 0	Cg = 0, 1	Special Scorings
v/+ = 1 (0)		V = 0	Cl = 0, 0	
v = 0 (0)		FY = 0	Ex = 0, 0	Lv1 Lv2
		YF = 0	Fd = 0, 0	DV = 0x1 0x2
		Y = 0	Fi = 0, 0	INC = 2x2 0x4
		Fr = 0	Ge = 0, 0	DR = 0x3 0x6
		rF = 0	Hh = 0, 0	FAB = 0x4 0x7
		FD = 2	Ls = 0, 0	ALOG = 0x5
Form Quality		F = 14	Na = 1, 0	CON = 0x7
			Sc = 0, 0	Raw Sum6 = 2
FQx FQf MQual SQx			Sx = 0, 0	Wgtd Sum6 = 4
+ = 0 0 0 0			Xy = 0, 0	
o = 14 9 1 0			Id = 0, 0	AB = 1 CP = 0
u = 3 3 0 0				AG = 0 MOR = 0
- = 2 2 0 0				CFB = 0 PER = 0
none = 0 — 0 0	(2) = 5			COP = 1 PSV = 2

Ratios, Percentages, and Derivations

R = 19	L = 2.80		FC:CF+C = 1: 2	COP = 1 AG = 0
			Pure C = 1	Food = 1
EB = 1: 3.0	EA = 4.0	EBPer = 3.0	SumC′:WSumC = 1:3.0	Isolate/R = 0.11
eb = 2: 2	es = 4	D = 0	Afr = 0.46	H: (H)Hd(Hd) = 1: 3
	Adj es = 4	Adj D = 0	S = 0	(HHd) : (AAd) = 2: 1
			Blends:R = 2:19	H+A:Hd+Ad = 11: 6
FM = 1 : C′ = 1	T = 0		CP = 0	
m = 1 : V = 1	Y = 0			
			P = 6 Zf = 7	3r+(2)/R = 0.42
a:p = 3: 0	Sum6 = 2		X+% = 0.74 Zd = -1.5	Fr+rF = 1
Ma:Mp = 1: 0	Lv2 = 0		F+% = 0.64 W:D:Dd = 7:11: 1	FD = 0
2AB+Art+Ay = 4	WSum6 = 4		X-% = 0.11 W:M = 7: 1	An+Xy = 0
M- = 0	Mnone = 0		S-% = 0.00 DQ+ = 2	MOR = 0
			Xu% = 0.16 DQv = 0	

SCZI = 0	DEPI = 5*	CDI = 3	S-CON = 3	HVI = No	OBS = No

253

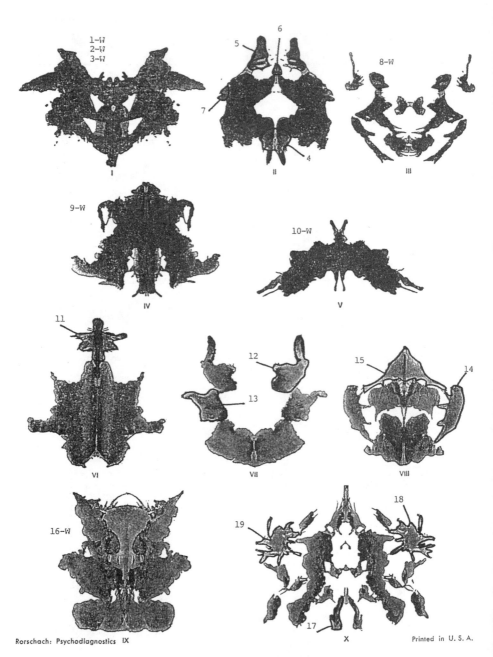

FIG. 10.1. Location choices of Ms. Anderson.

but she never becomes intently involved in studying the cards as a way of being able to elaborate on what they suggest to her. To the contrary, as noted in Table 10.1, she puts 7 of the 10 cards down immediately after her final response, without continuing to look them, without bothering to hand them back to the examiner, and without displaying any interest in being shown the next one.

In her expressive style, moreover, Ms. Anderson consistently avoids being pinned down or committing herself. Four of her responses (13, 14, 15, and 19) are "like" something (as in "pig-like") rather than actually something. On Card III she says that two dancers "could be men as well as women" and "could be bowing to each other as well as dancing," and on Card V she declines to choose between butterfly and moth after reporting parts of each. At times she resorts to a rather flip style of describing the blots instead of reporting what she sees. On Response 4 she says, "I'm seeing butterflies everywhere"; on Response 9, "Let's call him a creature, how about that?"; on Response 10, "These are inkblots, right . . . a moth . . . that's where I come from on that one"; and on Response 11, "This one isn't as perfectly side by side as the others"). She also shows some intellectualized language that takes on a stilted quality, as in Card I being "definitely insect oriented."

Hence there is good reason to consider this a guarded high *Lambda* record, which has two important implications for the interpretive process. First, many of the structural variables in the protocol, particularly those in the control cluster, will have to be interpreted cautiously and may be misleading if taken at face value. Second, not much richness is to be expected in the content themes of the responses, although any clues to underlying dynamics that break through despite Ms. Anderson's guardedness are likely to be especially meaningful.

As for her manner of attending to experience, Ms. Anderson's high *Lambda* itself could possibly identify the narrowly focused and overly simplified style of processing information that is usually associated with this Rorschach finding. If so, she may well be the kind of person who characteristically prefers to be in familiar circumstances, find simple solutions to problems, and overlook or ignore anything that might be distressing or disruptive. On the other hand, we may be seeing in this protocol a product of situational guardedness, which not uncommonly characterizes the records of people who are being examined for administrative rather than clinical purposes. In that case, the Rorschach data may not represent a full and open expression of her personality style and coping capacities, and we may be seeing in this woman's protocol only a fraction of what there is to see about her. In particular, we should be cautious about assuming that she operates in a high *Lambda* style in her life outside of this examination, except in situations that threaten her as the Rorschach may be threatening her.

Nevertheless, going beyond the indications that she is situationally closed off rather than open to experience, we can infer from the data in the information-processing, mediation, and ideation clusters that Ms. Anderson is a cognitively well-functioning person. She organizes information efficiently ($Zd = -1.5$), looks at the world about the way most people do ($W:D:Dd = 7:11:1$), and perceives events realistically and conventionally ($X - \% = .11$; $Xu\% = .16$, $P = 6$). The fact that her $W:M$ ratio is unbalanced (7:1) may be attributable to a restricting effect of her high *Lambda* guardedness on her M production. Similarly, her low $DQ+ = 2$ probably relates to her minimal investment in the Rorschach task rather than to any pronounced deficit in integrative capacity (which would be unlikely in view of her educational and professional accomplishments).

With respect to her ideational functioning, Ms. Anderson appears to be capable of thinking logically and coherently ($WSum6 = 2$). The fact that her narrowed focus of attention allowed just one M, one FM, and one m response to appear means that her total number of active and passive movements is not large enough for the ratio between them to have any reliable interpretive significance. Likewise, her low EA of 4 limits any inferences that can be drawn from her EB or $FM + m$ concerning the adaptability of her ideational style. On the other hand, Ms. Anderson's $INTELL = 4$ is noteworthy. Although not at the usual cutting point for identifying an intellectualizing defensive style, this finding in a brief record, especially when considered together with her intellectualized language style as previously noted, suggests that Ms. Anderson may indeed rely on this kind of mechanism in coping with distressing situations.

Stress Management Issues

As already noted, this protocol provides a good example of how high *Lambda* in a brief record can result in misleading structural data concerning capacities for control and stress management. What we have here is a "hunkered-down" record, as identified by the combination of $D = 0$ and $EA = 4.0$. It would be mistaken to interpret this $D = 0$ in the usual way as signifying adequate frustration tolerance, adaptive capacity for self-control, and relative freedom from subjectively felt distress. The fault with such an interpretation resides in the low EA, which identifies an unreliable $D = 0$ in which psychological equilibrium is maintained only by avoiding stressful situations, and in which even modest amounts of stress can cause considerable psychological pain and loss of self-control.

The question here is whether Ms. Anderson is really an $EA = 4$ person, that is, someone who has well below average capacities for coping with life's demands. Her history of accomplishment, her apparently successful marriage, and the absence of any history of psychological incapacity make it unlikely that her low *EA* reflects anything other than her situational guard-edness. Accordingly, in a record of this type it becomes difficult to draw any conclusions with confidence concerning the actual level of her coping capacities (*EA*), how much stress she is experiencing (*es*), or even whether she prefers ideational or affective ways of dealing with her experience (*EB* style). All that can be said for sure in this regard is that her coping capacities were sufficient for her to give an adequate number of responses (i.e., *R* > 13) without becoming overtly upset or resistive in the process, even while finding ways to limit how much she was revealing about herself.

Affective Issues

Most notable among the affective features in Ms. Anderson's record is her elevated *DEPI* of 5, which indicates the presence of some depressive features and is consistent with the recent tearfulness she reports. Of the seven *DEPI* criteria, only one—*SumShd* > *FM* + *m* or *C'* > 2—is likely to result from situational distress (i.e., the production of numerous *Y*), whereas each of the other six criteria involve variables that have substantial retest correla-tions and therefore identify enduring rather than reactive aspects of depres-sion. Hence the *DEPI* = 5 is a reliable indication of persistent depressive features and in fact merits special attention for having emerged despite a narrowly focused record. Note in particular that Ms. Anderson's guarded-ness did not prevent evidence of ambivalent feelings (a *ColShd* Blend) and self-critical attitudes (a Vista) from emerging.

As already mentioned, the suggestion in the data that she has a perva-sively extratensive coping style (*EB* of 1:3.0) is unreliable because of her high *Lambda* and low *EA*. However, there are definite indications that she has difficulty modulating affect either sufficiently or pleasurably. She feels uncomfortable around affect, prefers to subvert feelings to thoughts, and generally avoids situations in which strong feelings are being exchanged (*INTELL* = 4; *Afr* = .46). Especially revealing in this regard is Response 8 on Card III, in which the two dancers "have an Oriental feeling, maybe because of the black and reds." In this response her blended *M.C'.C* accounts for half of her total *SumC* of 3.0, while at the same time her isolation of the pure *C* affect in talking about the "Oriental feeling" indicates that she would rather think about than experience emotions, and the *Col-Shd Bld* indicates how difficult it may be for her to sustain positive affect without having it sullied by some dysphoric concerns.

Personal and Interpersonal Issues

Ms. Anderson appears generally to have enjoyed adequate self-esteem in her life and to have viewed herself as being as capable and as worthwhile as most people (*3r* + *(2)/R* = .42). However, she appears presently to be struggling with some self-critical attitudes ($V = 1$) and to be attempting to compensate for them by reassuring herself of her adequacy in a compensatory narcissistic fashion ($Fr + rF = 1$). Keeping in mind that the Egocentricity Index is a highly stable variable that is generally unresponsive to situational influence, it is Ms. Anderson's average level of .42 that provides the basis for regarding the Vista and the Reflection, together with their interpretive significance, as being related to her current circumstances rather than to long-standing self-criticism or self-glorification. There is sufficient information in the brief background sketch to suggest at least one possible situational source of her being self-critical. If she had not moved from where she used to live—and note that, even in a guarded record, she referred, perhaps wistfully, to "where I used to live" on Response 5—she would not have gotten into the licensing difficulty that has been upsetting to her. Should this be a source of some negative self-regard, her compensatory needs to reassure herself of her adequacy to make good decisions most of the time, to practice her profession competently, and to control her use of alcohol could account for a situationally determined Reflection response.

As is typical of guarded high *Lambda* records, there are not many responses that are largely determined by projection and hence not many compelling content themes to consider. Nonetheless, the Sequence of Scores identifies an interpretively rich series of responses involving Card II, which begins with her Vista (Response 4) and is followed by her only two minus responses (Responses 5 and 6), her only *Dd* location response (Response 7), and the Oriental dancers on Card III (Response 8). After giving three *WFA* responses on Card I, she begins Card II with an apparent expression of some concern ("Geez") and then gives a response of a butterfly with "gossamer wings" and "silky . . . layers of tissue." There is something fragile about silky gossamer wings on a butterfly, and perhaps the self-critical attitude suggested by the Vista in this response has to do with Ms. Anderson feeling that if she were a stronger person, then she would not be in her present difficulties.

However this may be, the likelihood that her associations to Response 4 were distressing to her is strengthened by the deterioration in Response 5 to minus form "lobster claws." It may also be that the lobster claws were distressing to her in their own right, in that they reminded her of "where I used to live." Continuing with Response 6, Ms. Anderson fails to recover from her reality distortion on Response 5 and instead gives another minus, "the mouth and the lips" of a "gnawing insect." In one final attempt to recover on this card, Ms. Anderson directs her attention away from most of the blot to focus on one of the tiny side details (Dd31), to which she gives the nondescript unusual form response of "fish head."

Now comes Card III, on which in Response 8 she reconstitutes with a good form, cooperative, active, human movement Popular. However, she can accomplish this restitution only by employing some intellectualization and being noncommittal, and with the accompaniment of some uncertain feelings, all of which have been previously noted as characterizing this response. After this mixed success in opening up a bit, she then shuts down almost completely. Over the next four cards she gives five *Fo* responses, all with distancing apparent in their content categories [(H), Hd, A, (Ad), and Ay] or in putting the card down after a brief response or two. The only other movement responses in the record arc Popular animals running on Card VIII (Response 14) and a "volcanic eruption" on Card IX (Response 16). This kind of eruption response often suggests a potential for sudden, explosive loss of control, which is definitely out of keeping with the generally over-controlled tone of this protocol.

Notice, however, that before Ms. Anderson finishes her "eruption" response, she again ends up with a distancing type of response *process* description, rather than a response *experience* ("the pink and the peach are easier to tie in as an eruption"), and on Card X she returns to three brief, delimited responses: a good form *FC* "seahorses" (Response 17); a hesitatingly delivered "Medusa" (Response 18), which seems potentially significant as a self-image but is diluted in the inquiry ("They don't look like snakes coming out of a head, but they could be"); and a good form but qualified "crab-like thing" (Response 19).

With respect to her interpersonal relatedness, Ms. Anderson appears to have limited capacity to form close attachments to other people and little anticipation of being able to form intimate, mutually supportive, and collaborative relationships with them ($T = 0$, $COP = 1$). Interestingly, although she gives no Texture and does not come close to doing so on Card VI, where T is most likely to occur, she flirts with texture on Response 2, with a moth that has a "fuzzy little mouth." When asked about "fuzzy," however, she makes a point of denying use of texture by saying, "moths have a fuzzy mouth, but this does not look fuzzy." Although the thematic imagery in this guarded protocol is slim, this "fuzzy mouth" reference may combine with the mouths noted on Responses 6 and 13 to raise the possibility that she has some unmet needs to depend on and be nurtured by others. To add to any problem she may have in this regard, she gives some evidence of feeling uncomfortable in social situations and having difficulty dealing with people who are real, live, fully-functioning individuals [$H:(H)Hd(Hd) = 1:3$].

In Ms. Anderson's case, then, we have a good illustration of a guarded high *Lambda* record in which the subject reveals very little of her personality dynamics and not much can be said with confidence about her preferred coping style or adaptive capacities. There is evidence of depressive features, of some apparently situational concerns about her personal adequacy, and of some probably long-standing difficulties in relating comfortably and closely to other people. There is some suggestion that unmet dependency needs may be contributing to her difficulties. On the other hand, she displays fairly effective reliance on intellectual defenses and distancing to maintain her composure and avoid becoming upset or dysfunctional in any way, and her cognitive functioning appears intact. Accordingly, with respect to the referral question in this case, the Rorschach data did not present any reason for questioning her capacity to practice her profession in an appropriate and responsible manner.

CASE 2: MULTIPLE ADJUSTMENT PROBLEMS IN A SUBSTANCE ABUSING MAN WITH DIFFICULTY LIMITING HIS FOCUS OF ATTENTION

Mr. Baker is a 27-year-old single, Caucasian, recently graduated professional man who voluntarily entered the alcohol and drug rehabilitation unit of a psychiatric hospital for evaluation and treatment of a substance abuse problem of several years duration. As an undergraduate he had become depressed over the breakup of a relationship with a female classmate, which required his being medicated and having a brief hospital admission. Although he did not receive mental health care following this depressive episode, he did subsequently begin to drink heavily. In addition to abusing alcohol, sometimes to the point of blacking out, he developed a marijuana habit and occasionally used cocaine and LSD as well. At the time of his present admission to a drug rehabilitation unit, he was concerned about being able to find a job and sustain his relationship with a current girlfriend, both of which he considered unlikely unless he could overcome his drug dependence. Mr. Baker's Rorschach protocol follows in Tables 10.4, 10.5, and 10.6 and Fig. 10.2.

Stress Management Issues

Mr. Baker's Structural Summary indicates a valid record of 23 responses with an *S-CON* of 7. An *S-CON* of 7 falls one point short of the most efficient cutting score for this variable and is best taken as not documenting the presence of suicidal potential. On the other hand, it is advisable to examine an *S-CON* of 7 for the possibility that it constitutes what may be called a "high 7." For clinical purposes, a "high 7" on the *S-CON* can be defined as a score that falls only one point short on one or more variables of being an *S-CON* of 8 or more. In Mr. Baker's protocol, none of the five negative *S-CON* variables comes close to a critical level. Accordingly, his *S-CON* is a "low 7" and, as such, does not by itself warrant considering him suicidal at the present time.

TABLE 10.4
Rorschach Protocol of Mr. Baker

Responses	*Inquiry*

Card I

1. A butterfly.

E: *(Repeats response)*
S: Yes, the wings are here and the tentacles are here (D1), here are the eyes on his head, and there's a white pattern on his wings. The body cavity is here (D4), and the center here is where the wings branched out from when he was a caterpillar.

2. (If you look at it some more, you'll see some other things as well) Can I hold it upside down? (Any way you like) v This way, a Chinese building, pointed at the top.

E: *(Repeats response)*
S: A Ming-type dynasty, Chinese building, with the architecture open; it's a temple, ornate.

3. v A jack-o-lantern, for obvious reasons.

E: *(Repeats response)*
S: Here are the eyes, and there's a little pumpkin spout coming out of the head (Dd31) where the vine was, and these are the jagged teeth.

4. The bottom half of a snowflake.

E: *(Repeats response)*
S: It looks like a crystal, when water freezes.

E: What made it look like that?
S: The jagged parts and the symmetrical edges, and there are holes here; it looks like snowflakes you hang on a Christmas tree.

5. Maybe a bat.

E: *(Repeats response)*
S: A bat or butterfly; these, instead of tentacles on the butterfly (D1) could be claws, or arms, and these eyes (Dd22) would be ears. Plus the fact that it's black helps lend to my imagination that it could be a bat.

Card II

6. It looks like two rhinoceroses kissing, or battling; they're touching their horns.

E: *(Repeats response)*
S: The horns are here (D4), the heads are here, the torso here.

E: Is it the whole thing?
S: No, just the torso, the upper chest, ears, neck, and contact point.

(Continued)

TABLE 10.4
(*Continued*)

Responses	Inquiry
	E: You said they're kissing or battling.
	S: Well, they have their mouths together, and they're rubbing horns; but maybe they're battling, because rhinoceroses aren't into kissing.
7. v Looks like a terrier dog, a pit bull terrier. (*turns card a few times*) Can't make much more out of it.	E: (*Repeats response*)
	S: The ear, the nose are here; two pit bulls sniffing each other, sniffing noses.

Card III

Responses	Inquiry
8. Looks like two women's torsos reaching down, with a man's torso underneath them, reaching down into some kind of cauldron.	E: (*Repeats response*)
	S: They're two women, like washing or cooking something. The upper torso is like women, because they have breasts. The lower part—they're wearing high heeled shoes, but there's a penis shape here. It's like an avant-garde painting, a half torso, like the works of—I can't remember.
9. v This way it looks like a giant bug, or spider, a black widow with the red on its back like that.	E: (*Repeats response*)
	S: It's pretty obvious; a red spot on the back, the eyes and the teeth. These are little shoulder joints, or whatever they're called on spiders. It's just the top half of the spider.

Card IV

Responses	Inquiry
10. (*pause*) v It's kind of like a Christmas tree.	E: (*Repeats response*)
	S: The base of the tree is here, the trunk of the tree here, and a couple of branches or vines (D4). Or this (D1) could be a palm tree behind it with a long cylindrical leaf. The top of the tree is here, and this is where it would go into the ground.
11. v Looks like an x-ray of a back vertebra. Other than that I don't see much.	E: (*Repeats response*)
	S: Like a lumbar vertebra, with the canal here; the colors helped, the different shades of black and gray, like an MRI study.

(*Continued*)

TABLE 10.4
(Continued)

Responses	Inquiry
	E: How much is part of it?
	S: All of it. The coccyx is here (D3), the bone part is in the center, and maybe there is a building vertebra here (D2), but this (D4) is not part of it.

Card V

12. This looks a lot like a bat.

E: *(Repeats response)*
S: The ears, head, feet; a bat in flight, because the wings are extended.

13. v Maybe a little like two porpoises, leaping out of the water, out of the ocean or something. *(reads back of card)*

E: *(Repeats response)*
S: The ripply waves as they jump out; the head, the mouth part, the water is here, it's choppy, like a wave that got kicked up.

E: What made it look choppy?
S: The dolphins jumping out of the water make turbulence.

Card VI

14. This looks like a very fat cat.

E: *(Repeats response)*
S: The head, the whiskers, the body, the legs here; like animals are when lying down on the ground in a relaxed position, with legs out.

E: What suggests that it's very fat?
S: The body, it's wide, and it's pouched on the side; it would be a smaller body if it were a thin cat.

15. *(turns card several times)* Some kind of pelt hanging in a wall.

E: *(Repeats response)*
S: It's obvious. It's like a wild cat someone took the hide of and hung on a wall.

E: What makes it look like a pelt?
S: The width of it, it looks flat; the black and white look one-dimensional, flat. A pelt would have less height than an actual animal.

(Continued)

TABLE 10.4
(*Continued*)

Responses	Inquiry
16. > This looks kind of like a—maybe a thundercloud over a horizon, coming out over some water.	E: (*Repeats response*) S: The way a thundercloud rises vertically. The high part is here and the horizon here. This is a lake with a reflection here, a very calm and peaceful lake, and it's a little darker here, which makes it look some kind of land mass being reflected off the water.
17. v Looks like a man, two men, with a large nose and a goatee.	E: (Repeats response) S: The nose, the hair, the mouth, the goatee, and a bulgy eye. This lower part (D3) wouldn't have anything to do with it.
Card VII 18. Looks like two women stretching their necks forward to look at each other.	E: (*Repeats response*) S: The neck, the nose is here, and the chin; a bouffanty hairdo, kind of like Margo Simpson, this part being the torso, down to here (D2).
Card VIII 19. v Looks like an x-ray of a human skull, in technicolor.	E: (*Repeats response*) S: The orbital pits, the nasal cavity here, the mouth is here, and the mandible is here (D4). It's kind of hard to make anything out of it, but it's technicolor because of all the colors.
20. Looks like a panther crawling up a mountain.	E: (*Repeats responses 20 and 21*) S: It could be either one. There are colored rocks, and a mountain here, and a mouse or a panther. Maybe a panther, because it has no tail.
21. Or a mouse crawling up some colored rocks.	
Card IX 22. (*turns card several times, long delay*) Maybe a thermogram of a volcano, that's all I can see.	E: (*Repeats response*) S: It looks like it's hot here, the yellow, after erupting from the red. The green (D1) is a cooler color, would represent the ground, and the red (D6) would represent the hottest part, the area underground that is hotter than the lava coming out.

(*Continued*)

TABLE 10.4
(Continued)

Responses	Inquiry
Card X	
23. v A flower, like a tulip type of flower, maybe some bees flying around it, some kind of insects, pollenization bugs or whatever.	E: *(Repeats response)* S: The stem is here, the flower's reproductive organs here (D2), the pistil (D10) and the stamen. This (D7) is some kind of pollenizing insect. These are the leaves, these green things (D1), and these would be other different colored leaves here, off in the distance. The whole thing is like a flower garden, with one red tulip in the center and blue and yellow tulips here.

Although Mr. Baker's protocol is presented in this chapter to illustrate a low *Lambda* record, the first positive key variable is $D < AdjD$, which is an indicator of situation stress. When low *Lambda* people lack sufficient adaptive capacity to manage the abundance of complex mental and emotional activity to which their open style of attending to experience exposes them, they often develop psychological difficulties that are manifest more prominently in some cluster of Rorschach variables other than those loading on information processing. In Mr. Baker's case, given that his $CDI = 4$ is the next positive key variable after his $D < AdjD$, the cluster search order following Table 3.2 is controls, affect, self-perception, interpersonal perception, processing, mediation, and ideation. Hence, even though the manner in which Mr. Baker attends to experience sets the tone for his record, as Ms. Anderson's high *Lambda* did in her record, consideration of cognitive issues will come last in this discussion, following consideration of stress management, affective, and personal and interpersonal issues.

Concerning his management of stress, the Rorschach data indicate that Mr. Baker is basically a psychologically competent individual. He shows an *EA* of 7.0, which is normative and probably speaks to his having been able to complete his professional education. Unfortunately, however, his adaptive capacities fall far short of allowing him to cope adequately with his very high level of experienced stress, as indicated by an $es = 16$ that far exceeds normative levels. He is consequently in a serious stress overload ($D = -3$) that is likely to make him, at present, an anxious, tense, and irritable person with limited frustration tolerance and a noteworthy susceptibility to impulsiveness.

As for the sources of his high level of experienced stress, he appears to be unusually preoccupied with concerns about getting his needs met (*FM*

TABLE 10.5
Sequence of Scores for Mr. Baker

Card No.		Loc.	No.	Determinant(s)	(2)	Content(s)	POP	Z	Special Scores
I	1	WS+	1	FC'u		A		3.5	INC,DR
	2	Wo	1	Fu		Ay		1.0	
	3	WSo	1	Fu		Art		3.5	DV
	4	WSo	1	F-		Na,Art		3.5	
	5	Wo	1	FC'o		A	P	1.0	INC
II	6	D+		Mau	2	Ad		3.0	AG,FAB
	7	D+		FMau	2	Ad		3.0	COP,PSV
III	8	D+		Mau	2	H,Sx,Art,Cg		3.0	INC,COP
	9	D+		FC'.FC-		Ad		4.0	INC
IV	10	W+	1	FDo		Bt		4.0	DV
	11	Ddo	99	FYu		Xy			
V	12	Wo	1	FMao		A	P	1.0	
	13	Dd+	99	FMa.mpu	2	A,Na		2.5	
VI	14	Wo	1	FMpu		A		2.5	DV,ALOG
	15	Wo	1	mpo		Ad	P	2.5	
	16	W/	1	Fr.mp.YFo		Na,Cl		2.5	
	17	Do	4	Fo	2	Hd			DV
VII	18	D+	2	Mao	2	Hd	P	3.0	DV
VIII	19	DSo	6	FC-		An			INC
	20	D+		FMao		A,Ls	P	3.0	
	21	D+	1	FMa.CFo		A,Na	P	3.0	
IX	22	W/	1	ma.CFu		Na,Fi,Art		5.5	
X	23	W+	1	FMa.CF.FDo		A,Bt		5.5	DV

= 7) and about being in a situation in which he lacks control of his own destiny ($m = 4$). He also gives evidence of being more than normatively troubled by unpleasant internalized feelings that have a dysphoric quality ($C' = 3$). On the other hand, his *AdjD* reduces to −1, which suggests that he could be functioning reasonably were he not so worried about being trapped in circumstances outside of his control. In terms of treatment planning, Mr. Baker's combination of a normative *EA* with an abnormally elevated *es* indicates that he is the kind of person who does not need help to become more competent as much as he needs help to minimize or resolve his sources of stress. The $m = 4$ indicates further that gaining some relief from

TABLE 10.6
Structural Summary for Mr. Baker

Location Features	Determinants Blends	Single	Contents	S-Constellation
Zf = 20	FC'.FC	M = 3	H = 1, 0	NO . . FV+VF+V+FD>2
ZSum = 60.5	FM.m	FM = 4	(H) = 0, 0	YES . . Col-Shd Bl>0
ZEst = 66.5	Fr.m.YF	m = 1	Hd = 2, 0	NO . . Ego<.31,>.44
	FM.CF	FC = 1	(Hd) = 0, 0	NO . . MOR > 3
W = 12	m.CF	CF = 0	Hx = 0, 0	YES . . Zd > +- 3.5
(Wv = 0)	FM.CF.FD	C = 0	A = 8, 0	YES . . es > EA
D = 9		Cn = 0	(A) = 0, 0	YES . . CF+C > FC
Dd = 2		FC' = 2	Ad = 4, 0	YES . . X+% < .70
S = 4		C'F = 0	(Ad) = 0, 0	YES . . S > 3
		C' = 0	An = 0, 0	NO . . P < 3 or > 8
		FT = 0	Art = 1, 0	YES . . Pure H < 2
DQ		TF = 0	Ay = 0, 1	NO . . R < 17
. . . . . . (FQ-)		T = 0	Bl = 0, 0	7 . . . . . TOTAL
+ = 11 (1)		FV = 0	Bt = 1, 1	
o = 10 (2)		VF = 0	Cg = 0, 1	Special Scorings
v/+ = 2 (0)		V = 0	Cl = 0, 1	
v = 0 (0)		FY = 1	Ex = 0, 0	Lvl Lv2
		YF = 0	Fd = 0, 0	DV = 6x1 0x2
		Y = 0	Fi = 0, 1	INC = 5x2 0x4
		Fr = 0	Ge = 0, 1	DR = 1x3 0x6
		rF = 0	Hh = 0, 0	FAB = 1x4 0x7
		FD = 1	Ls = 0, 1	ALOG = 1x5
Form Quality	F = 4		Na = 3, 2	CON = 0x7
			Sc = 0, 0	Raw Sum6 = 14
FQx FQf MQual SQx			Sx = 0, 1	Wgtd Sum6 = 28
+ = 0 0 0 0			Xy = 0, 1	
o = 10 1 1 0			Id = 1, 0	AB = 0 CP = 0
u = 10 2 2 2				AG = 1 MOR = 0
- = 3 1 0 2				CFB = 0 PER = 0
none = 0 — 0 0	(2) = 6			COP = 2 PSV = 1

Ratios, Percentages, and Derivations

R = 23	L = 0.21	FC:CF+C – 2: 3	COP = 2 AG = 1
		Pure C = 0	Food = 0
EB = 3: 4.0 EA = 7.0 EBPer = N/A		SumC':WSumC = 3:4.0	Isolate/R = 0.65
eb = 11: 5 es = 16 D = -3		Afr = 0.28	H: (H)Hd(Hd) = 1: 2
Adj es = 12 Adj D = -1		S = 4	(HHd) : (AAd) = 0: 0
		Blends:R = 6:23	H+A:Hd+Ad = 9: 6
FM = 7 : C' = 3 T = 0		CP = 0	
m = 4 : V = 0 Y = 2			

			P = 6	Zf = 20	3r+(2)/R = 0.39
a:p = 10: 4	Sum6 = 14		X+% = 0.43	Zd = -6.0	Fr+rF = 1
Ma:Mp = 3: 0	Lv2 = 0		F+% = 0.25	W:D:Dd = 12: 9: 2	FD = 2
2AB+Art+Ay = 5	WSum6 = 28		X-% = 0.13	W:M = 12: 3	An+Xy = 2
M- = 0	Mnone = 0		S-% = 0.67	DQ+ = 11	MOR = 0
			Xu% = 0.43	DQv = 0	

SCZI = 2	DEPI = 5*	CDI = 4*	S-CON = 7	HVI = No	OBS = No

267

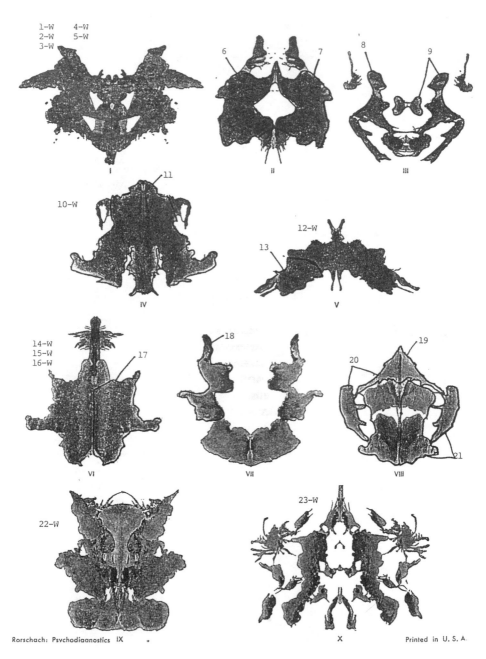

FIG. 10.2. Location choices of Mr. Baker.

his sense of powerlessness could very quickly help him feel and function more effectively than he is at the moment.

On the other hand, the control cluster variables identify two additional coping liabilities that could become important treatment targets in working with Mr. Baker if he were to enter psychotherapy. First, despite the adequate basic competence shown by his $EA = 7$, Mr. Baker gives evidence of serious difficulties in coping effectively with events in his life ($CDI = 4$). This combination of findings makes it highly likely that his interpersonal relationships are significantly impaired by poor social skills. As noted in chapter 5, an elevated CDI in the presence of an adequate EA typically indicates specific interpersonal incompetencies rather than more pervasive coping deficits and does not preclude solid accomplishment in noninterpersonal pursuits.

Second, Mr. Baker's difficulties in mustering adequate resources for coping with the substantial stresses in his life are exacerbated by his not having been able to establish a consistent manner of approaching decision-making situations. As an ambitent ($EB = 3{:}4.0$), he is likely to be an inconsistent and unpredictable person who vacillates ineffectively between reflective and expressive ways of dealing with experience and between conceptual and trial-and-error approaches to solving problems. In the absence of a preferred coping style, he probably feels as uncertain about what to expect of himself as others are about what to expect from him. He consequently may have an uncertain sense of his own identity and find it difficult to describe the kind of person he is.

Affective Issues

Mr. Baker's $DEPI$ of 5 identifies some depressive features in his present functioning and suggests that he has not fully escaped the vulnerability to becoming depressed that led to his being hospitalized a few years earlier. Clearly, there is a dysphoric tone to his depressive tendencies, as shown by the $C' = 3$ noted previously and by the presence of a stable Col-Shd Bld ($FC'.FC$) in his record. His difficulties in modulating affect pleasurably are indicated further by evidence that he is harboring considerable underlying anger or resentment ($S = 4$).

Mr. Baker also appears to be unusually aversive to emotionally charged situations and reluctant to become involved with people who are expressing strong feelings ($Afr = .28$). This preference to avoid or disengage from emotional interchange appears related in Mr. Baker's case to interpersonal concerns rather than to any basic incapacity to experience and express feelings. His use of color points to average ability to show affect ($SumC = 4.0$), freedom from emotional constriction ($SumC'{:}WSumC = 3{:}4.0$), and capacity for a mature and well-balanced blend of relatively reserved and relatively intense emotional displays ($FC{:}CF + C = 2{:}3$). His dysphoria and anger aside, Mr. Baker's openness to becoming aware of and expressing his feelings constitutes an important personality asset for him.

Personal and Interpersonal Issues

In contrast to the relatively meager amount of information concerning personal and interpersonal issues that emerged from Ms. Anderson's guarded high *Lambda* record, Mr. Baker's 23-response low *Lambda* (.21) record provides a rich source of inferences and speculations concerning how he views himself and his interpersonal world. To begin with, the depressive features noted with respect to affective dimensions of his personality do not appear associated with difficulties in maintaining adequate self-esteem and positive self-regard. The data suggest that he compares himself favorably with other people ($3r + (2)/R = .39$), and he does not give evidence of self-critical attitudes ($V = 0$) or negative views of his body or bodily functioning ($MOR = 0$).

To the contrary, the fact that he has a Reflection response suggests that he is a self-centered person who tends to overrate his merits and capacities and to attribute difficulties he encounters to the actions of others or to events outside of his control, rather than to any shortcomings or misdeeds on his part. Consistent with his apparent self-righteous need to assert that his way of doing things is the correct way, he comments on Response 3 that Card I is "a jack-o-lantern, for obvious reasons"; that the black widow spider he sees on Card III (Response 9) is "pretty obvious"; and, about a "pelt" on Card VI (Response 15) that "It's obvious." It may also be that the response on Card VI of "a very fat cat" captures in part an actual or idealized self-image as a person to be admired and envied, given that the expression "fat cat" often signifies a person who is wealthy, influential, self-satisfied, and "has it made."

Because psychologists examining patients with adjustment difficulties commonly encounter Reflection responses, they may at times underestimate the clinical implications of this finding. Whereas 20% of persons with diagnosed character disorder, 35% of men with antisocial personality, and 48% of borderline patients have Reflections in their records, $Fr + rF > 0$ occurs in only 7% of nonpatients (J. E. Exner, 1986, 1993, chap. 12; Gacono & Meloy, 1994, chap. 7). Accordingly, with just his single Reflection, Mr. Baker is demonstrating nonnormative narcissistic tendencies that may be contributing to adjustment difficulties, especially in his interpersonal relationships.

Before turning to Mr. Baker's interpersonal orientation, however, there is more to say about his sense of personal identity. Although he evidences adequate capacity for introspection ($FD = 2$), his examination of himself appears to result in numerous ambivalent and unwelcome self-images. Note first of all that in giving 23 relatively unguarded responses he is able to manage only one pure H. This $H = 1$ in an open, full-length record indicates limited success in forming a stable sense of identity based on identifications with real people in his life.

As might be expected, then, the images Mr. Baker projects in his Rorschach responses convey considerable uncertainty about what kind of person he is and would like to be. Response 6 on Card II depicts "rhinoceroses kissing or battling." Which is it, and which is he, a kissing rhinoceros or a battling rhinoceros? He has difficulty deciding, but finally opts for battling, "because rhinoceroses aren't into kissing." Aside from what this comment may suggest about aversion to tender interpersonal interaction, could it reflect some underlying attitudes he has about what big, powerful, macho figures with big horns do and what they do not do?

Continuing with this theme, Mr. Baker's next response on Card II is "a terrier dog, a pit bull terrier." This response also suggests identity confusion, in the sense that terriers are usually regarded as docile pets and pit bulls as aggressive combatants, even though pit bulls are a type of terrier. Finally to be considered in this regard are Responses 20 and 21, which in sequence describe the Popular animal figures on Card VIII first as a "panther" and then as a "mouse." Which is it, and how does he see himself in his own underlying fantasy, as a large and powerful predator or as a small and insignificant creature? Literally, in other words, is he a man or is he a mouse?

Mr. Baker's unsettled self-image extends beyond his manliness to his gender role in general. Most striking in this regard is his percept in Response 8 on Card III of figures that are women's torsos in the upper part "because they have breasts" and men's torsos in the lower part because "there's a penis shape here." He intellectualizes this response and prevents it from being a Level 2 *INCOM* by making it into "an avant-garde painting." With respect to the dynamic implications of this thematic imagery, however, the fat is already in the fire. Intellectualized or not, such impressions of figures having both male and female sexual anatomy strongly suggest underlying uncertainty and concerns about gender-role identity.

The extent to which Mr. Baker's underlying identity uncertainty causes him concerns that disrupt his mental functioning can be seen in the sequence of his responses to Cards II and III. The rhinoceroses kissing or battling, the pit bull terrier, and the bisexual torsos occur successively in Responses 6, 7, and 8, and the disruptive impact of these images shows up in Response 9. Here we see a breakdown in functioning adequacy manifest in a perceptually inaccurate (minus form), arbitrarily reasoned (*INCOM*), and emotionally dysphoric (*FC'.FC*) response involving a "black widow spider" that has teeth and "shoulder joints."

Consider further the possible dynamic significance in a response with prominent projected elements (as attested by the minus form level and the *INCOM*) involving association to a black widow spider, an organism generally believed to devour its sexual partner after copulation. Could this be a man who is fearful of sexual intimacy with women or is terrified by such a prospect? Although only tentative speculation, this question illustrates how potentially fruitful hypotheses can be generated by dynamically oriented thematic analysis. Along with his gender-role uncertainty, possible fears of intimacy would merit further exploration in efforts to understand this man and treat him, were he to become a patient in psychotherapy.

Moving on to implications of the data for the adequacy of Mr. Baker's interpersonal relatedness, his Rorschach responses identify numerous social concerns that, together with his difficulties in establishing a comfortable sense of identity, may well have contributed to his substance abuse. On the positive side, he appears to be a reasonably empathic person who can perceive the nature and motives of other people accurately ($M- = 0$) and who is as likely as most people to anticipate collaborative relationships with others ($COP = 2$). On the other hand, he gives evidence of limited interest in people ($SumH = 3$), long-standing incapacity to form close bonds of attachment to others ($T = 0$), and a striking lack of involvement with people who play an important part in his life ($ISOL = .65$). These findings, together with the affective cluster data of $Afr = .28$ and $S = 4$ and his previously noted $Fr + rF = 1$, suggest that he is basically an angry, avoidant, and self-centered person who resents other people for not meeting his needs. He may go through the motions of establishing close and enduring interpersonal relationships, but he is seldom likely to allow himself to become intimately involved with another person.

Cognitive Issues

As noted in introducing this record, Mr. Baker is unusually open to experience ($Lambda = .21$) and, quite unlike high $Lambda$ individuals, tends to be the kind of person who has difficulty maintaining an adaptive level of detachment and objectivity in his dealings with the world. Instead, he is prone to becoming overly involved in whatever he is doing, to making matters more complex than they need to be (i.e., making mountains out of molehills), and to losing clear focus on events in his life. People with abundant coping capacities can sometimes manage a low $Lambda$ orientation productively, as was elaborated in chapter 5, and for them it may even be an asset. However, for people such as Mr. Baker, in whom a modest EA is overwhelmed by a huge es, low $Lambda$ almost always proves maladaptive. Accordingly, this data constellation identifies the following treatment target whenever it occurs: In Rorschach language, turning some of Mr. Baker's es components into pure F responses would raise his $Lambda$, reduce his D-, and alleviate the stress overload that appears to be contributing to both emotional and behavioral problems in his life.

Unfortunately, Mr. Baker's information-processing problems do not end with his low *Lambda*. In addition, he gives evidence of limited capacity to organize information effectively ($Zd = -6$). As an underincorporator, he is prone to hasty and careless decision making in which he fails to take adequate account of all the information he should consider before coming to conclusions about what to think or how to act. He does display some intellectual prowess and some good capacity to synthesize aspects of his experience ($DQ+ = 11$), but these cognitive assets may be of little use to him so long as he continues to have difficulty focusing his attention economically and efficiently on one matter at a time.

With respect to his cognitive mediation, Mr. Baker is basically capable of recognizing conventional reality and perceiving people and events realistically ($P = 6$; $X - \% = .13$). Nevertheless, his $X - \%$ of .13 and an $S - \%$ of .67 also indicate some propensity for lapses in judgment when he becomes angry, and his $Xu\%$ of .43 identifies an unusually strong preference to define the world in his own terms and to do things his own way. This type of aversion to conformity commonly accompanies sensation-seeking behavior, and the unconventionality reflected in his elevated $Xu\%$ may have contributed to his being drawn to substance use as a way of relieving the psychological pain of his earlier depressive experiences.

Turning finally to Mr. Baker's ideational functioning, the test data identify some personality assets but also some additional sources of likely adjustment difficulties. On the positive side, there is no indication that he is excessively committed to ideational modes of dealing with experience, because as an ambitent he is far from being pervasively introversive, nor is he inclined to favor fantasy over reality as a way of solving problems ($Mp = 0$). On the other hand, he is much more likely than most people to have trouble thinking clearly and logically ($WSum6 = 28$), he tends to use intellectualization as a way of distancing himself from events ($INTELL = 5$), and he displays a rigid and inflexible frame of reference ($a:p = 10:4$).

The $WSum6 = 28$ is of particular concern, because it constitutes an elevation on this variable that usually identifies formal thought disorder. However, the data in this regard illustrate the importance of examining the composition of deviant summary scores for possible mitigating features that attenuate their seeming significance for psychopathology. In Mr. Baker's case, all 14 of the Critical Special Scores he gives are of the Level 1 variety, which identify mild rather than severe cognitive slippage, and 11 of them involve *DV* or *INCOM*, which as pointed out in chapter 5 are the two relatively benign Critical Special Scores.

As for the three instances of more serious cognitive slippage, his *DR* on Response 1 consists of a comment on the butterfly's previous form as a caterpillar and is only slightly off task. His *FABCOM* on Response 6 involves animals in human movement, which is a type of *FABCOM* more indicative of a childish lapse than a major breakdown in logicality. His *ALOG* on Response 14 is coded for seeing a "very fat cat" because it has a wide body, whereas "it would be a smaller body if it were a thin cat." This appears to be an instance of taking blot size literally as object size, as in the prototypical example of "It must be a big one, because the blot fills almost the entire card." Mr. Baker's *ALOG* is less blatantly circumstantial than this prototype, however, and some coders might legitimately question whether Response 14 warrants a Special Score at all. Considered in light of its composition, then, Mr. Baker's *WSum6* of 28 demonstrates far greater than average susceptibility to instances of mild cognitive slippage, but it probably does not identify pathologically disordered thinking.

The sequence of Mr. Baker's responses as well as his *INTELL* = 5 provide clues to when and how he utilizes intellectualization as a defense. He receives three of his five *INTELL* points on this index in Responses 2, 3, and 4 on Card I, which involve one *Ay* and two *Art* contents. These three responses follow his signaling some distress in his opening response, a butterfly with tentacles, "eyes on his head," "a white pattern on his wings," and an earlier life as a caterpillar, which resulted in codes indicative of dysphoria (*FC'*) and cognitive slippage (*DV* and *DR*). Given the depressive features already noted in his record, it is reasonable to hypothesize that he was having an immediate negative reaction to the dark coloration of Card I. A *C'* occurring on the very first response, as a way of signing in, often bespeaks psychological investment in being, feeling, and presenting oneself as a depressed person.

At any rate, following this apparent arousal of dysphoria occasioned by Card I and reflected in Response 1, Mr. Baker distances himself from painful affect by focusing attention in Response 2 on an impersonal object that is far removed in space and time from anything occurring in his life—an *Ay* Chinese building from the days of the Ming dynasty. He then follows with two decorative *Art* contents, the jack-o-lantern on Response 3 and the "snowflakes you hang on a Christmas tree" on Response 4. It may even be that his association to decorating a Christmas tree, which most people would regard as a pleasurable experience, represents a further effort to turn away from or deny his Card I dysphoria.

What we see, then, is a man who is quite susceptible to feeling gloomy and who attempts to defend himself against negative affect with intellectualization and perhaps some denial as well. As for the adequacy of his defenses in helping him recover from episodes of gloom, the data in Response 5 suggest mixed success. On the one hand, after having employed intellectualization in three successive responses, two of them with unusual form and one a minus, he is finally able in this fifth response to Card I to give his first ordinary form percept, the Popular bat. Yet, even in this recovery response, he cannot escape a dysphoric tone (another FC'), nor can he avoid an instance of mild cognitive slippage (the $INCOM$ of a bat with "claws or arms"). Further evidence that his intellectualizing serves him poorly in sparing him distress appears in the sequence of Responses 8 and 9 on Card III, which have previously been analyzed for their thematic imagery. In Response 8, which involves the torsos that are half men and half women, he takes intellectual distance by putting the figures into a painting (the Art). However, his defensiveness in this instance does not prevent the dysphoric and perceptually distorted ($FC'.FC$-) black widow spider from emerging in Response 9.

Lastly, with respect to Mr. Baker's unbalanced $a{:}p$ ratio, this finding indicates that he is relatively inflexible in his thinking and the kind of opinionated person who is set in his ways and disinclined to consider points of view that differ from those he already holds. This kind of ideational rigidity, like the $a{:}p$ ratio by which it is measured, tends to be a stable and persistent personality characteristic, and, as would be expected, it is likely to pose an obstacle to progress in psychotherapy. In common with most other trait-related Rorschach variables, however, an unbalanced $a{:}p$ ratio can be modified in psychotherapy, and this feature of Mr. Baker's cognitive style should be among the treatment targets in his case (see Weiner, in press; Weiner & Exner, 1991). At the same time, whoever may be treating him should be alerted that the Rorschach indications of his disinterest in changing his mind predict slow progress and resistance to self-examination in the initial phases of treatment and some risk for early dropout.

To summarize the findings in Mr. Baker's case, he presents a low *Lambda* record in which evidence of inability to maintain a detached and delimited focus of attention is accompanied by indications of multiple adjustment difficulties that have probably resulted, at least in part, from his excessive subjectivity in dealing with experience. He is anxious and depressed, as well as unable to manage comfortably the amount of stress he is experiencing or to take pleasure in his life. He is distant and isolated from other people and, although basically a competent individual, he lacks adequate social skills. He is confused and uncertain about his personal identity, especially in relation to issues of gender role. He has not developed a consistent coping style, is likely to vacillate unproductively in how he chooses to deal with situations, and is only moderately successful in attempting to use mechanisms of intellectualization and denial to defend against painful psychological awareness. Although Mr. Baker is not seriously disturbed, the breadth of his adjustment difficulties and the inadequacy of his defenses leave him chronically exposed to subjectively felt distress and ineffective coping. This persistent distress and ineffectiveness, in combination with tendencies toward nonconformity and sensation seeking, may account for his having turned to self-medication with drugs. Mr. Baker's low *Lambda* identifies a primary target for his treatment. If he could be helped to narrow his frame of reference and impose a bit more objectivity on his way of attending to experience, he might well be able to minimize his susceptibility to becoming distressed and thereby reduce his needs to self-medicate.

11

Using Ideation

Using ideation refers to the ways in which people think about their experiences and the conclusions they draw concerning what these experiences mean. As elaborated in chapter 5, adequate adaptation depends on being able to think logically, coherently, flexibly, constructively, and in moderation. People whose thinking tends to be illogical, incoherent, and inflexible or who are prone to being overly fanciful and excessively ruminative, on the other hand, have functioning liabilities that frequently result in adjustment difficulties.

Problems in using ideation adaptively appear on the RIM in the form of deviations from normative expectation in the ideational cluster of variables listed in Table 3.1. As shown in Table 3.2, the Comprehensive System interpretive search strategy places initial emphasis on these variables when $SCZI$ > 3 or when EB is introversive. $SCZI$ > 3 usually identifies serious adjustment problems attributable to ideational dysfunction, although it is possible for a $SCZI = 4$ to reflect poor reality testing in the absence of disordered thinking. As elaborated by J. E. Exner and Weiner (1995, chap. 5) and Weiner (1998b), examiners should be alert to this particular finding, because it constitutes a "false positive 4" for schizophrenia.

In contrast to an elevation on $SCZI$, an introversive EB identifies preference for an ideational approach to experience that, depending on the adequacy of other aspects of an individual's personality functioning, may be associated with either serious or mild adjustment difficulties or with no adjustment difficulties at all.

The two cases presented in this chapter involve serious psychological disorder in which ideation plays a major role, but they illustrate different levels of ideational abnormality. The first record was given by a chronically paranoid schizophrenic man recently hospitalized following an episode of decompensation, and in his record abnormal ideation, particularly as manifest in disordered thinking, stands at the core of his disturbance. In the second record, given by an adolescent girl with anorexia nervosa, an introversive *EB* directs initial attention to the ideational cluster of variables, but the patient's manner of thinking is less a maladaptive aspect of her disturbance than an overly controlled and emotionally inhibited personality style that colors how her disturbance is expressed.

CASE 3: EMOTIONAL BREAKDOWN IN A PARANOID SCHIZOPHRENIC MAN

Mr. Carter is a 45-year-old Caucasian man who was voluntarily admitted to the inpatient psychiatric service of a university hospital with a chief complaint of "I'm depressed, I'm lifeless, and I have no motivation to go on." He reported that 8 years previously, while living in another part of the country, he had been hospitalized with a diagnosis of paranoid schizophrenia. He was discharged after 1 month's treatment with antipsychotic drugs and continued in outpatient medication management. He was subsequently rehospitalized on five occasions, each time in relation to having paranoid thoughts and for a duration of approximately 30 days.

Mr. Carter has been twice married and divorced. His first marriage lasted 18 years, and he has three grown children from that union. He was married to his second wife for 3 years and has a 2-year-old child from that marriage. After divorcing his second wife about a year ago, he moved back to his original part of the country to be close to his parents and older children, with whom he states he felt happier than with his second wife. Five months prior to his present hospitalization, he responded to a request from his second wife to return to her home to assist her in caring for their child. Since moving 2,000 miles to rejoin his second wife, Mr. Carter has been unable to find work, his car has been repossessed, and he has become despondent, with reported sleep disturbance, loss of appetite and weight, and episodes of restlessness and racing thoughts. On interview he was alert and oriented, his speech was coherent and relevant, and he denied any paranoid ideation. He was referred for psychological evaluation to clarify differentiation of his long-standing diagnosis of paranoid schizophrenia from possible schizoaffective or bipolar disorder. Mr. Carter's Rorschach protocol follows in Tables 11.1, 11.2, and 11.3 and Fig. 11.1.

Cognitive Issues

Mr. Carter's Structural Summary indicates a valid record of 22 responses, no elevation on the *S-CON*, and a first positive key variable of *SCZI* > 3. Hence, the order for searching the clusters in his record, following Table 3.2, is

TABLE 11.1
Rorschach Protocol of Mr. Carter

Responses	Inquiry
Card I	
1. Kinda looks like—in the—on top it looks like two gorillas with their hands up, down the middle of the picture.	E: (*Repeats response*) S: There's the hands (D1), the heads (Dd22), and the faces. E: I'm not sure where you're seeing it. S: It's this part here (Dd21).
2. If you stretch it out, it looks like two spacemen, in space suits, down the center of the picture. That's all I can make out.	E: (*Repeats response*) S: That could be part of the whole central. This part looks like gorillas (Dd21), but if you go all the way down, it looks like spacemen. E: What helps you see the space suits? S: It's awful bulky.
Card II	
3. (*pause*) Down the center, it looks like two praying hands.	E: (*Repeats response*) S: Up here (D4), it just looks like two praying hands.
4. Kinda looks like two bear cubs, the black portion of it.	E: (*Repeats response*) S: This portion—bears or pigs, or lambs. E: What makes it look like that? S: The ears (Dd31) and the noses here (D4).
5. The two red things on top look like outer space things, like two individuals talking to each other. That's all.	E: (*Repeats response*) S: Like you see on TV, in the cartoons. You can see the eyes here. E: How much of them are you seeing? S: All of them, and here are the eyes and the hands sticking out.
Card III	
6. I see a bow tie right in the center.	E: (*Repeats response*) S: It's right here, this part is shaped like a bow tie.
7. These look like two individuals holding onto a coffee table.	E: (*Repeats response*) S: Here's the individuals here, and here's the coffee table (D7). They're both holding on to it, and they got their back in a big arch, and their shoes are real high, like high-heeled shoes.

(*Continued*)

279

TABLE 11.1
(*Continued*)

Responses	Inquiry
8. On the bottom it looks like a person's face. Their eyes are covered up. And that's it.	E: (*Repeats response*) S: The eyes look like they're covered up with a big long cotton—or mask. Here's the face (D8), and the eyes, covered up. E: What made them look covered up? S: You can't see the eyes.
Card IV 9. This one looks like some kind of monster with big feet, real big feet, and a long tail. That's it on this one.	E: (*Repeats response*) S: The feet are here, the tail here, and the head up here.
Card V 10. This looks like a bat, just like a bat. It looks like a bat with a snail's head on it. That's all I can make out of this one. (*continues to look intently at card*)	E: (*Repeats response*) S: The bat portion is here, the feet here, and the snail's head is right here (D6). E: The bat has a snail's head on it? S: That's right.
Card VI 11. This one reminds me of an insect on the top portion. Some kind of bug.	E: (*Repeats response*) S: It's right here (D3). E: How does it look like a bug to you? S: It just looks like some kind of big moth or something.
12. The other part reminds me of a land mass, and then a highway down the middle.	E: (*Repeats response*) S: There's a mass of land here (D1), with a highway here (D12). E: What made it look like a land mass? S: It just looks like a blotch of land, sand, and gravel, and here it's darkened, like it's a roadway.
13. This it kinda reminds me of—as in South America, where our lord Jesus is standing on top of a big mountain, the statue of him. That's what it reminded me of when I first saw it, that famous statue on a mountain in South America. That's all.	E: (*Repeats response*) S: That statue stands on a big mountain (Dd34) in Rio, I think. Jesus stands straight up, with his hands outstretched. I bet you never got that one before.

(*Continued*)

TABLE 11.1
(Continued)

Responses	Inquiry
Card VII	
14. This reminds me of two girls looking at each other, with pony tails.	E: *(Repeats response)* S: I see the head, and the pony tail sticking straight up.
15. On the bottom it looks like somebody standing on guard. It looks like a small entrance to somewhere. On top of it you could see the sun horizon—the sun looking over the top of it. That's it.	E: *(Repeats response)* S: A guard, standing guard at an entrance. This is the entrance here (Dd26). E: What suggested an entrance? S: It just starts to open up here, and the sun horizon is here. E: The sun horizon? S: It looks like a sunset, over a lake, the darker part is the reflection, like a lake. Wait, I made a mistake. The entrance is not here (Dd26), it's here (Dd27).
Card VIII	
16. I see a face of some kind of native African, all dressed up. I can see the head real plain, eyes, nose. The face is real vivid, and it has a headdress on it. That's all.	E: *(Repeats response)* S: The head is here (D4), with the headdress, and the face is here (DS3). E: What suggests it to you? S: It's what they wear. It just looks like his dress, and his makeup. I've seen it in movies. E: What makes it look like makeup? S: Just the way the eyes are, and the mouth.
17. On the side it looks like two animals. I can't make out what kind they are.	E: *(Repeats response)* S: Two animals. I can't make out what kind they are. I've never seen animals that shape before.
Card IX	
18. *(long pause)* Inside, the green portion—I see eyes—part of an animal. Maybe the head of a deer. That's all I see in this one.	E: *(Repeats response)* S: Yes, maybe a deer. The head—two deers, like they're looking out.

(Continued)

281

TABLE 11.1
(Continued)

Responses	Inquiry
Card X	
19. *(pause)* This looks like—*(laughs)*—two little grubs, or strange creatures, holding up an instrument.	E: *(Repeats response)* S: Two grubs here (D8), and the instrument here. Their hands are here, like they're holding it up. E: It's an instrument? S: It just looks like a long pipe or something.
20. The two portions on the side kinda look like crabs.	E: *(Repeats response)* S: Yeah, these two on the sides look just like crabs.
21. The one in the center reminds me of a pelvic bone.	E: *(Repeats response)* S: This part here (D6) looks like one.
22. The other part looks like a lady's face is covered up by a horse. On both sides. There are two ladies, on each side, and half their face is covered up, like by a horse.	E: *(Repeats response)* S: Are you sure it was on this one (*response reread*). I don't think it was this one—oh, I see it—it looks like a mouth and an eye, and it looks like a horse over them. It looks like an old horse from Black Bart days. It just reminds me of that horse, and the cartoon.

ideation, mediation, processing, controls, affect, self-perception, and interpersonal perception.

With respect to his ideation, Mr. Carter presents dramatic evidence in his Rorschach responses of seriously impaired capacity to think logically, flexibly, constructively, and in moderation. First of all, his *WSum6* of 18 identifies disordered thinking, particularly with respect to a predilection for arbitrary reasoning. Note that his *WSum6* = 18 is being interpreted as evidence of thought disorder, whereas Mr. Baker's *WSum6* = 28 was not interpreted as such in chapter 10. As mentioned in discussing Mr. Baker's data, accurate interpretation of *WSum6* requires attention to its composition as well as its total. It is in its components that Mr. Carter's *WSum6* is pathological. Whereas all of Mr. Baker's 14 Critical Special Scores were of the Level 1 variety and 11 were either *DV* or *INCOM*, 2 of Mr. Carter's Critical Special Scores are sufficiently bizarre to be coded Level 2. These include an *INCOM2* on Response 10 of "a bat with a snail's head" and a *FABCOM2* on Response 22 involving a "lady's face" that is somehow "covered up by a horse."

As another way of grasping the difference between the records of these two men, Mr. Baker's *WSum6* of 28 is twice the number of his 14 Critical

TABLE 11.2
Sequence of Scores for Mr. Carter

Card No.		Loc.	No.	Determinant(s)	(2)	Content(s)	POP	Z	Special Scores
I	1	Ddo	21	FMp-	2	A			
	2	D+	4	Fo	2	H,Cg		4.0	DV
II	3	D+	4	Mau	2	Hd		3.0	
	4	Do	6	Fo	2	A	P		
	5	D+	2	Mpu	2	(H)		5.5	PER
III	6	Do	3	Fo		Cg			
	7	D+	1	Mao	2	H,Hh,Cg	P	3.0	
	8	D+	7	FD-		Hd,(Hd)		3.0	
IV	9	Wo	1	Fo		(A)		2.0	
V	10	Wo	1	Fu		A		1.0	INC2
VI	11	Do	3	Fo		A			
	12	Dv	1	YFu		Ls,Sc			DV
	13	Dd+	99	Mpo		H,Ls,Art		2.5	
VII	14	D+	1	Mp.mpo	2	Hd	P	3.0	
	15	Dd+	99	Mp.FY-		H,Na		3.0	DV
VIII	16	DS+	3	F-		Hd,Cg,Ay		4.0	PER
	17	Do	1	Fo	2	A	P		
IX	18	DdSo	99	FMp-	2	Ad			
X	19	D+	11	Mau	2	A,Id		4.0	FAB
	20	Do	1	Fo		A	P		
	21	Do	6	F-		An			
	22	D+	1	FD-	2	Hd,A		4.0	FAB2

Special Scores, whereas Mr. Carter's *WSum6* (18) is three times the number of his Critical Special Scores (6). In other words, Mr. Carter does not show cognitive slippage very often in his record, but the slippage is considerable and the result sometimes bizarre when he does slip. This finding seems consistent with the fact that, although he has been hospitalized on several previous occasions for schizophrenia, he is at present complaining of depression rather than paranoid ideation and was noted to speak coherently and relevantly during his admission interview.

As for flexibility in his thinking, Mr. Carter gives evidence (as did Mr. Baker) of being rigid and set in his ways, the kind of person who knows what he knows, believes what he believes, and does not readily entertain

TABLE 11.3
Structural Summary for Mr. Carter

Location Features	Determinants		Contents	S-Constellation
	Blends	Single		

Location Features	Blends	Single		Contents		S-Constellation
Zf = 13	M.m	M	= 5	H	= 4, 0	NO . . FV+VF+V+FD>2
ZSum = 42.0	M.FY	FM	= 2	(H)	= 1, 0	NO . . Col-Shd Bl>0
ZEst = 41.5		m	= 0	Hd	= 5, 0	YES . . Ego<.31,>.44
		FC	= 0	(Hd)	= 0, 1	NO . . MOR > 3
W = 2		CF	= 0	Hx	= 0, 0	NO . . Zd > +- 3.5
(Wv = 0)		C	= 0	A	= 7, 1	NO . . es > EA
D = 16		Cn	= 0	(A)	= 1, 0	NO . . CF+C > FC
Dd = 4		FC′	= 0	Ad	= 1, 0	YES . . X+% < .70
S = 2		C′F	= 0	(Ad)	= 0, 0	NO . . S > 3
		C′	= 0	An	= 1, 0	NO . . P < 3 or > 8
		FT	= 0	Art	= 0, 1	NO . . Pure H < 2
DQ		TF	= 0	Ay	= 0, 1	NO . . R < 17
. . . . . . (FQ-)		T	= 0	Bl	= 0, 0	2 . . . . . TOTAL
+ = 11 (4)		FV	= 0	Bt	= 0, 0	
o = 10 (3)		VF	= 0	Cg	= 1, 3	Special Scorings
v/+ = 0 (0)		V	= 0	Cl	= 0, 0	
v = 1 (0)		FY	= 0	Ex	= 0, 0	

				Contents		Special Scorings		
		YF	= 1	Fd	= 0, 0		Lv1	Lv2
		Y	= 0	Fi	= 0, 0	DV = 3x1		0x2
		Fr	= 0	Ge	= 0, 0	INC = 0x2		1x4
		rF	= 0	Hh	= 0, 1	DR = 0x3		0x6
		FD	= 2	Ls	= 1, 1	FAB = 1x4		1x7
		F	= 10	Na	= 0, 1	ALOG = 0x5		
				Sc	= 0, 1	CON = 0x7		
				Sx	= 0, 0	Raw Sum6 = 6		
				Xy	= 0, 0	Wgtd Sum6 = 18		

Form Quality

	FQx	FQf	MQual	SQx		Id = 0, 1		
+	= 0	0	0	0		AB = 0	CP = 0	
o	= 10	7	3	0		AG = 0	MOR = 0	
u	= 5	1	3	0		CFB = 0	PER = 2	
-	= 7	2	1	2		COP = 0	PSV = 0	
none	= 0	—	0	0	(2) = 11			

Ratios, Percentages, and Derivations

R = 22		L = 0.83		FC:CF+C	= 0: 0	COP = 0 AG = 0
				Pure C	= 0	Food = 0
EB = 7: 0.0	EA = 7.0	EBPer = 7.0		SumC′:WSumC	= 0:0.0	Isolate/R = 0.18
eb = 3: 2	es = 5	D = 0		Afr	= 0.47	H: (H)Hd(Hd) = 4: 7
	Adj es = 4	Adj D = +1		S	= 2	(HHd) : (AAd) = 2: 1
				Blends:R	= 2:22	H+A:Hd+Ad = 14: 7
FM = 2 : C′ = 0 T = 0				CP	= 0	
m = 1 : V = 0 Y = 2						

				P = 5	Zf = 13	3r+(2)/R = 0.50
a:p = 3: 7		Sum6 = 6		X+% = 0.45	Zd = +0.5	Fr+rF = 0
Ma:Mp = 3: 4		Lv2 = 2		F+% = 0.70	W:D:Dd = 2:16: 4	FD = 2
2AB+Art+Ay = 2		WSum6 = 18		X-% = 0.32	W:M = 2: 7	An+Xy = 1
M- = 1		Mnone = 0		S-% = 0.29	DQ+ = 11	MOR = 0
				Xu% = 0.23	DQv = 1	

SCZI = 5*	DEPI = 3	CDI = 3	S-CON = 2	HVI = Yes	OBS = No

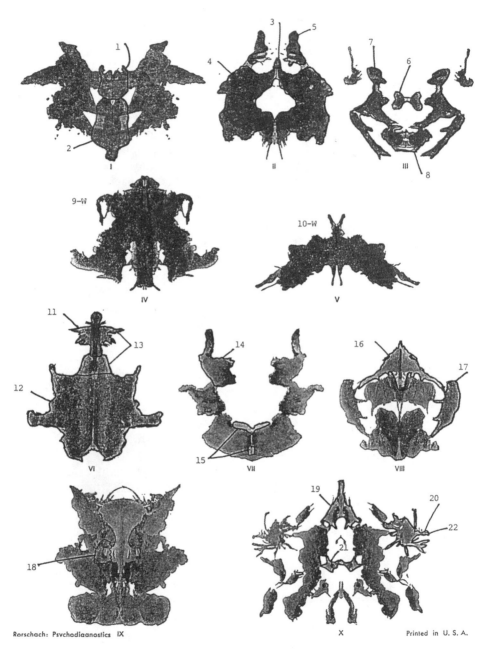

FIG. 11.1. Location choices of Mr. Carter.

the possibility of changing his mind about anything ($a:p = 3:7$). He additionally appears to have limited capacity for thinking constructively about his problems and actively contemplating how best to deal with them. Instead, his $Ma:Mp = 3:4$ suggests that he is prone to deal with problems by fantasizing about how other people or fortuitous events will resolve them, rather than by seeking his own solutions to them.

Finally of concern in Mr. Carter's thinking is an excessive commitment to ideational ways of approaching problem-solving and decision-making situations at the expense of adequate channels for emotional awareness and expression. As someone who is pervasively introversive ($EB = 7:0.0$), he has little tolerance for emotionality and cannot allow himself the freedom to take any action without first ruminating about its consequences. Moreover, as a pervasively introversive person whose $WSumC$ is 0.0, he has virtually no adaptive capacity to be in touch with his own feelings and share them with others, and it will be almost impossible for him to behave in a casual, relaxed, spontaneous manner unfettered by contemplation and deliberation. People thus devoid of adaptive capacities for recognizing and displaying affect are highly susceptible to being overwhelmed by it. Unable to modulate emotion, they become markedly overwrought when painful emotions are unavoidably thrust on them. This implication of Mr. Carter's 7:0.0 EB is reflected in his dramatic presenting complaint of being so depressed that "I'm lifeless, and I have no motivation to go on."

The data in Mr. Carter's mediation and processing clusters provide further evidence of the serious psychological disorder that has interfered with his adjustment for at least the last several years. He does show normative capacity to recognize conventional reality ($P = 5$) and to focus attention on common and ordinary aspects of his experience ($W:D:Dd = 2:16:4$). These capacities may account for his having been able to function outside of a hospital setting prior to his current breakdown, especially if, as his history suggests, he was living in a fairly protected environment with support from his parents and grown children.

On the other hand, what we can we see at present is reality testing that is compromised by pathological tendencies to misperceive events ($X-\% = .32$), and a focus of attention that takes excessive notice of unusual details ($Dd = 4$). Taken together, these last two findings identify some persistent difficulty in sizing up situations accurately and exercising good judgment in deciding what to do about them. This liability could have a bearing on his apparently ill-advised reunion with his second wife, which subjected him to demands he was not capable of handling.

Continuing with his information processing, Mr. Carter appears to be a man who, despite the inflexible and sometimes illogical conclusions he draws, and despite the frequently distorted impressions on which these conclusions are based, is normatively open to experience ($Lambda = .83$). Along with taking in appropriate amounts of information, he is capable of organizing this information efficiently (Zd = +0.5). Although he is thus neither a high or low *Lambda* person and neither an underincorporator or overincorporator, there are some unusual contrasts in his information-processing style. On the one hand, he makes slightly more than an average amount of effort to organize his experience (Zf = 13), and he displays above average capacity to synthesize elements of this experience ($DQ+$ = 11). Yet, he pays little attention to global aspects of his experience or to seeing things in their entirety, and instead opts for a very concrete, economical, and delimited way of looking at the world ($W:D$ = 2:16). Consistent with his infrequent effort to attain a W response, his $W:M$ ratio of 2:7 suggests a man who has characteristically set low goals for himself, has kept his reach well within his grasp, and, perhaps because of his serious disorder, has never been able to utilize fully the achievement potential indicated by his $DQ+$ of 11 and seven M responses.

Overall, Mr. Carter's cognitive data are consistent with his history of diagnosed schizophrenic disorder and would strongly suggest schizophrenia even if this were his first admission. The $SCZI$ of 5, based on his demonstrating both disordered thinking ($WSum6$ = 18) and impaired reality testing ($X - \%$ = 32), is fairly conclusive in this regard and much less likely than a $SCZI$ = 4 to be a false positive. Thinking disorder with an elevated $WSum6$ may occur in other schizophrenia spectrum disorders, such as paranoid delusional disorder and schizotypal personality disorder, and it may also appear in bipolar disorder, which was a possibility mentioned in the referral question. However, schizophrenia spectrum disorders other than schizophrenia itself ordinarily do not involve overt psychosis, as defined by impaired reality testing and measured on the RIM by poor form level. Hence the elevated $X - \%$ in this thought-disordered man makes it likely that he is schizophrenic rather than merely delusional or schizotypal.

As for bipolar disorder, Mr. Carter's record differs in many respects from usual expectation in persons with hypomanic or cyclothymic conditions. Absent are such defining characteristics of bipolar disorder as an emotionally expressive style and intense, labile affectivity, as manifest in both numerous C' and a large $WSumC$ with a predominance of $CF + C$ responses; a rambling, tangential, and loosely associated flow of predominantly positively toned ideas sometimes juxtaposed with gloomy thoughts that are quickly denied, as manifest in long, involved responses containing many DRs and strikingly cheerful, optimistic imagery, sometimes alternating with morbid and pessimistic imagery as well; and a high energy level with considerable subjective involvement in events, as manifest in a large R, a low *Lambda*, and numerous complex Blends. The absence of these and other bipolar characteristics, many of which are illustrated in the case of Ms. Fisher in chapter 12, makes it unlikely that Mr. Carter has a bipolar disorder (see Weiner, 1998b).

With respect to his impaired reality testing, an elevated $X - \%$ along with a false positive $SCZI = 4$ could appear in persons who are not schizophrenic but are nevertheless either psychotically disturbed or seriously impaired in their capacity to exercise sound judgment. These include depressed or hypomanic people with psychosis, persons with organic psychoses, and individuals with severe character problems. Psychopathic prison inmates and chronically delinquent adolescents exemplify character disordered individuals who frequently have difficulty anticipating the consequences of their actions and often show poor form level in their Rorschach responses. However, none of these types of psychotic or character disordered individuals who give an elevated $X - \%$ should show disordered thinking as well, unless like Mr. Carter they have a schizophrenic disorder.

Proceeding further with the issue of differential diagnosis in this case, Mr. Carter's Rorschach data also reflect the previously diagnosed paranoid features of his condition. Noteworthy in this regard is the positive *HVI* indicated on his Structural Summary. Although a positive *HVI* is not by itself diagnostic of paranoid disorder, it does identify an orientation to the world characterized by anger, hypervigilant scanning of the environment for possible sources of danger, and a distant and distrustful stance in relation to people. As noted in chapter 5, subjects can elevate on *HVI* and display all of these personality characteristics without being diagnosably paranoid. On the other hand, people who are in fact paranoid almost invariably elevate on this index, except when they give carefully guarded and generally unrevealing records.

Along with his positive *HVI*, which is included among the information-processing variables in Table 3.1, Mr. Carter's cognitive data are consistent with paranoid thinking in two other respects: his pervasively introversive approach to experience (the *EBPer*) and his predilection for excessive use of fantasy in solving problems (the *Mp > Ma*), both of which identify traits consistent with delusion formation. This is not to say that being overly ideational and excessively fanciful document that someone is delusional. Rorschach data cannot be taken as conclusive evidence that delusions or any other specific symptoms of disorder are present. The best way to determine whether people have some symptom is to ask them, just as the presence of some behavior problem, such as substance abuse, can be identified more reliably by direct inquiry than by any pattern of Rorschach scores. On the other hand, Rorschach findings do reflect personality characteristics reliably, and they may accordingly identify fertile soil in which certain kinds of symptoms and particular types of problems are likely to take root and flourish. In Mr. Carter's case, then, his being overly ideational and excessively fanciful serve to increase the possibility of his developing delusional thoughts.

Finally, it is interesting to note with respect to his cognitive functioning that Mr. Carter's paranoia is not evident in how he attends to experience. He earns a point on *HVI* by virtue of doing a bit more organizing than most people (the *Zf* of 13), but he does not show any inclination to scan the environment carefully (he is not an overincorporator). The paranoia in his protocol emerges mainly in data concerning his interpersonal relatedness, to which we will turn after considering stress management and affective issues. The fact that interpersonal issues will come last in this particular interpretive sequence, as shown in Table 3.2, is consistent with his current clinical status, in which paranoid ideation was not a presenting complaint and was not observed on interview when he was admitted to the hospital.

Stress Management Issues

The data in Mr. Carter's control cluster indicate that he is a psychologically stable individual who, were it not for a slightly above average level of situational anxiety ($Y = 2$), would be more comfortable with himself than most people are and would be well insulated against becoming emotionally upset or losing self-control ($D = 0$ and $AdjD = +1$). A finding of $AdjD > 0$ in a person with diagnosable psychological disorder usually identifies chronic disturbance involving ego-syntonic symptom formation, a long prior history, and a likely future course of persistent adaptive difficulty. Like the Rorschach data concerning his cognitive functioning, these implications of his positive *AdjD* are consistent with his clinical history.

Although Mr. Carter's normative range *CDI* of 3 does not give reason for concern about his being able to manage his everyday affairs adequately, the composition of his *D* and *AdjD* scores illustrates a pattern of findings in which apparently stable stress management, even when associated with chronic disorder, may be ephemeral. First of all, his average *EA* of 7.0 is suspect as an index of adequate adaptive capacities because, as already noted, his pervasively introversive *EB* style (7:0.0) indicates markedly deficient channels for coping with affective experience. Second, his *es* of 5 is below average and, in the context of an average length record ($R = 22$) with a normative range *Lambda* (.83), identifies concerted effort to keep distressing thoughts and feelings out of his conscious awareness.

This combination of an *EBPer* and a low *es* indicate that Mr. Carter's psychological equilibrium is precarious. If he is allowed by people and circumstances to function in his preferred ways, he will be able for the most part to conduct himself in a stable, predictable, unexpressive, and undramatic albeit chronically disturbed manner. However, as already anticipated, being compelled to deal with affect or being prevented from suppressing upsetting thoughts and feelings will put him at considerable risk for becoming psychologically overwhelmed and no longer able to function in a comfortable and purposeful fashion. This may be exactly what happened to him as a consequence of his leaving a supportive and probably undemanding environment to come help his second wife and young child and thereby subjecting himself to pressures and responsibilities beyond his capacities to manage. Now we see him in the hospital in a state of decompensation, not overtly psychotic or paranoid, but clearly overwhelmed and complaining of being lifeless and unable to go on with his life.

Affective Issues

Unfortunately, with respect to Mr. Carter's adaptive capacities, there is not much to say about the manner in which he modulates affect beyond observing that he avoids doing so as much as possible. As previously noted, he is dramatically unable to modulate affect sufficiently ($WSumC = 0.0$). As for being able to modulate affect pleasurably, his $C' = 0$, $Col\text{-}Shd\ Bld = 0$, and normative range $S = 2$ are probably less an indication that he is a happy man enjoying his life than a result of his active suppression of affective experience of any kind. His extreme aversion to affect helps to explain why his $DEPI = 3$, weighed against his presenting complaint ("I'm depressed") is a false negative finding. $DEPI$ in general is an index notable more for its specificity than its sensitivity; that is, an elevation ($DEPI > 4$) is very likely to identify depressive features or an affective spectrum disorder, but a low score ($DEPI < 5$) cannot and should not be taken as a basis for ruling out these possibilities (see J. E. Exner & Weiner, 1995, chap. 5).

Nevertheless, the composition of Mr. Carter's $DEPI$ reveals that depressive elements are not entirely lacking in his protocol. The 14 variables in the $DEPI$ index measure aspects of depression involving dysphoric affect, negative cognitions, low energy level, and withdrawal from interpersonal interaction. Among these, affective variables account for the largest share of the variance in $DEPI$, and Mr. Carter's total avoidance of affective experience is likely to have held down his score on this index. Yet he does give evidence of negative self-attitudes ($3r + (2)/R = .50$ with $Fr + rF = 0$), limited energy (Blends = 2), and interpersonal withdrawal ($COP = 0$), each of which generates a point on $DEPI$. As for dysphoric affect, Mr. Carter appears to be a man who is more likely to talk about or admit feeling depressed when asked about it directly than he is to express sadness and gloom when he is completely free to avoid doing so, as when giving Rorschach responses.

Personal and Interpersonal Issues

As just mentioned, Mr. Carter appears to have long-standing difficulty in maintaining adequate self-esteem. His elevated Egocentricity Index in the absence of any Reflections indicates that he is characteristically inclined to be a self-focused individual who pays a lot of attention to himself but does not derive much pleasure from dong so. Nevertheless, he seems at present to be free of any self-critical attitudes ($V = 0$) or any concerns about the adequacy of his body and bodily functioning ($MOR = 0$). As additional personality assets, he gives evidence of being able to form a stable sense of identity based on identifications with real people in his life ($H = 4$), and he shows average capacities to examine himself and maintain adequate self-awareness ($FD = 2$). This adaptive capacity for introspection does not of course preclude the possibility that his occasionally faulty reality testing and illogical reasoning will influence what he concludes about himself when he introspects.

With respect to Mr. Carter's thematic imagery, the presence in his protocol of seven minus form and seven M responses indicate the likelihood of dynamically revealing content despite his affective constraint and his being a man of relatively few words (as indicated by the brevity of his statements on both the free association and inquiry portions of the examination). The first of these 14 projected responses is his initial effort on Card I, which provides especially telling evidence of how vulnerable he is to being initially overwhelmed by new, unfamiliar, and relatively unstructured demands. Presented with an inkblot containing an easily observable Popular, and being someone who eventually gives five Ps, he hesitates and stammers ("Kinda looks like—in the—on top it looks like"), restricts his attention to a small and unusual detail, and gives as his first response the minus form percept of "gorillas with their hands up." He shows some recovery on Response 2, the ordinary form "spacemen," and gives only one additional minus over the next 12 responses. Then, beginning with Response 15, 5 of his last 8 responses have minus form quality, the last of which, Response 22, is also his worst response, the Level 2 *FABCOM*.

This sequence suggests that he is a man who is holding on by a thread. Initially overwhelmed, he pulls himself reasonably well together and functions realistically for a brief period of time, after which he runs out of gas and, in the continued absence of structure and support, falls increasingly prone to disordered thinking and poor reality testing. These shifts occur in the context of a record in which he seems intent on being careful and controlled and preventing any cognitive slippage from emerging. As evidence of his cautious approach, note the previously mentioned brevity of his statements; note that he does not turn any of the cards to examine them from a different perspective, but restricts himself to a single viewing position; and note the extended pauses that precede his first response on Cards II, IX, and X.

Turning to Mr. Carter's interpersonal orientation, he displays well above average interest in people ($SumH = 11$), and his normative range $ISOL$ of .18 gives no indication that he is isolated from people who play an important part in life. However, the fact that he pays so much attention to people contributes to his previously noted elevation on *HVI*, as do an apparent difficulty anticipating or forming close bonds of attachment to others ($T =$ 0) and a tendency to be hypercritical and reluctant to take things at their face value ($H + A{:}Hd + Ad = 14{:}7$). As further interpersonal liabilities, he appears likely to feel uncomfortable in social situations ($H{:}(H)Hd(Hd) = 4{:}7$), to avoid collaborative interactions in ways that limit his appeal as a friend or companion ($COP = 0$), and at times to lack empathic understanding of other people (of his seven *M*s, only three are ordinary form, with three being unusual and one minus). Taken together, these data identify Mr. Carter as an interpersonally distant, cautious, and suspicious person who very much needs privacy and personal space, both physical and psychological, in order to avoid feeling ill at ease.

The thematic imagery in this record graphically bears out the paranoid orientation suggested by the structural data already discussed. Following the guidelines presented in chapters 4 and 6 for identifying revealing thematic imagery, the Sequence of Scores suggests that the most significant content theme in the record is likely to occur in Response 15, which is a three-bagger by virtue of projected elements suggested by a minus form level, an *M*, and an embellishment (the *DV*). As it turns out, this response to an unusual detail involving D6 and parts of Dd25 in Card VII depicts "somebody standing on guard" at "a small entrance to somewhere" with "the sun horizon" over the top of it. The possible meanings of "sun horizon" and its implications do not seem to lead in any particularly compelling direction. The "entrance" seen in this location suggests possible associations to female sexuality and perhaps concerns about approaching or allowing others to approach it closely. Although a more compelling source of hypotheses than the "sun horizon," this particular "entrance" response could be interpreted in numerous other ways as well, none of which relates to any repetitive themes in the record.

By contrast with the unclear meaning of "sun horizon" and the uncertain significance of "entrance," the subject's association to "standing on guard," in the context of a minus response, has transparent implications for troubling and disorganizing concerns about being protected against possible sources of harm. Generally speaking, imagery involving actions or accoutrements of protection, along with circumstances that prevent one from seeing or recognizing exactly what is out there in the environment or make one feel an object of scrutiny, identify the types of suspicion and fearfulness that characterize paranoid individuals. In Mr. Carter's case, his Rorschach responses contain repetitive themes of protection, concealment, and scrutiny.

Regarding accoutrements of protection, Mr. Carter gives an unusual number of Clothing responses (4), which accounts for one of his points on *HVI*. Notable among these is Response 2 involving spacemen in "space suits" that are "awful bulky." Bulky space suits provide considerable protection for the individual inside, while at the same time they conceal from view just what the person inside looks like. Response 8 is a minus form percept of "a person's face" in which "their eyes are covered up" by some kind of "long cotton" object or a mask. On Response 17, he "can't make out what kind" of animals he is seeing, and on Response 22, in a minus form *FAB2*, he sees "ladies" about whom he says, "half of their face is covered up, like by a horse."

As for feeling an object of scrutiny, numerous "eye" and "face" responses often indicate concern about being looked at or watched by others, especially when they involve poor form level and thereby reflect both projection and sufficient distress to cause a breakdown in reality testing. Mr. Carter mentions the eyes of his percepts on six occasions (Responses 1, 5, 8, 16, 18, and 22), five of which are in minus form percepts. In three of these minus responses he mentions "face" as well, most notably in Response 16 on Card VIII. In this response he reports "a face of some kind of native African" and then, despite its poor form, says that he "can see the head real plain," including the eyes and nose.

Finally of note in this record is a convergence of structural and thematic data that identify passive-dependent features in Mr. Carter's personality makeup. We saw earlier that, unlike many individuals who become paranoid, he does not display much anger or resentment ($S = 2$). It may be that instead of being a hostile, aggressive, tendentious type of paranoid person who resists being beholden to anyone, he is instead an insecure, troubled, and needy paranoid individual who is looking for help even while worrying about whether he can trust anyone who offers to be helpful.

The evidence in this regard begins with his $a:p$ ratio of 4:7 and the absence of any *AG* responses despite a total of 10 responses with movement. Because the $a:p$ ratio is generally quite stable over time, it identifies in Mr. Carter's case an abiding disposition to defer to the wishes and preferences of others, to be a follower rather than a leader, and to let other people make decisions for him and shoulder responsibilities that should be his. The $AG = 0$ must be interpreted cautiously, because it does not necessarily imply a lack of assertiveness on his part. Nevertheless, it can be said that his Rorschach responses do not contain any positive indications of his being likely to act assertively or aggressively in his relationships with others.

As for his imagery, examine how he responds to Card II, which is the initial presentation in the RIM of bright red color and (as discussed in chap. 4) often elicits associations to anger, aggression, blood, and animals who are hurt or hurting each other. It is already known that he chooses not to articulate any of these card pull elements (*WsumC*, *S*, *MOR*, and *AG* are all zero). Instead, in Response 5 on Card II he gives "two praying hands," and in Response 6 he reports the Popular animals but sees them as "bear *cubs*." These two responses suggest a self-image as a helpless, needy, dependent creature who can do no more for himself than reach out for succorance and hope that God, if not humankind, will come to his aid.

The religiosity suggested by the "praying hands" in Response 3 is expressed even more dramatically in Response 13 on Card VI, in which he sees the statue of "our lord Jesus," which "is standing on top of a big mountain" and is "straight up, with his hands outstretched." The absence of any indicators of grandiosity in his record makes it unlikely that Mr. Carter is identifying with "our lord Jesus" and seeing himself as a saintly or divine person. Rather, given his low self-esteem, neediness, and passive-dependent orientation, it seems more likely that Jesus is on his mind as a potential savior and source of deliverance from his difficulties. In concluding this response by saying, "I bet you never got that one before," he communicates how important his religious faith is to him and perhaps also how special he believes he is to have included his Lord in his test responses.

In conclusion, Mr. Carter's tersely delivered but nevertheless revealing record demonstrates the patterns of disordered thinking, inaccurate perception, and interpersonal caution and distancing that typically reflect paranoid schizophrenic disorder. In addition, his personality stability and ego-syntonic stance suggest that his disorder is chronic and long standing. Interesting in this case, however, is the apparent fact that he is presently in fairly good remission and presents neither with the psychotic breakdown nor the paranoid ideation that have led to his previous hospitalizations. Instead, being a pervasively ideational man with extremely limited capacities to deal with affective experience, being a man with limited coping capacities who depends for his psychological equilibrium on avoiding demanding responsibilities and emotionally stressful situations, and having left an apparently supportive environment for a situation in which he was faced with demands beyond his capacities to manage, he has now decompensated in the form of a depressive reaction characterized by helplessness and despair. Although his passive-dependent as well as paranoid nature has probably contributed to the depressive quality of his present condition, his affective impoverishment makes bipolar disorder extremely unlikely. He is a man desperately in need of supportive therapy and environmental realignment to allow him to return to remitted status as a paranoid schizophrenic individual who can function comfortably and with adequate self-control if he is given sufficient structure and can be spared from having to take care of rather than depend for care on other people.

CASE 4: OBSESSIVE-COMPULSIVE FEATURES IN AN ADOLESCENT GIRL WITH ANOREXIA NERVOSA

Deborah is a 13-year, 10-month-old Caucasian girl who for the past year has been feeling lonely and alienated from her friends. In her words, "I was feeling confused and down on myself, and I didn't like the way I was or who

I was." Six months prior to this examination she began to decrease her food intake and also began binge eating and purging by putting a finger down her throat: "I felt I could control something by not eating." Along with beginning a pattern of vomiting three to five times a day, Deborah undertook a strenuous exercise program in which she did aerobics for 30 minutes every night before going to bed. Her continued weight loss, combined with her apparent depression and social isolation, led to her being admitted to an inpatient psychiatric facility, emaciated and severely undernourished.

After her admission, Deborah elaborated having felt helpless and hopeless during the past few months, sleeping poorly, and having little energy. Her social isolation has involved decreasing interest in seeing her friends and increasing amounts of time spent at home. According to her parents, she has been compliant at home and agreeable about everything except her food intake. She helps with cleaning, cooking, and taking care of a younger brother. Deborah stated further that she felt losing weight would help her "fit in better" with her friends. She does not have currently have a best friend, she says, and has not yet shown any interest in boys or been involved in any sexual activity. She denies any alcohol or drug use. She had her menarche 2 years ago, was physically healthy and not having any psychological problems prior to her recent weight loss, and reportedly was a happy child who did well in school and had many friends. She comes from a stable and intact family and has enjoyed a comfortable home life with her parents and younger brother. Deborah's Rorschach protocol follows in Tables 11.4, 11.5, and 11.6 and Fig. 11.2.

TABLE 11.4
Rorschach Protocol of Deborah

Responses	Inquiry
Card I	
1. It looks like a face of some kind of animal, a fantasy type creature. There are strange ears or wings up there, and eyes.	E: (*Repeats response*) S: The eyes are here (DdS30), the mouth is here (DdS29), the horns (D1), the ears (D7), and a pointy chin or beard.
E: If you keep looking you'll see some other things as well. S: I don't know, I don't really see anything. (*continues to look intently at card*) Nothing, there's nothing else.	E: You said it looks strange. S: Yes, it just looks strange, I don't know why.

(Continued)

TABLE 11.4
(*Continued*)

Responses	Inquiry
Card II	
2. It looks like two people, holding their hands against each other.	E: (*Repeats response*) S: They are profiles and they're kneeling and they have their hands up against each other.
3. These red look like faces. These faces look like straight normal faces.	E: (*Repeats response*) S: Yes, right here. E: You said they're straight normal faces. S: They're people but not realistic. E: How do you mean? S: They're not real people, but they look like people.
4. This face looks sad.	E: (*Repeats response*) S: These look like sad faces here (a Dd including D3). E: What suggests sad faces? S: Everything is kind of long and droopy, like they're crying—it's so sad.
5. Here it looks like the profile of a laughing face.	E: (*Repeats response*) S: The outline of the nose, the eye socket, and the mouth laughing. The mouth is real wide open, it's laughing.
Card III	
6. This looks like two people leaning over something, over a pot or a bowl of some kind.	E: (*Repeats response*) S: The people are here, bent at the waist, and this is a pot or bowl. They are cooking or putting something into the pot.
7. It looks like a butterfly in the middle. I don't know what his (D2) is. (*laughs*)	E: (*Repeats response*) S: It's here. E: Yes, but what about the blot makes it look like a butterfly? S: The wings and the body in the middle.

(*Continued*)

TABLE 11.4
(Continued)

Responses	Inquiry
Card IV	
8. It looks like a big monster or something really tall, with a tail and feet here.	E: (*Repeats response*) S: The taller part is the bigger part up her, like he's looking down, the big tail is there (D1), and it looks like he has long baggy sleeves on, or shaggy hair.
	E: Shaggy hair? S: It doesn't look like he's wearing clothes, he looks kinda furry.
	E: Why furry? S: It's so bumpy, and the texture of it looks like fur.
Card V	
9. This one looks like a moth or a butterfly.	E: (*Repeats response*) S: The wings, the head here. Butterflies don't have ears and these look like ears, so maybe it's a bat.
Card VI	
10. It looks like a leaf, and there's some kind of bug on the stem.	E: (*Repeats response*) S: The stem is here and the leaf part is here, and some kind of bug with wings is crawling on the stem.
	E: What made it look like a leaf? S: Just the shape, like a maple leaf or something.
Card VII	
11. These two things look like two girls with their hair fixed kind of weird.	E: (*Repeats response*) S: The hair is in a ponytail, sticking straight up, and the two girls are here (D1), here's their faces, eyes, nose, and mouth.
12. Underneath them is a jester with a funny hat.	E: (*Repeats response*) S: These two (D3) are jesters, their heads with those funny kind of hats.
13. And this down here looks like a tunnel or hallway that goes back.	E: (*Repeats response*) S: This (D6) looks like a tunnel going back.
	E: What helps you see it as going back? S: Just the shape, and it looks kinda dark in there.

(*Continued*)

TABLE 11.4
(Continued)

Responses	Inquiry
Card VIII	
14. It looks like two tigers or something climbing up a mountain.	E: (Repeats response) S: It looks like tigers climbing up mountains, a range of mountains here and this is a valley.
	E: What made it look like a valley? S: It looks like it's going down, everything goes down into that area.
Card IX	
15. It looks like fire, with a stream of water shooting up through the middle and some smoke.	E: (Repeats response) S: It looks like fire here (D6), and the dark greenish (D1), it's firey looking.
	E: What suggests fire? S: The colors, the red and the orange up here (D3). It's firey looking.
	E: What suggests smoke? S: The coloring, and its rounded like clouds.
Card X	
16. Two seahorses.	E: (Repeats response) S: They're here.
	E: What makes them look like seahorses? S: The shape, and they're curly at the end.
17. Maybe some fish.	E: (Repeats response) S: These little things (D2).
	E: I'm not sure I'm seeing them like you are. S: They just look like fish to me. They have that kinda shape like a fish.
18. This could be coral.	E: (Repeats response) S: That's here (D1). It's spiky, like stuff in the ocean. A lot of coral is spiky like this.
19. And some kind of animals guarding some kind of statue behind them.	E: (Repeats response) S: It's at the top (D11). Two animals of some kind, guarding the statue.
	E: I'm not sure about the animals. S: I don't know, sort of like little mice or rats. See the legs?

TABLE 11.5
Sequence of Scores for Deborah

Card No.		Loc.	No.	Determinant(s)	(2)	Content(s)	POP	Z	Special Scores
I	1	WSo	1	Fo		(Ad)		3.5	
II	2	D+	6	Mp-	2	H		3.0	COP
	3	Do	2	F-	2	Hd			
	4	Ddo	99	Mp-	2	Hd			MOR
	5	Ddo	99	Mau		Hd			
III	6	D+	1	Mao	2	H,Hh	P	3.0	
	7	Do	3	Fo		A			
IV	8	Wo	1	Mp.FD.FTo		(H)		2.0	
V	9	Wo	1	Fo		A	P	1.0	
VI	10	W+	1	FMau		A,Bt		2.5	
VII	11	Do	1	Fo	2	Hd	P		
	12	D+	3	Fu	2	Hd,Cg		1.0	
	13	Do	6	FVo		Ls			
VIII	14	W+	1	FMa.FDo	2	A,Ls	P	4.5	
IX	15	W/	1	ma.CFu		Fi,Na,Cl		5.5	
X	16	Do	9	Fu	2	A			
	17	Do	3	Fu	2	A			
	18	Do	1	Fu	2	Ls			
	19	D+	11	Mp.FDu	2	A,Art		4.0	FAB

Cognitive Issues

Deborah's Structural Summary indicates a valid record of 19 responses, and the *S-CON* is not applicable for persons under age 15. She does not elevate any of the first seven key variables, each of which is typically associated with some form of symptomatic or characterological disorder. The fact that she does not show an entry point prior to the *EB* style variable is consistent with her psychologically healthy developmental history and indicates that, her recent onset eating disorder aside, she is a relatively well-integrated girl with good ego-strength. The first positive key variable is her introversive *EB*, which calls for an interpretive search order proceeding through the ideation, processing, mediation, controls, affect, self-perception, and inter-personal perception clusters (see Table 3.2).

TABLE 11.6
Structural Summary for Deborah

Location Features	Determinants		Contents	S-Constellation
	Blends	Single		

Location Features	Blends	Single		Contents		S-Constellation
Zf = 10	M.FD.FT	M = 4		H = 2, 0		. . FV+VF+V+FD>2
ZSum = 30.0	FM.FD	FM = 1		(H) = 1, 0		. . Col-Shd Bl>0
ZEst = 31.0	m.CF	m = 0		Hd = 5, 0		. . Ego<.31,>.44
	M.FD	FC = 0		(Hd) = 0, 0		. . MOR > 3
W = 6		CF = 0		Hx = 0, 0		. . Zd > +- 3.5
(Wv = 0)		C = 0		A = 7, 0		. . es > EA
D = 11		Cn = 0		(A) = 0, 0		. . CF+C > FC
Dd = 2		FC' = 0		Ad = 0, 0		. . X+% < .70
S = 1		C'F = 0		(Ad) = 1, 0		. . S > 3
		C' = 0		An = 0, 0		. . P < 3 or > 8
		FT = 0		Art = 0, 1		. . Pure H < 2
DQ		TF = 0		Ay = 0, 0		. . R < 17
. . . . . . (FQ-)		T = 0		Bl = 0, 0		x . . . . . TOTAL
+ = 6 (1)		FV = 1		Bt = 0, 1		
o = 12 (2)		VF = 0		Cg = 0, 1		Special Scorings
v/+ = 1 (0)		V = 0		Cl = 0, 1		
v = 0 (0)		FY = 0		Ex = 0, 0		Lv1 Lv2
		YF = 0		Fd = 0, 0		DV = 0x1 0x2
		Y = 0		Fi = 1, 0		INC = 0x2 0x4
		Fr = 0		Ge = 0, 0		DR = 0x3 0x6
		rF = 0		Hh = 0, 1		FAB = 1x4 0x7
		FD = 0		Ls = 2, 1		ALOG = 0x5
Form Quality		F = 9		Na = 0, 1		CON = 0x7
				Sc = 0, 0		Raw Sum6 = 1
FQx FQf MQual SQx				Sx = 0, 0		Wgtd Sum6 = 4
+ = 0 0 0 0				Xy = 0, 0		
o = 8 4 2 1				Id = 0, 0		AB = 0 CP = 0
u = 8 4 2 0						AG = 0 MOR = 1
- = 3 1 2 0						CFB = 0 PER = 0
none = 0 — 0 0		(2) = 11				COP = 1 PSV = 0

Ratios, Percentages, and Derivations

R = 19	L = 0.90		FC:CF+C = 0: 1	COP = 1 AG = 0	
			Pure C = 0	Food = 0	
EB = 6: 1.0	EA = 7.0	EBPer = 6.0	SumC':WSumC = 0:1.0	Isolate/R = 0.42	
eb = 3: 2	es = 5	D = 0	Afr = 0.46	H: (H)Hd(Hd) = 2: 6	
	Adj es = 5	Adj D = 0	S = 1	(HHd) : (AAd) = 1: 1	
			Blends:R = 4:19	H+A:Hd+Ad = 10: 6	
FM = 2 : C' = 0 T = 1			CP = 0		
m = 1 : V = 1 Y = 0					

		P = 4	Zf = 10	3r+(2)/R = 0.58	
a:p = 5: 4	Sum6 = 1	X+% = 0.42	Zd = -1.0	Fr+rF = 0	
Ma:Mp = 2: 4	Lv2 = 0	F+% = 0.44	W:D:Dd = 6:11: 2	FD = 3	
2AB+Art+Ay = 1	WSum6 = 4	X-% = 0.16	W:M = 6: 6	An+Xy = 0	
M- = 2	Mnone = 0	S-% = 0.00	DQ+ = 6	MOR = 1	
		Xu% = 0.42	DQv = 0		

SCZI = 2	DEPI = 3	CDI = 3	S-CON = N/A	HVI = No	OBS = No

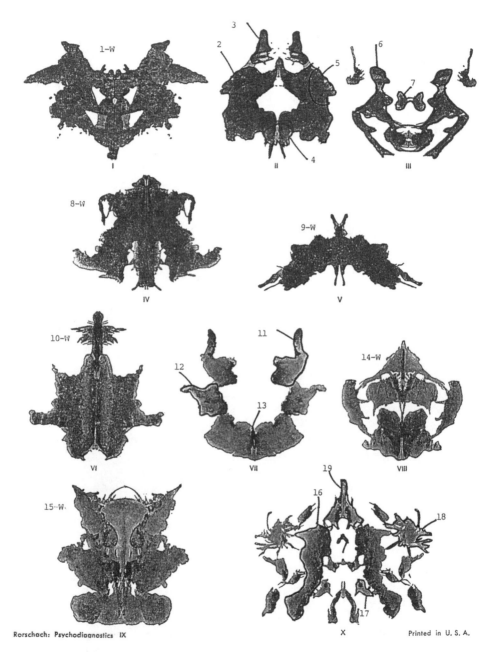

FIG. 11.2. Location choices of Deborah.

Looking first at her ideational functioning, Deborah appears capable of thinking about her experience in a logical, coherent, and flexible manner ($WSum6 = 4$; $a:p = 5:4$). The single instance of cognitive slippage in her record is a *FABCOM* on Response 19, her final response, which consists of a somewhat childish but hardly pathological impression of animals ("mice or rats") in human movement ("guarding some kind of statue"). On the other hand, she does give evidence of difficulty in thinking constructively about problems that arise in her life and seems inclined instead to excessive fantasizing about events that will solve her problems ($Ma:Mp = 2:4$).

Of further concern with respect to her adaptation is her excessive investment in ideational ways of dealing with experience at the expense of adequate channels for emotional expression. Like Mr. Carter in the previous case, Deborah is pervasively introversive ($EB = 6:1.0$). She is fortunately not as susceptible as Mr. Carter to becoming overwhelmed by affect, given that her *WSumC* is 1.0, compared to his 0.0. Nevertheless, in contrast to her not appearing to think inflexibly (the $a:p$), she is quite inflexible when it comes to exchanging contemplation for an intuitive or affect-driven style of decision making (her *EB*). Allowing emotion to influence what she says and does is not an acceptable option for her, acting on a whim is not in her repertoire, and coming to any conclusions or formulating any plans without first thinking them through carefully would be foreign to her nature.

With respect to her processing of information, Deborah's *Lambda* of .90 in the context of her 19-response record is reminiscent of the guardedness shown by Ms. Anderson in chapter 10. Although not as guarded as Ms. Anderson and not quite reaching the criterion of *Lambda* > .99 used to define a high *Lambda* record, Deborah does seem likely to view her life with a narrow frame of reference and to seek simple and economical solutions to problems. In this vein, she is capable of organizing information efficiently ($Zd = -1.0$), but she shows some potentially maladaptive processing in her Economy Index ($W:D:Dd$) and her Aspiration Ratio ($W:M$). In her $W:D:Dd = 6:11:2$ she gives further indication of viewing the world economically in terms of its details at the expense of striving for a more global perspective. By giving just six W in a record with six M, moreover, she (similarly to Mr. Carter in the preceding case) may be inclined to set modest goals for herself and to doubt her ability to achieve as much success as other people with whom she compares herself.

Deborah's patterns of perceiving people and events demonstrates the importance of looking closely at form-level scores. Her $X-\%$ of .16 indicates that she is more likely than most people to form distorted impressions of what is happening around her and consequently to display instances of poor judgment. Note, however, that all three of her minus responses occur on Card II and that two of these are M responses involving pairs. This observation illustrates the utility of examining the sequence and homogeneity of minus responses, as recommended in the cognitive mediation cluster of variables shown in Table 3.1. The data indicate that Deborah's lapses in reality testing are neither pervasive nor random, but are instead limited to and aroused by situations that confront her with strong affective stimulation and/or elicit associations to interpersonal relationships.

As for her conventionality, Deborah's adequate number of D locations and her normative range $P = 4$ indicate that she is capable of looking at the world as most people do and recognizing conventional reality when she chooses to. However, her extremely elevated $Xu\%$ of .42 identifies a strong preference to resist conformity, to establish herself as a unique individual in her own right, and to do things her own way. In the case of Mr. Baker in chapter 10, an elevated $Xu\%$ was noted to be associated with sensation-seeking behavior and possibly to have played a role in his susceptibility to drug use, which usually shows an inverse relationship to conventionality (Weiner, 1992, chap. 10). How then in Deborah's case does nonconformity as suggested by the Rorschach jibe with her apparently comfortable home life, conservative life style, and lack of any known sexual activity, substance use, or conduct problem? At least a partial answer to this question may be provided by her anorexia, with which she is dramatically opposing the wishes of her parents that she should eat and be well, while at the same time she is engaging in an entirely self-conceived and self-directed course of action that has set her uniquely apart from most other people, as a physically emaciated and socially isolated girl now receiving treatment in a psychiatric hospital.

Stress Management Issues

Deborah appears to have basically adequate resources for coping with everyday experience ($EA = 7.0$; $CDI = 3$). Although her pervasively introversive EB may temper somewhat the adaptive capacity suggested by an EA of 7, her previously noted access to at least a little emotionality ($WsumC = 1.0$) protects her from being totally overwhelmed by emotionally charged events. In addition, the fact that she is experiencing only modest amounts of stress ($es = 5$) means that her coping capacities are sufficient for her to deal with the demands in her life without becoming unduly upset by them ($D = 0$). As a $D = 0$ person, she is likely to be relatively free of overt anxiety, tension, nervousness, and irritability and instead to be a relatively calm, relaxed, self-content, and self-controlled individual.

But, how could a girl who is starving herself to death and has become cut off from social relationships she previously enjoyed display so little subjectively felt distress on the Rorschach? One answer to this question lies in the nature of anorexia nervosa, a condition in which the ill person, most commonly an adolescent girl, is typically satisfied with what she is doing to herself and likely to become upset only when others interfere with her efforts to lose weight (see Kimmel & Weiner, 1995, chap. 13). What anorexic girls want most of all is to be left alone to do things their own way. Although they may regret social isolation that results from their self-imposed restrictions on their lives, as Deborah appears to do, they regard this as an acceptable price to pay for the satisfaction they derive from avoiding food, losing weight, and maintaining a tightly controlled schedule of weight-reducing activities. Hence a $D = 0$ pattern is not a surprising finding in young people with anorexia and is consistent with the general peace of mind Deborah was displaying prior to being brought to the hospital by her parents.

Nevertheless, even though she is a $D = 0$ person experiencing relatively little subjectively felt distress, and despite her giving just 19 responses with a *Lambda* approaching 1.00, and even though these 19 responses are for the most part brief and unelaborated, Deborah does allow some glimpses of underlying concerns to emerge in her Rorschach responses. The nature of these concerns is identified in discussing the affective, personal, and interpersonal issues apparent in her protocol.

Affective Issues

As already noted, Deborah's adjustment is handicapped by her inability to modulate affect sufficiently. With only a single color response in her record—a *CF* fire and clouds on Card IX—she demonstrates very little capacity to become aware of her own feelings or to share them with others. Her *FC:CF + C* of 0:1 suggests further that she is inclined to be fairly intense and dramatic on those rare instances when she becomes emotional and that she is markedly deficient in the kind of stable, reserved, and well-modulated emotionality that promotes good social adaptation in adolescents and adults. As also noted previously, the sequence of three minus responses in a row on being handed Card II shows how readily her sense of reality and the appropriateness of her judgment can be disrupted when she is confronted with situations that for most people are emotionally arousing.

There is little indication in Deborah's Rorschach that she is unable to modulate affect pleasurably, however. Her *C'* and *Col-Shd Bld* are both zero, and there is no elevation in either her *SumShd* or her *S*. As in the preceding case of Mr. Carter, on the other hand, neither these data nor her *DEPI* of 3 should be interpreted as ruling out depression. Like Mr. Carter, Deborah is a pervasively introversive individual who does not easily recognize or readily express dysphoric affect, and she is accordingly relatively unlikely to elevate on *DEPI*. Nevertheless, she does receive *DEPI* points for showing signs of self-critical attitudes ($V = 1$), low self-esteem (elevated Egocentricity without Reflections), and interpersonal withdrawal and isolation ($COP = 1$; $ISOL = .32$), and she just barely avoids a further point for avoidance of emotional involvement ($Afr = .46$). Keep in mind that Deborah has complained of such characteristic symptoms of depression as feeling helpless and hopeless, lacking energy, and having difficulty sleeping. Together with the structural data just mentioned, compelling Rorschach evidence of Deborah's being depressed appears despite her *DEPI* of 3 in the imagery of Response 4 on Card II: faces that "look sad" because they are "long and droopy like they are crying."

Personal and Interpersonal Issues

Where better to begin commentary on how Deborah views herself than with the sad, droopy, and crying faces just noted from Response 4 on Card II. This is the only such dysphoric response in the record, and (as elaborated in chap. 6) some interpretive caution may be dictated by its not being part of a repetitive theme. However, drawing once more on the discussion in chapter 6, we can see that Response 4 constitutes a dramatic three-bagger projection (human movement, minus form, and morbid embellishment); stands out for this reason in the Structural Summary as the response most likely to reveal Deborah's self-image; embodies transparent symbolic significance (sad and crying means depressed and unhappy); and breaks through in the context of a generally unexpressive and unemotional record. Accordingly, Response 4 strongly suggests that, despite her surface composure, her satisfaction with the way of life she has chosen for herself, and her apparent conviction that she has been doing the right thing, underneath it all Deborah is a psychologically miserable girl.

And how else does she view herself? On Card I she signs in with a "fantasy-type creature" that has "strange ears or wings" and turns out just to "look strange, I don't know why." In Response 11 on Card VII she reports the Popular "girls" but sees them with "their hair fixed kind of weird." Could it be that she is or has been seeing herself as strange or weird, and as somehow different from other people, especially her former friends? Could this be an almost-14-year-old girl whose former friends have matured to the point of becoming involved in dating and sexuality and in dressing and looking like young women, while Deborah, not yet having developed any interest in boys, comes to have increasingly less in common with these friends and to be increasingly estranged from them? If so, could her anorexia be serving the purpose of maintaining a childlike figure lacking sexual characteristics and removing her from the adolescent arena of heterosexuality for which she feels unprepared?

These latter speculations are based on the dynamics of anorexia rather than the Rorschach data, although the possible self-image of strangeness and weirdness projected into Responses 1 and 11, as well as numerous other features of this protocol, are consistent with typical social and behavioral manifestations of this disorder. To continue with the Rorschach data themselves, the sequence of Deborah's responses following the two strange/weird responses and her crying face on Response 4 provide some clues to the nature and adequacy of her defensive operations. After Response 1, she merely puts a lid on. Despite the ready availability of the Popular on Card I, she declines to report anything after the strange creature ("I don't really see anything"), and she continues to say "There's nothing else" even while looking at the blot intently. In this instance, then, she imposes control by simply ceasing to respond, and she is able to do so without her comments indicating any apparent distress.

In a much different manner, she follows the minus form sad and crying face on Response 4 with an unusual form "profile of a laughing face" on Response 5. Thus, her dysphoria on Response 4 is turned off by blatant denial, as if to say "I don't see a crying face, I see a laughing face." The fact that Response 5 is accurately perceived, even though unusual, suggests that this defense works effectively for her. Interestingly, denial along with distorted perception often contribute to even severely malnourished anorexic patients feeling good about themselves and failing to recognize the gravity of their illness. They continue to perceive their emaciated bodies as looking good or, if anything, still too fat, and they steadfastly deny that they are doing anything harmful to themselves.

Following the girls with weird hair on Response 11, Deborah delivers another self-image response that may or may not constitute an adequate recovery—the "jester with a funny hat" in Response 12. Like the "clown" response discussed in chapter 6, this "jester" can have two very different kinds of meaning. Is this a happy jester who is entertaining others and having a good time in the process, or is this a ridiculous looking jester at whom others laugh, with little consideration for the person's feelings? However this may be, Card VII ends on a dysphoric and self-critical note in Response 13, as reflected in the *FV* coding. Looking at D6, which is ordinary form for vagina, Deborah reports "a tunnel or hallway that goes back" and says it "looks kinda dark in there." At least one possible implication of this response is a negative, distasteful, perhaps even self-loathing attitude toward her sexuality, which would be one more finding consistent with the underlying dynamics in many instances of anorexia nervosa.

The structural data bearing on Deborah's self-perception indicate that she is capable of adequate introspection ($FD = 3$) and, to a limited extent, of identifying with other people ($H = 2$). However, the imbalance in her human contents, with $H:(H)Hd(Hd) = 2:6$, suggests that her developing sense of identity is to this point based less on identifications with actual people in her life as they really are than with partial objects and imaginary figures.

Interestingly, Deborah does not evidence any unusual preoccupation with or negative attitudes toward her body or bodily functioning ($An + Xy$

= 0; *MOR* = 1). This lack of expressed somatic concerns despite her considerable attention to the appearance of her body and her failing health speaks
to the denial and selective perceptual distortion she displays, in common
with most anorexic patients. On the other hand, her elevated *3r* + *(2)/R* of
.58 indicates that she pays an inordinate amount of attention to herself,
probably at the expense of paying adequate attention to others, and her *Fr*
+ *rF* = 0 indicates that she does not derive much pleasure from looking at
herself. She is consequently likely to compare herself unfavorably to other
people and, as implied by her previously noted Vista response, to be critical
of herself and lacking in self-regard.

With respect to her interpersonal stance, Deborah appears to be adequately interested in other people (*SumH* = 8) and to have adaptive capacities to form close attachments to others (*T* = 1). On the other hand, her
H:(H)Hd(Hd) = 2:6 suggests that she feels uncomfortable in social situations,
and she gives evidence of being isolated from relationships to people who
are important to her (*ISOL* = .32) and withdrawn from collaborative interactions with others (*COP* = 1). There is also some indication in her fantasy in
Response 19, in which the animals are "guarding some kind of statue," of
needs to protect herself against possible sources of danger in the environment.

Of further note is the previously observed indication that Deborah is
inclined to misperceive the implications interpersonal relationships (*M-* =
2), which is typically associated with impaired empathic capacity. The extent
to which even thinking about interpersonal interactions distresses her is
apparent in the sequence of her already mentioned Card II responses. In
Response 2 she appears to become sufficiently upset by her association to
"people holding their hands against each other" that she produces a minus
form-quality response. In Response 3 she is unable to recover from this
distressing association. She attempts to set things right by seeing faces that
are "straight normal" and then taking distance by suggesting that they are
"not really people," but she ends up with another minus human response.
Then in Response 4 she articulates the minus form "sad" and "crying" faces.
Not until the "laughing face" on Response 5 can she recover from the
distress apparently caused on Response 2 by her thinking about people
involved in a pleasant and cooperative interaction—perhaps because for her
such an interaction, especially with her peers, has become only a faint
memory and a highly desirable but presently unobtainable part of living.
After Response 2, she gives no further imagery involving cooperative interactions. For her, the prospect of such relationships may have become something better put out of mind than yearned for without hope of finding them.

In summary, Deborah's Rorschach illustrates maladaptive consequences
of an overly ideational personality style in a generally well-integrated and
psychologically capable young girl who, apparently as a consequence in

part of some difficulties in making the developmental transition through pubescence, became severely anorexic at age 13 and determined to avoid gaining weight. Her contemplative, self-controlling, and nonconforming style has led to her forming and implementing deliberate routines of food avoidance and strenuous exercise, and her denial and perceptual distortions have contributed to her conviction that she is doing well and doing the right thing for herself. Although saddened by the social isolation and deprivation of peer relationships that has attended her disorder, and although apparently troubled at a deeper level by aversion to sexual maturation, she is superficially comfortable, satisfied with herself, and likely to be pleasant and agreeable, up to the point where she is encouraged or pressured to give up her anorexia.

Although consistent with personality patterns often seen in young people with anorexia, the Rorschach data are in no way diagnostic of this disorder. Likewise, Deborah's pervasively ideational style, affective inhibition, and emphasis on control through self-imposed routines often accompany obsessive-compulsive symptom formation. Obsessive-compulsive disorder, like eating disorder and substance use disorder, must be identified from observable behavior and cannot be diagnosed from Rorschach data, and in Deborah's record the compelling evidence for an obsessive-compulsive style provided by an elevation on the Obsessive Index is not present. However, the features of her record noted in this case example can be put in the "fertile soil" category, that is, an orientation to dealing with experience that, other things being equal, is conducive to the emergence of obsessive-compulsive symptoms.

12

Modulating Affect

As elaborated in chapter 5, modulating affect concerns the manner and comfort with which people process their emotional experience. Affect modulation accordingly comprises how people manage feelings arising within themselves and also how they deal with the feelings of others and with emotionally charged situations in general. Well-developed capacities to modulate affect sufficiently, pleasurably, and in moderation constitute personality assets that contribute to good adjustment. Conversely, people who process affect in a constricted, dysphoric, or overly intense manner are displaying functioning incapacities or impairments that are likely to interfere with their adaptation.

Deficient or impaired affective modulation appears on the RIM in deviations from normative expectation on the affective cluster of variables listed in Table 3.1. The Comprehensive System search strategy shown in Table 3.2 calls initial attention to this cluster of variables when $DEPI > 5$ or when a subject's EB is extratensive. A $DEPI > 5$ usually identifies the presence of some type of affective disorder, whereas being extratensive merely identifies an expressive approach to experience and, like being introversive, has no necessary implications for adjustment difficulty or psychological disorder.

The two cases presented in this chapter both show a $DEPI = 6$ and illustrate numerous features of depression, but the context in which these two persons were examined and the composition of their records differ markedly. The first case was a court referral requesting aid in the sentencing of a woman with numerous prior arrests and convictions but no history of overt psychological disturbance or mental health treatment. Aside from its depressive features, her Rorschach protocol is notable for indications of subjectively felt distress and severely impaired interpersonal coping skills. The second record was given by a psychiatrically hospitalized woman with a several-year history of depressive episodes, suicide attempts, prior hospitalizations, and ongoing treatment with medication and psychotherapy. In this protocol, the depressive features are accompanied by indications of mood variability and some disruption in her cognitive functioning.

CASE 5: UNSUSPECTED DEPRESSION IN A WOMAN LEADING TWO LIVES

Ms. Evans is a physically very attractive, 26-year-old Caucasian woman who is presently incarcerated after having been arrested and charged with grand larceny in a jewel robbery she helped to perpetrate. She has been convicted of robbery on three previous occasions and served some prison time, although her sentences have been suspended or reduced subsequent to her providing information that led to other arrests. In each of her robberies she worked with a male accomplice who orchestrated the crime and told her what to do. Her work history includes short periods of employment as a sales clerk, a cashier, a waitress, and a topless dancer, and she openly admits to working on and off as a hooker. She disclaims any problems about being a prostitute and says, "You gotta get by the best way you can, and that's all I got to make it with." Ms. Evans has been married and divorced and has an 8-year-old son. After her divorce she lived briefly with several different men and on one occasion had an abortion. For the last 2 years she has been living alone with her son.

Contrary to what might be expected from this history of criminality and instability, Ms. Evans is an intelligent woman with a Full Scale WAIS–R IQ of 118. She had never seen a mental health professional prior to the current examination, and there is no evidence of her ever having been considered to have psychological problems. Further investigation revealed that she has been keeping a neat apartment for herself and her son, belongs to the PTA at his school, and did a year's service as a den mother for the Cub Scouts. She states she got involved in the current robbery in order get some money to take her son on a vacation trip over the Christmas holidays. Her current view of the situation that led to her being arrested is that she was "being stupid as usual." She was pleasant and cooperative at the time of the examination, but she said that she was depressed at being in jail and she concerned about her son, who has been placed in a foster home pending the outcome of her case.

The judge who referred Ms. Evans for evaluation was undecided concerning her sentencing. He asked specifically whether she is sincerely involved with caring for her son, capable of responding to treatment, and appropriate for being placed on probation, or whether instead if her appearance of domestic normality is a contrived and inadequate basis for sparing her the 10- to 20-year prison term her record would warrant. In clinical terms, then, the referral question is whether Ms. Evans is a neurotically disturbed woman who has been acting out and is relatively amenable to change, or whether she is a psychopathic woman who is antisocial and relatively refractory to change. In more general terms concerning this woman who has been leading two lives, is the real Ms. Evans the concerned parent and den mother or the uncaring prostitute and thief? Her Rorschach protocol follows in Tables 12.1, 12.2, and 12.3 and Fig. 12.1.

Affective Issues

Ms. Evans' Structural Summary indicates a valid record of 22 responses, no elevation of the *S-CON*, and, as already noted, a first positive key variable consisting of *DEPI* = 6. The order for searching the clusters in her record, as indicated in Table 3.2, is therefore affect, controls, self-perception, interpersonal perception, processing, mediation, and ideation.

TABLE 12.1
Rorschach Protocol of Ms. Evans

Responses	Inquiry
Card I	
1. It could be a butterfly I suppose. It looks damaged.	E: (*Repeats response*) S: The wings make it look like that, and they're ragged like they are damaged, and this is the body part.
2. The center could be a bug with the antlers coming out of the head.	E: (*Repeats response*) S: Like a roach or something; it has the look of a roach, kind of shiny in parts like the shell that roaches have.
3. The black makes me think of a bat too.	E: (*Repeats response*) S: Well, it's the same as for the butterfly, but I see it different, like it's black and the ragged edged parts go better for a bat, and see the feet up here too. (*points*)
4. That center could be a nude person too, its back is to me. The bottom part is pretty clear but the top is vague.	E: (*Repeats response*) S: Down here are the calves, I guess it's a woman but maybe not. It doesn't look like she has any clothes on, you can see the butt.

(Continued)

TABLE 12.1
(*Continued*)

Responses	Inquiry
	E: I'm not sure I see it as you do.
	S: It's just this part (D3), you can't see the upper part well, but the head must be up here somewhere. Here is the butt and the ankles and the feet, and you can see the indentation where the butt is.
Card II	
5. This looks like two hand puppets, like they are fighting. They're all red.	E: (*Repeats response*)
	S: This red thing looks like two hands with cloth puppets on them, and the puppets have teeth and facial features and it looks like they are fighting.
6. The bottom part looks like a woman's vagina.	E: (*Repeats response*)
	S: It just looks like that, you can see the lips folded back like.
	E: Folded back?
	S: The coloring there makes it look like there is a separation and they are folded back, the shades like, see?
Card III	
7. This looks like a couple people fighting over this thing down here. It looks like a bag of something.	E: (*Repeats response*)
	S: The black blobs each represent a person holding onto this thing here, like pulling at it, sort of fighting over it, and see here are the legs and heads and arms.
8. v This red think looks like a—abortions.	E: (*Repeats response*)
	S: Well, they look like children, but not very well formed, and they're bloody, like it would be if it were aborted. The cord is still there, see the little heads and bodies?
Card IV	
9. (*laughs*) That's really furry, you know, like a rug of some kind.	E: (*Repeats response*)
	S: Yeah, it looks like all fur, like a rug. I thought of a blanket, but it has like leg parts, so I thought of a rug or something like that.
	E: I'm not clear about what makes it look like fur.
	S: It just does (*rubs card*). It just has all the marks on it, like fur.
10. This side thing could be snakes' heads, like they was slithering out of a bush or something.	E: (*Repeats response*)
	S: Well it's like the head and neck parts, like a snake, and this part could be the bush and they're coming out of it. See it's all dark like a bush might be, black, you know?

(*Continued*)

TABLE 12.1
(*Continued*)

Responses	Inquiry

Card V

11. Oh, a bat I guess.

E: (*Repeats response*)
S: It's like the first one, all black with the wings out, flying along and the feet are out in front.

12. v This looks like two legs growing out of something like a body, but there's no body, just two legs.

E: (*Repeats response*)
S: You know, there's no feet either, just the legs with the stumps of feet here, like something left over from an explosion or something. I think they must be legs from a war or something, just laying there.

Card VI

13. That's a penis if I ever saw one.

E: (*Repeats response*)
S: It has the shape of one, a real good likeness, like when they're stiff, like ready to go.

14. v There's a lot of sex on this one. Here's a vagina too.

E: (*Repeats response*)
S: It's really opened up, like it's ready for that stiff one. You can see the lips rolled back, like the other one.

E: Rolled back?
S: Yeah, it looks lighter inside as compared with the outside, like if the lips are rolled back. If you look at yourself in the mirror that's what you see.

15. You know, this whole bottom part looks like fur too, like another blanket or rug, just pretty furry.

E: (*Repeats response*)
S: It sure looks like fur. It must be a blanket or a rug, see it has legs here (*points*) so it must be a rug, a big ole bear rug.

E: What makes it look like fur?
S: It's like the other one, the spots there create a furry appearance. (*rubs card*)

Card VII

16. This looks like pieces of bread all broken up.

E: (*Repeats response*)
S: It's like somebody just pulled some bread apart, you know, like Italian or French bread. It looks grainy, like bread looks.

E: Grainy?
S: Oh, you know, yeah, grainy, see, the differences in the color make it look grainy, like a grainy substance.

(*Continued*)

TABLE 12.1
(*Continued*)

Responses	Inquiry
17. It could be a couple of kids arguing with each other. They have funny hats on, like feathers.	E: (*Repeats response*) S: Just the faces of a couple of kids, see the nose and mouths are here, and these are the funny hats, and like features up here. (*points*)

Card VIII

18. This is pretty, it looks like a diagram that shows two animals, crawling up each side.	E: (*Repeats response*) S: Yeah, well the whole thing is some sort of diagram, I don't know ... It probably means something but I don't know what. It's all colored to have meaning, but I don't know what. But these animals are crawling up each side, like rats or something, see the legs and this is the body.
19. This is like a sex thing again, you know, like a vagina. It's got all the inside flesh exposed.	E: (*Repeats response*) S: Well, it's got all that color like flesh, and it's got fine distinctions of the color, like flesh, and this is the slit, and the opening is deeper cause it's darker in here, like the folds of it, you know what I'm talking about?

Card IX

20. This top looks like two creatures having a watergun fight; the water is shooting out of these things.	E: (*Repeats response*) S: Yeah, they're pretty weird, like not real people, more like witches, and they are shooting at each other with these things, like a water fight, and here is the water shooting out.

Card X

21. This looks like two ants in combat with each other about something, this stick I guess.	E: (*Repeats response*) S: They're clinging to it, like each one felt that he had to have it, and they're pulling until one gives in and the other goes away. See here they are and this is the thing they want.
22. The pink looks like a worm, no not a worm like in the ground, but a worm that turns into a butterfly, like it's happening.	E: (*Repeats response*) S: It's like all pink, like a worm that's turning into a butterfly, raw and new, like it was in the process of doing it, like it was moving even like a worm.

TABLE 12.2
Sequence of Scores for Ms. Evans

Card No.		Loc.	No.	Determinant(s)	(2)	Content(s)	POP	Z	Special Scores
I	1	Wo	1	Fo		A	P	1.0	MOR
	2	Do	4	FYo		A			INC
	3	Wo	1	FC'o		A	P	1.0	
	4	Do	3	Fo		Hd,Sx			
II	5	D+	2	Ma.FCo	2	(Hd)		5.5	AG
	6	Ddo	24	FVo		Hd,Sx			
III	7	D+	1	Mao	2	H,Id	P	3.0	AG
	8	Do	2	CFo	2	Hd,Bl,Sx			MOR
IV	9	Wo	1	TFo		Ad		2.0	
	10	D+	4	FMa.C'F.FDo	2	Ad,Bt		4.0	INC
V	11	Wo	1	FMa.FC'o		A	P	1.0	
	12	Ddo	99	Fu	2	Hd			MOR
VI	13	Do	6	Mao		Hd,Sx			
	14	Ddo	33	Ma.FVu		Hd,Sx			
	15	Do	1	TFo		Ad	P		
VII	16	Wv	1	FYu		Fd			MOR
	17	D+	1	Mao	2	Hd,Cg	P	3.0	AG
VIII	18	W+	1	FMa.CFo	2	A,Art	P	4.5	FAB
	19	Ddo	23	FC.FVu		Hd,Sx			
IX	20	D+	3	Ma.mao	2	(H),A	P	2.5	AG
X	21	D+	11	Mao	2	A,Bt		4.0	AG,FAB
	22	Do	9	FMp.FCo		A			INC

Regarding her affect, Ms. Evans is clearly more capable than Mr. Carter and Deborah in chapter 11 of processing affective experience sufficiently. Although she is an introversive person who prefers ideational to expressive ways of dealing with situations (*EB* = 7:3.5), her *WSumC* of 3.5 is normative for introversive nonpatient adults. Moreover, her *SumC':WSumC* of 3:3.5 does not indicate any constriction in her current capacity to recognize and display her feelings. As an additional personality strength, Ms. Evans' *FC:CF* + *C* of 3:2 demonstrates balanced capacities to process affect either in relatively formal and reserved ways or in relatively casual and relaxed ways, with a normative adult preference for the former.

TABLE 12.3
Structural Summary for Ms. Evans

Location Features

Zf	= 11
ZSum	= 31.5
ZEst	= 34.5
W	= 6
(Wv	= 1)
D	= 12
Dd	= 4
S	= 0

DQ

......	(FQ-)
+	= 7 (0)
o	= 14 (0)
v/+	= 0 (0)
v	= 1 (0)

Determinants

Blends

M.FC
FM.C'F.FD
FM.FC'
M.FV
FM.CF
FC.FV
M.m
FM.FC

Single

M	=	4
FM	=	0
m	=	0
FC	=	0
CF	=	1
C	=	0
Cn	=	0
FC'	=	1
C'F	=	0
C'	=	0
FT	=	0
TF	=	2
T	=	0
FV	=	1
VF	=	0
V	=	0
FY	=	2
YF	=	0
Y	=	0
Fr	=	0
rF	=	0
FD	=	0
F	=	3

Contents

H	= 1, 0
(H)	= 1, 0
Hd	= 8, 0
(Hd)	= 1, 0
Hx	= 0, 0
A	= 7, 1
(A)	= 0, 0
Ad	= 3, 0
(Ad)	= 0, 0
An	= 0, 0
Art	= 0, 1
Ay	= 0, 0
Bl	= 0, 1
Bt	= 0, 2
Cg	= 0, 1
Cl	= 0, 0
Ex	= 0, 0
Fd	= 1, 0
Fi	= 0, 0
Ge	= 0, 0
Hh	= 0, 0
Ls	= 0, 0
Na	= 0, 0
Sc	= 0, 0
Sx	= 0, 6
Xy	= 0, 0
Id	= 0, 1

S-Constellation

YES	.. FV+VF+V+FD>2
YES	.. Col-Shd Bl>0
NO	.. Ego<.31,>.44
YES	.. MOR > 3
NO	.. Zd > +- 3.5
YES	.. es > EA
NO	.. CF+C > FC
NO	.. X+% < .70
NO	.. S > 3
NO	.. P < 3 or > 8
YES	.. Pure H < 2
NO	.. R < 17
5	..... TOTAL

Special Scorings

		Lv1	Lv2
DV	=	0x1	0x2
INC	=	3x2	0x4
DR	=	0x3	0x6
FAB	=	2x4	0x7
ALOG	=	0x5	
CON	=	0x7	
Raw Sum6 =	5		
Wgtd Sum6 =	14		

AB	= 0	CP	= 0
AG	= 5	MOR	= 4
CFB	= 0	PER	= 0
COP	= 0	PSV	= 0

Form Quality

	FQx	FQf	MQual	SQx
+	= 0	0	0	0
o	= 18	2	6	0
u	= 4	1	1	0
-	= 0	0	0	0
none	= 0	—	0	0

(2) = 9

Ratios, Percentages, and Derivations

R = 22	L = 0.16

EB = 7: 3.5	EA = 10.5	EBPer = 2.0
eb = 5: 10	es = 15	D = -1
	Adj es = 14	Adj D = -1

FM = 4 :	C' = 3	T = 2
m = 1 :	V = 3	Y = 2

FC:CF+C	= 3: 2
Pure C	= 0
SumC':WSumC	= 3:3.5
Afr	= 0.29
S	= 0
Blends:R	= 8:22
CP	= 0

COP = 0	AG =	5
Food	=	1
Isolate/R	=	0.09
H: (H)Hd(Hd)	=	1:10
(HHd) : (AAd)	=	2: 0
H+A:Hd+Ad	=	10:12

	P = 8	Zf = 11		3r+(2)/R = 0.41
a:p = 11: 1	Sum6 = 5	X+% = 0.82	Zd = -3.0	Fr+rF = 0
Ma:Mp = 7: 0	Lv2 = 0	F+% = 0.67	W:D:Dd = 6:12: 4	FD = 1
2AB+Art+Ay = 1	WSum6 = 14	X-% = 0.00	W:M = 6: 7	An+Xy = 0
M- = 0	Mnone = 0	S-% = 0.00	DQ+ = 7	MOR = 4
		Xu% = 0.18	DQv = 1	

SCZI = 0	DEPI = 6*	CDI = 4*	S-CON = 5	HVI = No	OBS = No

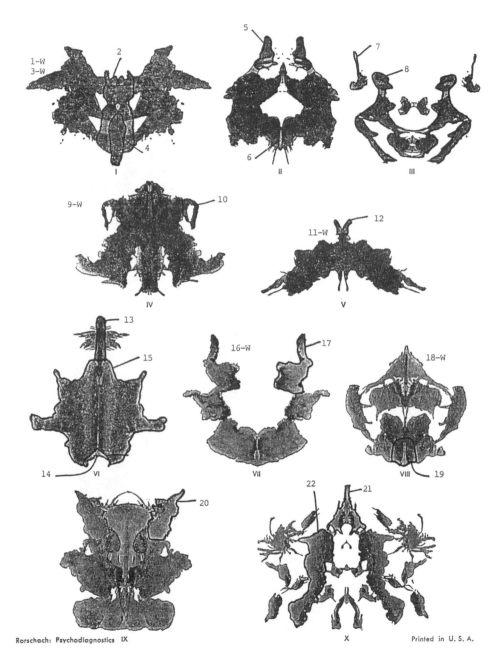

FIG. 12.1. Location choices of Ms. Evans.

At the same time, however, Ms. Evans' *Afr* of .29 indicates that she tends to avoid emotional interaction with her environment and to back away from situations in which feelings are being exchanged. *Afr* and *FC* are among the most stable variables in the Structural Summary, with 3-year stability coefficients in adults of .90 and .86, respectively. Hence there is reason to wonder why a woman with adequate capacities to modulate affect sufficiently and in moderation should characteristically have been so reluctant to become involved in emotionally charged situations. As one possible explanation of this finding, which was also noted in the case of Mr. Baker in chapter 10, the pairing of an adequate *WSumC* and a balanced and mature *FC:CF + C* with a dramatically low *Afr* often indicates emotional withdrawal that has less to do with avoiding affect than with avoiding the kinds of interpersonal situations in which affect is likely to become aroused. As already anticipated and is elaborated further in Ms. Evans' case, interpersonal issues do in fact figure prominently in her Rorschach and no doubt in her checkered life history as well.

Affective components of depression emerge not only in Ms. Evans' emotional withdrawal, but also in a limited capacity to modulate affect pleasurably. She gives evidence of being a sad and unhappy person who is experiencing considerable painful internalized affect, is emotionally quite distressed, and is rarely able to enjoy herself without having mixed feelings about what she is doing (*C′* = 3; *Col-Shd Bld* = 1; *SumShd* = 10 with *SumShd* > *FM + m*). Interestingly, however, she does not display any of the anger or resentment that commonly accompany feeling depressed (*S* = 0). This absence of any indication of oppositional tendencies, like her emotional withdrawal, has some implications for compliance in interpersonal relatedness and may contribute to understanding her criminal history as an accomplice who did what she was told.

The compelling evidence of dysphoria and withdrawal in Ms. Evans' affective cluster is consistent with her complaint of being depressed about being in jail, but it contrasts with the apparent fact that she has not previously been identified or treated as a depressed person, nor did the present court referral mention anything about her seeming depressed. Against this background, *DEPI* is not particularly sensitive to reactive or situational depression (as was noted in discussing Ms. Anderson in chap. 10), but rather elevates in association with endogenous types of depression and persistent disposition to recurring episodes of depression (see J. E. Exner & Weiner, 1995, chap. 6; Weiner, 1998b). An intriguing question, then, concerns how Ms. Evans could be so obviously depressed and depression-prone, as revealed by her Rorschach data, and not have shown her dysphoria to others in ways that would have led to her affective disorder having been identified.

Ms. Evans' introversive style provides some explanation of how she could have a previously unsuspected depressive disorder. As someone who by nature prefers to manage herself and her life in ideational rather than expressive ways, she is less likely than an extratensive person to display her feelings and make them known to other people. Combined with her low *Afr*, her introversiveness thus serves to conceal her dysphoria from view and minimize the likelihood of her being identified as a depressed person in need of mental health care. It is not uncommon for painful affects to go at least partly unnoticed in introversive people, which in clinical settings can result in underdiagnosis of an affective disorder or an underestimate of its severity.

In parallel fashion, cognitive dysfunction may escape notice in extratensive people, who are more inclined to show the world how they feel than how they think, and the clinical result may be inadequate recognition of underlying thought disorder in such individuals. In instances of such divergence between symptom patterns and coping style, Rorschach data can prove especially helpful in identifying affective or cognitive dysfunction that is obscured by aspects of personality style and goes undetected in a clinical interview.

Stress Management Issues

Ms. Evans' control cluster of variables illustrates the potential information value of the relationship between *EA* and *CDI*. With respect to being able to muster adequate resources to cope with the demands of everyday living, she gives evidence of having above average adaptive capacities (*EA* = 10.5) involving a well-established but not inflexible preferred coping style (*EB* = 7:3.5). Yet, she also gives evidence of being seriously limited in her capacities to cope effectively with experience (*CDI* = 4). As discussed in chapter 5, the combination of an adequate *EA* and an elevated *CDI* typically identifies a pattern in which a basically competent person is markedly deficient in specific social skills and/or is having considerable difficulty establishing and maintaining comfortable and rewarding interpersonal relationships. In Ms. Evans' case, her good *EA* could be the basis of her life as capable and concerned mother and respectable community participant, whereas her *CDI* could hold the key to her other life as an ineffective felon and compliant accomplice.

The control cluster also reveals that Ms. Evans' adaptive capacities are not now and have not previously been sufficient for her to manage comfortably the stresses in her life. The *D* and *AdjD* of −1 indicate mild but persistent and long-standing susceptibility to becoming anxious, tense, irritable, and unable to tolerate frustration. With respect to one of the differential diagnostic issues in this case, the minus *AdjD* merits further attention because of its implications for chronic discomfort, dissatisfaction with oneself, and ego-alien symptom formation, as contrasted with the implications of *AdjD* =

0 for peace of mind, self-acceptance, and ego-syntonic symptom formation, if any. With respect to one of the differential diagnostic issues in this case, Ms. Evans' $AdjD = -1$ along with her $DEPI = 6$ point more toward symptomatic disorder with features of anxiety and depression than to characterological disorder with features of psychopathy.

With respect to the most likely origins of Ms. Evans' subjectively felt distress, the six variables that contribute to her extremely elevated es of 15 fall into two groups. On the one hand, her $FM = 4$, $m = 1$, and $Y = 2$ are all within normal limits, indicating that neither intrusive ideation $(FM + m)$ nor feelings of hopelessness (Y) constitute a source of difficulty for her. On the other hand, the dysphoria identified by her $C' = 3$ has already been discussed as an affective issue, and she also shows elevations in Vista and Texture that lead into the examination of personal and interpersonal issues suggested by her protocol.

Personal and Interpersonal Issues

Ms. Evans appears to be a woman who generally has enjoyed adequate self-esteem $(3r + (2)/R = .41)$. The previously mentioned long-term stability of the Egocentricity Index, which includes a 3-year retest correlation of .87, makes it likely that she has characteristically been able to compare herself favorably to other people. It is further noteworthy with respect to the referral question that she does not show the heightened self-centeredness that would be indicated by an elevated Egocentricity Index, nor does she display the self-glorification and other narcissistic features that would be suggested by the presence of Reflections. Although her average Egocentricity Index and the $Fr + rF = 0$ do not preclude the possibility of psychopathic personality features, they make a diagnosis of antisocial personality considerably less likely than it would be if these indicators of self-centeredness and narcissism were present (see Gacono & Meloy, 1994, chap. 7).

Despite her generally adequate level of self-esteem, however, Ms. Evans gives evidence of some extremely negative and self-critical attitudes toward herself. Her three Vistas in particular point to considerable self-recrimination and regret concerning aspects of the kind of person she is and how she has lived her life. Whereas her average Egocentricity Index suggests that she considers herself a basically decent and capable person, the $V = 3$ is analogous to standing back and looking at herself and her conduct and detesting what she sees. Her recent arrest as well as her prior law breaking and her prostitution could well be contributing factors in her negative self-regard, and the comment she made on interview about "being stupid as usual" is consistent with this hypothesis.

The elevated Vista introduces a cognitive element into her depression, namely, thinking badly about herself as well as feeling badly, and the presence of four *MOR* responses in her record adds to this depressive mix the likelihood that she harbors some unusually negative attitudes toward her body and its functions. The thematic imagery in these *MOR* responses conveys in particular a view of herself as damaged goods. In her very first response she signs in with a butterfly that "looks damaged," as if to say that, above all else, "This is what I am." She continues this theme of damage in Response 8 on Card III, with "abortions" that "look like children" but are "not very well formed." This response may reflect distressing recollections of her own abortion, which could be a source of lingering remorse as well as of concerns about having been physically harmed by it. Response 12 on Card V echoes concerns about being physically harmed in a gruesome percept involving "legs with the stumps of feet here, like something left over from an explosion." Her final *MOR*, in which an item of food ("pieces of bread") is seen as damaged ("all broken up") in Response 16 on Card VII, suggests that she cannot prevent negative expectations from intruding on even ordinary aspects of getting daily nurturance.

Ms. Evans' four *MOR* responses considered together with her six *Sx* contents, one *Bl*, and five *AG* responses present a picture of concerns about harm often seen in persons who have in fact been victimized by trauma. Determining whether this is the case would require sources of information beyond the RIM, which can help to identify posttraumatic stress disorder (see Weiner, 1997a) but does not provide any reliable index of whether and how a person may have been victimized. On the other hand, Ms. Evans' imagery in these responses, especially those containing human movement, reveal some additional aspects of how she views herself and her relationships to others.

A particularly informative sequence begins with Response 4 on Card I, which is the first of her six *Sx* responses. The content is an ordinary form nude woman whose bottom part "is pretty clear," including "the indentation where the butt is," but whose "top is vague" and "whose head must be up here somewhere." This is the first of 11 human content responses in Ms. Evans' record, only two of which include heads—the "abortions" in Response 8 and "faces of a couple of kids" in Response 17 on Card VII. Her other nine human contents are all *Hd* percepts involving people seen from the waist down, and in three of these she reports a "vagina" (Responses 6, 14, and 19).

Could it be that Ms. Evans' self-image is dominated by perceptions of herself as being important only for what she has below the waist? Without doubt she is far more preoccupied with sexuality than most people. Her six *Sx* responses—which include in addition to the three "vagina" contents the "butt" on Response 4, the "abortions" on Response 8, and a "penis" on Response 13—contrast sharply with normative expectations. Only 4% of adult nonpatients give any *Sx* responses at all, and the normative mean frequency of *Sx* in this reference sample is just .07. Could Ms. Evans' attention to genitals and the striking absence of heads in her human percepts indicate that, despite her high average intelligence, she demeans herself as a brainless person whose thoughts and ideas have no worth and whose coin for dealing with people and events in her life is minted mainly by what she can do with her body and not with her mind? She says almost as much when she comments about her work as a prostitute, "That's all I got to make it with."

Returning to the sequence following Response 4, Ms. Evans begins Card II with an M in Response 5 of "Two hand puppets, like they are fighting." Her possible identification here with hand puppets suggests a self-image as someone who, even when behaving aggressively, does what other people would have her do. Hand puppets have no life or will of their own and are as brainless as people who have no heads; they just do whatever is orchestrated by the hand inserted in them. This aspect of how Ms. Evans seems inclined to view herself may have a bearing on the actual circumstances of her robberies, in which she appears to have been a willing but compliant accomplice.

The hand puppets are followed on Response 6 by "a woman's vagina" in which "you can see the lips folded back" because of the "coloring" and "shades." This response is significant in two respects beyond the Sx content alone. First, the sexual organ is not only named ("vagina") but is also elaborated in further anatomical detail ("the lips folded back"). Such elaborations of sexual anatomy, together with any attribution of movement to it, increase the likely intensity of the sexual preoccupation suggested by its presence. Second, by adding Vista to the response through inferring its folded appearance from the shading, Ms. Evans may be providing some indication that she is not as comfortable as she would have us believed with identifying herself primarily as a sexual being and prostituting herself. The pairing of V with a content theme in this manner frequently indicates that distasteful affects and self-critical attitudes are associated with it.

Similar responses recurring throughout Ms. Evans' record affirm these implications of Response 6. On Card VI she delivers two Sx responses that involve both anatomical detail and human movement. Response 13 on Card VI is "a penis if I ever saw one" that is "stiff, like ready to go," and Response 14 on the same card, following a comment that "There's a lot of sex on this one," uses Vista and depicts a "vagina" that is "really opened up, like it's ready for that stiff one." The final Sx content in Response 19 on Card VIII is "a sex thing again, you know, like a vagina," and it also includes shading and descriptive detail ("this is the slit"). Of the three Vistas in this record, then, all of them occur in "vagina" responses, which lends further weight to the inference that Ms. Evans is a woman with both generally adequate self-esteem and some very critical self-attitudes specific to her sexual nature and sexual activities. Considering her history of prostitution, of transient live-in arrangements with numerous men, and of a possibly traumatic abortion, she may be susceptible to thinking that her vagina, as the organ of her sexuality, has been the source of much of the trouble in her life.

As for the remainder of the responses in Ms. Evans' protocol that are likely to contain projected features of her self-image, two of her seven *M* responses are the just noted *Sx* responses on Card VI, and the remaining five are notable mainly for the aggressive interactions they depict: the hand puppets fighting on Response 5; "a couple people fighting over this thing down here" on Response 7; "a couple of kids arguing" on Response 17; "two creatures having a watergun fight" on Response 20; and "two ants in combat" on Response 21. Before turning to the interpersonal implications of these five aggressive *M* responses, there is some additional information concerning Ms. Evans' self-perception to be gleaned from her four *FM* responses.

Two of these *FM* response are unelaborated Populars with little idiographic significance: a flying bat on Card V and crawling animals on Card VIII. The other two *FM* responses contain the thematic imagery of "snakes' heads, like they was slithering out of a bush" (in Response 10 on Card IV) and, as her way of signing out, "a worm that's turning into a butterfly, raw and new, like it was in the process of doing it" (in Response 22 on Card X). The "I am" technique described in chapter 6 provides a way of speculating about the possible implications of the imagery projected in these responses for how she views herself. Could she be a slithering snake, as evil and untrustworthy as is embodied in common conceptions of what it means to be "a snake in the grass"? Or, is she a previously pathetic little creature (a worm) now evolving into something beautiful to be admired (a butterfly)? Perhaps she views herself in both ways, and perhaps the positive tone of her sign-out response speaks to some determination to turn her life around and entirely replace her identity as prostitute with her identity as den mother.

Looking next more fully into Ms. Evans' relationships with others, her interpersonal cluster of variables bears out the adaptive difficulties anticipated in commenting on her having an elevated *CDI* despite an adequate *EA*. In terms of interpersonal assets, she does display substantial interest in people (*SumH* = 11), adequate capacity to form attachments to other people and to anticipate forming intimate relationships with them ($T > 0$), and no apparent problem in perceiving other people and their actions realistically (of her seven *M* responses, six have ordinary form quality, one is unusual, and none is minus). In addition, she does not give evidence of being isolated from people who play an important part in her life (*ISOL* = .09).

On the other hand, the suggestion of interpersonal withdrawal that emerged in considering Ms. Evans' *Afr* = .29 is reinforced by two noteworthy findings in the interpersonal cluster of variables. Her *COP* = 0 and her *H:(H)Hd(Hd)* = 1:10 indicate that she is likely to feel uncomfortable in social situations in which she has to deal with real and well-functioning people; she rarely anticipates collaborative relationships with others, even in the context of intimacy; and she is likely to have been an outlier in groups to which she has belonged, a fringe member rather than an integral participant and someone more likely to go unnoticed than to be popular or well-liked.

To the extent that these interpersonal liabilities as suggested by the Rorschach findings are in fact characteristic of her interactions with people, they may provide some clue to her having opted for prostitution, an activity in which the participants seldom conduct themselves as real people or as they would in their real lives, but instead play out certain roles in a circumscribed interaction with a clearly demarcated beginning and end. Likewise, her social discomfort in real-life relationships and limited spirit of collaboration may have contributed to her having had only transient close relationships with men, many of whom appear to have exploited rather than nurtured her.

As support for these last two hypotheses, Ms. Evans' previously noted total of five AG responses indicates that, along with not anticipating a cooperative spirit in interpersonal relationships, she sees the world as a highly competitive place in which people can be expected to struggle aggressively and assertively with each other for what they want to have. Subjects with such substantial elevations in AG are typically firm believers in the oft-heard phrase, "It's a jungle out there," and often they adopt an aggressive and assertive stance that they regard as necessary to holding their own in a hard and unsympathetic world. It may be that interpersonal attitudes of this kind made it possible for Ms. Evans to commit crimes without showing any apparent concern for the victims of these crimes, even though she gives evidence of regret and remorse for having gotten herself in trouble and jeopardizing her home life and custody of her son.

Does this mean that, despite the indications in her record of persistent subjectively felt distress and ego-alien symptom formation, Ms. Evans is a psychopathic individual with an antisocial personality disorder? Her being basically an ideational person with mature capacities to process affect and a woman who gives little indication of being angry, self-centered, or narcissistic makes such a diagnostic inference unlikely. Of special note in this regard is the presence of T in her record, which indicates a capacity for attaching to and caring about others that is rarely seen in psychopathic individuals. Compared to the 89% of nonpatient adults who have at least one T in their record, $T > 0$ has been found in just 29% of antisocial women (Gacono & Meloy, 1994, chap. 4). Ms. Evans in fact shows an elevated T of 2, which suggests more than ordinary neediness for physically and psychologically close relationships to people.

Ms. Evans' elevated T could represent a persistent neediness for closeness or for at least a semblance of intimacy that could have participated in her susceptibility to becoming sexually promiscuous. As discussed in chapter 5, it is also possible that her $T = 2$ is a reactive rather than persistent elevation, in which case she may be feeling interpersonally needy as a consequence of being deprived of her customary intimacy with her son. Should this be the case, her $T = 2$ would not only argue against psychopathy, but would also give reason to believe that the appearances of her having a close and caring relationship with her son are genuine rather than contrived.

Cognitive Issues

The variables in Ms. Evans' processing and mediation clusters indicate that she attends to her experience in an open, efficiently organized, conventional, and realistic manner. If anything, her low *Lambda* of .16 in combination with her *SumShd* = 10 indicates that she becomes overly involved in emotional reactions to events in her life and that she would probably feel better and function more effectively if she could narrow her focus a little and be a bit more objective and detached in dealing with her experience. Phrased in Rorschach language, recommended treatment targets suggested by these observations would include transforming some of Ms. Evans' shading and achromatic color into pure *F*, which would raise her *Lambda* and make her *AdjD-minus* into an *AdjD* = 0.

To continue with the noteworthy personality strengths reflected in these two clusters, Ms. Evans gives evidence of being a well-organized person who is capable of grasping relationships between events and examining situations without becoming excessively or insufficiently attentive to their details ($Zf = 11$; $DQ+ = 7$; $Zd = -3$). She pays adequate notice to common and ordinary details of living that most people notice, she recognizes conventional realities in her environment, and she consistently forms accurate impressions of what she sees happening around her ($W:D:Dd = 6:12:4$; $P = 8$; $X - \% = 0.00$). If anything, her eight Popular and zero X- indicate more than usual attention to being conventional and accurate in giving Rorschach responses.

In light of the reasons why Ms. Evans is being examined, these particular findings could reflect some determination on her part to give a good account of herself. However, before being tempted to regard these indications of good reality testing as misleading, we need to appreciate that they have not emerged in the context of a guarded record. To the contrary, Ms. Evans has given an average length, low *Lambda* record containing rich thematic imagery. Moreover, the fact that she was able to avoid lapsing into perceptual inaccuracy even while giving vivid *Sx* responses involving Vista and morbidity speaks to her considerable capacity to retain realistic perspectives even while dealing with situations that are very troubling to her.

Two additional aspects of Ms. Evans' location choice should be noted. First, in contrast to her generally conventional focusing, her *Dd* = 4 constitutes some excessive attention to unusual details rarely noticed by most people. Three of these *Dd* locations occur with *Sx* content (Responses 6, 14, and 19), and the fourth involves the *MOR* on Response 12. Hence, despite her generally conventional focus of attention, Ms. Evans, when faced with concerns about her sexuality and about being damaged goods, may make some unusual choices in what she decides to pay attention to. Second, like Mr. Carter and Deborah in chapter 11, she shows an Aspiration Ratio with fewer *M* than *W* responses (*W:M* = 6:7). As noted in discussing these previous cases, people whose *M* does not exceed their *W* frequently show a pattern of conservative goal setting in which their aims and accomplishments fall well below what their talents and abilities would have allowed them to achieve. The contrast between Ms. Evans' high average intelligence and her spotty work history seems consistent with this Rorschach index of under-achievement.

Finally, with respect to her ideation, Ms. Evans appears capable of thinking logically and coherently about the meaning of her experience. Her *WSum6* = 14 does approach the range in which some question might be raised about tendencies toward disordered thinking. However, three of her five Critical Special Scores are Level 1 *INCOM* responses; a fourth is a childish rather than seriously inappropriate *FABCOM* on Response 21, which is the "ants in combat"; and the fifth one is a *FABCOM* on Response 18 in which the Popular animals "are crawling up the side" of what "looks like a diagram." Taken together, these five responses provide little basis for concern about the adequacy of Ms. Evans' reasoning. Similarly, she does not show any maladaptive inclination to use fantasy as a way of solving problems or intellectualization as a way of handling affect (*Ma:Mp* = 7:0; *INTELL* = 1), and her normative range *FM* + *m* = 5 gives no evidence that she is bothered by intrusive ideation.

Ms. Evans' ideational cluster of variables does identify one noteworthy liability, however. Her unbalanced *a:p* ratio of 11:1 indicates that she is markedly inflexible in how she thinks about herself and events in her life. She is consequently likely to be quite set in her ways, disinclined to consider changing any of her opinions or beliefs, and reluctant to entertain any perspectives different from those she already holds. This personality characteristic commonly constitutes an obstacle to progress in psychotherapy, as noted earlier, for the obvious reason that almost all forms of psychotherapy involve helping people in one way or another to change how they look at themselves and their experiences.

With further respect to Ms. Evans' treatment prognosis, the Rorschach data identify numerous personality characteristics typically associated with good likelihood of a person's remaining in and benefiting from psychotherapy. These include her being a relatively well-integrated person with basically adequate coping capacities and no apparent disturbances in thinking or reality testing; a psychologically distressed person with overt manifestations of anxiety and depression; a person who has adequate channels for expressing her feelings and revealing her underlying concerns; and someone who, although perhaps interpersonally competitive and withdrawn, is interested in people and capable of forming attachments to them (see Weiner, in press). The main obstacle to her becoming profitably involved in psychotherapy, from a clinical perspective, would be her previously noted inflexibility and apparent aversion to thinking in new and different ways.

In summary, Ms. Evans' Rorschach protocol provides a wealth of information bearing on her past and present circumstances and on diagnostic and treatment issues related to the questions raised in the court referral. First, despite no prior history of suspected psychological disorder or mental health treatment, she is a distressed, dysphoric, withdrawn, and self-denigrating woman who has probably been disposed to depressive episodes in the past and who is seriously in need of treatment for her present depressive disorder. Second, her personality style and attitudes toward herself and other people are consistent with neurotic symptom formation, including neurotic acting out, but do not suggest psychopathy or antisocial personality formation. Third, concerns about sexuality, an image of herself as being worthwhile only as a sexual object, and strong needs for intimate interpersonal relationships may have been contributing factors in her previous life as a prostitute and thief, whereas basic personal competence, intact cognitive functioning, and mature emotionality have allowed her to function adequately in her other life as parent and den mother. Fourth, despite some inflexibility in her thinking, she displays considerable potential for becoming involved in and benefiting from psychotherapy. Finally, consistent with the previous four conclusions, the Rorschach data suggest that she is indeed sincerely attached to and concerned about her son and is capable of being a good mother to him.

CASE 6: SUICIDAL AND HOMICIDAL TENDENCIES IN A SEVERELY DEPRESSED WOMAN WITH PROBABLE BIPOLAR DISORDER

Ms. Fisher is a 39-year-old, African-American mother of two children who was admitted to a psychiatric hospital complaining of being depressed and having had escalating suicidal and homicidal ideation during the preceding 2 months. This is her third psychiatric hospitalization in the past 3 years, with the previous two admissions having been occasioned by her overdosing with prescribed medication. She reports having frequent arguments with her husband, being angry with him to the point of being "blinded by rage," and having 2 days ago purchased a gun with the intent "to kill him and then myself." This marriage was the first for both Ms. Fisher and her husband, who has been successful in a middle management career, and they have remained together despite a recently dysfunctional relationship. The reasons why she has thought of killing him are unclear to this point in the evaluation.

Ms. Fisher has been more or less depressed since a hysterectomy 4 years ago and has been treated continuously since that time with outpatient psychotherapy and antidepressant medication, with obviously limited success. On admission to the hospital she was described as a soft-spoken person who nevertheless alternated between being argumentative and tearful when first interviewed and demonstrated psychomotor retardation, limited concentration, depressed affect, and some seemingly paranoid ideation. She was diagnosed as having major depressive disorder and referred for psychological evaluation of her diagnostic status and treatment needs as well as her present danger to herself and others, especially her husband. Ms. Fisher's Rorschach protocol follows in Tables 12.4, 12.5, and 12.6 and Fig. 12.2.

Affective Issues

Ms. Fisher's Structural Summary shows a valid record of 14 responses with an $S\text{-}CON$ of 7. Although $R = 14$ meets the minimum criterion for sufficient length to yield a generally reliable Rorschach protocol, records with fewer than 20 responses may be guarded and consequently limited in how much they reveal

TABLE 12.4
Rorschach Protocol of Ms. Fisher

Responses	*Inquiry*
Card I	
1. (*pause–deep sigh–pause*) At first glance it looks like an evil cat's face (*pause*). Without the jagged edges and stuff, it— (*tails off and falls silent*).	E: (*Repeats response*) S: A face, the ears here (Dd34), the eyes (DdS30), the mouth (Dds29). It's evil because of all the jagged edges. Or it's been in a fight, tattered skin, it's fur is tattered.
	E: What makes it look like fur? S: Because of the way it's painted, it looks like it has texture. The dark spots are like blood, although they're not red.
2. When I look at it deeply, I see some sort of moth, no, a bat, that's been through some turbulence—because its wings and body are kind of tattered.	E: (*Repeats response*) S: These things on the the head (D1), the body, the wings here. It's all tattered, with holes in it, and there's color on the bat. It's not all black, it could be black and white, or black and grey.

(Continued)

TABLE 12.4
(Continued)

Responses	*Inquiry*

Card II

3. *(sigh—pause)* Man—it's a hard day today. It looks like a spaceship, trying to blast off. But these are two bear-like monsters or beings that are trying to prevent them from blasting off. But the process continues, and it's trying to blast off, and the flames, the fire coming out burns them. Their heads are up, and they're shooting fire and venting their pain. You see it through their body. But it's a controlled thing.

E: *(Repeats reponse)*
S: The spaceship is here (DS5) and they're here (D1), and this (D4) is how they're trying to prevent it. But it's still in the process of blasting off, and this (D3) is the fire, and it's burning their legs, and this (red in D1) is the pain that's going through them, and this (D2) is their fury.

Card III

4. *(pause)* Well—I'm not sure *(pause; becomes tearful and cries softly)*. I'm sorry. It looks like—*(pause)* I see two things. Two women, as identified by these—protrusions, and they're fighting over something—something broken in half—and this is fury—they're angry. And also they have high heeled shoes.

E: *(Repeats response)*
S: They have breasts and high-heeled shoes. It looks like a tug of war. This (D7) was one thing, and they pulled it in half, fighting over it. Their fury is here (D2 and D3).

5. But then I also see it as an outline of a man, his bow tie and tuxedo, but not these things up here.

E: *(Repeats response)*
S: Not the whole man, just the face, neck, and he has a tuxedo shirt and a bow tie, and this is his jacket.

E: What makes it look like it does?
S: The way it's shaped, and it's a red bow tie.

Card IV

6. This looks like a big fuzzy giant monster, looking down at you. He has big feet, so he can step all over you—stomp you—hooked arms, so he can hook you, take you where he wants, and it looks like he has a stinger, too.

E: *(Repeats response)*
S: He's looking down, he looks massive, because of the bulk of his body. Big feet and boots and fur.

E: What suggests fur?
S: Again, because of the texture. A little head, but he's powerful—eyes, neck, and big hooked arms (D4), it makes him look evil, and the feet scare you, they're so big, and this (D1) looks like a stinger of some kind.

(Continued)

TABLE 12.4
(*Continued*)

Responses	Inquiry
Card V	
7. (*long pause*) I see two things. One is some kind of dangerous insect.	E: Antennae, the back of the body, and wings, but the wings look like they have claws, so they could catch you, or they have venom, so they could hurt you.
8. Either two crocodiles or two alligators, lying flat. The feet are here, the mouth, and they're butted up against each other, or its a mirror of one. They look like they've been mangled or killed, because they're not smooth. It looks like they've been injured or gutted.	E: (*Repeats response*) S: They're butted up against each other, but it looks like they're broken up, lying flat. It's probably a mirror image, or it could be two of them. E: You said they're not smooth. S: They're just mangled up.
Card VI	
9. It's either a—coyote that's been splattered on the road—run over several times, to flatten it. But I don't see no blood, so it's probably just a rug, a coyote skin. If it's a coyote that's been run over, it looks like a cartoon. Run over by a big Mack truck with wide tires.	E: (*Repeats response*) S: The head, nose, whiskers are here, and fur here, depicted by texture, the way it's painted. Feet, legs, the backbone, and the butt.
Card VII	
10. It just looks like smoke from a fire, and it looks like water on the horizon, and like smoke from a fire.	E: (*Repeats response*) S: It's after the fire has gone out. Here's the origin of the fire (D6). It looks like water here, and the horizon. E: What makes it look like smoke? S: They way it's painted.
Card VIII	
11. (*long pause—sigh—pause*) I don't know—I can see a woman's pelvis here, reproductive organs, but I can't see it as a whole picture. These animals look like they're trying to take over this woman and control her—or—it could represent—seeing how this is red, it could be the bad thing in the woman. The bad things are leaving the woman, like she's cleansing her body.	E: (*Repeats response*) S: What I see is the pelvic bone here (D7), and it's coming out of her body and forming the shape of animals (D1). She could be having a hysterectomy, I don't know. E: You mentioned reproductive organs. S: It's just the pelvis, the bony structure, and the coloring, the red, like blood, you know.

(Continued)

330

TABLE 12.4
(Continued)

Responses	Inquiry
Card IX	
12. Somebody peeking through some shrub for some reason, someone who has evil eyes. That's all.	E: (Repeats response) S: Somebody is here, the head, the eyes here (DdS22), vicious eyes. It's doing something bad, and these are all the flowers, the shrubs. It could be a Martian or an extraterrestrial, because there is like a glow up here, like a global type head (DS8). E: What suggests the shrubs? S: I like flowers, and I like color. He's trying to see what's going on, or getting ready to pounce on someone.
Card X	
13. This truly looks like a woman's body—various parts, and ovaries, a a jacket here. It looks like you're looking right through her skin into her body. The head is up here, an oblong head, with bulgy eyes. She's making a fashion statement. There's fur on her jacket. She looks like she's wealthy, and because of her wealth, she can dress as she pleases. She has freedom and can do what she wants to do.	E: (Repeats response) S: Here's the head (D14), eyes, ears, and earrings, and this (D8) is a fur color. E: How does it look like fur? S: The coloring and texture, and the jacket is here (D9), but you can see right through her. These (D2) are her ovaries, and this (D6) is her bra. This (D3) is a wishbone, and I don't know where a wishbone goes in the body. This (D10) could be her feet.
14. I see crabs in here, two sets of crabs.	E: (Repeats response) S: The two sets of crabs are here (D1) and here (D7).

about a subject's personality processes, especially if they have a high *Lambda* (as in the case of Ms. Anderson in chap. 10). In Ms. Fisher's case, however, the Structural Summary shows that she was sufficiently open to give a low *Lambda* of .27, sufficiently involved to produce several complex Blends, and sufficiently responsive to articulate a number of long and elaborate responses. Accordingly, there is good reason to expect that this 14-response record will reliably identify many aspects of her personality structure and dynamics.

Regarding the *S-CON* = 7, an analysis of the kind conducted with Mr. Baker's *S-CON* = 7 in chapter 10 yields less sanguine results than in his case. With just one more *FD* than the two in her record and/or one less than her two *H*, she could have an *S-CON* = 8 or an *S-CON* = 9. Accordingly, the

TABLE 12.5
Sequence of Scores for Ms. Fisher

Card No.		Loc.	No.	Determinant(s)	(2)	Content(s)	POP	Z	Special Scores
I	1	WSo	1	FTo		Ad,Bl		3.5	MOR,ALOG
	2	WS+	1	FC'o		A	P	3.5	MOR
II	3	WS+	1	ma.Ma.CFo	2	Sc,(A),Fi		4.5	FABCOPAGABMOR
III	4	W+	1	Ma.Co	2	H,Id	P	5.5	AB,MOR,AG
	5	DS+	1	FC-		Hd,Cg		4.5	
IV	6	Wo	1	Mp.FD.FTo		(H),Cg	P	2.0	
V	7	Wo	1	Fo		A		1.0	INC
	8	D+	4	Fu	2	A		2.5	MOR,DV
VI	9	Wo	1	FTo		(A),Sx	P	2.5	MOR
VII	10	Wv	1	YFu		Fi			
VIII	11	D+	1	Ma.CF-		An,Bl		3.0	DR2
IX	12	WS+	1	Ma.FD.CFu		(H),Bt		5.5	AG
X	13	Dd+	21	FY.FT-		H,Cg,Sx		4.0	INC2,DR
	14	Do	1	Fo	2	A	P		

Rorschach findings identify a "high 7" on the *S-CON* and suggest that Ms. Fisher should for the present be considered at risk for doing harm to herself. In particular, given her history of overdosing with medication, ingestion of her prescribed drugs should be closely monitored while she is in the hospital and following her discharge to outpatient care as well.

As in the preceding case of Ms. Evans, Ms. Fisher's first positive key variable is *DEPI* = 6, and the sequence for searching her variable clusters is affect, controls, self-perception, interpersonal perception, processing, mediation, and ideation. The *DEPI* = 6 provides compelling evidence for the presence of an affective disorder (see J. E. Exner & Weiner, 1995, chap. 6; Weiner, 1998b) and, in common with many people who are depressed, Ms. Fisher shows in her affective cluster some aversion to becoming involved in affectively charged situations (*Afr* = .40), a heavy burden of stressful affect (*FM* + *m:SumShd* = 1:7), and a considerable amount of underlying anger and resentment (*S* = 5).

As further manifestations of her depression, Ms. Fisher's low *R* and test behavior convey the sense of psychomotor retardation observed during her admission interview. Despite having a lot to say once she got a response

TABLE 12.6
Structural Summary for Ms. Fisher

Location Features	Determinants Blends	Single	Contents	S-Constellation
Zf = 12	m.M.CF	M = 0	H = 2, 0	NO .. FV+VF+V+FD>2
ZSum = 42.0	M.C	FM = 0	(H) = 2, 0	NO .. Col-Shd Bl>0
ZEst = 38.0	M.FD.FT	m = 0	Hd = 1, 0	YES .. Ego<.31,>.44
	M.CF	FC = 1	(Hd) = 0, 0	YES .. MOR > 3
W = 9	M.FD.CF	CF = 0	Hx = 0, 0	YES .. Zd > +- 3.5
(Wv = 1)	FY.FT	C = 0	A = 4, 0	NO .. cs > EA
D = 4		Cn = 0	(A) = 1, 1	YES .. CF+C > FC
Dd = 1		FC' = 1	Ad = 1, 0	YES .. X+% < .70
S = 5		C'F = 0	(Ad) = 0, 0	YES .. S > 3
		C' = 0	An = 1, 0	NO .. P < 3 or > 8
		FT = 2	Art = 0, 0	NO .. Pure H < 2
DQ		TF = 0	Ay = 0, 0	YES .. R < 17
. . . . . .(FQ-)		T = 0	Bl = 0, 2	7 . . . . . TOTAL
+ = 8 (3)		FV = 0	Bt = 0, 1	
o = 5 (0)		VF = 0	Cg = 0, 3	Special Scorings
v/+ = 0 (0)		V = 0	Cl = 0, 0	
v = 1 (0)		FY = 0	Ex = 0, 0	Lv1 Lv2
		YF = 1	Fd = 0, 0	DV = 1x1 0x2
		Y = 0	Fi = 1, 1	INC = 1x2 1x4
		Fr = 0	Ge = 0, 0	DR = 1x3 1x6
		rF = 0	Hh = 0, 0	FAB = 1x4 0x7
		FD = 0	Ls = 0, 0	ALOG = 1x5
Form Quality		F = 3	Na = 0, 0	CON = 0x7
			Sc = 1, 0	Raw Sum6 = 7
FQx FQf MQual SQx			Sx = 0, 2	Wgtd Sum6 = 25
+ = 0 0 0 0			Xy = 0, 0	
o = 8 2 3 3			Id = 0, 1	AB = 2 CP = 0
u = 3 1 1 1				AG = 3 MOR = 6
- = 3 0 1 1				CFB = 0 PER = 0
none = 0 – 0 0		(2) = 4		COP = 1 PSV = 0

Ratios, Percentages, and Derivations

R = 14	L = 0.27	FC:CF+C = 1: 4	COP = 1 AG = 3
		Pure C = 1	Food = 0
EB = 5: 5.0	EA = 10.0 EBPer = N/A	SumC':WSumC = 1:5.0	Isolate/R = 0.07
eb = 1: 7	es = 8 D = 0	Afr = 0.40	H: (H)Hd(Hd) = 2: 3
	Adj es = 7 Adj D = +1	S = 5	(HHd) : (AAd) = 2: 2
		Blends:R = 6:14	H+A:Hd+Ad = 10: 2
FM = 0 : C' = 1 T = 4		CP = 0	
m = 1 : V = 0 Y = 2			

		P = 5	Zf = 12	3r+(2)/R = 0.29
a:p = 5: 1	Sum6 = 7	X+% = 0.57	Zd = +4.0	Fr+rF = 0
Ma:Mp = 4: 1	Lv2 = 2	F+% = 0.67	W:D:Dd = 9: 4: 1	FD = 2
2AB+Art+Ay = 4	WSum6 = 25	X-% = 0.21	W:M = 9: 5	An+Xy = 1
M- = 1	Mnone = 0	S-% = 0.33	DQ+ = 8	MOR = 6
		Xu% = 0.21	DQv = 1	

SCZI = 3	DEPI = 6*	CDI = 2	S-CON = 7	HVI = No	OBS = No

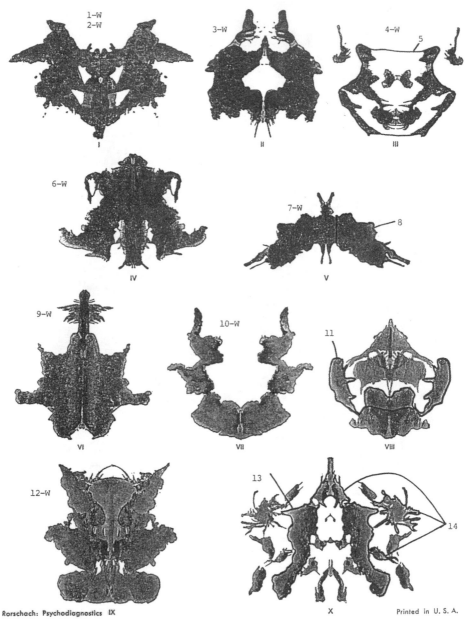

underway, she still could muster only enough mental energy to generate 14 responses. As noted in the protocol, she frequently paused either before beginning or in the process of delivering a response, sometimes for an extended period of time. Often her responses were punctuated by deep sighs, and on one occasion (Card III) she became tearful and sobbed for several minutes. On Card II, after a sigh and a pause, she began with "Man—it's a hard day today."

Surprisingly, however, Ms. Fisher's structural data do not include any elevations on the variables labeled in chapter 5 as the "dysphoric duo." Her normative range $C' = 1$ and $ColShd\ Bld = 0$ provide no basis for inferring either that she is feeling sad or is having difficulty enjoying herself. Moreover, she displays unmistakable evidence of a free-flowing affective style that stands in sharp contrast to the emotional constriction and tightly moderated emotional expression usually seen in persons who are depressed. Her $SumC':WSumC$ of 1:5 indicates that she rarely keeps her feelings bottled up or denies them free expression, and her $FC:CF + C$ of 1:4 indicates that she is an emotionally intense person who typically expresses her feelings in a dramatic, expansive, and rapidly shifting fashion. Such Rorschach manifestations of affective excess and lability in a person who presents as clinically depressed and has a $DEPI > 5$ usually points to concurrent hypomanic features and the presence of a cyclothymic or bipolar disorder.

The possibility of bipolar rather than unipolar depression in Ms. Fisher's case receives further support from the previously noted quantity of her verbiage. The length of her responses during both the free association and the inquiry is apparent from the amount of space they occupy on the printed page. Most depressed persons who can muster only 14 responses can also find only a few words to say about them. Ms. Fisher, despite a slow rate of speech and her frequent pauses, found a good deal to say and was quite able and willing to say it. As an additional perspective on this diagnostic clue, depressed people with psychomotor retardation are usually difficult to examine with the Rorschach, because they offer little information spontaneously and require a delicate inquiry in which the examiner's need to probe enough to code the responses must be balanced against causing the subject excessive distress. By contrast, records that flow with little guidance from the examiner, contain detailed free associations that require little inquiry, and include sharply focused replies to inquiry questions, when given by depressed subjects, provide reason to wonder whether there are hypomanic features as well in the person's clinical picture.

Stress Management Issues

The data in Ms. Fisher's control cluster suggest that she is a psychologically competent person with generally adequate coping capacities and no pronounced difficulties in meeting the usual demands of everyday living. Her

EA of 10 is slightly above average, and her *CDI* = 2 is well within normal limits. Furthermore, her adaptive capacities appear sufficient for managing comfortably the amount of stress she is experiencing (*D* = 0). In fact, were it not for a slight elevation in situationally determined distress (*Y* = 2), she would be functioning with an above average degree of self-content, unflappability, and insulation against subjectively felt distress (*AdjD* = +1). The well-documented corollaries of such *D* and *AdjD* scores include individuals being in a stable state of psychological equilibrium and being able to impose adequate control on their behavior.

As in sorting out the evidence of excessive and labile emotionality in a depressed person, it is now necessary to reconcile the control cluster implications of adaptability and stability with the clinical history of this over-dosing and thrice-hospitalized woman who has purchased a gun with the intention of using it to kill her husband and herself. This reconciliation can begin with the fact discussed in chapter 5 that neither good adaptive capacities nor stability preclude psychological disorder. Being psychologically resourceful (as indicated by an at least average *EA*) may minimize a person's susceptibility to psychopathology, but sufficiently pathogenic biological or environmental influences can induce psychopathology no matter what a person's level of adaptive capacity. Being psychologically stable means being consistent and relatively unlikely to change, not necessarily being well-adjusted. Being in a state of equilibrium (as indicated by *D* and *AdjD* scores of 0) can accompany psychological good health, but it can also reflect chronic symptomatic or characterological disorder, and it can even occur in people who are consistently and predictably volatile and unstable.

As for self-control, the discussion in chapter 5 indicated further that having good frustration tolerance and being unlikely to act impulsively, as indicated by *D* = 0, does not preclude being an action-oriented person who chooses not to impose much self-restraint and who may, as a consequence of poor judgment or evil intent, behave in reckless, disruptive, and ill-advised ways that endanger their own safety or the safety of others. Impulsivity, it was pointed out, is indexed on the Rorschach by a minus D-score and consists of losing control and behaving in uncharacteristic ways that the individual feels uncomfortable about and regrets later on. Behavior that is inadequately controlled by choice, rather than as a consequence of incapacity to exert self-control, comprises objectionable and self-defeating conduct that is characteristic of how the individual usually acts, feels natural and comfortable to the person, and seldom leads to sincere regrets or apologies. As noted in chapter 5, this characterological proclivity to inadequately controlled behavior in the presence of *D* = 0 is indexed on the Rorschach by such variables as a high *Lambda*, a pervasively extratensive *EB*, a substantial predominance of *CF* + *C* over *FC*, and infrequent *FM* responses.

Of these four variables possibly associated with problem behavior attributable to characteristic manifestations of personality style rather than uncharacteristic loss of self-control, Ms. Fisher shows neither a high *Lambda*
nor pervasive extratensiveness. She does have a markedly unbalanced *FC:CF*
+ *C* ratio, as already discussed, and her *FM* = 0 suggests that she may be
the kind of person who has little conscious awareness of need states because she translates her needs into action as soon as they arise. In combination with her *S* = 5, her unmodulated use of color and *FM* = 0 are consistent
with the overt expression of anger and hostility noted in her clinical history.
Whether her expressions of anger and hostility are likely to involve poor
judgment is an important question to be considered when examining her
cognitive functioning.

To complete the analysis of the control cluster variables, two other
features of the data indicate that Ms. Fisher's *EA* = 10 does not reflect as
much adaptive capacity as it might suggest. First, she has an ambitent *EB*
style (*M:SumC* = 5:5.0), which means that she is likely to be inconsistent and
unpredictable in how she chooses to act. Second, the composition of her
average level *es* = 8 differs markedly from normative expectation. Half of
her *es* total comes from four *T* responses, which constitutes an unusually
high elevation on this variable and suggests some extremely distressing
affect associated with unmet needs for close and intimate relationships
with people.

Personal and Interpersonal Issues

With respect to her image of herself, Ms. Fisher appears to have normative
capacities for self-awareness (*FD* = 2) and some at least marginal capacities
to form a sense of identity based on identifications with real people in her
life (*H* = 2). On the other hand, her *H:(H)Hd(Hd)* of 2:3 raises the possibility
that her sense of self may be based more on identifications with imaginary
figures or partial objects rather than real objects in her life. Of greater
concern, however, are indications that she has chronically had little esteem
for herself (*3r + (2)/R* = .29) and holds some very negative attitudes toward
her body and its functions (*MOR* = 6). A sequence analysis of the thematic
content of her six *MOR* responses reveals just how intensely Ms. Fisher
regards herself as a damaged object.

The record opens with four consecutive Morbids, a dramatic and extended "sign-in" documenting that Ms. Fisher identifies and presents herself
to the world mainly as someone who is tattered and broken, has had bad
things done to her body, and is a shambles of what she once was and would
like to be. Response 1 involves the face of a cat that has "been in a fight,"
has "tattered skin," and whose "fur is tattered." In Response 2 on Card I
there is a bat "that's been through some turbulence" and whose "wings and

body are kind of tattered"; on inquiry the bat is described further as "all tattered, with holes in it." On Card II, Response 3 focuses on two "bear-like monsters or beings" who are in a fire that is "burning their legs" and who are "venting their pain." Response 4 on Card III involves two women fighting over something that is "broken in half."

After three subsequent responses without such morbidity, Ms. Fisher continues this theme in Response 8 on Card V with "crocodiles or alligators" that have "been mangled or killed" and that look like "they've been injured or gutted," and in Response 9 on Card VI with "a coyote that's been splattered on the road, run over several times to flatten it." For good measure, she adds that the coyote has been "run over by a big Mack truck with wide tires."

In addition to the implications of these six *MOR* responses for negative self-imagery, they occur in the context of some other revealing response characteristics. Both Response 1 and Response 9 combine morbidity with Texture, suggesting some linkage in Ms. Fisher's psyche between concerns about having a damaged body and concerns about lacking as much closeness and intimacy as she would like to experience in her relationships with people. The appearance of *T* in the initial response to Card I is normatively very unusual and provides particularly good reason to believe that she sees and presents herself as being a very needy as well as a damaged person. In Response 2, the morbidity occurs in connection with the only *FC'* in her record. This combination and the sequence of the first two responses on Card I suggest that Ms. Fisher, although not experiencing much depressive affect, is nevertheless susceptible to becoming dysphoric when self-perceptions as a damaged and emotionally deprived person prey on her mind.

The next two Morbids are embedded in complex responses that also show anger and assertiveness and may indicate how Ms. Fisher attempts to defend herself against the type of painful self-perceptions apparent in her first two responses. The morbidity persists in Responses 3 and 4, along with her previously noted delays in responding. However, the *FT* and *FC'* seen in Responses 1 and 2 are gone, replaced by active movement and bright color (an $m^a.M^a.CF$ in Response 3 and an $M^a.C$ in Response 4). Admittedly, there is some card pull involved in choosing different determinants on Cards II and III than on Card I. Nevertheless, there is plenty of gray-black and shading available on Cards II and III, should a subject be disposed to use it in formulating a response, and there is no necessity to articulate the red on these cards.

What appears to be happening in Response 3 is that the figures are still being harmed ("the fire coming out burns them"), but they are no longer passive and demoralized victims. Instead, they are actively asserting themselves, "trying to prevent [a spaceship] from blasting off," and their affect, as symbolized by the red color, has turned to "fury." In Response 4, the women who are fighting are angry (with their "fury" once more symbolized by the red color), and it is no longer they who are "broken" but instead the object they have pulled in half. In terms of defense, then, the painful neediness, dysphoria, and victimization manifest in the first two responses has been replaced in the next two responses by an active struggle against opposing forces and people and by active striving and direction of anger outward rather than internally.

Such defensive maneuvers sometimes prove adaptive in warding off depression. In Ms. Fisher's case, however, the defensiveness goes too far. The externally directed anger becomes "fury," the expression of affect is intellectualized and poorly modulated (*AB* on Responses 3 and 4; *CF* on Response 3 and *C* on Response 4), and her reasoning becomes illogical in the process (the *FABCOM* on Response 4). Moreover, the sequel to her defensive efforts on Responses 3 and 4 does not show good recovery, but further deterioration instead: Response 5 involves a minus form quality "outline of a man, his bow tie and tuxedo." Consistent with the previously noted implications of her expansive affective style for hypomanic features, we may be seeing here a strained and excessive defensive reaction against depression in which determined denial, unusually energetic striving, and intense outer-directed affect are associated with bipolar disorder.

Further examination of those responses with prominent projected elements identifies two additional significant themes in Ms. Fisher's imagery. First, she appears to be a woman who is unusually concerned about sources of danger in her environment and specifically about being at the mercy of people who can control her and might intentionally do her harm. Her *M.FD.FT* in Response 6 on Card IV is particularly striking as a representation of a powerful figure that holds appeal and might tempt one into a close relationship ("a big fuzzy giant"), but that one should best keep some distance from (the *FD*) because of its dangerousness: "He has big feet, so he can step all over you—stomp you—hooked arms, so he can hook you, take you where he wants, and it looks like he has a stinger, too." Her *M-* in Response 11 on Card VIII involves animals that "look like they're trying to take over this woman and control her," and her remaining *M* in Response 12 on Card IX depicts "somebody peeking through some shrub for some reason, someone who has evil eyes." This projection of threat onto the environment also appears in the cat with tattered fur on Response 1, which has an "evil cat's face," and in Response 7 on Card V of a "dangerous insect." Although as someone with *T* in her record she does not elevate on *HVI*, Ms. Fisher nevertheless displays in these images considerable propensity to develop paranoid ideation, which was noted on her admission interview.

The other significant theme in Ms. Fisher's imagery appears in Responses 11 and 13. In Response 11, the minus form woman who is being controlled by animals is seen only as a "pelvis" and "reproductive organs" and is described as possibly "having a hysterectomy." Asked about the reproductive organs, she retreats from this impression and, perhaps showing some adaptive use of denial, says that what she sees is "just the pelvis" and some blood. On Response 13, which is also a minus, she reports "a woman's body" and "ovaries" that you can see by "looking right through her skin into her body." The disorganizing distress that Ms. Fisher experiences in the "hysterectomy" response is apparent from its minus form quality and her inability to give any other response on Card VIII. In the "ovaries" response the similar implications of the minus form quality are accentuated by the substantial cognitive slippage indicated by the Level 2 *INCOM*, which is coded for the impossible transparency effect of seeing both external and internal features of the body, and the *DR*, the content of which is quite interesting in its own right, in the following way.

Ms. Fisher is obviously very distressed about being a damaged, victimized, and externally controlled object, and her particularly upsetting concerns about reproductive organs are consistent with her actual history of having become depressed following a hysterectomy. Note then how she deals in Response 13 with the cumulative impact of these concerns having been brought visibly close to the surface by the Rorschach stimuli. She produces an off-task fantasy elaboration of this transparent woman with "an oblong head" and "bulgy eyes" in which the woman is seen as "making a fashion statement" and described further: "There's fur on her jacket, she looks wealthy, and because of her wealth she can dress as she pleases; she has freedom and can do what she wants to do." Is it difficult to imagine that the wealthy, well-dressed, and free woman in Ms. Fisher's fantasy is an ideal for her, perhaps a dream beyond her grasp? Such recourse to utopian fantasy often characterizes the defensive efforts of people who are using Pollyannish denial to ward off depression and who may as a consequence show features of bipolar disorder.

With respect to the remaining structural data concerning Ms. Fisher's interpersonal relatedness, her previously noted $T = 4$ identifies both adequate capacities to form close attachments to people and the likelihood that she is presently a lonely person who feels very much deprived of the kinds of love, affection, and intimacy she would like to have in her life. She is somewhat uncomfortable in social situations ($H:(H)Hd(Hd) = 2:3$), and she appears to view interpersonal interactions as more likely to be competitive than collaborative ($COP = 1$; $AG = 3$). However, despite the paranoid propensities noted in her imagery, she seems to have retained adequate interest in people ($SumH = 5$) and does not give evidence of being unusually isolated from others ($ISOL = .07$).

Cognitive Issues

The cognitive data in Ms. Fisher's protocol indicate first of all that, in attending to her experience, she is less able than most people to deal with situations in a detached and objective manner. As shown by her low *Lambda* of .27, she tends instead to become overly involved in events and to make even routine matters more complicated than they need to be. Like Ms. Evans in the previous case, she would probably feel better and function more effectively if she could be helped to narrow her frame of reference and approach situations in a more matter-of-fact way. In Rorschach terms, what she needs in treatment is a focus on putting some more pure F into her life.

Along with her low *Lambda*, Ms. Fisher's difficulty in doing things the easy way is reflected in her *W:D:Dd* ratio of 9:4:1 and in her being an overincorporator ($Zd = +4$). By using only four D locations compared to her nine W, she is showing little of the economy of effort that is associated with attending to the readily apparent details rather than the global aspects of everyday experience. Similarly, in her positively elevated Zd she is displaying an inclination to seek out and gather more information than is necessary for efficient problem solving and careful decision making. Instead, this finding suggests that she typically solves problems rather slowly as a consequence of being excessively careful in the process. This style of processing information differs from usual expectation in hypomanic individuals, who are typically more hasty and careless in decision making than Ms. Fisher appears to be. At the same time, the unusual care with which she examines situations may be associated with the concerns she has about being controlled or victimized and with her apparent susceptibility to paranoid ideation.

The way in which Ms. Fisher attends to her experience is also notable for her propensity to misperceive events in her life. Her $X-\% = .21$, although not in the psychotic range ($X-\% > .29$), is sufficiently high to identify a substantial likelihood of lapses in judgment based on poor reality testing. Note, on the other hand, that two of the three minus form responses she produces in this 14-response record are associated with her apparently pressing concerns about her reproductive organs: the woman "having a hysterectomy" on Response 11 and the "ovaries" in Response 13. Accordingly, it may be that her distortion of reality and tendency to exercise poor judgment are not generally characteristic of how she behaves, but are instead adaptive liabilities that emerge primarily in situations that bring her reproductive functioning to mind.

Finally, the data bearing on Ms. Fisher's use of ideation contain no indication that she is an excessively contemplative or ruminative person. As an ambitent ($EB = 5:5.0$), she has no particular commitment to being deliberative about what she observes, even though as a low *Lambda* overincorporator she is likely to observe widely and takes in a considerable amount of information. She also does not give evidence of using fantasy to excess as a way of solving problems ($Ma:Mp = 4:1$), nor does she seem inclined to excessive use of intellectualization as a defense ($2AB + Art = Ay = 4$).

However, her ideational data are notable for indications of inflexibility and probable thought disorder. Of these, the inflexibility is the easier and more straightforward adaptive liability to identify. In her unbalanced $a:p$ ratio of 5:1 she demonstrates, as did Ms. Evans in the previous case, considerable resistance to changing how she thinks. She is likely to be set in her ways, disinterested in perspectives different from those she already has, and unreceptive to suggestions that she consider altering her opinions about anything. As noted in other instances, such cognitive rigidity is typically an obstacle to progress in psychotherapy and is often associated with early dropout from treatment. In Ms. Fisher's case, her 4-year history of unsuccessful outpatient therapy may well reflect some resistance to change as measured in this Rorschach index of cognitive rigidity.

As for disordered thinking, Ms. Fisher's $WSum6 = 25$ is beyond the minimum criterion for this variable on the Schizophrenia Index ($SCZI > 17$) and strongly suggestive of incoherent association and illogical reasoning. However, as noted in discussing Mr. Baker's $WSum6 = 28$ in chapter 10 and Mr. Carter's $WSum6 = 18$ in chapter 11, the composition of this score must be considered carefully before any conclusions are drawn from it. Resembling Mr. Carter's data more than Mr. Baker's, the nature of Ms. Fisher's seven Critical Special Scores does not minimize the maladaptive significance of her elevated $WSum6$. Four of these seven scores involve serious rather than mild instances of cognitive slippage (two DR, one $FABCOM$, and one $ALOG$), and two of the seven are of the bizarre Level 2 variety that is rarely given by subjects who are not thought disordered.

Ms. Fisher's Critical Special Scores also illustrate the manner in which the composition of $WSum6$ can help in differentiating schizophrenic thought disorder from the forms of disordered thinking often seen in persons with bipolar disorder. Schizophrenic thinking is usually dominated by illogical reasoning and expressed in terse, unelaborated statements that the person takes no pleasure in discussing further. Disordered thinking in bipolar persons, by contrast, is usually dominated by loose associations and expressed in long, rambling, tangential discourse that the individual enjoys delivering and is happy to expand on if asked to do so.

As someone who appears to have a bipolar disorder but is also presently depressed and somewhat paranoid, Ms. Fisher does not display either of these two forms of thought disorder exclusively. Note, however, that her Critical Special Scores include two DR but only one FAB; that she gives a Level 2 DR but no Level 2 $FABCOM$; that, although she is not always enjoying herself while elaborating her responses, her DR in Response 13 involves the very upbeat image of the wealthy and well-dressed woman free to do what she wants; and that elaboration rather than terseness characterizes each of the seven $WSum6$ responses. In each of these respects, she gives evidence of the type of thought disorder more likely to occur in bipolar than in schizophrenic disorder (see Weiner, 1998b).

In summary, the Rorschach findings help to identify Ms. Fisher as a chronically depressed woman with severely negative attitudes toward herself. At the same time, the data provide a study in contrasts. She is an unstable and unpredictable person whose inconsistency is nevertheless an apparently stable and persistent aspect of her personality functioning. Her instability revolves largely around defenses aimed at warding off depression, as a consequence of which she does not display much dysphoria but instead gives evidence of numerous bipolar features, most particularly a dramatic and expansive affective style.

In addition, Ms. Fisher appears to be an angry and needy woman who feels victimized in a hostile world and who harbors both paranoid ideation and suicidal and homicidal tendencies that must be taken seriously. Although she appears at the moment to be adequately in control of herself, there is reason to speculate that her hysterectomy 4 years earlier has played a significant role in her becoming disturbed and that brooding about her reproductive capacity may engender lapses in her capacities to think clearly and exercise realistic judgment. Structured supportive treatment and close monitoring of her course are clearly indicated by these test results.

13

Managing Stress

Ordinary everyday living requires people to confront decision-making and problem-solving situations that make demands on their psychological resources. The discussion in chapter 5 noted that managing stress adaptively consists of people having sufficient adaptive capacities to meet the demands they are experiencing, whereas inability to cope with life's demands in some satisfactory fashion constitutes inadequate stress management and typically leads to maladaptive consequences. As further noted in chapter 5, adequate resources for minimizing subjectively felt distress and maintaining a consistent coping style promote successful adaptation and a sense of well-being. Conversely, a combination of insufficient resources, excessive experienced stress, and inconsistent coping efforts can be expected to contribute to a wide range of adjustment difficulties.

Strengths and weaknesses in stress management are measured on the RIM by variables listed in the control cluster and situation-related stress array in Table 3.1. As shown in Table 3.2, the Comprehensive System search strategy gives initial attention to this cluster in three circumstances: (a) when $D < AdjD$, which suggests the presence of some significant situational distress; (b) when $CDI > 3$, which identifies substantial deficits in coping capacities; and (c) when $AdjD > 0$, which points to persistent and long-standing subjectively felt distress related to individuals' inability to muster sufficient resources to cope with the demands in their life.

Each of these three circumstances has characterized cases discussed in previous chapters. Mr. Baker in chapter 10 displayed all three of these indications of impaired capacities for stress management and indeed did show multiple adjustment difficulties, but his record was selected for presentation primarily to illustrate a low *Lambda* protocol. Mr. Carter in chapter 11 gave evidence of some situational distress ($D < AdjD$), but his first positive key variable was the $SCZI = 5$ that identified the schizophrenic features in his disorder. In chapter 12, Ms. Evans had an $Adj = -1$ and an elevated CDI of 4, and Ms. Fisher showed some mild situational distress ($D = 0$ and $AdjD = +1$), but the most salient Rorschach finding in both of their cases was the depressive disorder evidenced by the $DEPI = 6$. The illustrations in the present chapter involve two cases in which $D < AdjD$ provides the entry point into the record and constitutes the only positive finding among the first seven key variables listed in Table 3.2.

As discussed in chapter 3, the first seven key variables examined in the Comprehensive Search strategy generally alert examiners to the likelihood of some type of symptomatic, characterological, or developmental disorder. Following these first seven key variables, the eighth one in the list pertains to whether the person is displaying preference for an introversive or extratensive coping style, which has no necessary implications for psychopathology. Subjects whose records reach this eighth key variable without flagging an entry point on any of the preceding seven are often reasonably well-integrated individuals who are more likely to have an adjustment disorder, or no disorder at all, than a disorder that would be diagnosed on Axis I or Axis II of the *DSM-IV*. Although far from providing a precise or infallible index of the presence or severity of diagnosable psychological disorder, this distinction between the first seven entry points identified by key variables and the rest of the variables in Tables 3.2 and 3.3 often proves useful as a rough guide to whether a Rorschach protocol is identifying substantial adjustment difficulties and need for treatment.

Accordingly, in the two cases that follow, it is reasonable to expect that, were it not for some situational anxiety, these two persons would be getting along fairly well in their lives. As becomes evident, however, the positive implications of elevating only on $D < AdjD$ among the first seven key variables does not preclude either noteworthy adjustment difficulties or problematic life situations. The cases involve two different kinds of persons in two different situations. Case 7 is an Hispanic teenage gang member charged with complicity in two murders who was examined with respect to his competency to stand trial and sanity at the time of the alleged offenses. Although not seriously disturbed, he displays limited coping skills, poor judgment, and a maladaptive inclination to do what he is told. Case 8 is a Caucasian dental student doing poorly in school and complaining of concentration difficulties. His coping skills are generally adequate, but he demonstrates major problems in his interpersonal relationships.

CASE 7: A TEENAGE GANG MEMBER CHARGED WITH BEING AN ACCESSORY TO MURDER

Luis is a 15-year-old Hispanic boy living with his father in a small apartment in an inner-city neighborhood. For the last 2 years he has spent his life mainly on the streets, in the company of a group of older boys who occasionally work for pay at unskilled jobs but are mostly concerned with finding "easy" money (usually through petty criminal activity), "hanging out" (which usually means making a nuisance of themselves in their neighborhood and various other public places where they "cruise"), and protecting their turf. In this group Luis has been treated much like a mascot or little brother, someone who is protected and taken care of but also expected to do chores and run errands for other group members.

It happened one day that the group captured and took to a deserted location two boys whom they believed had broken into one of the group member's homes and stolen some money and marijuana that he was safeguarding for the group. After some discussion in which Luis says he was not included, he was dispatched by the group to find a particular person and bring this person to the location where the two suspected "robbers" were being held. According to Luis, he had no idea why he was being sent to fetch this person or what would happen subsequently. He was aware, however, that this person's street name was "Shooter."

Knowing where to look, Luis found Shooter and brought him back to where the two captive boys were being held. Someone turned on a radio and put the volume up high. Then Shooter took out a revolver and shot both boys through the head in gangland execution style. Luis was then given a blanket and told to roll up the bodies and help load them into a vehicle, which he did. The group then dispersed, and Luis went home, showered, and threw away the clothes he had been wearing. That evening he told his father what had happened and his father took him to the police station, where he gave a full report of the crime. All of those involved were subsequently arrested and charged with kidnaping and murder.

Prior to this incident, Luis had been picked up by the police on several occasions for drunkenness, loitering, and running away, but he had never been arrested. He began drinking beer and smoking marijuana at age 13 and has been a heavy user of both substances since that time. He managed to complete nine grades in school, but in the last few years he had done poorly and frequently been truant. He has no history of psychological disorder, and his measured Wechsler IQ is 91. Prior to being arrested on this occasion, his typical day was spent "hanging around, smoking weed and drinking, and not doing much else." He regrets the fact that two people were killed and says it was "a terrible thing to see." He says he had nothing to do with planning the crime, however, and helped to dispose of the bodies because he was afraid not to: "That dude with the gun was right there, mean-looking, and I was scared he'd shoot me too if I didn't do what they said."

The public defender requested an examination of Luis to determine if there were any indications that he was incompetent to stand trial or might have been legally insane at the time of his complicity in this crime. When examined, Luis presented as a neatly groomed, pleasant looking, soft-spoken, and somewhat pudgy boy of average height whose appearance and demeanor did not fit the usual stereotypes of teenage gang delinquents. He was calm and relaxed, despite his circumstances, and he cooperated fully with the test procedures. Luis' Rorschach protocol follows in Tables 13.1, 13.2, and 13.3 and Fig. 13.1.

Stress Management Issues

Luis' Structural Summary indicates a valid record of 27 responses, no elevation on the *S-CON*, a first positive key variable of $D < AdjD$, and a next positive key variable of an extratensive *EB* (0:4.5). The order for searching the cluster in his record, following Table 3.2, is accordingly controls, affect,

TABLE 13.1
Rorschach Protocol of Luis

Responses		*Inquiry*
Card I		
1. A bunny rabbit.	E:	*(Repeats response.)*
	S:	The ears are here (Dd34). It just looks like a face.
2. A wolf. That's it, I think.	E:	*(Repeats response)*
	S:	Then I thought of a wolf. It's a mean face.
	E:	What makes it look mean?
	S:	The way the eyes look, the shape of them.
Card II		
3. Face, a face that looks bloodied up, the nose and mouth.	E:	*(Repeats response)*
	S:	The eyes are here (D2), the cheekbone here (D1). It looks like blood running over it, not running, but all over the face and down here (D3). The nose is here (D4) and the mouth here (DS5).
4. It looks like a heart right there. That's all.	E:	*(Repeats response)*
	S:	It's right here. It looks like a heart, plus it's red.

(Continued)

TABLE 13.1
(*Continued*)

Responses	Inquiry
Card III	
5. It looks like a bow, a red bow, right there.	E: (*Repeats response*) S: Right there, it looks like a red bow.
6. A bell, a bell that goes ching, ching.	E: (*Repeats response*) S: The way it comes down like this (*points*), and the ching thing is here (Dd31).
	E: I'm not sure where you're seeing it. S: It's right around here somewhere (indefinite D1).
7. It looks like a dress too. That's all.	E: (*Repeats response*) S: All of it, except this (D2) looks like a dress, because of the bow.
	E: I'm not sure what makes it look like a dress. S: It's just the way it is.
	E: Can you help me a little more to see it? S: It's how they get a round dress, and that's it, and this looks like the place where ladies have their titties (Dd32).
Card IV	
8. It looks like a dude hung on a tree. He's got boots on.	E: (*Repeats response*) S: It looks like boots there (D6) and a tree here (D1), and it looks like a face up here (D3), and the body is on the tree.
	E: How do you mean, the body is on the tree? S: It's not really hung on it, but stuck to it.
9. It looks like two ducks on the side.	E: (*Repeats response*) S: It looks like a duck with a beak. I've seen black and white ducks before, and it looks like them, just the head of them.
10. It looks like a snake, a cobra, right there at the top. That's it.	E: (*Repeats response*) S: It looks like the head of a cobra, like a king cobra. It has these things on the side.
Card V	
11. Looks like a bat.	E: (*Repeats response*) S: The head, it's wings, and the legs are there.

(*Continued*)

TABLE 13.1
(*Continued*)

Responses	Inquiry
12. A butterfly.	E: (*Repeats response*) S: It looks just like a butterfly too, because of the wings and these antler things coming out.
13. And two alligators right there.	E: (*Repeats response*) S: It looks like mouths right there, and it looks like the mouth is open a bit. A long face, like an alligator, and bumps on it. Just the head.
14. And a bunny's head at the top, right here.	E: (*Repeats response*) S: Because of the ears, it just looks like the head and face, the shape of it.
Card VI 15. v^it looks like a tomahawk right there.	E: (*Repeats response*) S: One of the Indian things (*gestures with a chopping motion*). This part (D5) and this part (D3), but without all this (D4).
16. Looks like a dog's face right there, and over there too. I really don't see nothing in this one.	E: (*Repeats response*) S: The nose, a long face, and a little part like eyebrows, on both sides.
Card VII 17. Looks like a girl's face—two girls' faces—with their pony tails up. It looks like they have little bitty bodies and long neck, and they've got a tail. I don't really see nothing else in it.	E: (*Repeats response*) S: The pony tail is up, it's here (D5), and there's hair and eyes, a nose and a mouth, and long necks. E: And you see the bodies? S: Yes, that's their little bitty body with no arms on it (D3), and it looks like they've got a tail (Dd21). E: They've got a tail? S: Yes.
Card VIII 18. > Looks like a type of animal in the red.	E: (*Repeats response*) S: It looks like an animal, legs here, a tail, and a face here. There's a little bump for an ear and a dot for an eyeball.

(Continued)

349

TABLE 13.1
(*Continued*)

Responses	Inquiry
19. Like a dinosaur on top.	E: (*Repeats response*) S: It looks like a dinosaur body, with the head going down here. It's got that real long body and long neck.
20. In a way, it looks like a woman's lingerie thing right here. That's all I see.	E: (*Repeats response*) S: This looks like the stomach part (Dd2) and up here (D5) it looks like where it ties together. E: What suggests lingerie? S: The color, I guess.
Card IX 21. I can't see nothing in this one. (*pause*). Here it looks like Washington DC—the president's thing, right here, the White House.	E: (*Repeats response*) S: The way it goes up here, the cone thing (DdS32), and down there would be the square post. E: What suggests it? S: Just the cone part, with the structure down here.
Card X 22. Looks like those things that look like question marks—seahorses. And it looks like they're drinking something.	E: (*Repeats response*) D: The way they're curved, and this blue thing (D6) is going up to their mouth like they're drinking something, I don't know what it is.
23. Looks like two spiders here.	E: (*Repeats response*) S: One on each side, just look like spiders.
24. Up top it looks like two horses pulling something.	E: (*Repeats response*) S: Here they are (D8), and it looks like they have wire things or ropes connected to what they're pulling. E: What does it look like they're pulling? S: I don't know.
25. Looks like yellow birds.	E: (*Repeats response*) S: There are two yellow birds here (D2).
26. And two more yellow birds here.	E: (*Repeats response*) S: Yes, these (D15) are the other birds.
27. And a bunny rabbit, with something green coming out of his eyes. That's all.	E: (*Repeats response*) S: Right here, the nose and ears, and this green thing is something coming out of his eyes, something green and I don't know what it is.

TABLE 13.2
Sequence of Scores for Luis

Card No.		Loc.	No.	Determinant(s)	(2)	Content(s)	POP	Z	Special Scores
I	1	Wo	1	Fu		Ad		1.0	
	2	WSo	1	FMpo		Ad		3.5	
II	3	WS+	1	CF-		Hd,Bl		4.5	MOR
	4	Do	3	FC-		An			
III	5	Do	3	FCo		Cg			
	6	Ddo	99	F-		Id			DV
	7	D+	1	F-		Cg,Sx		4.0	
IV	8	W+	1	mpo		H,Bt,Cg	P	4.0	FAB2
	9	Do	4	FC'o	2	Ad			PER
	10	Ddo	30	Fu		Ad			
V	11	Wo	1	Fo		A	P	1.0	
	12	Wo	1	Fo		A	P	1.0	PSV,INC
	13	Do	10	FMpo	2	Ad			
	14	Do	6	Fo		Ad			
VI	15	Ddo	99	Fu		Ay			
	16	Ddo	24	Fu		Ad			
VII	17	Do	2	mpo	2	Hd	P		INC2
VIII	18	Do	1	Fo		A	P		
	19	Do	4	Fo		A			
	20	Do	5	FC-		Cg			
IX	21	DdSo	99	Fu		Sc			
X	22	D+	9	FMau	2	A		4.0	
	23	Do	1	Fo	2	A	P		
	24	D+	8	FMa-	2	A,Id		4.0	COP
	25	Do	2	FCu	2	A			
	26	Do	15	FCo	2	A			
	27	D+	10	mp.CFu		Ad,Id		4.0	FAB

self-perception, interpersonal perception, processing, mediation, and ideation.

Beginning with the control cluster variables, then, the first and very
important finding to emerge from this record concerns Luis' limited coping
capacities. Even though his *CDI* = 3 is in the normative range, his *EA* of just
4.5 indicates that he lacks sufficient adaptive resources to function capably
in ordinary kinds of everyday situations. This limited capability has nothing

TABLE 13.3
Structural Summary for Luis

Location Features	Determinants		Contents	S-Constellation
	Blends	Single		

Location Features	Blends	Single		Contents		S-Constellation
Zf = 10	m.CF	M = 0		H = 1, 0		NO . . FV+VF+V+FD>2
ZSum = 31.0		FM = 4		(H) = 0, 0		NO . . Col-Shd Bl>0
ZEst = 31.0		m = 2		Hd = 2, 0		YES . . Ego<.31,>.44
		FC = 5		(Hd) = 0, 0		NO . . MOR > 3
W = 6		CF = 1		Hx = 0, 0		NO . . Zd > +- 3.5
(Wv = 0)		C = 0		A = 9, 0		YES . . es > EA
D = 16		Cn = 0		(A) = 0, 0		NO . . CF+C > FC
Dd = 5		FC′ = 1		Ad = 8, 0		NO . . X+% < .70
S = 3		C′F = 0		(Ad) = 0, 0		NO . . S > 3
		C′ = 0		An = 1, 0		NO . . P < 3 or > 8
		FT = 0		Art = 0, 0		YES . . Pure H < 2
DQ		TF = 0		Ay = 1, 0		NO . . R < 17
. . . . . . (FQ-)		T = 0		Bl = 0, 1		4 . . . . . TOTAL
+ = 6 (3)		FV = 0		Bt = 0, 1		
o = 21 (3)		VF = 0		Cg = 3, 1		Special Scorings
v/+ = 0 (0)		V = 0		Cl = 0, 0		
v = 1 (0)		FY = 0		Ex = 0, 0		

				Lv1	Lv2
	YF = 0	Fd = 0, 0			
	Y = 0	Fi = 0, 0	DV = 1x1	0x2	
	Fr = 0	Ge = 0, 0	INC = 1x2	1x4	
	rF = 0	Hh = 0, 0	DR = 0x3	0x6	
	FD = 0	Ls = 0, 0	FAB = 1x4	1x7	
Form Quality	F = 13	Na = 0, 0	ALOG = 0x5		
		Sc = 1, 0	CON = 0x7		
		Sx = 0, 1	Raw Sum6 = 5		

	FQx	FQf	MQual	SQx	Contents	Special Scorings
					Xy = 0, 0	Wgtd Sum6 = 18
+	= 0	0	0	0	Id = 1, 2	
o	= 13	6	0	1		AB = 0 CP = 0
u	= 8	5	0	1		AG = 0 MOR = 1
-	= 6	2	0	1		CFB = 0 PER = 1
none	= 0	—	0	0	(2) = 8	COP = 1 PSV = 1

Ratios, Percentages, and Derivations

R = 27	L = 0.93		FC:CF+C = 5: 2	COP = 1 AG = 0
			Pure C = 0	Food = 0
EB = 0: 4.5	EA = 4.5	EBPer = 4.5	SumC′:WSumC = 1:4.5	Isolate/R = 0.04
eb = 7: 1	es = 8	D = -1	Afr = 0.59	H: (H)Hd(Hd) = 1: 2
	Adj es = 6	Adj D = 0	S = 3	(HHd) : (AAd) = 0: 0
			Blends:R = 1:27	H+A:Hd+Ad = 10:10
FM = 4 : C′ = 1 T = 0			CP = 0	
m = 3 : V = 0 Y = 0				

			P = 6	Zf = 10	3r+(2)/R = 0.30
a:p = 2: 5	Sum6 = 5		X+% = 0.48	Zd = +0.0	Fr+rF = 0
Ma:Mp = 0: 0	Lv2 = 2		F+% = 0.46	W:D:Dd = 6:16: 5	FD = 0
2AB+Art+Ay = 1	WSum6 = 18		X-% = 0.22	W:M = 6: 0	An+Xy = 1
M- = 0	Mnone = 0		S-% = 0.17	DQ+ = 6	MOR = 1
			Xu% = 0.30	DQv = 0	

SCZI = 3	DEPI = 4	CDI = 3	S-CON = 4	HVI = No	OBS = No

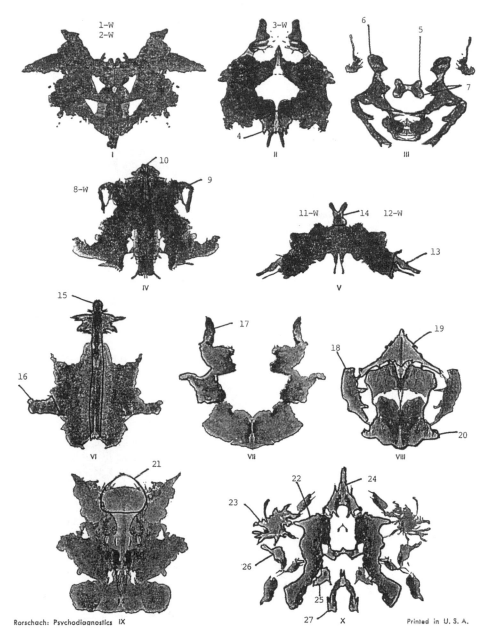

FIG. 13.1. Location choices of Luis.

to do with his being 15 years old and not yet a mature adult. The kinds of functioning capacities measured by *EA* are shared equally by nonpatient adolescents and adults, and the mean for *EA* happens to be exactly the same in the adult and 15-year-old nonpatient reference samples (8.82). What a low *EA* does suggest in a young person is a developmental arrest that, in the absence of a diagnosable developmental disorder, is usually attributable to a psychologically deprived childhood in which the young person lacked parental figures who could model and teach effective ways of coping.

Luis' *EA* identifies coping liabilities not only in its low total but also by virtue of its unbalanced composition. His 4.5 *EA* derives entirely from a *WSumC* of 4.5 in the absence of any *M*. This extremely unbalanced *EB* of 0:4.5 indicates good capacities to process affect but virtually no capacity to use ideation as a way of dealing with experience. In the case of Mr. Carter in chapter 11, an *EB* = 7:0.0 reflected his being an excessively contemplative and deliberative man whose lack of channels for experiencing or expressing feelings made him susceptible to being overwhelmed by affective experience. Luis' case shows the opposite extreme, a boy who is almost totally incapable of preceding action with thought, who makes decisions entirely on the basis of how he feels at the moment, and who rarely if ever contemplates alternative courses of action or solves problems by giving consideration to their origins or consequences. In short, he is limited by his coping inadequacies to being a reactive person who does what his environment demands rather than a proactive person who imposes himself on his environment.

Despite his limited and unbalanced coping capacities, Luis has managed to keep himself relatively free from subjectively felt distress. As can be seen from the *Adjes* = 6 and the fact that his *Lambda* = .93 approaches identifying him as a high *Lambda* person, he generally keeps the demands he experiences at a minimum by maintaining a narrow and uncomplicated frame of reference and keeping unpleasant thoughts and feelings out of his conscious awareness. These inferences from the Rorschach data would appear to fit closely the lifestyle he has chosen for himself, that is, as a fringe member of a delinquent gang who neither works nor attends school, hangs around all day, and does what he is told without bothering to think very much about it. As for the control cluster variables, his low *Adjes* combines with his low *EA* to produce an *AdjD* = 0, which indicates that he has for the most part and over time been functioning in a comfortable and self-satisfied albeit hunkered-down way without experiencing much tension, nervousness, or irritability and without being prone to impulsive losses of self-control.

Nevertheless, Luis appears at present to be experiencing some situational anxiety, particularly with respect to concerns about having no control over his fate, which is in the hands of the judicial system that will decide what happens to him (*m* = 3). As a consequence, his *es* = 8, although still below mean expectation in 15-year-olds, is too much for his *EA* of 4.5 to handle, and he has a $D = -1$. The $D < AdjD$ index of situation-related stress provided the entry variable for examining this record, as already noted, and it is no surprise that Luis gives evidence of experiencing a little more distress and uneasiness than he would if he were not in jail awaiting trial. What is surprising is that, given the gravity of his offense and the penalties he could be facing, Luis is not displaying more distress than he is. It may be that his above average *Lambda*, indicating as it does proclivities for dealing with experience in a detached and uninvolved manner, explains in part why he is not more overtly distressed in response to his circumstances.

Affective Issues

Luis' previously mentioned capacities for adaptive modulation of affect constitute a personality asset and may account for his acceptance among the group of older boys, who apparently liked and looked after him without ever abusing him. More specifically in terms of the data, he appears capable of modulating affect sufficiently, recognizing and expressing emotions without constriction, and feeling comfortable in emotionally arousing situations without needing to withdraw from them (*Afr* = .59; *SumC':WSumC* = 1:4.5). In addition, there is little indication in the data that he has difficulties modulating affect pleasurably. There is no *ColShd Bld* in the record, the $C' = 1$ is in the normative range, and the *SumShd* = 1 is below average and probably speaks to his working successfully to keep painful affect out of his awareness. He does show a slightly elevated $S = 3$, indicating more than a usual amount of underlying anger and resentment, but he otherwise appears quite at peace with himself emotionally and fully capable of enjoying his life.

As a further adaptive capacity of note, Luis seems beyond his years in the maturity with which he manages his feelings. The *FC:CF + C* ratio of 5:2 indicates that he can be either relatively restrained and moderate in expressing affect or relatively spontaneous and intense, with an adultlike preference for relatively reserved emotionality. At the same time, his giving just one Blend response, considered together with his *Lambda* = .93, suggests that he generally keeps his emotional life simple and uncomplicated and would rather keep detached from situations than become deeply involved in them.

Personal and Interpersonal Issues

In contrast to his comfortable and sufficient modulation of his affective experience, Luis gives evidence of numerous maladaptive attitudes toward himself and his interpersonal world. He appears to compare himself unfavorably to other people and to have long-standing problems maintaining adequate self-esteem ($3r + (2)/R = .30$); he shows little capacity to step back and examine himself and his behavior in an introspective manner ($FD = 0$); and he has not yet been able to establish a sense of his own identity on the basis of identifications with real people in his life ($H = 1$). The responses most notable for their projected elements, which include one *MOR* and six minus forms, indicate in addition that his calm exterior conceals troubling concerns about the world being a dangerous place and about becoming involved with girls. Because almost all of his other responses involve either movement, form distortion, cognitive slippage, or some other embellishment, it is informative in this case to examine the entire sequence of his first eight responses.

On Card I Luis signs in with "a bunny rabbit," which conveys a sense of childish, playful innocence far removed from what one might expect to find in an accused gang murderer. This theme suggestive of immaturity and a self-image of being small, weak, and helpless reappears in "a bunny's head" on Response 14 and in another "bunny rabbit" on Response 27, which is his sign-out response. Notice that by this time, perhaps as a consequence of the distressing impact of the intervening imagery, this last bunny rabbit is flawed by the *FABCOM* embellishment of "something green coming out of his eyes."

The second response on Card I is a face of a wolf that is "mean" because of "the way the eyes look." This frightening image of looking into the face of a mean-looking wolf sets the stage for Card II, in which, confronted with the implications of anger, aggression, and harm often associated with the bright red color on the blot, he temporarily loses his hold on reality and gives two of his six minus form responses.

The first of these two minuses, in Response 3, is perhaps the most dramatic and revealing percept in the record: a morbid *CF-* of "a face that looks bloodied up" and that "has blood running over it." This response quite likely signifies what in his mind can happen to you if you antagonize the wrong people, which could be a persistent concern molded by his years on the street and recently exacerbated by seeing two people murdered in front of his eyes. The "heart" that follows in Response 4 is not elaborated in any thematically significant way, and its minus form quality, as well as his failure to report the Popular on this card, probably constitutes a carryover from the distress caused by the stimulus qualities of Card II and his initial association to it in Response 3.

On Card III he again misses the Popular, but he shows some recovery in Response 5 with an ordinary form *FC* of "a red bow." This recovery is short-lived, however, and he follows with two seemingly bland but nevertheless minus Responses on 5 and 6, a "bell" and a "dress." Note, however, that his elaboration of this dress on inquiry concludes with his pointing out "the place where ladies have their titties." Like the bunny rabbits, this reference to "ladies" and their "titties" reflects neither the thought content nor the language usage expected in an inner-city gang delinquent. Beyond suggesting immaturity in general, this response has the specific ring of latency-age rather than typically adolescent ways of fantasizing and talking about the opposite sex.

These themes of fearfulness and psychosexual immaturity are echoed in subsequent responses. On Card VII in Response 17 he gives the ordinary form Popular of "girls' faces," but he describes them as having "little bitty bodies" and adds the Level 2 *INCOM* of their looking "like they've got a tail." What kinds of girls are these, with little bitty bodies and tails? The childish language aside, they are not likely to be pubescent girls with developing figures, and, with tails attributed to them in this illogical fashion, they could have some phallic properties that spare Luis from contemplating how females actually look below the waist. In similar fashion, his percept in Response 20 on Card VIII of "a woman's lingerie thing" resembles a latency age rather than adolescent form of expression. These speculative hypotheses, although not yet documented as fact, suggest a scenario in which Luis interacts with the older members of his group not as a 15-year-old boy mature beyond his years, but rather as a teenage child who has not yet begun to grapple with the psychosexual developmental tasks of middle adolescence.

As for his fearfulness, Luis reports two other suggestive images. Following the first seven responses, which as noted include four minus percepts apparently attributable to arousal of concerns about being harmed, he recoups in part with an ordinary form Popular in Response 8 on Card IV. However, this response turns into a Level 2 *FABCOM* involving "a dude" initially seen as "hung on a tree" and later described as "not really hung on it, but stuck to it." Like getting your face bloodied up, being hung on a tree depicts something very bad, even fatal, that can happen to you. Changing being "hung" to being "stuck" to the tree, which is a strained and illogical way of trying to defend against contemplating the fatal consequences of the former, still leaves the "dude" (presumably a self-image) in a helpless position. The other image suggestive of seeing the world as a dangerous place appears in Response 13 on Card V, which involves "alligators" whose "mouth is open a bit."

Some additional structural data help to round out the Rorschach picture of Luis' interpersonal orientation. He does not give any indication of being isolated from people who play an important part in his life (*ISOL* = .04). At the same time, however, he shows little interest in people, little capacity to form close bonds of attachment to others, and little inclination to anticipate collaborative and mutually supportive interpersonal relationships (*SumH* = 3; *T* = 0; *COP* = 1). What Luis does display is a proclivity for passivity and subservience in his interpersonal relationships. His *a:p* of 2:5 suggests that he is by nature a person who defers to others, would much rather follow than lead, and prefers to let decisions, initiatives, and responsibility rest in other people's hands. This well-defined and probably stable feature of his personality style probably helps further to explain how he could be content as an errand boy and hanger-on in the group to which he belonged and, as a result of doing what he was told, has become an accessory to murder.

Cognitive Issues

With respect to how he attends to his experience, Luis' Rorschach data illustrate the maladaptive implications of a high *Lambda* occurring in a record of adequate length. As in the case of Deborah in chapter 11, his *Lambda* = .93 does not quite meet the criterion of *Lambda* > .99 for identifying a high *Lambda* person, but it is still high enough to identify a narrow frame of reference and an oversimplified approach to dealing with life situations. As further evidence of Luis' characteristic and self-imposed restriction on his focus attention, note that in the free association he limits his 27 responses to brief statements; on inquiry he responds tersely, almost grudgingly, and makes the examiner's task difficult; and he explicitly controls how much he will report by saying "That's it" or "That's all" after his final response on six cards (I, II, III, IV, VIII, and X) and by saying that he sees "nothing else" on two other cards (VI and VII).

Whereas high *Lambda* in a brief record ($R < 20$) suggests guardedness, as discussed in chapter 5 and illustrated in the case of Ms. Anderson in chapter 10, high *Lambda* in a record of at least average length indicates an action-oriented inclination to plow straight ahead in problem situations, as if with blinders on, looking neither left nor right and ignoring subtle nuances of what might be appropriate or acceptable behavior in these situations. Not surprisingly, then, people who give a substantial *Lambda* in the context of a full-length record are at risk for behaving without adequate circumspection in ways that break the rules, are offensive to others, and get them in trouble—all of which characterize the criminal acts with which Luis is charged.

Within his narrow frame of reference, Luis is capable of organizing information efficiently ($Zd = 0.0$), and his use of 16 D locations and articulation of 6 Popular responses indicates that he is capable of paying adequate attention to conventional aspects of reality. Nevertheless, he is far from conventional in the impressions he forms of what he pays attention to. His $X + \% = .48$ indicates that more than half of the time he fails to see things the way most people do. Instead, he interprets events either unrealistically or idiosyncratically. His $X - \% = .22$ is not in the psychotic range ($X - \% > .29$) but nevertheless indicates that he is frequently likely to show poor judgment. His $Xu\% = .30$ indicates that he often forms unique impressions of what is going on around him and is consequently likely to defy conventionality in what he chooses to think and do.

With further respect to his reality testing, however, it is significant that all six of Luis' minus form responses occur on colored cards (II, III, VIII, and X), and four of them occur within a span of five responses to Cards II and III. In light of the significance already attributed to his responses on these cards, it seems reasonable to infer that his difficulties in perceiving situations accurately and exercising good judgment are not as much pervasive as they are specifically related to aroused concerns about being around or victimized by angry and aggressive actions by others.

In similar fashion, Luis' ideational variables indicate that he is not likely to display illogical or incoherent thinking any more frequently than might be normal for a 15-year-old ($Sum6 = 5$), but that he is capable of fairly seriously disordered thinking on those occasions when cognitive slippage occurs ($WSum6 = 18$). However, the context in which his two most serious lapses in logic appear suggests a specific dynamically determined breakdown rather than random or pervasively disordered thinking. One of these include the Level 2 *FABCOM* in Response 8 on Card IV, in which he appeared to be struggling to escape the anxiety and fearfulness aroused by Cards II and III and to be viewing himself as someone who could be "hung" or "stuck." The other one is the Level 2 *INCOM* in Response 17 on Card VII, in which it seems likely that his percept of girls "with tails" was heavily influenced by concerns related to his psychosexual maturation. His giving just five Critical Special Scores and showing these mitigating contextual factors in the two coded as Level 2 make it unlikely that Luis is thought disordered or has any condition in which disordered thinking is a defining characteristic.

Three other features of Luis' thinking should be noted. As already mentioned, his pervasively extratensive *EB* of 0:4 indicates that he has extremely limited capacity to use ideation effectively in solving problems or making decisions. Second, his *a:p* ratio of 2:5 suggests not only the behavioral passivity previously mentioned but also some inflexibility in the beliefs he holds and the behavior patterns he prefers. Third, his $FM + m = 7$ is elevated beyond the normal range and suggests that he may be maladaptively preoccupied with worries and concerns (i.e., intrusive ideation) and as a result may be experiencing difficulties in concentration.

In summary, then, Luis is a boy in jail charged with a serious crime and understandably worried about what will happen to him. His predicament and the behavior that led to it, as well as his 2 years on the street as a member of a delinquent gang of older youth, are likely to have emerged as a consequence of his being an insecure and unattached boy, an action-oriented boy with little capacity to think about what he does before doing it, a passive boy accustomed to and comfortable in doing what others would have him do, and a boy whose fears of being harmed can interfere with his reasoning and reality capacities and result in his having occasional but serious lapses in judgment and good sense.

Applying legal criteria to the referral question in Luis' case, none of these Rorschach findings provide a basis for considering him presently insane or as possibly having been so at the time of his offense. Similarly, although competency to stand trial depends on whether defendants can understand the charges against them and participate effectively in their own defense and hence cannot be directly measured by psychological tests, the Rorschach findings do not identify any reasons to expect that Luis would be incapable in either respect.

CASE 8: CONCENTRATION DIFFICULTY IN AN ACADEMICALLY DYSFUNCTIONAL DENTAL STUDENT

Mr. Hart is a 23-year-old Caucasian dental student who recently completed the second year of his program and was suspended for poor grades, pending the outcome of an evaluation for learning disability. He had received this dispensation after reporting to his dean that difficulty concentrating and completing written examinations, rather than an inadequate grasp of the material, were responsible for his academic failure. When interviewed, Mr. Hart stated that he had always been a highly active person and since childhood could never sit still in front of a television screen, unless he was playing a video game. He stated further that his preference ran to active sports in which "I push myself to the limit," especially one-person, high-excitement sports like snowboarding and surfing. Team sports never appealed to him, he said, because "there's too much sitting and waiting."

The presenting school achievement problems and the developmental suggestions of an overactive, restless, stimulus-seeking temperament initially suggested the possibility of long-standing and previously undiagnosed attention deficit hyperactivity disorder with an adult manifestation in impaired ability to concentrate and take written examinations at the level required in a professional degree program. However, thorough examination of Mr. Hart's cognitive and intellectual functioning identified high average intelligence (a Full Scale WAIS–R IQ of 118) without any indications of neuropsychological dysfunction, impaired learning capacities, or deficit in basic academic skills. Hence it fell to the RIM to identify whether any features of his personality functioning could account at least in part for his inability to perform adequately in dental school. Mr. Hart's Rorschach protocol follows in Tables 13.4, 13.5, and 13.6 and Fig. 13.2.

TABLE 13.4
Rorschach Protocol of Mr. Hart

Responses	*Inquiry*
Card I	
1. It looks like a viking face mask, with places for the eyes here.	E: (*Repeats response*) S: Here's where the eyes would look through (DdS30), and the place to breathe is here (DdS29). The horns are up here (D1), and it's meant to scare the opponent. This part (D3) would be the muzzle of the face. E: The muzzle? S: Yes.
2. It also looks like a skull to me.	E: (*Repeats response*) S: Like the dried out skulls in the desert, a picture of an animal that's been eaten. E: What reminds you of a dried out skull? S: The bony structures.
3. It also reminds me of a cross-section through the brain. It looks like gray matter in the middle with the gray matter around it, like we saw in anatomy.	E: (*Repeats response*) S: We did this in dental school. The spinal tracts are here, and it's symmetrical. E: What made it look like gray matter? S: The gray centered in the middle, with the white parts in the surrounding areas.
4. It also looks like an angel diving into water, with the water splashing into the sides.	E: (*Repeats response*) S: The body, the arms spread out and the wings here (D7), as she dives in, and this would be the splash off to the sides.
Card II	
5. This one also reminds me of a cross-section through the spinal cord, with the pathways here.	E: (*Repeats response*) S: It just looks like it, the symmetry, with the cord in the center.
6. (*pause*) It looks like a skinned animal laid out flat on the carpet, with part of the body missing. I don't see the significance of the red—I can't find anything for it.	E: (*Repeats response*) S: It's skinned, like a raccoon—spread out—they made a carpet out of it, but the middle part is missing. E: What makes it look like an animal skin? S: The symmetry, and the way it's laid out flat. The head would be up here, and the snout is here (D4), with appendages on either side.

(Continued)

TABLE 13.4
(Continued)

Responses	Inquiry
	E: You mentioned the significance of the red?
	S: I couldn't make much of it, except the bottom red (D3) now looks like a butterfly.

Card III

7. This first strikes me as a happy face, a clown figure.

E: (*Repeats response*)
S: The eyes are here (Dd32), the nose area (S), bangs around the face (D2), the mouth (D7), and a smile here (DdS23), the grimacing of the face.

E: What suggests a clown?
S: My parents used to have a painting that was kind of similar, the color scheme, the bright reds. It was almost creepy, and this reminds me of it.

E: The color scheme?
S: Just the bright reds contrasted against the gray and black.

E: And it was almost creepy?
S: As a child, the big huge face of the clown was almost scary looking.

8. The silhouette of a frog, or maybe even a crab.

E: (*Repeats response*)
S: Like the way a frog looks, the legs, the body, and the head region, the basic shape of it.

E: You said maybe even a crab.
S: The same thing, but more like a frog.

9. It also reminds me of the red nucleus of the brain stem, these two regions at the bottom.

E: (*Repeats response*)
S: A cross-section through the brain, again.

10. Taking it all together, maybe it looks like a red butterfly, flying between two people sitting by a lake, out in nature. That's it.

E: (*Repeats response*)
S: The butterfly is here (D3), and one person is sitting on one side, with the head, leg, body and arm here, and one on the other, looking at each other—a male and a female.

E: A male and a female?
S: That's the way I'd like to picture the scenario, I guess.

(Continued)

TABLE 13.4
(Continued)

Responses	Inquiry
	E: And the lake?
	S: The couple could be on a picnic. I don't see a lake, but they could be beside one.

Card IV

11. Reminds me of Godzilla, like looking up at him from an ant's perspective.	E: *(Repeats response)*
	S: Looking up at him, with his tail coming down from behind. The legs are coming at you. It's so tall that the arms are very small.
12. Looks like a caterpillar coming out from beneath some leaves or branches.	E: *(Repeats response)*
	S: A close-up view, with the caterpillar here (D1) emerging.
	E: And there are leaves or branches?
	S: It could be dirt or branches.
	E: What makes it look like that?
	S: I'm just using my imagination, just trying to put the caterpillar in some situation.
13. > It also looks like a reflection of a swan sitting on the water, with clouds in the background, thunder clouds, cumulo-limbus or whatever. That's it.	E: *(Repeats response)*
	S: The swan silhouette is here (D4), and the reflection is in the lake on the other side.
	E: What suggests thunder clouds?
	S: They look like storm clouds, dark, thick, and vertically positioned.

Card V

14. This one reminds me of a bat, with its wings open. That's about it.	E: *(Repeats response)*
	S: Seen from above, like a bat flying, the tail, the wings, and the head.

Card VI

15. < Looks like a mystical dragon to me.	E: *(Repeats response)*
	S: Flying this way. This is the wing coming off to the side, and the head is here.
16. Also looks like American Indian art, something you'd see on terrycloth, some kind of design. That's all.	E: *(Repeats response)*
	S: The pattern reminds me of feathers.
	E: How does it look like feathers?
	S: Just multiple feathers in a pattern, with multiple lengths.

(Continued)

TABLE 13.4
(*Continued*)

Responses	*Inquiry*
Card VII	
17. Looks like a pig's face.	E: (*Repeats response*) S: A cartoon character, a pig's face looking at you. The eyes are here (D2), the ears up here (D5), the snout (DS10), and the mouth part (D4).
18. I also see like—two gargoyles, on either side, looking in opposite directions.	E: (*Repeats response*) S: It's real clear. I see the teeth, the nose, horns sticking out here (Dd21). They're looking down, like gargoyles you'd see on top of a building.
19. And two rabbits standing up looking in opposite directions also.	E: (*Repeats response*) S: The feet, the tail, the body, the ears sticking up here, on both sides.
Card VIII	
20. A very pretty color scheme. It could be a coat-of-arms design.	E: (*Repeats response*) S: It just reminds me of a coat-of-arms. They have a lot of different colors like this, and a symmetrical pattern.
21. Looks like two lions crawling up on either side of the design.	E: (*Repeats response*) S: Four legs, the head, walking up on either side.
22. I can also see a face in the bottom side of the picture. It looks like a startled face, startled appearing.	E: (*Repeats response*) S: The eyes (Dd33), the mouth here, the nose here—the face has a shocked-like expression, the way the mouth is drawn in.
23. I can see a crown above the face. That's about it.	E: (*Repeats response*) S: The crown is on top of the head (D4 & D5). E: How does it look like a crown? S: It comes to a point at the top, and it's colorful, and it rests on the head.
Card IX	
24. It reminds me of the monster from "Aliens."	E: (*Repeats response*) S: The mouth, the eyes, the nose here in the center (DS8), and the horns up here (D3).
25. It also reminds me of a saggital section through a human head, maybe a frontal view.	E: (*Repeats response*) S: The frontal section through a skull, the nasal cavity, the sinuses, and the orbits.

(Continued)

TABLE 13.4
(Continued)

Responses	Inquiry
Card X	
26. > Happy looking colors. It looks cheerful, like springtime.	E: *(Repeats response)* S: Basically, all of the colors remind me of spring, the yellow, the green, the pink— and the blue would be symbolic of water.
27. It looks like a yellow canary on a branch.	E: *(Repeats response)* S: Two yellow canaries (D15), and the branch is here (D7).
28. It looks like the Eiffel tower on top. *(puts card down)*	E: *(Repeats response)* S: This part on top just looks like the Eiffel tower.

Stress Management Issues

Mr. Hart's Structural Summary indicates a valid record of 28 responses with an *S-CON* = 7 and a first positive key variable of $D < AdjD$. As noted in discussing the cases of Mr. Baker in chapter 10 and Ms. Fisher in chapter 12, an *S-CON* of 7 always bears examination to determine if it is a "high 7," that is, a value close enough to being an *S-CON* = 8 to raise concern about suicidal potential. Note on the Structural Summary that, of the five *S-CON* criteria that are negative, three are within a single point of being positive. Specifically, if he had either one more *FD*, one more *S*, or one fewer *P* in his record, he would have an *S-CON* of 8. This finding qualifies Mr. Hart as a "high 7" on the *S-CON*, and it provides sufficient basis for keeping the possibility of some self-harmful tendencies in mind as the rest of the data are being formulated. Such concerns are warranted further by the fact that his *DEPI* = 5, although not meeting the criterion of *DEPI* > 5 for constituting a positive key variable, is high enough to identify probable depressive features in his present functioning.

As for the sequence in which the clusters of variables should be searched in Mr. Hart's case, the $D < AdjD$ calls for beginning with the control cluster, as it did in the previous case of Luis. Unlike Luis, however, Mr. Hart's Rorschach data do not move from the $D < AdjD$ key variable down to *EB* style before further elevations appear to indicate substantial adjustment difficulty in addition to the situational distress. Mr. Hart has a Reflection in his record, which means that the sequence for searching the variable clusters, as indicated in Table 3.2, will differ from the sequence followed for Luis

TABLE 13.5
Sequence of Scores for Mr. Hart

Card No.		Loc.	No.	Determinant(s)	(2)	Content(s)	POP	Z	Special Scores
I	1	Wso	1	Fo		(Hd),Ay		3.5	DV
	2	Wo	1	Fo		An		1.0	MOR
	3	Wo	1	FC'u		An		1.0	PER
	4	W+	1	Ma.mpo		(H),Na		4.0	
II	5	DSo	6	Fu		An		4.5	
	6	Do	6	mpu		Ad			MOR
III	7	Wo	1	Mp.CF.C'F-		(Hd),Art		5.5	DV,PER
	8	Do	1	F-		A			
	9	Do	2	Fu		An			
	10	D+	1	Mp.mao	2	H,A	P	4.0	DR
IV	11	Wo	1	FDo		(A)		2.0	
	12	W+	1	FMpo		A,Bt		4.0	
	13	W+	1	FMp.Fr.C'F.FDo		A,Na,Cl		4.0	DV
V	14	Wo	1	FMao		A	P	1.0	
VI	15	Wo	1	FMau		(A)		2.5	
	16	Do	3	Fu		Art			
VII	17	WSo	1	FMp-		(Ad)		4.0	
	18	Do	3	Fu	2	(Hd),Art			
	19	Ddo	99	FMpu	2	A			
VIII	20	Wo	1	CFo		Art		4.5	
	21	Do	1	FMpo	2	A	P		
	22	Do	2	Mp-		Hd,Hx			
	23	Do	8	FCu		Id			
IX	24	Wo	1	Fu		(Ad)		5.5	
	25	Wo	1	F-		An		5.5	
X	26	Wv	1	C		Na			AB
	27	D+	15	FCo		A,Bt		4.0	
	28	Do	11	Fo		Sc			

and will consist of controls, self-perception, interpersonal perception, affect, processing, mediation, and ideation.

With respect to Mr. Hart's ability to manage stress, he gives evidence of an average level of psychological resources for meeting demands of living, and he does not display any serious deficits in coping capacity ($EA = 8.5$; $CDI = 3$). On the other hand, he appears to have some difficulty maintaining

TABLE 13.6
Structural Summary for Mr. Hart

Location Features	Determinants Blends	Single		Contents		S-Constellation
Zf = 17	M.m	M	= 1	H	= 1, 0	NO .. FV+VF+V+FD>2
ZSum = 60.5	M.CF.C'F	FM	= 6	(H)	= 1, 0	YES .. Col-Shd Bl>0
ZEst = 56.0	M.m	m	= 1	Hd	= 1, 0	YES .. Ego<.31,>.44
	FM.Fr.C'F.FD	FC	= 2	(Hd)	= 3, 0	NO .. MOR > 3
W = 15		CF	= 1	Hx	= 0, 1	YES .. Zd > +- 3.5
(Wv = 1)		C	= 1	A	= 7, 1	YES .. es > EA
D = 12		Cn	= 0	(A)	= 2, 0	YES .. CF+C > FC
Dd = 1		FC'	= 1	Ad	= 1, 0	YES .. X+% < .70
S = 3		C'F	= 0	(Ad)	= 2, 0	NO .. S > 3
		C'	= 0	An	= 5, 0	NO .. P < 3 or > 8
		FT	= 0	Art	= 2, 2	YES .. Pure H < 2
DQ		TF	= 0	Ay	= 0, 1	NO .. R < 17
...... (FQ-)		T	= 0	Bl	= 0, 0	7 ..... TOTAL
+ = 5 (0)		FV	= 0	Bt	= 0, 2	
o = 22 (5)		VF	= 0	Cg	= 0, 0	**Special Scorings**
v/+ = 0 (0)		V	= 0	Cl	= 0, 1	
v = 1 (0)		FY	= 0	Ex	= 0, 0	Lv1 Lv2
		YF	= 0	Fd	= 0, 0	DV = 3x1 0x2
		Y	= 0	Fi	= 0, 0	INC = 0x2 0x4
		Fr	= 0	Ge	= 0, 0	DR = 1x3 0x6
		rF	= 0	Hh	= 0, 0	FAB = 0x4 0x7
		FD	= 1	Ls	= 0, 0	ALOG = 0x5
Form Quality		F	= 10	Na	= 1, 2	CON = 0x7
				Sc	= 1, 0	Raw Sum6 = 4
FQx FQf MQual SQx				Sx	= 0, 0	Wgtd Sum6 = 6
+ = 0 0 0 0				Xy	= 0, 0	
o = 12 3 2 1				Id	= 1, 0	AB = 1 CP = 0
u = 10 5 0 1						AG = 0 MOR = 2
- = 5 2 2 1						CFB = 0 PER = 2
none = 1 — 0 0		(2) = 4				COP = 0 PSV = 0

Ratios, Percentages, and Derivations

R = 28	L = 0.56	FC:CF+C = 2: 3	COP = 0 AG = 0
		Pure C = 2	Food = 0
EB = 4: 4.5 EA = 8.5 EBPer = N/A		SumC':WSumC = 3:4.5	Isolate/R = 0.36
eb = 10: 3 es = 13 D = -1		Afr = 0.47	H: (H)Hd(Hd) = 1: 5
Adj es = 11 Adj D = 0		S = 3	(HHd) : (AAd) = 4: 4
		Blends:R = 4:28	H+A:Hd+Ad = 12: 7
FM = 7 : C' = 3 T = 0		CP = 0	
m = 3 : V = 0 Y = 0			

		P = 3	Zf = 17	3r+(2)/R = 0.25
a:p = 4:10	Sum6 = 4	X+% = 0.43	Zd = +4.5	Fr+rF = 1
Ma:Mp = 1: 3	Lv2 = 0	F+% = 0.30	W:D:Dd = 15:12: 1	FD = 2
2AB+Art+Ay = 7	WSum6 = 6	X-% = 0.18	W:M = 15: 4	An+Xy = 5
M- = 2	Mnone = 0	S-% = 0.20	DQ+ = 5	MOR = 2
		Xu% = 0.36	DQv = 1	

SCZI = 2	DEPI = 5*	CDI = 3	S-CON = 7	HVI = Yes	OBS = No

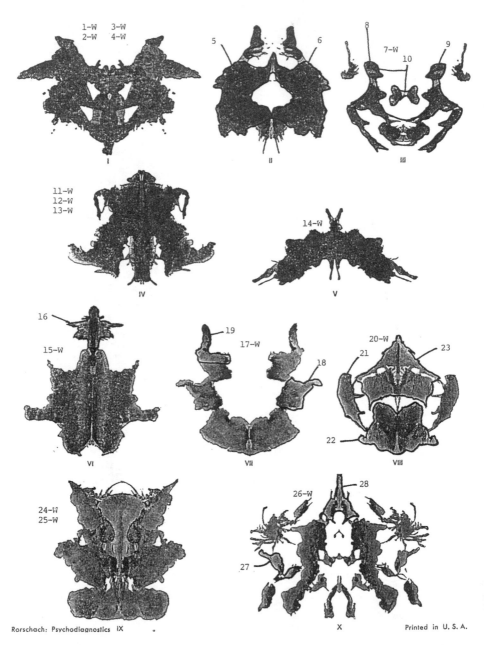

FIG. 13.2. Location choices of Mr. Hart.

consistency in how he chooses to deal with his experience. His $EB = 4{:}4.5$ indicates that he is adaptively capable of making decisions and solving problems in either an ideational ($M = 4$) or expressive ($WSumC = 4.5$) manner, but that he is maladaptively incapable of settling on a clear preference for conducting himself primarily in one way or another. As an ambitent, then, he is more likely than most people to be inconsistent and unpredictable in his behavior, to be perceived by others as a highly changeable person, and to be uncertain himself of how he can expect himself to think, feel, and act from one situation or moment in time to another.

As for his situational anxiety, the data indicate that Mr. Hart is presently a little anxious, tense, and irritable and perhaps a bit more likely than most people to have difficulty tolerating frustration and exercising self-control ($D = -1$). The mildness of these manifestations of subjectively felt distress reflect the fact that the stresses he is experiencing exceed his coping capacities only slightly, and the excess stress is attributable in part to elevated concerns about being presently involved in circumstances over which he has little control and in which his destiny is out of his hands ($m = 3$). Were it not for this situationally related anxiety, he would be in a comfortable state of psychological equilibrium, not necessarily without problems and concerns, but with sufficient adaptive capacity to avoid becoming unduly upset by them ($AdjD = 0$). As noted in discussing the preceding case of Luis, an elevation in m leading to $D < AdjD$ occurs commonly in people who are being evaluated to provide information that will be used in making decisions about what will happen to them, whether they are in jail awaiting trial or have been suspended from school and are hoping for readmission.

Personal and Interpersonal Issues

The data in Mr. Hart's self-perception cluster of variables identify, first of all, some narcissistic features by which he is apparently trying to compensate for difficulties he has in maintaining adequate self-esteem. On the one hand, his $Fr + rF = 1$ rarely occurs in nonpatient adults (only 7% of whom show $Fr + rF > 0$) and suggests some tendencies to admire himself excessively and externalize responsibility for his personal difficulties, rather than to admit to shortcomings or limitations on his part. On the other hand, he does not display the self-centeredness that typically characterizes narcissistic people and is manifest on the RIM in an elevated Egocentricity Index. Instead, his $3r + (2)/R$ of .25 falls well below the normal range, receives a point on *DEPI*, and indicates that he tends to compare himself unfavorably to other people and view them as being more capable and personally attractive.

As discussed in chapter 5, this pairing of Reflections with a low Egocentricity Index suggests long-standing low self-esteem that Mr. Hart defends against by compensatory efforts to convince himself and others of what a fine person he is, much in the Adlerian sense of developing a "superiority complex" as a way of avoiding the distressing awareness of feeling inferior. Put in other terms, subjects with Reflections in their Rorschach record but no elevation in Egocentricity are unlikely to be primarily narcissistic people. Instead, such individuals are likely to be showing secondary or compensatory narcissistic features that represent strained defensiveness rather than relaxed and natural self-assurance and a trait-based inflation of self-esteem.

Despite the narcissistic defensiveness apparently generated by his basically low self-esteem, Mr. Hart does not display any indication of self-critical attitudes or negative views of his body and its functioning ($V = 0$; $MOR = 2$), and he also shows normative capacities to examine himself in an introspective manner ($FD = 2$). However, paralleling the inconsistent coping style he demonstrates in his ambitent EB, he does not appear to have been successful to this point in his life of forming a stable sense of his own identity. The $H:(H)Hd(Hd) = 1{:}5$ indicates that he has not been able to form identifications with real people in his life as a basis for deriving his own sense of the kind of person he is, but has instead identified mainly with imaginary figures—that is, with people who have not in actuality participated in his life—or with partial rather than complete objects.

Turning to further details of Mr. Hart's self-image as suggested in his thematic imagery, the Sequence of Scores identifies two responses that are particularly likely to contain revealing content. On the basis of their involving both human movement and minus form quality, and thereby constituting what were identified in chapter 4 as two-bagger responses in terms of their projected elements, these two critical responses are the two $M-$ in the record, Response 7 on Card III and Response 22 on Card VIII.

In delivering Response 7 as his initial response to Card III, Mr. Hart says, "This first strikes me as a happy face, a clown figure." From this free association statement through the inquiry, this Response 7 is a vivid study in contrasts that identifies several respects in which this young man's life is confused and uncertain. To begin with, seeing a "happy" figure suggests a sense of well-being and a positive outlook on life, but seeing only the "face" rather than the entire figure suggests as well some difficulties in identifying and feeling comfortable with a whole person, rather than with just part of what a person is like.

Moreover, this is not even a real person, but instead an imaginary or "pretend" figure, a clown, and the dual image of "clown" as both an entertaining figure to be applauded and a foolish figure to be laughed at has been noted several times in previous chapters. As always in such responses, especially when their minus form quality indicates that the themes they contain are especially important and probably quite distressing to the individual, considerable weight should be given to their implications for how subjects view themselves. In this instance, then, is the "clown" with whom this man identifies an entertainer, a buffoon, or a little of both?

In the inquiry, Mr. Hart complicates this percept further by referring to "a smile here, the grimacing of the face." In these few words the pleasant image of a smiling happy face turns into something much different, a grimacing face. He then goes on to recall a painting "my parents used to have" that resembled his percept and that was "almost creepy" and "almost scary looking." He notes additionally the contrast between the red and the gray-black colors in this image, thereby giving a *CF.CF'* blend that indicates ambivalent affect, suggests anhedonia, and receives a point on the *DEPI* index. Thus, this dramatic and personally meaningful *M-* response is a mixture of positive and negative self-images and euphoric and dysphoric affect.

On Response 8, Mr. Hart attempts to gain some distance from the distress apparent in Response 7 by opting for a narrowly focused pure *F* response involving an animal seen only in bare outline, the "silhouette of a frog." As a minus response signifying a breakdown in reality testing, however, Response 8 reflects the continuing maladaptive impact of the issues raised in his mind by Response 7. On Response 9, he is able to recover more adequately by drawing on his studies of head and neck anatomy to produce an unusual but at least accurately perceived form of a brain stem section. A full restitution of his adaptive capacity is achieved in Response 10, in which he gives a good form *M* response consisting of the Card III Popular human figures. In addition to being structurally sound, this Response 10 recoups positively toned imagery in the form of a male and female who "could be on a picnic." The importance to him of being able to turn his fantasy to this pleasant impression is apparent in his saying, "That's the way I'd like to picture the scene, I guess." Perhaps this scene also represents a kind of idyllic male–female relationship he would like to capture in his real-world life.

Pursuing the self-perception implications of the Card III sequence of responses, note that Mr. Hart continues to recover in Card IV with a series of six accurately perceived responses (four ordinary and two unusuals) that begin with Response 11 on Card IV and conclude with Response 16 on Card VI. However, the structurally adequate percept of "Godzilla" on Response 11 is seen from "an ant's perspective." Is Mr. Hart's identification with the powerful Godzilla portrayed in this response, or is it with the perspective of the insignificant ant looking up at Godzilla? The eight animal figures he sees in the blots provides a tentative answer to this question. These comprise the previously noted frog on Response 8, a butterfly on 10, a caterpillar on 12, swans on 13, a bat on 14, rabbits on 19, lions on 21, and a canary on 27. Taken together, these animal contents suggest more than an ordinary focus on small and powerless animals, which may well have a bearing on how he views himself and converge with the other Rorschach indications that he has a low opinion of himself.

As for the interpersonal implications of the Card III sequence, the next breakdown in reality testing following this card occurs in Response 17, leading off Card VII. On this card, which is usually seen as depicting women or children, he misses the Popular and begins with a minus form "pig's face." The other two responses on this card are unusual form "gargoyles" and "rabbits," both of which are unremarkable except for the fact that they are both "looking in opposite directions." Could Mr. Hart in fact have some difficulties relating comfortably to women, and could his fantasies about heterosexual encounters range in tone from the idyllic picture of sharing a picnic with a woman (Response 10) to the distressing prospect of having women look the other way when he is around (Responses 18–19)? As is always the case when such indefinite imagery is interpreted in such speculative ways, these are questions to be considered carefully but not conclusions to be taken seriously, at least not until other test and case history data confirm their validity.

Returning now to the second of the *M*- responses in Mr. Hart's record, Response 22 and the context in which it occurs inject another possible dynamic into the Rorschach picture of his inner life. He sees in this response on Card VIII "a startled face" that "has a shocked-like expression." Using the "I am" technique described in chapter 6 for grasping self-imagery projected into Rorschach responses, there is little difficulty in perceiving Mr. Hart as a person who feels startled or shocked by events in his life. Perhaps being unpleasantly taken by surprise refers merely to his failing academically and being suspended from school after a history of solid if not spectacular achievement that extended through the first year of his dental program. He does, after all, in one more *M* percept not yet mentioned, Response 4 on Card I, appear to identify with being an "angel." Angels are pure and good and do no wrong, and they should not have such bad things happen to them as being forced to leave school. Even if correct, however, such readily available inferences should not preclude wondering why a particular image appeared when and where it did in the Rorschach sequence.

In this instance, the startled face appears in the context of three other responses to Card VIII that seem to have a singular theme not seen elsewhere in the record. Response 20 is "a coat-of arms design" and Response 23 is "a crown," both of which convey concerns about status and accomplishment and commonly characterize the records of persons who attach considerable importance to "being somebody," that is, somebody who is recognized, admired, envied, and influential. The other image on Card VIII is the "lions" in Response 21, which as already noted stands alone among Mr. Hart's animal responses as the only one involving a large and powerful figure. Perhaps these lions on Card VIII have something in common with the Godzilla on Card IV that is seen "from an ant's perspective." In considering earlier whether Mr. Hart was identifying primarily with the ant or with Godzilla, the weight of the evidence was seen as favoring self-perception as being relatively small, weak, and powerless. However, these lions on Card

VIII and Mr. Hart's attention to symbols of power and status on this same card suggest that he may also fantasize at times about being or becoming a superior person. Such additional complexity in his inner life would be consistent with the previous observation concerning his probable recourse to compensatory narcissism as a defense against feeling unworthy or inferior to other people.

With further respect to Mr. Hart's interpersonal relationships, his previously noted difficulties in identifying with real people in his life appear to be just one aspect of problematic social interactions. Although his *SumH* = 6 indicates adequate interest in people, the unbalanced *H:(H)Hd(Hd)* ratio of 1:5 makes it likely that he is uncomfortable in social situations. His elevated *ISOL* = .36 suggests further that he is in fact socially isolated and not involved on a regular basis with many people who play an important part in his life. His two *M-* responses exceed the normal range and indicate in addition a shortfall in empathic capacity that may result in his misperceiving the actions and intentions of other people and consequently responding to them in socially inappropriate ways.

Of even greater concern with respect to Mr. Hart's interpersonal adaptation, he gives evidence of serious liabilities in his capacities to anticipate interpersonal intimacy, security, and collaboration. As a person with *T* = 0, *COP* = 0, and a positive *HVI*, he is an interpersonally cautious and distant man who is hyperalert to possible sources of danger in his environment and rarely reaches out for physically or psychologically close contact with people. The imagery of his initial, sign-in response conveys further his hypervigilant stance in relation to the interpersonal world: "a viking mask" that is "meant to scare the opponent." This response shows a powerful and dangerous figure (the viking) whose true nature is concealed from view (by the mask) and has bad intentions toward the viewer (why else would he be confronting an "opponent" while wearing "something meant to scare"?).

Mr. Hart's hypervigilance does not reach the proportions of paranoia that were seen in the case of Mr. Carter in chapter 11. Unlike Mr. Carter, he does not demonstrate dramatic needs for protection or concerns about being under the scrutiny of others, nor, as is noted shortly, does he display any penchant for the kinds of illogical reasoning that contribute to delusion formation. Although not demonstrating paranoia, Mr. Hart is nevertheless seriously handicapped in trying to establish and enjoy comfortable interpersonal relationships by virtue of limited capacities to form close and secure attachments to others. As one additional interpersonal liability, his *a:p* = 4:10 indicates that he is unlikely to take initiative or assert himself in social situations. Instead, he is the kind of person who sits back and waits for others to act first in creating and sustaining a relationship and in the process tends to defer to other people's preferences. Such passivity often results in individuals being left alone and resenting other people for not being more actively attentive to their needs and for allowing them to adopt a subservient position.

Affective Issues

Mr. Hart appears adaptively capable of modulating his affective experience sufficiently, as indicated by an $Afr = .47$, a $WSumC = 4.5$, and a normal range Constriction Ratio of $SumC':WSumC = 3:4.5$. He is thus neither withdrawn from affective experience, limited in his ability to recognize his feelings, nor constricted in his channels for expressing emotion. At the same time, however, there is ample evidence that the feelings he recognizes and the emotions he expresses are often unpleasant for him. His C' of 3, the presence of a *ColShd Bld* (the *CF.C'F* on Response 7), and an $S = 3$ indicate that he is more likely than most people to feel sad and gloomy, to have difficulty enjoying himself, and to struggle with underlying feelings of anger and resentment. These indications of dysphoria, anhedonia, and anger, together with the low self-esteem and isolation discussed as personal and interpersonal issues, account for his receiving the five points on *DEPI* that were noted initially as evidence of depressive features in his present personality functioning.

As noted in discussing the personal and interpersonal significance of the sequence of Mr. Hart's responses to Card III, however, his affective experience embraces pleasure and enthusiasm as well as anhedonia and dysphoria. Despite being depressed with $C' = 3$ and a *ColShd Bld = 1*, he manages a $WSumC$ of 4.5 that includes two CF and one C. Such access to relatively unmodulated use of color rarely characterizes depression, except in depressed people who cycle through phases of emotional exuberance and affective spontaneity. Note in this regard that the creepy and scary clown's face in Response 7 on Card III starts out being happy and smiling, and in Response 26 on Card X, which is his pure C, he gives the almost euphoric percept of "Happy looking colors. It looks cheerful, like springtime."

The indications in these data of alternating cycles of gloomy reserve and delighted enthusiasm are reminiscent of the juxtaposed depressive and hypomanic features of Ms. Fisher's protocol in chapter 12. Although Mr. Hart does not match the intensity of Ms. Fisher in these respects or show as she did other indications of probable bipolar disorder, he does seem likely to have some cyclothymic features and to be highly variable in his energy level as well as in his mood states and self-attitudes.

A final personality characteristic suggested by Mr. Hart's affective variables concerns his previously noted elevation in S. Whenever the Rorschach data give reason to believe that a person is feeling unusually angry or resentful, the interpersonal cluster of variables should be examined to estimate whether the person is likely to express this anger in assertive or passive ways. There are no AG responses in Mr. Hart's record, and his probable behavioral passivity was previously noted in commenting on the $a:p = 4{:}10$. Accordingly, the data suggest a strong likelihood of his translating his resentments into passive–aggressive patterns of behavior.

Cognitive Issues

Mr. Hart attends to his experience about as openly as most people do, neither focusing his attention too narrowly on events occurring around him nor becoming excessively distracted by them ($Lambda = .56$). On the other hand, consistent with his previously noted HVI stance, he is an overincorporator who tends to examine situations extensively, take in more information than he can process efficiently, and allow even slight uncertainty to deter his coming to conclusions ($Zd = +4.5$). Being an overincorporator, he is likely to be very thorough in his work but also excessively careful at the expense of finishing tasks in a timely fashion. This overincorporative style of approaching tasks contrasts sharply with the carelessness, impetuousness, and distractibility that usually accompany concentration difficulties associated with attention deficit hyperactivity disorder. Moreover, overincorporation can contribute to academic underachievement in its own right, especially by fostering a plodding, ruminative, compulsive way of taking written examinations in which nonproductive puzzling over the meaning of questions and constant rechecking and revising of answers result in failure to complete tests. In light of Mr. Hart's reported difficulty passing examinations despite being adequately prepared for them, the possibility of an inefficient overincorporative approach to taking tests would be important to consider in developing a treatment plan.

Also of note in how Mr. Hart attends to his experience is the frequency of his W responses. Even in a record of 28 responses, the 15 W he gives represents an unusually global approach to experience and far exceed what might be expected in a record with just 4 M. In discussing the Aspiration Ratio ($W{:}M$) in the case of Ms. Evans in chapter 12, the observation was made that giving no more W than M is often associated with conservative goal setting and failure to achieve at the level of a person's talents and abilities. In Mr. Hart's case, the $W{:}M = 15{:}4$ suggests the opposite: an unusually high level of ambition and aspiration that may involve some grandiosity on his part and relate to the compensatory narcissism and emphasis on status noted in discussing his self-image.

Except for his apparently limited empathic capacities, Mr. Hart seems able to perceive his experiences realistically. His $X-\% = .18$ is beyond the normative range and suggests that he is more likely than most people to show lapses in judgment. However, his level of perceptual inaccuracy falls well below the criterion for psychotically impaired reality testing ($X-\% >$

.29), and two of his minus percepts involve the *M-* responses that identify his specifically interpersonal misperceptions. Although being thus generally in adequate touch with reality, Mr. Hart gives evidence of being highly unconventional in how he chooses to look at situations in his life. His normatively low $P = 3$ and unusually high $Xu\% = .36$ identify a disinterest in endorsing conventional modes of response and a preference for rejecting conventionality in favor of being a free spirit who does things his own way on his own terms. Should other sources of information confirm such non-conformity on his part, a good question to raise would concern how comfortable and content he has been with dentistry as his career goal and with the regimented demands of his dental school curriculum. Discontent in either of these respects, like an overincorporative test-taking style, could be contributing to his academic difficulties independently of any possible specific learning handicap.

Regarding his ideational functioning, Mr. Hart is fully capable of thinking logically and coherently about relationships between events (*WSum6* = 6), but in other respects the ways in which he uses ideation add further impediments to effective functioning. He is in addition an inflexible person who is set in his ways and neither accustomed to nor interested in changing what he thinks about himself, other people, or the world in general (*a:p* = 4:10). He is inclined to use fantasy excessively as a way of solving problems and to forsake constructive planning for daydreaming about how someone else or a lucky turn of events will solve his problems for him (*Ma:Mp* = 1:3). He is inclined to rely heavily on intellectualization as a defense by which he insulates himself against dealing directly and in a personally involved manner with thoughts and feelings that command his attention (*INTELL* = 7).

Finally of note, Mr. Hart gives evidence of an unusually high level of intrusive ideation in his *FM + m* = 10. This elevation on *FM + m* indicates considerable preoccupation with troublesome thoughts that resist being ignored or pushed out of conscious awareness. Fretting about unmet needs (*FM*) and worrying about the effects of events over which people have no control (*m*) are the usual components of such intrusive ideation. As illustrated in the preceding case of Luis, intrusive ideation of this kind typically interferes with concentration, and, with a level of 10 *FM + m*, Mr. Hart can be expected to find it extremely difficult to maintain his concentration on any task. This test result has obvious implications for his poor academic performance and reported concentration difficulties, independently of any possible distractibility related to an attention disorder.

To summarize, the case of Mr. Hart presents an interesting illustration of academic failure initially suspected as attributable to a learning disability or previously undiagnosed attention deficit hyperactivity disorder but understandable on psychological grounds alone. Although never having previously come to mental health attention or having received any psychological treatment, Mr. Hart gives evidence of being not only situationally anxious but also chronically disposed to cyclical moods and episodes of depression. He is additionally handicapped by an uncertain sense of self-esteem, with compensatory narcissism being employed to ward off feelings of inferiority, a distant and distrustful stance in his interpersonal relatedness, and a proclivity for passive–aggressive patterns of behavior.

These previously unnoticed and untreated adjustment difficulties would by themselves be sufficient to account for instances of academic failure. In addition, Mr. Hart's Rorschach responses identify an overincorporative style, which can lead to specific maladaptive work habits, and a high level of intrusive ideation, which can cause significant concentration difficulties. Whether through a focus on his test-taking style or on broader characterological liabilities that must be contributing to adjustment difficulties in his life, numerous treatment targets identified by the Rorschach data are likely to provide fruitful avenues for being of help to this young man.

14

Viewing Oneself and Relating to Others

Being able to view oneself in favorable and thorough ways that maintain adequate self-esteem, promote positive regard, enhance self-awareness, and foster a stable sense of identity are personality assets that contribute to good psychological adjustment. Conversely, as elaborated in chapter 5, negative self-attitudes and an insufficient grasp of the kind of person an individual is constitute adaptive liabilities that make people susceptible to adjustment difficulties. In relating to others, adequate capacities to become comfortably involved, anticipate intimacy and security, and be appropriately collaborative and assertive characterize good adjustment, whereas disinterest, discomfort, disengagement, distrust, and excessive dominance or passivity in interpersonal relationships typically pave the way for disappointment, discontent, and psychological disorder.

As noted in introducing the case studies in chapter 9, devoting a single chapter to individuals viewing themselves and relating to others does not signify that these two dimensions of adaptation are any less important to adjustment than the four dimensions discussed in chapters 10 through 13. On the contrary, because of their transcendental importance to psychological good health and happiness, personality strengths and weaknesses in how people view themselves and how they relate to others have already been illustrated at length in discussing their manifestations on the Rorschach. Moreover, these two dimensions of adaptation share theoretical and practical implications for object relatedness in general, and individual Rorschach responses, particularly in their thematic imagery, often provide clues simultaneously to how both the self and others are represented and viewed.

Object relatedness is reflected on the Rorschach in the self-perception and interpersonal perception clusters of variables listed in Table 3.1. The two cases presented in this chapter were selected to illustrate different contexts in which narcissistic self-centeredness can lead to behavioral and emotional problems. Both have an entry point determined by a first positive key variable of $Fr + rF > 0$, and both concern seemingly well-adjusted and gainfully employed adults with no prior history of mental health care. However, the first subject is an extratensive man whose poorly controlled temper and alleged domestic violence have raised questions about his dangerousness, and the second is an introversive woman whose inability to relate pleasantly to coworkers is threatening to derail her career.

CASE 9: VIOLENCE POTENTIAL IN A MAN WHO HAD TO HAVE HIS OWN WAY

Mr. Ingram is a 27-year-old Caucasian man who was referred for evaluation by a marriage counselor with whom he and his wife of 4 years had been talking since separating a few months earlier. He has an associate degree in computer technology and for the last 7 years has worked steadily for a large firm, doing hardware repair and receiving regular salary increases. He met his wife at age 21 when she was 18, and during 2 years of dating prior to their marriage they had frequent and mutually enjoyable sexual relations. She has been employed throughout their marriage as a secretary in a bank.

After the first year of their marriage, according to his report and with the concurrence of his wife, they began to grow apart. Although continuing to have frequent sexual relations, they often disagreed about minor matters, came to feel they shared few interests in common, and began to spend increasing amounts of time apart, he with his male friends and she with her female friends. Four months prior to this examination, there was an incident in which Mr. Ingram lost his temper and struck his wife several times. At around the time of this assault, she had a miscarriage while 3 months pregnant. It is unclear whether Mr. Ingram's violent outburst was precipitated by his being upset with his wife for miscarrying (which is his story) or occurred prior to and possibly precipitated the miscarriage (which is her version of what happened). At any rate, Mr. Ingram's wife left their home later that same day and moved into her parents' home in a nearby neighborhood. Her parents, appalled by her bruises, called the police, who arrested Mr. Ingram and took him to the county jail. His wife declined to press charges, however, and he was released the next day.

Over the next several weeks the Ingrams saw each other at marital counseling sessions, during which Mr. Ingram pleaded with his wife to go on dates with him and consider returning to their home. She declined to do either and indicated instead that she was thinking about filing for divorce. Mr. Ingram was dismayed by these rebuffs, and on two occasions, while speaking with her on the telephone, threatened to assault her physically if she refused to go out with him. In the counseling sessions he expressed contrition for his actions and said that he is still deeply in love with his wife, wants to make a good home for her, and hopes that ultimately they will have children. At the same time as he expresses contrition, however, he states that his wife's resistance to reconciliation is due to her mother and her friends "turning her against me," and for his part he says, "I'll keep coming to this counseling for as long as it takes to get her back."

The marriage counselor requested psychological consultation to assist in evaluating Mr. Ingram's personality strengths and weaknesses, assessing whether his contrition is sincere, and determining whether he posed a risk of potential violence. Three days after this evaluation was conducted, and following a telephone conversation in which his wife refused once more to see him, Mr. Ingram went to her parents' house and knocked on the door. When his wife opened the door, he took out a gun, shot her through the heart, and then killed himself with the same weapon. Mr. Ingram's Rorschach protocol follows in Tables 14.1, 14.2, and 14.3 and Fig. 14.1.

TABLE 14.1
Rorschach Protocol of Mr. Ingram

Responses	*Inquiry*
Card I	
1. It looks like a moth.	E: (*Repeats response*)
	S: These are the antennae and the wings, and it's hard to tell a female moth from a male moth, I don't know which it is.
2. (*long pause*) (If you look some more you'll find some other things as well) Okay, a leaf.	E: (*Repeats response*)
	S: A leaf from an oak tree or something, and it's dying because it's dark and fragmented, and these are holes in it. (*points*)
Card II	
3. It looks like a bug on a windshield, all squished, what's left of him.	E: (*Repeats response*)
	S: This is the blood, and he is just smushed out?
	E: The blood?
	S: It's red and it's smeared all over. When he hit his body just like separated, see the hole in the center, just flattened.

(Continued)

TABLE 14.1
(Continued)

Responses	Inquiry
4. If you forget the red it could be like two dogs.	E: *(Repeats response)* S: Not the red, but here, their feet are down here, they're standing on their hind feet, they have little ears, and it's like they're jumping up and doing a little dance together, playing, and this dark spot is the eye, you can see ears, noses, and the eyes. (*points*)
5. Or a blossom on a flower that opens up, like maybe a lily if you look in it.	E: *(Repeats response)* S: The white part is like when you look down into a flower like a lily, and around it is where the petals come up. E: I'm not sure I see it the way you do. S: The white is the center, down in, and this darker part would be the petals. E: What makes it look down in? D: I don't know, I guess the white just looks lower than the black.
Card III 6. v It looks like some type of bug with its mouth here and legs here, not the whole bug though.	E: *(Repeats response)* S: I see the legs and the feet and that's his mouth, with his pincers like beetles have (D8). Maybe it's a black widow with red marking on it, but it's more of a beetle. I guess some beetles have red marks too, whatever; it's the kind of bug I wouldn't want to look at very long. E: You said it's not the whole bug? S: Yeah, something is missing. Where it's white some of it should be black like the rest, like it's decayed in some places.
Card IV 7. > This looks like a bank on a shoreline and an old tree stump that has rotted away, and this is the reflection here.	E: *(Repeats response)* S: Here is the shoreline and this is the tree stump and limb, and this is the reflection of it down here.
8. This way it really looks like a frog with a tail.	E: *(Repeats response)* S: These are his feet (D6), his head (D3), and his tail (D1).

(Continued)

TABLE 14.1
(*Continued*)

Responses	Inquiry

Card V

9. This looks as though it's a bat.

E: (*Repeats response*)
S: The wings and feet are behind him as he flies by, and his arms are out at the end of the wings, a pretty weird bat.

10. Or it would look like another moth.

E: (*Repeats response*)
S: The same principle as the bat, with little antennae and wings, and it's in flight.

11. < This way it could be a tree stump sticking out of the water, and this would be the reflection.

E: (*Repeats response*)
S: This (center line) is the shore line, like still water, and that's the shape of the tree stump, and this is the reflection of it down here, like you would get during the day when the sun is shining. Just a tree stump, an old dead tree.

Card VI

12. This looks like it could be like when people kill an animal and take the hide from it; maybe a flattened out hide of an animal.

E: (*Repeats response*)
S: I have been to places and seen where they have done that to an animal, and it looks like this. Some jerk shot an animal and will hang it on the wall.

E: I'm not sure how you're seeing it.
S: The head, the neck, and the hide. It's already been skinned, and you can see where the legs had been. (*points*)

13. > This way it seems to be a reflection of bushes and plant growth here, and this is a reflection in the water.

E: (*Repeats response*)
S: The shoreline is here, and this could be a dead tree stump and weeds, and this is the bushes, with all of it reflecting down here.

Card VII

14. This looks like two people looking at each other, with the nose here and the mouth, and with a feather in their head, stretching their necks out to stare at each other.

E: (*Repeats response*)
S: The head here, the feather, nose, mouth, neck, like they're glaring at each other, really mad, you know, like they had been arguing and didn't settle anything and now they're just staring at each other, a couple of kids I guess, just this top part.

(*Continued*)

TABLE 14.1
(Continued)

Responses	Inquiry
15. > If you look at it this way it looks like ice sticking out of the water, and this is a reflection on a vertical basis, a mirror image of itself.	E: *(Repeats response)* S: It all looks like it would be ice or something, but it's a mirror image because of this water and these icicles hanging out here, dripping. E: Dripping? S: See the edges, they're irregular, like drops of water, like it is dripping, melting.
Card VIII 16. < This looks like an animal. He's coming from this rock here, and this is water here, and this is the reflection, and the animal is climbing on a stump or something.	E: *(Repeats response)* S: Here, the rock, you can tell it's a colored stone, like out west, the shoreline and this looks like a dog or something, like he's stepping from the stone to a stump or something, maybe another stone or maybe a dead tree, probably a dead tree. He just wants to get across the water, here, this blue is the water, and he doesn't want to get wet.
Card IX 17. v This looks like some type of a plant, a pink flower, and this is its stem coming up from the ground, with green foliage.	E: *(Repeats response)* S: This is the ground (D3), and the stem, and this up here is the pink flower itself, and the green foliage below it; some sort of tropical plant I guess, maybe an orchid or something.
Card X 18. This reminds me of lungs, and these would be the bacteria, and these are antibodies going to combat the bacteria that's in our system.	E: *(Repeats response)* S: The pink (D9) is the lungs, mine are not pink because I smoke, and this is the throat (D11), and these are germs and all these other things are antibodies attacking the germs. They're all different colors, like each color is a different kind of antibody, each one has its own special job to do to protect the lungs. I hope they're protecting mine like that, because my lungs are probably in worse shape than these.

TABLE 14.2
Sequence of Scores for Mr. Ingram

Card No.		Loc.	No.	Determinant(s)	(2)	Content(s)	POP	Z	Special Scores
I	1	Wo	1	Fo		A		1.0	DR
	2	WSo	1	FC'o		Bt		3.5	MOR
II	3	WSv	1	C		Ad,Bl			MOR,DV
	4	D+	6	Mao	2	A	P	3.0	COP,FAB
	5	DdSo	99	FV-		Bt		4.5	
III	6	DdSo	99	FC'.FC-		Ad		4.5	MOR
IV	7	W+	1	Fro		Ls		4.0	MOR
	8	Wo	1	Fu		A		2.0	INC
V	9	Wo	1	FMao		A	P	1.0	INC
	10	Wo	1	FMao		A		1.0	PSV
	11	W+	1	Fru		Na		2.5	MOR
VI	12	Wo	1	Fo		Ad	P	2.5	PER
	13	W+	1	Fro		Ls		2.5	MOR
VII	14	D+	1	Mao	2	Hd,Id		3.0	AG,DR
	15	WS+	1	Fr.mp-		Na		4.0	DV
VIII	16	W+	1	FMa.Fr.CFo		A,Na	P	4.5	MOR
IX	17	W+	1	CFo		Bt		5.5	
X	18	W+	1	FMa.FC-		An,A		5.5	AG,DR

Personal and Interpersonal Issues

Mr. Ingram's Structural Summary indicates a valid record of 18 responses with an *S-CON* = 8 and a first positive key variable of $Fr + rF > 0$. Keeping in mind that $S\text{-}CON > 7$ is a conservative criterion for suicidal risk and rarely yields false positives, the *S-CON* elevation in this case calls for an immediate clinical response. Depending on what is most appropriate to the circumstances, this response should include some combination of immediately notifying the referral source of patients' likelihood of engaging in suicidal behavior, giving direct feedback to patients concerning the suicidal potential suggested by their Rorschach responses, and alerting people in patients' support systems to the importance of observing them closely for manifestations of self-destructive impulses. It does not matter in instances of an elevated *S-CON* whether the subject has previously reported suicidal ideation

TABLE 14.3
Structural Summary for Mr. Ingram

Location Features	Determinants Blends	Single		Contents		S-Constellation
Zf = 17	FC'.FC	M	= 2	H	= 0, 0	NO . . FV+VF+V+FD>2
ZSum = 54.5	Fr.m	FM	= 2	(H)	= 0, 0	YES . . Col-Shd Bl>0
ZEst = 56.0	FM.Fr.CF	m	= 0	Hd	= 1, 0	YES . . Ego<.31,>.44
	FM.FC	FC	= 0	(Hd)	= 0, 0	YES . . MOR > 3
W = 14		CF	= 1	Hx	= 0, 0	NO . . Zd > +- 3.5
(Wv = 1)		C	= 1	A	= 6, 1	YES . . es > EA
D = 2		Cn	= 0	(A)	= 0, 0	YES . . CF+C > FC
Dd = 2		FC'	= 1	Ad	= 3, 0	YES . . X+% < .70
S = 5		C'F	= 0	(Ad)	= 0, 0	YES . . S > 3
		C'	= 0	An	= 1, 0	NO . . P < 3 or > 8
		FT	= 0	Art	= 0, 0	YES . . Pure H < 2
DQ		TF	= 0	Ay	= 0, 0	NO . . R < 17
. . . . . (FQ-)		T	= 0	Bl	= 0, 1	8 . . . . . TOTAL
+ = 9 (2)		FV	= 1	Bt	= 3, 0	
o = 8 (2)		VF	= 0	Cg	= 0, 0	Special Scorings
v/+ = 0 (0)		V	= 0	Cl	= 0, 0	
v = 1 (0)		FY	= 0	Ex	= 0, 0	Lvl	Lv2
		YF	= 0	Fd	= 0, 0	DV = 2x1	0x2
		Y	= 0	Fi	= 0, 0	INC = 2x2	0x4
		Fr	= 3	Ge	= 0, 0	DR = 3x3	0x6
		rF	= 0	Hh	= 0, 0	FAB = 1x4	0x7
		FD	= 0	Ls	= 2, 0	ALOG = 0x5	
Form Quality		F	= 3	Na	= 2, 1	CON = 0x7	
				Sc	= 0, 0	Raw Sum6 = 8	
FQx FQf MQual SQx				Sx	= 0, 0	Wgtd Sum6 = 19	
+ = 0 0 0 0				Xy	= 0, 0		
o = 11 2 2 1				Id	= 0, 1	AB = 0	CP = 0
u = 2 1 0 0						AG = 2	MOR = 7
- = 4 0 0 3						CFB = 0	PER = 1
none = 1 — 0 1		(2) = 2				COP = 1	PSV = 1

Ratios, Percentages, and Derivations

R = 18	L = 0.20		FC:CF+C	= 2: 3	COP = 1 AG = 2
			Pure C	= 1	Food	= 0
EB = 2: 4.5	EA = 6.5	EBPer = 2.3	SumC':WSumC	= 2:4.5	Isolate/R	= 0.61
eb = 5: 3	es = 8	D = 0	Afr	= 0.20	H: (H)Hd(Hd)	= 0: 1
	Adj es = 8	Adj D = 0	S	= 5	(HHd) : (AAd)	= 0: 0
			Blends:R	= 4:18	H+A:Hd+Ad	= 7: 4
FM = 4 : C' = 2 T = 0			CP	= 0		
m = 1 : V = 1 Y = 0						

			P = 4	Zf = 17	3r+(2)/R = 0.94
a:p = 6: 1	Sum6	= 8	X+% = 0.61	Zd = −1.5	Fr+rF = 5
Ma:Mp = 2: 0	Lv2	= 0	F+% = 0.67	W:D:Dd = 14: 2: 2	FD = 0
2AB+Art+Ay = 0	WSum6	= 19	X-% = 0.22	W:M = 14: 2	An+Xy = 1
M-	= 0	Mnone	= 0	S-% = 0.75	DQ+ = 9	MOR = 7
			Xu% = 0.11	DQv = 1	

SCZI = 2	DEPI = 5*	CDI = 3	S-CON = 8*	HVI = No	OBS = No

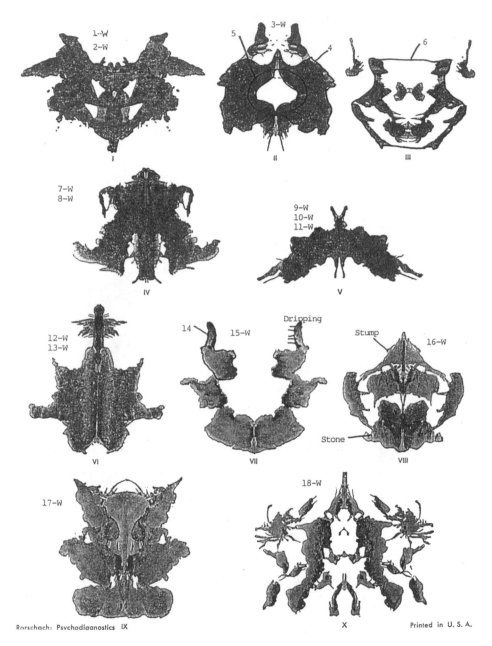

FIG. 14.1. Location choices of Mr. Ingram.

or been noted to be self-harmful. The *S-CON* data are sufficiently strong to warrant suicidal precautions when it is elevated, whatever a person's prior history. Such precautions would have been taken in Mr. Ingram's case, perhaps with results that would have prevented the tragedy that ensued, had there been enough time after the Rorschach was given to complete the examination and notify his counselor of the results.

The entry data are noteworthy in two other respects as well. First, the *DEPI* = 5 does not meet the *DEPI* > 5 criterion for constituting a positive key variable and beginning interpretation with the affective cluster of variables, but it is large enough to indicate significant depressive features in Mr. Ingram's present condition. Second, the *R* = 18 satisfies the criterion of *R* > 13 necessary to indicate a generally valid record, but nevertheless raises the possibility that his protocol will provide somewhat limited information. However, like Ms. Fisher in chapter 12, who gave only 14 responses but was sufficiently open to experience to have a *Lambda* = .27, Mr. Ingram combines his below average *R* with a low *Lambda* of .20. As in Ms. Fisher's case, then, and in contrast to the guarded record of Ms. Anderson in chapter 10 (which has an *R* = 19 and a *Lambda* = 2.80), Mr. Ingram's protocol would be expected to contain abundant clues to the kind of person he is and to the nature of his inner life. The search strategy in this case, following Table 3.2, will proceed through the self-perception, interpersonal perception, controls, affect, processing, mediation, and ideation clusters.

The obvious key to Mr. Ingram's self-perception appears in his giving five Reflections and an Egocentricity Index of .94. With respect to his level of self-esteem, these findings indicate that he is an extraordinarily selfish, self-focused, and self-centered individual who characteristically places his needs above those of others, feels entitled to have what he wants, extols his own virtues, and attributes his difficulties to the actions of others or to circumstances beyond his control rather than to any shortcomings or limitations on his part. As noted in chapter 5, some caution must be exercised in interpreting *Fr* + *rF* = 5 as necessarily demonstrating more prominent narcissism than *Fr* + *rF* = 1. Consider, however, that Mr. Ingram produces five Reflections and two Pairs in just 18 responses, and furthermore that the magnitude of the Egocentricity Index is highly stable over time, with a 3-year retest correlation of .87. Hence the narcissism observed thus far in the Rorschach data is undoubtedly well-established and of long standing.

Significantly, however, the picture of inflated self-esteem changes dramatically in Mr. Ingram's case when attention shifts to his self-regard. The relevant data illustrate the seemingly paradoxical circumstance discussed in chapter 5, in which persistently placing a high value on oneself independently of changing circumstances (high self-esteem) is accompanied by specific negative self-attitudes that arise in response to problematic events (low self-regard). Structural evidence of the latter comprises a Vista response, indicative of self-criticism, and *MOR* = 7, indicative of unusually strong negative attitudes toward the body and its functioning.

The thematic imagery in Mr. Ingram's *MOR* responses also suggests some likely origins of his experiencing low self-regard despite a generally high level of self-esteem. Response 2 on Card I is a dysphoric *FC'* involving an oak leaf that is "dying." Response 6 on Card III is an emotionally ambivalent and inaccurately perceived *FC'.FC-* involving a bug in which "something is missing ... like it's decayed in some places." Responses 7, 11, 13, and 16, occurring respectively on Cards IV, V, VI, and VIII, all depict "tree stumps" that are "dead" or "rotted away." This repetitive and fairly transparent imagery suggests the distinct possibility that it is he who is decayed in some places and has some part missing, and that what is missing from his life is symbolized by the tree, which is now a dead and rotting stump that can no longer function as it once did and as he needs it to function in order to feel good about himself and sustain his self-regard.

If this thread of inference is valid, the Rorschach data may be demonstrating the pattern of needs and adaptive jeopardy typically associated with phallic narcissistic character disorder. What Mr. Ingram needs to sustain his sense of adequacy is regular and frequent heterosexual intercourse, which he enjoyed with his wife from the beginning of their dating relationship and even during the otherwise strained years of their marriage. There is no indication that he has ever been involved or even considered becoming involved with other women. Now the separation has deprived him of the opportunity to demonstrate his phallic capacity, and his wife's reluctance to see him and her thinking of filing for divorce has threatened him with indefinite prolongation of this deprivation. Small wonder, then, that he is distraught, showing features of depression, determined to get her back, and willing to continue in the marital counseling "for as long as it takes." Note, however, that he does not say anything about being willing to change his behavior or the kind of person he is as a way of convincing his wife to return to him.

One further *MOR* percept in the record not yet mentioned occurs in Response 3 on Card II, in an interesting sequence leading to his Vista in Response 5. Response 3 begins Card II with "a bug on a windshield" that is "all squished" with blood "smeared all over." Although morbid, this response does not have the self-denigrating qualities of his other six *MOR*, and it may be that in this instance he is identifying as an aggressor with whoever squished the bug, rather than with the victim of the squishing. If so, and keeping in mind the difficulties his aggressive and assaultive behavior have caused him, Response 4 that follows can be seen as an adaptive but nevertheless defensive and somewhat strained effort to take distance from a show of aggression. He begins by saying, "If you forget the red," which may be what he would like to do, along with the anger it typically suggests. He then gives his only *COP* in the record, a good form *M* but one involving a *FABCOM* and some forced gaiety: two dogs who are "jumping up and doing a little dance together, playing." He then follows in Response 5 with a minus form Vista, as if regrets and self-criticisms related to his having behaved aggressively toward his wife have not been fully expunged by the happy image of the dogs playing. His distress in this regard appears to carry over to Card III, on which in Response 6 he gives the previously noted *FC'.FC- MOR* and misses the Popular human figures.

Returning to the structural data bearing on Mr. Ingram's self-perception, he demonstrates two additional personality liabilities that typically contribute to adjustment difficulties. First, the *FD* = 0 indicates very little capacity for self-awareness. As much as he may become absorbed with what an admirable and deserving person he is or what a deprived and nonfunctioning person he is, he lacks sufficient psychological mindedness to step back and examine his own behavior in an introspective manner. Second, the *H:(H)Hd(Hd)* = 0:1 points to a substantial deficit in being able to form a stable sense of his own identity on the basis of forming identifications with real people in his life. Given what has already been observed about his probable phallic narcissism, it could be that his uncertain sense of identity includes or even revolves around underlying and strongly defended against uncertainty about his masculinity.

This last hypothesis lends some meaning to the unusual way in which he signs into the record with his first response. The free association in Response 1 is unremarkable: "It looks like a moth." In the inquiry, however, he adds the tangential remark, "It's hard to tell a female moth from a male moth, I don't know which it is." This loose and off-task association results in the response being coded as a *DR*, which suggests that the thematic imagery in the response reflects concerns sufficiently bothersome to intrude on his ideational functioning and cause some cognitive slippage. As for the nature of these concerns, it seems unlikely that he or most other people for that matter are troubled by whatever difficulties there may be in identifying the gender of moths. It seems more likely that he is displaying thinly disguised concerns about discerning whether people are men or women, which should not be troublesome at all unless the individual is experiencing difficulty in establishing a comfortable sense of masculinity or femininity.

The fact that Mr. Ingram produces only a single human content in his 18 responses, and this one an *Hd*, signifies that he not only has little capacity to identify with people but also little interest in people at all. As noted in chapter 5, narcissistic features combined with a strong interest in people often result in a type of "nice narcissism" in which friends and companions are sought and cultivated as an appreciative audience whom the individual attempts to please. By contrast, narcissism without genuine interest in people can produce a pattern of "nasty" narcissism in which other people are ignored or used and exploited to an individual's own ends, with little regard for their welfare, little concern about pleasing them, and attention only to getting them to do what the individual wants to have done.

The likelihood that Mr. Ingram is this second kind of narcissist is enhanced by indications in the data that people seldom play an important part in his life ($ISOL$ = .61); he rarely anticipates collaborative relationships with people (COP = 1); he has little capacity to form close attachments to others; he rarely anticipates or reaches out for intimacy; and he is inclined to relate to people as objects and from a distance, rather than as fellow human beings up close (T = 0). He does, on the other hand, appear to be reasonably empathic when he chooses to pay attention to people (both of his M responses are good form), and he shows a normal range of assertiveness (AG = 2) without any indications of behavioral passivity ($a:p$ = 6:1). It may well be that in his work, away from his wife and the likely role of their sexual relationship in sustaining his sense of adequacy, his interpersonal distance and disinterest have not prevented him from performing effectively doing computer hardware repairs and having little need to become involved with people.

With further reference to Mr. Ingram's wife, the thematic imagery in Card VII, which includes his other M and a minus form response not yet mentioned, presents a possibly revealing sequence. Response 14 consists of the Popular heads of "two people looking at each other," and on inquiry they are elaborated as "glaring at each other" and then, in another off-task and tangential DR, they are described as being "really mad, you know, like they had been arguing and didn't settle anything." Although other possibilities could be suggested, this response would appear to be a transparent portrayal of Mr. Ingram and his wife, two people who have had substantial disagreements that remain unresolved, at least not to his satisfaction. In Response 15, at least partly in reaction to distress caused by his associations to unresolved arguments in Response 14, he displays a temporary lapse in reality testing (minus form quality), some cognitive slippage in an awkward choice of words (a DV for "a reflection on a vertical basis"), and an unusual blend of determinants that captures both feeling helpless to control events (m) and feeling worthy and blameless (Fr).

Against this backdrop of concern and defensiveness, the imagery he produces in Response 15 consists of "ice sticking out of the water," which he later described as "icicles hanging out there, like it's dripping, melting." Two possibilities come to mind concerning the symbolic significance of this response, both of which could apply. First, the chilly imagery of the "ice," produced immediately following the image of two people arguing, could represent his own feelings of coldness toward his wife, whom he needs to have as an object in his life but not as someone to love, or it could indicate coldness he attributes to his wife for being uncaring and unresponsive to his needs and wants. Second, the melting icicle "hanging out there" could, in concert with the repetitive imagery of the dead or rotting tree stumps, constitute just one more expression of the distress being caused by deprivation of opportunities to perform sexually.

Affective Issues

Mr. Ingram has adequate capacities to experience and express feelings, and he does not give evidence of any constriction in being able to make his feelings known to others ($WSumC = 4.5$; $SumC':WSumC = 2:4.5$). He additionally shows adaptive capacity to process affect in both relatively reserved and relatively expansive ways ($FC:CF + C = 2:3$). He is likely to be a little more spontaneous than most adults in displaying emotion, and his pure C in Response 3, which was the smear of blood where a bug had been "squished," suggests that at times he may become quite intense when expressing anger. By and large, however, his capacities to modulate affect sufficiently and in moderation are within normal limits and constitute a personality strength that has probably contributed to his having no prior history of psychological disorder.

Note, however, that his $Afr = .20$ falls well below normative expectation and indicates avoidance of emotionally arousing situations and withdrawal from interactions in which strong feelings are being exchanged. Typically, such affective avoidance and withdrawal occur in the context of deficits in basic capacities to experience and express feelings; that is, people with such deficits remove themselves from emotionally charged situations because they are poorly equipped to handle them. When, as in this case, a low Afr appears along with ample evidence of adequate capacities to process affect, the subject's problem is usually interpersonal rather than affective; that is, emotional interchange is avoided as a manifestation of interpersonal withdrawal and not because of insufficient modulation of affect. Mr. Ingram's preference to distance himself from close and involved relationships with other people has already been noted in discussing his $T = 0$, $COP = 1$, $SumH = 1$, and $ISOL = .61$, and his low Afr appears related to the implications of these findings.

As would be expected from the initial observation that a $DEPI = 5$ in Mr. Ingram's protocol identifies some depressive elements in his condition, he is at present having difficulty modulating affect pleasurably. Although his $C' = 2$ is within normal limits, his previously noted $FC'.FC$ blend indicates an ambivalent affective tone and a likelihood that he is not finding much pleasure in his life. In addition, and of considerable significance in light of the referral question and outcome in this case, he gives evidence in an $S = 5$ of being a very angry man. Having already noted in the interpersonal cluster of variables that he shows a normal range level of assertiveness (AG

= 2) and no indications of behavioral passivity ($a:p$ = 6:1), there is little reason to expect that he will express his anger passively. An AG = 2 and $a:p$ = 6:1 do not by themselves constitute risk factors in the evaluation of violence potential. In combination with an elevation in S, however, they decrease the likelihood that the person's considerable anger will be discharged through indirect channels and accordingly increase the risk of direct confrontation with the object of the anger.

Stress Management Issues

Mr. Ingram has somewhat marginal but still normative range psychological resources for coping with everyday experience. His EA = 6.5 is below average but does not meet the criterion of EA < 6.0 for a point on the CDI. His CDI = 3 is also within normal limits, and his stress management capacities are strengthened further by a well-defined but not pervasive EB style ($M:WSumC$ = 2:4.5). These data indicate that he is likely to behave in a reasonably consistent and predictable manner, to have at his disposal sufficient adaptive capacity to deal with average amounts of life stress, and to employ both ideational and expressive strategies in problem-solving and decision-making situations, with a preference for the latter.

Of particular importance in the data are indications that Mr. Ingram's coping capacities are adequate to meet the demands he is facing in his life. As attested by the D = 0 and $AdjD$ = 0, he is now and has been in a comfortable state of equilibrium in which he is experiencing little subjectively felt distress and is relatively unlikely to feel anxious, tense, or irritable. Moreover, the D and $AdjD$ scores indicate that he has average capacities to tolerate frustration and is no more inclined than most people to lose control of himself or act impulsively. The known facts in this case call for careful reconciliation of these control cluster data with how Mr. Ingram felt and what he did. The D = 0 and $AdjD$ = 0 scores indicate that he is generally comfortable and at peace with himself, which is consistent with his narcissism, and they indicate a degree of stability that suggests a well-entrenched narcissistic personality disorder. They do not, however, preclude his feeling angry or depressed or having underlying concerns about his masculinity that are making him determined to get his wife back into his life.

As for Mr. Ingram's conduct, the D = 0 and $AdjD$ = 0 scores indicate that he is not inclined to behave impulsively, but they do not preclude his acting in ways that are harmful to himself or others. When D = 0 and $AdjD$ = 0 people commit acts of violence or behave in other ill-advised ways, they do so not as a consequence of losing self-control and impetuously doing things they would ordinarily refrain from doing. Instead, such people do bad things as a consequence of having decided to take certain actions that are consistent with their usual ways of behaving and that proceed according to more or less deliberate plan. In Mr. Ingram's case, he carefully and deliberately carried out acts of violence that were a predictable extension of his being an angry, assaultive, hot-tempered, and self-centered person. In these circumstances, his disposition to take ill-advised actions was probably increased by his general preference for doing things rather than thinking about them (as already noted in Mr. Ingram's extratensive *EB* style) or by poor judgment concerning the consequences of his actions (as is identified next as a liability in his cognitive functioning). However, impulsivity and loss of self-control are not necessary ingredients of either general misconduct or specific acts of violence, and the implications of $D = 0$ and $AdjD = 0$ accordingly do not preclude either.

Cognitive Issues

As indicated by his previously noted low *Lambda* of .20, Mr. Ingram is quite open in attending to experience, alert to the nuances of what is going on around him, and less inclined than most people to appraise situations in a detached and objective manner. His low *Lambda* suggests further that he rarely deals with situations in a simple or economical way, but is instead inclined to make matters more complicated than they need to be. His aversion to limiting his focus to just the obvious and easily manageable aspects of situations appears as well in the $W{:}D{:}Dd = 14{:}2{:}2$. His disregard or disdain for what is readily apparent, as reflected in his using only two D locations in his 18 responses, is paired with a marked emphasis on striving for global impressions of what he sees, as shown by his 14 W responses. When compared with the presence of just two M in his record, these 14 W suggest some unusually high aspirations or expectations, perhaps indicative (as in the case of Mr. Hart in chap. 13) of some grandiosity in association with his narcissism.

Nevertheless, the data indicate that Mr. Ingram can organize information efficiently, without taking in less information than he needs in making decisions or more information than he can process in a timely fashion ($Zd = -1.5$). He shows normal range capacities to recognize conventional reality and does not appear inclined to form unconventional impressions of what he sees ($P = 4$; $Xu\% = .11$). On the other hand, he is much more likely than most people to misperceive the nature and meaning of events ($X-\% = .22$). Although his $X-\%$ does not reach the level of $X-\% > .29$ used as a criterion for psychotic loss of contact with reality, it is sufficiently high to identify the considerable likelihood of Mr. Ingram's exercising poor judgment. The elevated frequency of inaccurate form perception he shows typically contributes to distorted impressions of what events signify, mistaken assessments of what people intend, and faulty anticipations of the consequences of his actions.

The additional fact that three of Mr. Ingram's four minus responses involve use of white space sheds further light on the nature of his susceptibility to exercising poor judgment. The $S - \% = .75$ is well above the criterion of $S - \% = .40$ for identifying a substantial role of anger in precipitating instances of impaired reality testing. These data accordingly indicate that Mr. Ingram has more of an anger problem than a reality testing problem. When he becomes angry, which he does often, his anger clouds his judgment, and he may then form impressions or decide on actions that he would reject were he not angry and consequently unable to see things clearly.

Finally with respect to his ideation, Mr. Ingram presents a situation, similar to that of Mr. Baker in chapter 11, in which a $WSum6 > 17$ suggests disordered thinking that, on closer inspection, is not demonstrated by the data. Of the eight Critical Special Scores he gives, none is of the Level 2 variety indicating serious cognitive slippage. The most heavily weighted Critical Special Score in his record is a Level 1 *FABCOM*, for which he receives 4 of his 19 points on *WSum6*. This *FABCOM* is the dogs "doing a little dance" in Response 4, and, as discussed in previous cases as well, a Level 1 *FABCOM* involving animals in human activity is more likely to indicate mild and temporary regression to a childish way of thinking than a persisting incapacity for logical reasoning.

Three other Critical Special Scores that contribute nine points to his *WSum6* are *DR* occurring in Responses 1, 14, and 18. The *DR* in Responses 1 and 14 have already been discussed in relation to significant personal concerns suggested by their content, and Response 18 involves a parting comment at the end of his last response that concerns his smoking habits and the condition of his lungs. Although clearly tangential, this closing comment seems to represent a need to forget the blots and talk about himself more than it does a dissociation in his thought processes. Examined closely, then, the composition of his *WSum6* does not appear to demonstrate the presence of thinking disorder.

There is likewise no indication in the ideational variables that Mr. Ingram thinks too much or too fancifully. He does not give evidence of an unusual amount of intrusive ideation ($FM + m = 5$), of using fantasy to excess as a way of solving problems ($Ma:Mp = 2:0$), or of relying heavily on intellectualization as a defense ($2AB + Art + Ay = 0$). However, his $a:p = 6:1$ does indicate that he tends to be rigid and inflexible in how he thinks about things and as a consequence is set in his ways and disinclined to alter his perspectives. This inflexibility on his part may well have played a role in how little was accomplished in the marital counseling sessions he attended with his wife and in how convinced she was that a reconciliation on any but his terms would not be possible.

In summary, the Rorschach data give good reason to believe that Mr. Ingram has a narcissistic personality disorder, little interest in becoming intimately involved with or placating other people, and likely underlying needs to sustain an uncertain sense of masculinity through frequent heterosexual activity. His self-centeredness and lack of concern for his wife's interests and needs, combined with his assaultive behavior toward her, led to a situation of separation and pending divorce that deprived him of something he wanted and needed badly—his wife at home and in his bed. Despite his basic stability, adequate coping resources, and general self-satisfaction, then, he arrived at a point of desperation in which, not being able to look forward to living with his wife again, he did not want to live without her either.

Being an angry man feeling entitled to have things his way, being an action-oriented man whose resentments often cloud his judgment, and being a depressed man rebuffed by his wife for what may be the last time, Mr. Ingram decided to end both of their lives and then calmly and systematically did so. His depression and suicidal tendencies were apparent as soon as this Rorschach had been scored, and the several features of the data that elevated the violence potential in this case were noted in the preceding discussion. There was unfortunately insufficient time between the evaluation and the tragedy that ensued to take steps that might have averted it.

CASE 10: INTEMPERATE OUTBURSTS JEOPARDIZING THE CAREER OF A SUCCESSFUL BUT SELF-CENTERED BUSINESSWOMAN

Ms. Jordan is a 33-year-old married woman with an MBA and a supervisory management position in a large company. She has recently come to the attention of her superiors because of complaints from her staff concerning her screaming and yelling at them over minor everyday problems of office management. She has no history of diagnosed psychological disorder or mental health treatment, but a penchant for intemperate outbursts has been noted for some years in her personnel file. Because of her management talent and value to her company, she was encouraged to admit herself at their expense to a prestigious psychiatric facility for a through diagnostic evaluation. Ms. Jordan resisted this recommendation, insisting there was nothing psychologically wrong with her, and a compromise was reached in which she agreed to undergo psychiatric and psychological assessment on an outpatient basis. Ms. Jordan's Rorschach protocol follows in Tables 14.4, 14.5, and 14.6 and Fig. 14.2.

Personal and Interpersonal Issues

Ms. Jordan's Structural Summary indicates a valid record of 23 responses with an unremarkable *S-CON* of 5 and a first positive key variable of $Fr + rF$ = 2. Her *Lambda* is far above average at .92 but short of the criterion of

TABLE 14.4
Rorschach Protocol of Ms. Jordan

Responses	Inquiry
Card I	
1. My first thought is a butterfly, kind of freaky looking.	E: (*Repeats response*) S: The wings are here, and the central body.
	E: It's freaky looking? S: It's like Halloween, a black flying creature.
	E: It looks like it's flying? S: Yes.
2. Or a bug of some sort	E: (*Repeats response*) S: It's the same, with wings and a central body.
3. (*pause*) I could see a lady in there too, with her arms up, and some sort of wild costume.	E: (*Repeats response*) S: The hands are here (D1) and the dress here. It has the silhouette of a woman here (D4).
	E: What suggests a wild costume? S: It's like the opera, and all this out here (D2) would be part of a wild costume.
Card II	
4. A vertebral body. These are real symmetrical. It looks like it was one thing, folded together and then opened up.	E: (*Repeats response*) S: The spinal column goes here (DS5), the vertebra is here (D6) and this (D2) is part of the process.
	E: Is it the whole thing? S: Yes.
5. Could be two people dancing, kicking up their legs together, putting their hands together, looking at each other.	E: (*Repeats response*) S: They're putting their hands together here (D4), their heads are here (D2), and the lower leg and knees are here, kicking up.
Card III	
6. Again, it looks like two people facing each other.	E: (*Repeats response*) S: The lower body and leg here, the upper body here, the arms extending out.
	E: How do you mean facing each other? S: They're looking at each other.

(Continued)

TABLE 14.4
(Continued)

Responses	*Inquiry*
7. Is it okay to turn it? (If you like) v This way it looks like a bug; I'm stuck on bugs and people.	E: *(Repeats response)* S: The front claws or legs are here (D5), and here are the eyes, the head, and the mouth (D7). E: How much of it do you see? S: It's part of the body, like a fly without wings. Flies have those big old eyes like this, but I don't know what to do with this part (D2).
Card IV 8. *(pause)* v *(pause)* ^ All I can think of is some kind of bug.	E: *(Repeats response)* S: The head here (D3) and the rest is the body. E: How much of this one do you see? S: All of it.
9. An oddly shaped tree.	E: *(Repeats response)* S: The trunk is here (D1), and it's almost like a Christmas tree except for these things hanging out to the sides. E: Things hanging out to the sides? S: I'm not sure what they are, but they're just hanging from the tree.
10. And a head of a member of the cat family—a leopard or cheetah.	E: *(Repeats response)* S: This is the nose (D1), the nostrils, eye, cheek, and these are ears (D4) and this is the top of the head (D3).
Card V 11. *(laughs)* A bug again, a bug with its wings spread.	E: *(Repeats response)* S: The whole thing, with the antennae up here.
12. Or a bat *(pause)* v *(pause)* ^ *(puts card down)*.	E: *(Repeats response)* S: The head and the wings.
Card VI 13. Looks like a cartoon cat that's been smashed—a cat skin rug.	E: *(Repeats response)* S: The whiskers, head, nose, front legs, back legs.

(Continued)

TABLE 14.4
(Continued)

Responses	Inquiry
	E: You said a cat skin rug?
	S: No, it's not a rug. It's a cat, flattened out, like in the cartoons, like a truck ran over it.
14. v *(pause)* An explosive cloud in the shape of a star.	E: *(Repeats response)*
	S: It took off down here (D3), and the rest is the big cloud.
	E: What made it look like a cloud?
	S: I've seen fireworks in the last few months, and it just reminds me of a fireworks explosion, I guess.
Card VII	
15. Two women with wild hairdos, facing each other. It looks like a bust of the women, mounted on some kind of partial base. All of these seem real symmetrical. v *(pause)* > *(pause)* *(puts down)*	E: *(Repeats response)*
	S: The nose, mouth, hair going up, shoulders, bust here. A statuette, mounted here on this base.
	E: They have wild hairdos?
	S: It's the way their hair is up in the air like this.
Card VIII	
16. Oh, that's pretty *(pause)* > a four-legged animal, a mirror image. It's like it's walking along rocks, by a creek, seeing its reflection in the creek. It reminds me of an otter. *(pause)* v < *(puts down)*	E: *(Repeats response)*
	S: The waterline is here, the animal walking along here, see its reflection.
	E: What made it look like rocks?
	S: Just getting int the water concept, walking along the water.
	E: Do you see the water?
	S: The waterline is here.
Card IX	
17. I like these colored ones. *(pause)* This reminds me of a deer, with antlers. Again it looks like a reflection.	E: *(Repeats response)*
	S: The antlers are here and the deer here (D3). The rest seemed rather abstract.
18. v Kind of like a paw, with five claws. ^ *(pause)* *(puts down)*	E: *(Repeats response)*
	S: These are the claws.
	E: What does it look like the claws of?
	S: Anything that has five claws, maybe a badger or beaver.

(Continued)

398

TABLE 14.4
(Continued)

Responses	*Inquiry*
Card X	
19. Ooh—a bullfinch.	E: *(Repeats response)*
	S: This part looks like a goldfinch.
	E: What about it suggested a goldfinch?
	S: It looks like the shape of a bird, and the black and yellow make me think of a goldfinch. That was the state bird where I grew up.
20. A green caterpillar.	E: *(Repeats response)*
	S: Here, both of these, shaped like a caterpillar and green.
21. Sand crabs.	E: *(Repeats response)*
	S: These two here are like sand crabs.
	E: How are they like sand crabs.
	S: The round oval shape with the legs coming out.
22. And these are two more sand crabs.	E: *(Repeats response)*
	S: There's just two more that look like that. We have a lot of them where I live now.
23. v ^ A human pelvic bone. I like the colors. They look like happy pictures.	E: *(Repeats response)*
	S: This part right here just reminds me of what the pelvic bone looks like.

Lambda > .99 for identifying a high *Lambda* protocol and beginning an interpretation with the information-processing cluster of variables. However, in contrast to the high *Lambda* guardedness seen in the case of Ms. Anderson in chapter 10, Ms. Jordan with her 23 responses, like Luis in chapter 13, appears to be presenting more of a high *Lambda* style than high *Lambda* guardedness, as these characteristics are distinguished in chapter 5. Following the guidelines in Table 3.2, further consideration of her possible high *Lambda* cognitive style will come near the end of an interpretive sequence that, as in the preceding case of Mr. Ingram, will proceed through the self-perception, interpersonal perception, controls, affect, processing, mediation, and ideation clusters of variables.

With respect to her self-perception, Ms. Jordan resembles Mr. Ingram in showing Reflection responses and an elevated $3r + (2)/R = .61$ that identify

TABLE 14.5
Sequence of Scores for Ms. Jordan

Card No.		Loc.	No.	Determinant(s)	(2)	Content(s)	POP	Z	Special Scores
I	1	Wo	1	FMa.FC'o		A	P	1.0	
	2	Wo	1	Fo		A		1.0	
	3	W+	1	Mpo		H,Cg		4.0	
II	4	WSo	1	Fu		An		4.5	
	5	W+	1	Mao	2	H		4.5	COP
III	6	D+	9	Mpo	2	H	P	4.0	
	7	Do	1	F-		Ad			
IV	8	Wo	1	F-		A		2.0	
	9	Wo	1	mpo		Bt		2.0	
	10	Wo	1	Fu		Ad		2.0	
V	11	Wo	1	FMpu		A		1.0	
	12	Wo	1	Fo		A	P	1.0	
VI	13	Wo	1	Fo		(A)		2.5	MOR
	14	Wo	1	ma-		Ex,Cl		2.5	PER
VII	15	W+	1	Mpo	2	Hd,Art	P	2.5	
VIII	16	W+	1	FMa.Fro		A,Ls	P	4.5	
IX	17	Do	3	Fro		A			
	18	Ddo	21	Fo	2	Ad			
X	19	Do	15	FC.FC'o	2	A			PER
	20	Do	4	FCo	2	A			
	21	Do	8	Fu	2	A			
	22	Do	7	Fo	2	A			
	23	Ddo	29	Fu		An			

stable and long-standing tendencies toward self-centeredness, self-admiration, externalization of blame, and a sense of entitlement. In contrast to Mr. Ingram's uncertainty and multiple sources of concern in relation to his self-image, however, Ms. Jordan appears comfortable, settled, and relatively nondefensive in relation to her high level of self-esteem. Her self-confidence and sense of superiority seem unsullied by negative self-regard or an unstable personal identity. She gives no evidence of critical self-attitudes or abnormal denigration of her body and its functions ($V=0$; $MOR=1$), and her $H:(H)Hd(Hd)$ = 3:1 suggests that she is normally capable of forming identifications with real people in her life and has been able to base a stable sense of her own identity

TABLE 14.6
Structural Summary for Ms. Jordan

Location Features	Determinants Blends	Single	Contents	S-Constellation
Zf = 15	FM.FC′	M = 4	H = 3, 0	NO . . FV+VF+V+FD>2
ZSum = 39.0	FM.Fr	FM = 1	(H) = 0, 0	YES . . Col-Shd Bl>0
ZEst = 49.0	FC.FC′	m = 2	Hd = 1, 0	YES . . Ego<.31,>.44
		FC = 1	(Hd) = 0, 0	NO . . MOR > 3
W = 14		CF = 0	Hx = 0, 0	YES . . Zd > +- 3.5
(Wv = 0)		C = 0	A = 11, 0	YES . . es > EA
D = 7		Cn = 0	(A) = 1, 0	NO . . CF+C > FC
Dd = 2		FC′ = 0	Ad = 3, 0	YES . . X+% < .70
S = 1		C′F = 0	(Ad) = 0, 0	NO . . S > 3
		C′ = 0	An = 2, 0	NO . . P < 3 or > 8
		FT = 0	Art = 0, 1	NO . . Pure H < 2
DQ		TF = 0	Ay = 0, 0	NO . . R < 17
. . . . . . (FQ-)		T = 0	Bl = 0, 0	5 . . . . . TOTAL
+ = 5 (0)		FV = 0	Bt = 1, 0	
o = 18 (3)		VF = 0	Cg = 0, 1	Special Scorings
v/+ = 0 (0)		V = 0	Cl = 0, 1	
v = 0 (0)		FY = 0	Ex = 1, 0	Lv1 Lv2
		YF = 0	Fd = 0, 0	DV = 0x1 0x2
		Y = 0	Fi = 0, 0	INC = 0x2 0x4
		Fr = 1	Ge = 0, 0	DR = 0x3 0x6
		rF = 0	Hh = 0, 0	FAB = 0x4 0x7
		FD = 0	Ls = 0, 1	ALOG = 0x5
Form Quality		F = 11	Na = 0, 0	CON = 0x7
			Sc = 0, 0	Raw Sum6 = 0
FQx FQf MQual SQx			Sx = 0, 0	Wgtd Sum6 = 0
+ = 0 0 0 0			Xy = 0, 0	
o = 15 5 4 0			Id = 0, 0	AB = 0 CP = 0
u = 5 4 0 1				AG = 0 MOR = 1
- = 3 2 0 0				CFB = 0 PER = 2
none = 0 — 0 0	(2) = 8			COP = 1 PSV = 0

Ratios, Percentages, and Derivations

R = 23	L = 0.92		FC:CF+C = 2: 0	COP = 1 AG = 0	
			Pure C = 0	Food = 0	
EB = 4: 1.0	EA = 5.0	EBPer = 4.0	SumC′:WSumC = 2:1.0	Isolate/R = 0.17	
eb = 5: 2	es = 7	D = 0	Afr = 0.53	H: (H)Hd(Hd) = 3: 1	
	Adj es = 6	Adj D = 0	S = 1	(HHd) : (AAd) = 0: 1	
			Blends:R = 3:23	H+A:Hd+Ad = 15: 4	
FM = 3 : C′ = 2 T = 0			CP = 0		
m = 2 : V = 0 Y = 0					

		P = 5	Zf = 15	3r+(2)/R = 0.61	
a:p = 4: 5	Sum6 = 0	X+% = 0.65	Zd = -10.0	Fr+rF = 2	
Ma:Mp = 1: 3	Lv2 = 0	F+% = 0.45	W:D:Dd = 14: 7: 2	FD = 0	
2AB+Art+Ay = 1	WSum6 = 0	X-% = 0.13	W:M = 14: 4	An+Xy = 2	
M- = 0	Mnone = 0	S-% = 0.00	DQ+ = 5	MOR = 1	
		Xu% = 0.22	DQv = 0		

| SCZI = 0 | DEPI = 3 | CDI = 3 | S-CON = 5 | HVI = No | OBS = No |

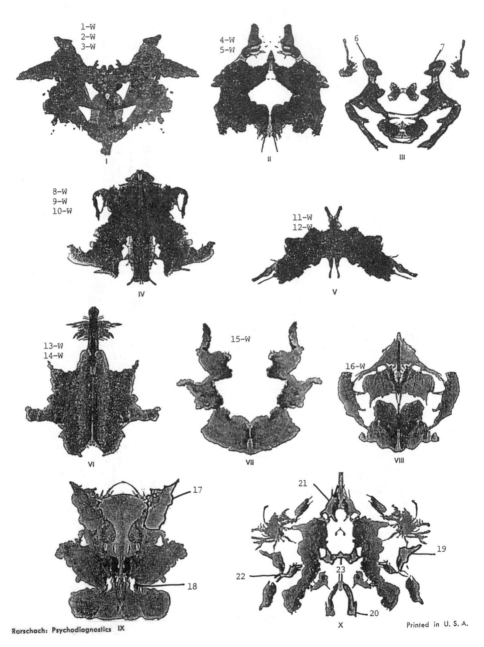

FIG. 14.2. Location choices of Ms. Jordan.

on such identifications. On the other hand, it is noteworthy in light of the problems that led to this consultation that her $FD = 0$ indicates limited psychological mindedness on Ms. Jordan's part and a corresponding likelihood that she has little capacity for self-awareness or introspection.

The responses in Ms. Jordan's record that involve prominent projected elements comprise one MOR, four M, and three minus responses, but these eight responses do not provide much additional information about how she views herself. The MOR occurs in Response 13 on Card VII and involves a "cartoon cat" that is "flattened out, like a truck ran over it." The frequent occurrence of this particular MOR limits its idiographic significance for Ms. Jordan, either in itself or in the sequence in which it occurs. The four M responses consist of "a lady with her arms up" in Response 1 on Card I; "people dancing" in Response 5 on Card II; people "looking at each other" in Response 6 on Card III; and "two women facing each other" in Response 15 on Card VII. None of these four M responses is elaborated in any way, except that the lady in Response 3 is described as having "some sort of wild costume" and the women in Response 15 as having "wild hairdos."

Because Responses 3 and 15 are not elaborated further, and because the "wild costume" and "wild hairdos" themes they contain do not appear elsewhere in the record, it is difficult to speculate with any confidence on their symbolic significance. Given that some qualities are being projected into these human percepts, however, it can be raised as question for further exploration whether something about being a wild woman constitutes a partial self-image or an attribution to others. For example, as a formal and proper businessperson with management responsibilities in a large company, could Ms. Jordan have some wishful fantasies about "letting her hair down" in some wild way, dressing in some outrageous fashion, and allowing herself to act more like a free spirit than a corporate manager? Or, on the contrary, is she entirely content with her personal style and circumstances and revealing in these responses some disapproval and denigration of women who groom, dress, and conduct themselves in outlandishly unconventional and irresponsible ways?

As for the three minus responses in the record, two of them occur consecutively in Response 7 on Card III and Response 8 on Card IV. Both of these are narrowly focused and unelaborated $F-$ "bug" responses that, in themselves, contain little indication of why Ms. Jordan became sufficiently upset at this point to lose sight of reality. Instead, analysis of the sequence suggests that her distress may derive from the two responses that precede these minus answers, which are Response 5 on Card II of "two people dancing" and Response 6 on Card III of "two people facing each other." How could these synthesized, pure H, ordinary form human movement responses, one a P and the other a COP, containing as they do numerous elements indicative of good ego strength, be serving as a source of distress in this instance? As one possible answer to this question, people who are experiencing problematic interpersonal relationships in their lives may be functioning sufficiently well to come to grips with the frequently seen human figures on Cards II and III and turn them into qualitatively good responses, but in the process of doing so they may also become upset by their unvoiced associations to impressions of two people interacting. Should Ms. Jordan have concerns or incapacities in her interpersonal relatedness, Response 5 and 6 could be responsible for the deterioration that follows in the form of two bland and otherwise difficult to explain minus responses. Accordingly, this sequence provides some basis for inferring that she does indeed have some interpersonal adjustment difficulties.

Pursuing her interpersonal stance further, note that Ms. Jordan recovers her capacity for accurate perception after Response 8 and gives only one more minus during the rest of her record, which occurs in Response 14 on Card VI. Response 14 is "an explosive cloud in the shape of a star" that she attributes on inquiry to the personal experience of having "seen fireworks in the last few months" and being reminded of them. The "cloud" and *PER* characteristics of this response, as well as her pause before giving it, suggest that it is more avoidant than it is revealing of any underlying dynamics. In this instance, the sequence is not particularly helpful either in accounting for her giving the minus form "star" shape. Response 13 is a *MOR*, but as already noted, is such a common *MOR* that it has little idiographic significance for body image problems.

However, it may be significant that in Response 13 she sees Card VI as a cat, says it is like "a cat skin rug," and then on inquiry rejects the rug concept and articulates her response without reference to the shading in the blot. Could it be that the commonly perceived textural quality of Card VI, together with the implications of *T* for interpersonal closeness and attachment, are upsetting to her and need to be avoided by disclaiming any "rug"? Perhaps similar dynamics are operating on Card IV, which as noted in chapter 4 follows Card VI as the second most likely card to elicit *T*. Note that prior to giving the minus form bug as her first response on Card IV, she pauses for some time and turns the card twice. Thus her difficulty in responding comfortably and generating good quality responses on Cards IV and VI may be due at least in part to her negative reaction to the textural quality of these blots, and this possibility is strengthened by structural data that bear further witness to interpersonal reserve.

On the positive side with respect to these structural data, Ms. Jordan's normative range *SumH* = 4, *H:(H)Hd(Hd)* = 3:1, and *ISOL* = .17 indicate that she is reasonably interested in people, feels comfortable in social situations, and is involved with people who play an important part in her life. In all three of these respects, her pattern of self-centeredness differs sharply from that of Mr. Ingram, whose narcissism was accompanied by limited interest in others and prominent interpersonal discomfort and isolation. Like Mr. Ingram, however, Ms. Jordan shows little capacity to form intimate attachments to other people and little inclination to anticipate or reach out for collaborative and mutually supportive relationships with them ($T = 0$; $COP = 1$). As a further point of comparison, the Rorschach data suggested that Mr. Ingram has difficulty feeling comfortable in social situations and getting along well with people whatever the circumstances, whereas Ms. Jordan appears able to feel comfortable socially and get along well personally provided that circumstances are sufficiently defined to limit intimacy and impose boundaries on closeness. As a further asset to her interpersonal functioning, Ms. Jordan's four accurately perceived M responses, with no M-, indicate that she is an adequately empathic person.

Finally with respect to Ms. Jordan's interpersonal functioning, it is noteworthy that her $a{:}p = 4{:}5$ approaches but does not quite meet the criterion of $p > a + 1$ for identifying behavioral passivity and interpersonal deference. A hint of such deference appears in her asking after Response 6 on Card III if she could turn the card. She did not turn the cards at all prior to this request for permission, but afterward did so frequently. She also displays in three PER responses some wish to explain herself to the examiner and let him know more about her. In addition to her previously noted reference to having seen fireworks in Response 14 on Card VI, her PER references occur in Responses 19 and 22 on Card X and consist of a "goldfinch" reported to be "the state bird where I grew up" and "sand crabs" of which "we have a lot of those where I live now."

To the extent that Ms. Jordan does tend by nature to be deferential to others and not particularly assertive ($AG = 0$), this personality characteristic could have some bearing on the difficulties she has encountered in her work situation. Sometimes people to whom giving orders and being in charge does not come naturally struggle a bit when their talents and energy result in their being placed in positions of responsibility in which they must assert themselves. Not finding it easy to impose authority in a relaxed and nonantagonistic manner, and not wanting to have their management careers derailed by their appearing too weak or mild mannered to elicit productivity and compliance from those reporting to them, such people may go to extremes in the other direction. Then they may become ranting, brow-beating, intemperate supervisors with very little tolerance for error and almost none for disagreement, not because of being angry or mean-spirited people, but because of wanting badly to succeed and not knowing how else to be in charge and get things done.

Although only fanciful to this point, and by no means a direct product of the Rorschach data, this scenario could help to account for the circumstances that resulted in Ms. Jordan's coming to the attention of her superiors and being asked to undergo a mental health evaluation. As we will see, she has some difficulty in dealing with affect that lends support to this line of inference about her problems on the job.

Stress Management Issues

The data in Ms. Jordan's control cluster of variables present some interesting contrasts with respect to her capacities to manage stress. On the one hand, her normative $CDI = 3$ and her $D = 0$ suggest that she is a basically competent person who can cope adequately with the demands of everyday life and can muster sufficient psychological resources to deal with the stresses in her life without becoming unduly upset by them. On the other hand, her low EA of 5.0 indicates well below average adaptive capacities, contributes a point to CDI, and comes as a surprise in a well-educated and occupationally achieving woman with a stable marriage and no history of developmental arrest or psychological breakdown.

The composition of Ms. Jordan's EB and D scores provides some explanation of these apparent discrepancies involving indices of her psychological competence. Her $EA = 5$ is based on a pervasively introversive EB style in which $M:WSumC = 4:1.0$. As in the cases of Mr. Carter and Deborah discussed in chapter 11, this type of imbalance indicates adequate capacities to employ ideation in dealing with experience but little ability to recognize or express feelings. Like Mr. Carter and Deborah, then, Ms. Jordan is susceptible to being overwhelmed by affectively charged or emotionally arousing situations and incapable of modulating her response to them in an adaptive manner.

As for her $D = 0$, Ms. Jordan demonstrates the "hunkered-down" posture (described in chap. 5 and also illustrated in the case of Ms. Anderson in chap. 10) in which an elevated *Lambda* combines with a below average *es* to make $D = 0$ possible despite a well below average *EA*. If she were not able to maintain such a narrow focus of attention and insulate herself as thoroughly against experiencing stress, and if her *es* of 7 were increased by just one point, which would bring it close to the mean *es* of 8.21 in nonpatient adults, then she would become a $D = -1$. In other words, in addition to having a specific liability in her coping capacities with respect to modulating affect, Ms. Jordan has very few adaptive resources in reserve for coping comfortably with even modest increases in the amount of stress to which she is subjected, and any sharp increase in stress could easily precipitate the kinds of impulsive acts and emotional outbursts seen in people with $D = -2$ or $D = -3$.

Affective Issues

As already noted, limited capacity to modulate affect adaptively constitutes a definite liability in Ms. Jordan's personality functioning. With respect to being able to modulate affect sufficiently, she does give evidence of normative willingness to become involved in emotionally charged situations and neither avoid nor withdraw from them (Afr = .53). Given how few affective tools she has to work with, her willingness in this regard suggests determination on her part to do what has to be done, and determination to succeed in difficult situations has probably contributed to her promising career.

Returning to the shortcomings in her emotional resources, however, the $SumC':WSumC$ = 2:1 and the $FC:CF + C$ = 2:0 identify marked constriction and stultifying inhibition in becoming aware of her feelings and being able to share them with others. What little affect she can experience is likely to remain bottled up inside, and what little affect she can express is likely to be formal, tepid, and reserved. Where Rorschach manifestations of casual, relaxed, spontaneous, expansive, intense, and free-flowing types of affective expression can be seen, in the $CF + F$, she has a 0. How, then, especially in view of the additional fact that she gives no Rorschach evidence of being an angry person (S = 1), can she be in trouble over screaming and yelling in anger at her subordinates in the office?

As an answer to this question, in addition to the explanatory considerations already suggested, $CF + C$ = 0 in an emotionally constricted person can create a susceptibility to emotional outbursts in the same way and for the same reasons as being pervasively introversive with a $WSumC$ = 1.0. In the absence of channels for regular, uncomplicated, and quickly forgotten discharge of minor irritations people feel toward each other, suppressed anger builds and gathers steam, like water in a pressure cooker. Then, often with little warning and in response to piddling events that constitute a last straw, festering irritation may explode into intense torrents of unwarranted and inappropriate verbal abuse.

Despite these affective difficulties, Ms. Jordan does not display the dysphoria shown by Mr. Ingram, who was seen as a narcissist deprived of his narcissistic supplies. She does have one *ColShd Bld*, indicating some ambivalent affect, but her C' = 2 is within normal limits. Likewise being free of the self-critical attitudes that plagued Mr. Ingram, she has an unremarkable *DEPI* = 3. Moreover, as a positive concluding note concerning affective issues, Ms. Jordan's comments on Cards VIII, IX, and X suggest that she may not be too far removed from achieving a more relaxed and light-hearted emotional stance. When shown Card VIII, she says, "Oh, that's pretty," following which she gives a percept of a landscape scene but does not articulate color at all. On being shown Card IX, she says, "I like these colored ones," but she then gives two responses without color. On Card X she begins with her two *FC* percepts, a "black and yellow bird" in Response 19 and a "green caterpillar" in Response 20, and then, after concluding in Response 23 with "a human pelvic bone," says, "I like the colors—they look like happy pictures."

Even modest translation of these affectively positive comments and Ms. Jordan's apparently just off-stage receptivity to emotionality into some additional articulation of *FC* and especially *CF* would greatly enhance the adaptive capacity suggested by her Rorschach protocol. Such enhancements in capacity to modulate affect could be a major treatment target in planning psychotherapy for her, and any progress toward this goal would very probably help soften her prickly nature as a supervisor.

Cognitive Issues

As mentioned in introducing her protocol, Ms. Jordan's *Lambda* = .92 in the context of 23 responses illustrates many features of a high *Lambda* style, as opposed to the high *Lambda* guardedness usually indicated by records with fewer than 20 responses (such as Ms. Anderson's in chap. 10). A high *Lambda* style Rorschach ordinarily does not conceal much from the examiner's view. What you see is pretty much what there is to see with respect to the subject's personality functioning. However, what there is to see in such persons is usually not very much, in the sense that they are narrowly focused and often hunkered-down individuals whose range of interests and activities is limited and who are intent on keeping their lives as simple and as uncomplicated as possible.

Some of these high *Lambda* style characteristics apply to Ms. Jordan (such as maintaining a *D* = 0 by hunkering down) and others do not (she has certainly not avoided challenge and complexity in her work), but this is consistent with the fact that she does not fully meet the criterion of *Lambda* > .99 for being considered a high *Lambda* person. Nevertheless, it is interesting to note that the high *Lambda* style characteristics discussed in chapter 5 include a propensity for behaving in ways that others find inappropriate or offensive, primarily as a result of the high *Lambda* person plunging straight ahead to solve problems in what seems to be the simplest way without paying adequate attention to subtle nuances they involve. Hence Ms. Jordan's elevation in *Lambda* may provide another clue to aspects of her personality style that have been contributing, along with her narcissism, to her insensitive and inconsiderate treatment of her staff.

It is also interesting to note that the manner in which Ms. Jordan handles the Rorschach cards supplements her *R* = 23 as an additional subtle basis for distinguishing her almost high *Lambda* style from high *Lambda* guardedness. As elaborated in chapter 7, guarded subjects typically do not spend much time looking at the blots and rarely bother to turn them as a way of searching out percepts. In Ms. Jordan's case, her protocol in Table 14.4 shows that she frequently paused while continuing to study the cards silently and engaged in a fair amount of card turning. Note, however, that her being thus involved in the response process did not generate much additional imagery. On Cards V, VII, VIII, and IX she continued to look at the blot and turn it one or more times after her final response, but then put it down without saying anything further. As an almost high *Lambda* style person, she was apparently keeping her focus narrowed and limiting the amount and complexity of what she was prepared to articulate. Not being a guarded high *Lambda* person, however, she did not hesitate to examine the cards in some detail and thus participate actively in the testing procedures.

The processing cluster of variables identify another possible source of Ms. Jordan's problems at work in the form of indications that she does not organize information very efficiently. Her $Zd = -10.0$ reveals her to be an underincorporator, the kind of person who makes careless decisions and comes to hasty conclusions as a result of not taking the time or spending the energy to consider enough relevant information beforehand. Hence we see another reason why she may at times say and do things that she would have refrained from saying or doing if she had contemplated her actions more thoroughly in advance. Also noteworthy in her processing is the unusual frequency of her W responses in comparison to her number of M responses ($W:M = 14:4$). As in the preceding case of Mr. Ingram, this $W:M$ pattern, with the emphasis on achieving global impressions, may signify a high level of aspiration and, given her narcissism, some grandiose or unrealistic expectations of much she will be able to accomplish.

In her perception of events, Ms. Jordan gives evidence of being able to recognize conventional reality and form mostly accurate impressions of what is happening around her ($P = 5; X - \% = 13$). Her $X - \%$ of .13 begins to approach a range that suggests occasional lapses in judgment, but two of her three minus responses consist of the bugs in Responses 7 and 8 that immediately follow some apparently distressing interpersonal content. Hence, as the nature of her presenting problem confirms, she may at times exercise faulty judgment subsequent to an interpersonal encounter, but there is no reason to believe that she has any basic incapacity in her reality testing.

Ms. Jordan is likewise fully capable of thinking about her experiences in a consistently logical, coherent, and flexible manner ($WSum6 = 0; a:p = 4:5$). As observed in discussing her pervasively introversive $EB = 4:1.0$, she tends to emphasize the products of her mind excessively in relation to the emanations of her heart. She is thus inclined to think too much and allow emotion too little place in how she conducts her life. As a further problem in this regard, she appears inclined to resort excessively to fantasy at the expense of constructive planning in solving problems ($Ma:Mp = 1:3$). She could probably function more effectively in her work and in other areas of her life as well if she were less tempted to deal with difficulties by daydreaming about how they will be resolved by good fortune or the efforts of someone else.

To summarize these Rorschach findings, the data indicate that Ms. Jordan is a well-integrated and reasonably well-functioning individual who gives no evidence of symptomatic disorder. Her personality style is marked by self-centeredness, interpersonal reserve, and a somewhat narrowly focused and excessively ideational approach to experience. Although she does not appear to be an angry or mean-spirited person, her limited channels for relaxed and spontaneous emotional expression create a susceptibility to emotional outbursts in which she goes suddenly from her customary cool contemplation to an intense affective outpouring without any gradual increments along the way. The episodes of intemperance that have distressed her subordinates at work probably derive in large part from this coping liability, and a treatment focus on allowing emotionality to become a more natural part of her life would likely be of considerable benefit to her. In addition to this core finding concerning the anger control problem that led to her being evaluated, other contributing personality characteristics suggested by her Rorschach responses include tendencies to come to conclusions and take action too hastily without sufficient attention to the nuances and complexities of situations, and some conflict between high achievement aspirations as a manager and some underlying uneasiness in having to assert authority over others.

References

Ainsworth, M. D. (1954). Problems of validation. In B. Klopfer, M. D. Ainsworth, W. G. Klopfer, & R. R. Holt, *Developments in the Rorschach technique: Vol. 1. Technique and theory* (chap. 14). Yonkers, NY: World Book.

Allport, G. W. (1937). *Personality: A psychological interpretation*. New York: Holt.

American Psychiatric Association. (1968). *Diagnostic and statistical manual of mental disorders (2nd ed.; DSM-II)*. Washington, DC: Author.

American Psychological Association. (1974). *Standards for educational and psychological tests*. Washington, DC: Author.

Anastasi, A., & Urbina, S. (1997). *Psychological testing* (7th ed.). New York: Prentice-Hall.

Aronow, E., & Reznikoff, M. (1976). *Rorschach content interpretation*. New York: Grune & Stratton.

Aronow, E., Reznikoff, M., & Moreland, K. (1994). *The Rorschach technique*. Boston: Allyn & Bacon.

Aronow, E., Reznikoff, M., & Moreland, K. L. (1995). The Rorschach: Projective technique or psychometric test? *Journal of Personality Assessment, 64*, 213–228.

Atkinson, L. (1986). The comparative validities of the Rorschach and MMPI. *Canadian Psychology, 27*, 238–347.

Baba, R. (1995). A comparative study of the Comprehensive System and a psychoanalytic sequence analysis. *Rorschachiana, 20*, 64–92.

Beck, S. J. (1930a). Personality diagnosis by means of the Rorschach test. *American Journal of Orthopsychiatry, 1*, 81–88.

Beck, S. J. (1930b). The Rorschach test and personality diagnosis. *American Journal of Psychiatry, 10*, 19–52.

Beck, S. J. (1968). Reality, Rorschach, and perceptual theory. In A. I. Rabin (Ed.), *Projective techniques in personality assessment* (pp. 115–135). New York: Springer.

Beck, S. J., Beck, A. G., Levitt, E. E., & Molish, H. B. (1961). *Rorschach's test: I. Basic processes* (3rd ed.). New York: Grune & Stratton.

Blatt, S. J. (1975). The validity of projective techniques and their clinical and research contributions. *Journal of Personality Assessment, 39*, 327–343.

Blatt, S. J. (1990). The Rorschach: A test of perception or an evaluation of representation. *Journal of Personality Assessment, 55*, 394–416.

Blatt, S. J., Brenneis, C., Schimek, J., & Glick, M. (1976). Normal development and psychological impairment of the concept of the object on the Rorschach. *Journal of Abnormal Psychology, 85*, 364–373.

Bohm, E. (1958). *A textbook in Rorschach diagnosis*. New York: Grune & Stratton. (Original work published 1951)

Bornstein, R. F. (1996). Construct validity of the Rorschach Oral Dependency scale: 1967–1995. *Psychological Assessment, 8*, 200–205.

Boyer, L. B. (1988). Effects of acculturation on the personality traits of Chiricahua and Mescalero Appaches: A Rorschach study. *British Journal of Projective Psychology, 32*, 2–17.

Brickman, A. S., & Lerner, H. D. (1992). Barren Rorschachs: A conceptual approach. *Journal of Personality Assessment, 59*, 165–175.

Brown, F. (1953). An exploratory study of dynamic factors in the content of the Rorschach protocol. *Journal of Projective Techniques, 17*, 251–279.

Burlatchuk, L. F., & Korzhova, E. Y. (1994). Projective approach to personality study in Soviet psychology: A summary of research. *Rorschachiana, 19*, 78–96.

Butcher, J. N., Nezami, E., & Exner, J. E., Jr. (1998). Psychological assessment in cross-cultural settings. In S. Kazarian & D. R. Evans (Eds.), *Cultural clinical psychology*. New York: Oxford University Press.

Cattell, R. B. (1946). *Description and measurement of personality*. New York: World Book.

Coonerty, S. (1986). An exploration of separation–individuation themes in the borderline personality disorder. *Journal of Personality Assessment, 50*, 501–511.

Cooper, S., H., Perry, J. C., & Arnow, D. (1988). An empirical approach to the study of defense mechanisms: I. Reliability and preliminary vaidity of the Rorschach Defense Scales. *Journal of Personality Assessment, 52*, 187–203.

Cooper, S. H., Perry, J. C., & O'Connell, M. (1991). The Rorschach Defense Scales: II. Longitudinal perspectives. *Journal of Personality Assessment, 56*, 192–201.

Gacono, C. B., & Meloy, J. R. (1994). *The Rorschach assessment of aggressive and psychopathic personalities*. Hillsdale, NJ: Lawrence Erlbaum Associates.

Dana, R. H. (1993). *Multicultural assessment perspectives for professional psychology*. Boston: Allyn & Bacon.

Dawes, R. M. (1994). *House of cards: Psychology and psychotherapy built on myth*. New York: The Free Press.

De Vos, G. A., & Boyer, L. B. (1989). *Symbolic analysis cross-culturally: The Rorschach test*. Berkeley: University of California Press.

Erikson, E. H. (1963). *Childhood and society* (2nd ed.). New York: Norton.

Exner, J. E., Jr. (1969). *The Rorschach systems*. New York: Grune & Stratton.

Exner, J. E., Jr. (1974). *The Rorschach: A comprehensive system*. New York: Wiley.

Exner, J. E., Jr. (1978). *The Rorschach: A comprehensive system: Vol. 2. Interpretation*. New York: Wiley.

Exner, J. E., Jr. (1980). But it's only an inkblot. *Journal of Personality Assessment, 44*, 562–577.

Exner, J. E., Jr. (1986). Some Rorschach data comparing schizophrenics with borderline and schizotypal personality disorders. *Journal of Personality Assessment, 50*, 455–471.

Exner, J. E., Jr. (1988). Problems with brief Rorschach protocols. *Journal of Personality Assessment, 52*, 640–647.

Exner, J. E., Jr. (1989). The search for projection. *Journal of Personality Assessment, 53*, 520–536.

Exner, J. E., Jr. (1991). *The Rorschach: A comprehensive system: Vol. 2. Interpretation* (2nd ed.). New York: Wiley.

Exner, J. E., Jr. (1993). *The Rorschach: A comprehensive system: Vol. 1. Basic foundations* (3rd ed.). New York: Wiley.

Exner, J. E., Jr. (Ed.). (1995). *Issues and methods in Rorschach research*. Mahwah, NJ: Lawrence Erlbaum Associates.

Exner, J. E., Jr. (1996). Critical bits and the Rorschach response process. *Journal of Personality Assessment, 67,* 478–494.

Exner, J. E., Jr. (1997a, March 14). *Empirical quality of the Comprehensive System.* Paper presented at Society for Personality Assessment Annual Meeting, San Diego, CA.

Exner, J. E., Jr. (1997b). The future of Rorschach in personality assessment. *Journal of Personality Assessment, 68,* 37–46.

Exner, J. E., Jr., Armbruster, G. L., & Mittman, B. (1978). The Rorschach response process. *Journal of Personality Assessment, 42,* 27–38.

Exner, J. E., Jr., & Exner, D. E. (1972). How clinicians use the Rorschach. *Journal of Personality Assessment, 36,* 403–408.

Exner, J. E., Jr., & Weiner, I. B. (1982). *The Rorschach: A comprehensive system: Vol. 3. Assessment of children and adolescents.* New York: Wiley.

Exner, J. E., Jr., & Weiner, I. B. (1995). *The Rorschach: A comprehensive system: Vol. 3. Assessment of children and adolescents* (2nd ed.). New York: Wiley.

Frank, G. (1977). On validity of hypotheses derived from the Rorschach: II. Interpretation of Card IV as "father" card and Card VII as "mother" card. *Perceptual and Motor Skills, 45,* 991–998.

Frank, L. K. (1939). Projective methods for the study of personality. *Journal of Psychology, 8,* 389–413.

Freud, S. (1958). Psycho-analytic notes on an autobiographical account of a case of paranoia (dementia paranoides). *Standard Edition, 12,* 9–84. (Original work published 1911)

Gacono, C. B., & Meloy, J. R. (1994). *The Rorschach assessment of aggressive and psychopathic personalities.* Hillsdale, NJ: Lawrence Erlbaum Associates.

Ganellen, R. J. (1996). Comparing the diagnostic efficiency of the MMPI, MCMI–II, and Rorschach: A review. *Journal of Personality Assessment, 67,* 219–243.

Goldfried, M. R., Stricker, G., & Weiner, I. B. (1971). *Rorschach handbook of clinical and research applications.* Englewood Cliffs, NJ: Prentice-Hall.

Hallowell, A. I. (1956). The Rorschach technique in personality and culture studies. In B. Klopfer, *Developments in the Rorschach technique* (Vol. 2, pp. 458–544). New York: Harcourt Brace Jovanovich.

Hertzman, M., & Pearce, J. (1947). The personal meaning of the human figure in the Rorschach. *Psychiatry, 10,* 413–422.

Hilsenroth, M. J., Fowler, J. C., & Padawer, J. R. (in press). The Rorschach Schizophrenic Index (SCZI): An examination of reliability, validity, and diagnostic efficiency. *Journal of Personality Assessment.*

Hilsenroth, M. J., Fowler, J. C., Padawer, J. R., & Handler, L. (1997). Narcissism in the Rorschach revisited: Some reflections on empirical data. *Psychological Asessment, 9,* 113–121.

Holt, R. R. (1967). Diagnostic testing: Present status and future prospects. *Journal of Nervous and Mental Disease, 144,* 444–465.

Kamano, D. K. (1960). Symbolic significance of Rorschach cards IV and VII. *Journal of Clinical Psychology, 16,* 50–52.

Kimmel, D. C., & Weiner, I. B. (1995). *Adolescence: A developmental transition* (2nd ed.). New York: Wiley.

Klein, A., & Arnheim, R. (1953). Perceptual analysis of a Rorschach card. *Journal of Personality, 22,* 60–70.

Klopfer, B., Ainsworth, M. D., Klopfer, W. G., & Holt, R. R. (1954). *Developments in the Rorschach technique: Vol I. Technique and theory.* Yonkers, NY: World Book.

Klopfer, B., Kirkner, F., Wisham, W., & Baker, G. (1951). Rorschach Prognostic Rating Scale. *Journal of Projective Techniques and Personality Assessment, 15,* 425–428.

Korchin, S. J., & Larson, D. G. (1977). Form perception and ego functioning. In M. A. Rickers-Ovsiankina (Ed.), *Rorschach psychology* (2nd ed., pp. 159–185). Huntington, NY: Krieger.

Krugman, M. (1938). Out of the inkwell: The Rorschach method. *Rorschach Research Exchange, 3-4,* 91–100.

Leichtman, M. (1996a). The nature of the Rorschach task. *Journal of Personality Assessment, 67,* 478–493.

Leichtman, M. (1996b). *The Rorschach: A developmental perspective.* Hillsdale, NJ: Analytic Press.

Lerner, P. M. (1991). *Psychoanalytic theory and the Rorschach.* Hillsdale, NJ: Analytic Press.

Lerner, P. M. (1993). Object relations theory and the Rorschach. *Rorschachiana, 18,* 45–57.

Lerner, P. M., & Lerner H. (1980). Rorschach assessment of primitive defenses in borderline personality structure. In J. Kwawer, H. Lerner, P. Lerner, & A. Sugarman (Eds.), *Borderline phenomena and the Rorschach test* (pp. 257–274). New York: International Universities Press.

Liaboe, G. P., & Guy, J. D. (1985). The Rorschach "father" and "mother" cards: An evaluation of the research. *Journal of Personality Assessment, 49,* 2–5.

Lindner, R. M. (1950). The content analysis of the Rorschach protocol. In L. E. Abt & L. Bellak (Eds.), *Projective psychology* (pp. 75–90). New York: Knopf.

Lunazzi de Jubany, H. (1992). *Lectura del psicodiagnostico* [Lectures in psychodiagnosis]. Buenos Aires: Editorial de Belgrano.

Masling, J. (1960). The influence of situational and interpersonal variables in projective testing. *Psychological Bulletin, 57,* 65–85.

Masling, J. M. (1997). On the nature and utility of projective tests and objective tests. *Journal of Personality Assessment, 69,* 257–270.

Masling, J. M. (1998). Interpersonal and actuarial dimensions of projective testing. In L. Handler & M. J. Hilsenroth (Eds.), *Teaching and learning personality assessment* (pp. 119–136). Mahwah, NJ: Lawrence Erlbaum Associates.

Masling, J. M., Rabie, L., & Blondheim, S. H. (1967). Obesity, level of aspiration, and Rorschach and TAT measures of oral dependence. *Journal of Consulting Psychology, 31,* 233–239.

Mattlar, C-E., & Fried, R. (1993). The Rorschach in Finland. *Rorschachiana, 18,* 105–125.

Mayman, M. (1977). A multidimensional view of the Rorschach movement response. In M. A. Rickers-Ovsiankina (Ed.), *Rorschach psychology* (2nd ed., pp. 229–250). Huntington, NY: Krieger.

McDowell, C., & Acklin, M. W. (1996). Standardizing procedures for calculating Rorschach inter-rater reliabiilty: Conceptual and empirical foundations. *Journal of Personality Assessment, 66,* 308–320.

Meyer, G. J. (1996). Construct validation of scales derived from the Rorschach method: A review of issues and introduction to the Rorschach Rating Scale. *Journal of Personality Assessment, 67,* 598–628.

Meyer, G. J. (1997). Assessing reliability: Critical correlations for a critical examination of the Rorschach Comprehensive System. *Psychological Assessment, 9,* 480–489.

Meyer, G. J., & Handler, L. (1997). The ability of the Rorschach to predict subsequent outcome: Meta-analysis of the Rorschach Prognostic Rating Scale. *Journal of Personality Assessment, 69,* 1–38.

Miale, F. R. (1977). Symbolic imagery in Rorschach material. In M. A. Rickers-Ovsiankina (Ed.), *Rorschach psychology* (2nd ed., pp. 421–454). Huntington, NY: Krieger.

Mindess, H. (1970). The symbolic dimension. In B. Klopfer, M. M. Meyer, & F. B. Brawer (Eds.), *Developments in the Rorschach technique* (Vol. 3, pp. 83–98). New York: Harcourt Brace Jovanovich.

Mullett, G. M. (1979). *Spider woman stories: Legends of the Hopi Indians.* Tucson, AZ: University of Arizona Press.

Offer, D., & Sabshin, M. (Eds.). (1991). *The diversity of normal behavior.* New York: Basic Books.

Ogawa, T. (1993). Contemporary trends in Rorschach research in Japan. *Rorschachiana, 18,* 93–104.

Parker, K. C. H., Hanson, R. K., & Hunsley, J. (1988). MMPI, Rorschach and WAIS: A meta-analytic comparison of reliability, stability, and validity. *Psychological Bulletin, 103,* 367–373.

Peterson, C. A., & Schilling, K. M. (1983). Card pull in projective testing. *Journal of Personality Assessment, 47,* 265–275.

Pine, F. (1990). *Drive, ego, object, and self.* New York: Basic Books.

Phillips, L., & Smith, J. G. (1953). *Rorschach interpretation: Advanced technique.* New York: Grune & Stratton.

Piotrowski, Z. A. (1957). *Perceptanalysis.* New York: Macmillan.

Piotrowski, Z. A. (1977). The movement response. In M. A. Rickers-Ovsiankina (Ed.), *Rorschach psychology* (2nd ed., pp. 189–227). Huntington, NY: Krieger.

Quintana, P. O., & Campo, V. (1993). The present status of the Rorschach test in Spain. *Rorschachiana, 18,* 26–44.

Raez de Ramirez, M. (1994). Rorschach's psychodiangosis in Peru. *Rorschachiana, 19,* 146–155.

Ranzoni, J. H., Grant, M. Q., & Ives, V. (1950). Rorschach "card pull" in a normal adolescent population. *Journal of Personality Assessment, 14,* 107–133.

Rapaport, D. (1942). Principles underlying projective techniques. *Character and Personality, 10,* 213–219.

Rapaport, D., Gill, M., & Schafer, R. (1968). *Diagnostic psychological testing* (Rev. ed. edited by R. R. Holt). New York: International Universities Press. (Original work published 1946)

Rausch de Traubenberg, N. (1993). The Rorschach: From percept to fantasm. *Rorschachiana: Yearbook of the International Rorschach Society, 18,* 7–25.

Richards, T. W. (1958). Personal significance of Rorschach figures. *Journal of Personality Assessment, 22,* 97–101.

Rorschach, H. (1942). *Psychodiagnostics: A diagnostic test based on perception.* Bern: Hans Huber. (Original work published 1921)

Rosenzweig, S. (1951). Idiodynamics in personality theory with special reference to projective methods. *Psychological Review, 58,* 213–223.

Schachtel, E. G. (1966). *Experiential foundations of Rorschach's test.* New York: Basic Books.

Schafer, R. (1954). *Psychoanalytic interpretation in Rorschach testing.* New York: Grune & Stratton.

Sendin, C. (1995). Nonpatient transcultural comparison. In *Proceedings Book, 14th International Congress of Rorschach and Projective Techniques* (pp. 207–212). Lisbon, Portugal: Gulbenkian.

Shapiro, D. (1977). A perceptual understanding of color response. In M. A. Rickers-Ovsiankina (Ed.), *Rorschach psychology* (2nd ed., pp. 251–301). Huntington, NY: Krieger.

Shontz, F. C., & Green, P. (1992). Trends in research on the Rorschach: Review and recommendations. *Applied and Preventive Psychology, 1,* 149–156.

Sines, J. O. (1960). An approach to the study of the stimulus significance of the Rorschach inkblots. *Journal of Projective Techniques, 24,* 64–66.

Smith, B. L. (1994). Object relations theory and the integration of empirical and psychoanalytic approaches to Rorschach interpretation. *Rorschachiana, 19,* 61–77.

Stricker, G., & Healey, B. J. (1990). Projective assessment of object relations: A review of the literature. *Psychological Assessment, 2,* 219–230.

Sugarman, A. (1991). Where's the beef? Putting personality back into personality assessment. *Journal of Personality Assessment, 56,* 130–144.

Sullivan, H. S. (1953). *The interpersonal theory of psychiatry.* New York: Norton.

Swift, J. (1726/1960). *Gulliver's travels.* Boston: Houghton Mifflin.

Urist, J. (1977). The Rorschach test and the assessment of object relations. *Journal of Personality Assessment, 41,* 3–9.

Vaz, C. E. (1995). Anxiety, productiveness, performance, and culture in the Rorschachs of a multiethnic group of adolescents. *Rorschachiana, 20,* 93–111.

Vernon, P. E. (1935). Recent work on the Rorschach test. *Journal of Mental Science, 81,* 894–920.

Weiner, I. B. (1977a). Approaches to Rorschach validation. In M. A. Rickers-Ovsiankina (Ed.), *Rorschach psychology* (2nd ed., pp. 575–608). Huntington, NY: Krieger.

Weiner, I. B. (1977b). Projective tests in differential diagnosis. In B. B. Wolman (Ed.), *International encyclopedia of neurology, psychiatry, psychoanalysis, and psychology* (pp. 112–116). Princeton, NJ: Van Nostrand Reinhold.

Weiner, I. B. (1986). Conceptual and empirical perspectives on the Rorschach assessment of psychopathology. *Journal of Personality Assessment, 50,* 472–479.

Weiner, I. B. (1989). On competence and ethicality in psychodiagnostic assessment. *Journal of Personality Assessment, 53,* 827–831.

Weiner, I. B. (1992). *Psychological disturbance in adolescence* (2nd ed.). New York: Wiley.

Weiner, I. B. (1994). The Rorschach Inbkblot Method (RIM) is not a test: Implications for theory and practice. *Journal of Personality Assessment, 62,* 498–504.

Weiner, I. B. (1995a). Methodological considerations in Rorschach research. *Psychological Assessment, 7,* 330–337.

Weiner, I. B. (1995b). Searching for Rorschach theory: A wild goose chase. In *Proceedings Book, 14th International Congress of Rorschach and Projective Methods* (pp. 23–32). Lisbon, Portugal: Gulbenkian.

Weiner, I. B. (1996). Some observations on the validity of the Rorschach Inkblot Method. *Psychological Assessment, 8,* 206–213.

Weiner, I. B. (1997a). Current status of the Rorschach Inkblot Method. *Journal of Personality Assessment, 68,* 5–19.

Weiner, I. B. (1997b). *Psychodiagnosis in schizophrenia.* Mahwah, NJ: Lawrence Erlbaum Associates. (Original work published 1966)

Weiner, I. B. (1998a). *Principles of psychotherapy* (2nd ed.). New York: Wiley.

Weiner, I. B. (1998b). Rorschach differentiation of schizophrenia and affective disorder. In G. P. Koocher, J. C. Norcross, & S. S. Hill (Eds.), *Psychologist's desk reference.* New York: Oxford University Press.

Weiner, I. B. (1998c). Teaching the Rorschach Comprehensive System. In L. Handler & M. J. Hilsenroth (Eds.), *Teaching and learning personality assessment* (pp. 215–233). Mahwah, NJ: Lawrence Erlbaum Associates.

Weiner, I. B. (in press). Rorschach Inkblot Method. In M. Maruish (Ed.), *The use of psychological testing in treatment planning and outcome evaluation* (2nd ed.). Mahwah, NJ: Lawrence Erlbaum Associates.

Weiner, I. B., & Exner, J. E., Jr. (1991). Rorschach changes in long-term and short-term psychotherapy. *Journal of Personality Assessment, 56,* 453–465.

Zubin, J., Eron, L. D., & Schumer, F. (1965). *An experimental approach to projective techniques.* New York: Wiley.

Author Index

Subject Index